ALTERNATIVE ENERGY

Political, Economic, and Social Feasibility

SECOND EDITION

CHRISTOPHER A. SIMON

University of Utah

ROWMAN & LITTLEFIELD
Lanham • Boulder • New York • London

Executive Editor: Traci Crowell
Assistant Editor: Deni Remsberg
Higher Education Channel Manager: Jonathan Raeder
Interior Designer: Rosanne Schloss

Credits and acknowledgments for material borrowed from other sources, and reproduced with permission, appear on the appropriate page within the text.

Published by Rowman & Littlefield
An imprint of The Rowman & Littlefield Publishing Group, Inc.
4501 Forbes Boulevard, Suite 200, Lanham, Maryland 20706
www.rowman.com

6 Tinworth Street, London SE11 5AL, United Kingdom

British Library Cataloguing in Publication Information Available

Library of Congress Cataloging-in-Publication Data

Names: Simon, Christopher A., 1968– author.
Title: Alternative energy : political, economic, and social feasibility / Christopher A. Simon, University of Utah.
Description: Second edition. | Lanham : Rowman & Littlefield, [2020] | Includes bibliographical references and index.
Identifiers: LCCN 2019043704 (print) | LCCN 2019043705 (ebook) | ISBN 9781538116364 (cloth ; alk. paper) | ISBN 9781538116371 (pbk ; alk. paper) | ISBN 9781538116388 (electronic)
Subjects: LCSH: Renewable energy sources—Government policy—United States. | Energy policy—United States. | Renewable energy sources.
Classification: LCC HD9502.U52 S544 2020 (print) | LCC HD9502.U52 (ebook) | DDC 333.79/4—dc23
LC record available at https://lccn.loc.gov/2019043704
LC ebook record available at https://lccn.loc.gov/2019043705

Dedicated to my parents,
Raffi G. and Susan M. Simon,
and
Kelly Nguyen

Brief Contents

★ ★ ★

List of Illustrations ix
Preface xi
About the Author xv

1 Why Alternative Energy and Fuels? 1

2 Studying Public Policy and Alternative Energy/Fuels 35

3 Alternative Energy/Fuels as a Public Policy Innovation 65

4 Solar Energy 101

5 Wind Energy 132

6 Geothermal Energy 159

7 New Century Fuels and Their Uses 185

8 Historical Precedents: Alternative Energy/Fuels and Legitimacy Issues 217

9 Conceptualizing Alternative Energy Policy and Future Directions 243

Index 265

Contents

★ ★ ★

List of Illustrations		ix
Preface		xi
About the Author		xv

1 Why Alternative Energy and Fuels?   **1**
Climate Change and Carbon   4
Energy and Water   7
Carbon-Based Fuels: Current and Future Availability   11
Common Fossil Energy Sources: U.S. Supply and Use   12
Culture Shifts and the Rise of Green Politics   16
Green Politics and Environmental Public Interest Groups   17
New Environmental Paradigm and Alternative Energy   19
Institutional Change and Influence   19
Global Demands and Conflict   26
Chapter Summary   27
References   29
Court Cases   34

2 Studying Public Policy and Alternative Energy/Fuels   **35**
Roles for Public Policy in Alternative Energy/Fuel Development   35
Policy Process   39
    Agenda Setting   41
    Policy Formation   42
    Policy Implementation   43
    Policy Evaluation   44
    Policy Termination/Change   45
Policy Types   46
Bottom-Up Policy Making/Top-Down Policy Making   48
Collaborative Policy Making   49

Federalism and Energy Policy   51
Policy Frameworks/Models   52
   Institutional Analysis and Development (IAD)   53
   Multiple Streams (MS)   55
   Advocacy Coalition Framework (ACF)   57
   Punctuated Equilibrium (PE)   58
   Policy Diffusion   58
   Narrative Policy Framework (NPF)   59
   Intergovernmentalism   60
Native Americans, Tribal Lands, and Renewable Energy   61
Chapter Summary   61
References   62

3 Alternative Energy/Fuels as a Public Policy Innovation   65
Defining Alternative Energy and Alternative Fuels   65
What Are Alternative Fuels?   68
Policy Innovation and Alternative Energy   68
The Waves of Policy Innovation   70
   Oil Shock I/Pre-PURPA 1970s (1973–1978)   71
   Secondary Oil Shock Period (1979–1982)   75
   Resurgence of Cheap(er) Petroleum and Growth
      of Deregulation (1983–1999)   77
   Bush I: EPAct Reauthorization (1992)   80
   Clinton and Post-EPAct 1992
      Reauthorization (1992–2005)   84
   Bush II: EPAct 2005 Reauthorization, ESIA 2007,
      FERC Order Innovations, and Electricity
      Markets (2001–2009)   87
   Obama: ARRA 2009, Coal Rules, and
      Paris Agreement (2009–2017)   92
   Trump: Resurgence of Coal and Reversal
      of Climate Policy (2017–present)   94
Chapter Summary   96
References   98

4 Solar Energy   101
What Is Solar Energy? How Does It Work?   101
Silicon-Based Photovoltaic Cells   103
Technical Feasibility of Solar Photovoltaics   105
Technical Feasibility of Solar Thermal   108
Economics of Solar Power   111
   Current Solar PV Energy Economic Infrastructure and
      Levelized Cost of Electricity   112
Economics of Solar Thermal—Concentrated Solar Power   115

Economic Development Impacts 116
Case Study—Rifle, Colorado: Using Solar Energy to
   Power Municipal Water and Sewer Systems 117
Federal Solar Energy Technologies Program 118
Major Federal Solar Incentives 122
   Commercial Incentives 122
   Personal Tax Incentives for Solar PV and Solar Thermal 123
State and Local Efforts 123
   California 124
   Honolulu, Hawai'i 125
Chapter Summary 125
References 127

5 Wind Energy **132**
What Is Wind Power? How Does It Work? 132
Technical Feasibility of Wind Power Systems 136
Economic Feasibility of Wind Power Systems 144
Political and Social Feasibility of Wind Energy 149
Chapter Summary 155
References 155

6 Geothermal Energy **159**
What Is Geothermal Energy? How Does It Work? 159
Case Study—California Job Growth and Geothermal Development 160
Safety, Environmental Damage, and Emission-Related Issues:
   Geothermal Energy 161
Technical Feasibility of Geothermal Energy 163
   Heat Pumps 163
   Other Forms of Direct Use 164
   Flash Steam Power 166
   Binary Systems 168
Economics of Geothermal Energy 172
Federal Geothermal Energy Programming 175
State and Local Efforts 177
Chapter Summary 178
References 179

7 New Century Fuels and Their Uses **185**
Fuel as a Concept 186
Natural Gas 189
Other Alternative Fuels 191
   Clean Diesel 191
   Biodiesel 191
   Ethanol 192
The Hydrogen Initiative 194

Hydrogen and Fuel Cells   196
  Technical Feasibility Issues   196
  Economic Feasibility Issues   199
Other Types of Fuel Cells Currently in Use and/or Development   201
  Alkaline Fuel Cells (AFC)   201
  Direct Methanol Fuel Cells (DMFC)   201
  Molten Carbonate Fuel Cells (MCFC)   202
  Phosphoric Acid Fuel Cells (PAFC)   203
  Solid Oxide Fuel Cells (SOFC)   204
Applications for Next-Generation Alternative Fuels, Fuel Cells   204
  Transportation   204
  Military Applications   206
  Residential   207
  Commercial   207
Chapter Summary   207
References   208

**8 Historical Precedents: Alternative Energy/Fuels and
    Legitimacy Issues   217**
Risk and Culture: Alternative Energy and Hidden Costs   219
Hydroelectric Dams   224
Nuclear Energy   229
The Rebirth of Nuclear Energy?   237
Chapter Summary   239
References   239

**9 Conceptualizing Alternative Energy Policy and
    Future Directions   243**
Future Directions   244
The Movement of Public Opinion   250
Concluding Remarks   258
References   262

Index   265

Illustrations

★ ★ ★

FIGURES

1.1	Domestic Petroleum Extraction in the United States, 1900–2017 (in bbls)	13
1.2	Coal Consumption in Electricity Generation, 1949–2017 (in short tons)	14
1.3	Natural Gas Consumption in Electricity Generation, 1997–2017 (in mcf)	15
2.1	Rivalry in the Gasoline Market	36
2.2	Inelasticity of Demand	38
2.3	Coercion, Policy, and Politics	47
2.4	U.S. Federal Budget Commitment to Alternative Energy (2014–2019)	52
3.1	Impact of Price Control on Demand	78
3.2	RTO/ISOs in the United States and Canada	86
3.3	Hydrogen Technology and Public Policy	88
4.1	Solar PV and Solar Thermal Electricity Production (2009–2018)	102
4.2	Schematic of an Si-Based Solar Cell	104
4.3	Domestic Photovoltaic Manufacturing Activities and Prices, United States (2010–2016)	114
5.1	Wind Electricity Production (2009–2018)	133
5.2	Wind System Design	133
5.3	Wind Turbine Blades	134
6.1	Geothermal Electricity Production (2009–2018)	159
6.2	Flash Steam Power Plant	160
6.3	U.S. Geothermal Provinces	162
6.4	Geothermal Use, 2017	165
7.1	U.S. B-100 Production and Consumption (2001–2018)	192
7.2	U.S. Ethanol Production (1981–2018)	193
8.1	Risk and Policy Solutions	220
9.1	Electricity Generation by Source (2009–2019)	261

PHOTOS

Low Water Levels at Hoover Dam	4
The Complexities of Public Policy	46
Students Collaborating in a Renewable Energy Lab	50
Gas Shortages	74
Thin Film Solar Array	107
A Power Tower in Nevada	110
A Parabolic Dish	111
Inside the Nacelle of a Wind Turbine	135
One Propeller Blade on a Semi Truck	137
Offshore Wind and a Transfer Vessel	143
Model of a House with a Heat Pump System	169
Drilling a Geothermal Well	170
Geothermal Energy Plant in Niland, California	171
A Steam Turbine Condenser	172
Rotor of a Turbine	175
LNG Storage	187
Ethanol Biorefinery Plant	195
Hydrogen Fuel Cell for an AFV	196
A Tidal Energy Turbine	224
Nuclear Power Plant	236

TABLES

4.1	Federal Commercial Solar Tax Credits	122
4.2	Solar PV and Solar Thermal	123
5.1	Blade Mass and Cost of Rotors	145
5.2	Land-Based Wind Turbine Scenario (2.16 MW Turbine)	147
5.3	Fixed Bottom Offshore Turbine Scenario (4.71 MW Turbine)	148
5.4	Floating Offshore Turbine Scenario (4.71 MW Turbine)	150
7.1	Energy Density	186
7.2	Natural Gas Consumption	189
7.3	Hydrogen Production Costs by Energy Source	200

TEXTBOXES

1.1	The New Environmental Paradigm	19
1.2	U.S. Department of Energy National Laboratories	26
3.1	Energy versus Power … and What Is Work (W)?	66
3.2	Some Issues to Consider When Studying Policy Innovation	70
5.1	St. Olaf Wind Turbine Case Study	152

Preface

★ ★ ★

The first edition of this book was published in 2007. At the time, the energy world was pondering major energy supply and security concerns. The United States was fighting a war in the Middle East. Matthew Simmon's book *Twilight in the Desert: The Coming Oil Shock and the World Economy* (2005), emphasizing the decline of Saudi oil, was still fresh in the minds of many energy policy analysts, policy makers, and concerned citizens. The National Petroleum Council Report *Balancing Natural Gas Policy: Fueling the Demands of a Growing Economy* (2003: 2) had recently called for greater energy conservation in light of "recent tightening of the natural gas supply/demand balance." Within a year of the book's publication, petroleum prices spiked at $178/bbl (in 2019 dollars) on the world market. Alternative energy was seen as one solution to the problems facing energy markets. The issue of climate change, while well known and understood, often seemed to take a back seat in the policy dialogue.

Shortly after the first edition was published, Dr. Ted Batchman, then dean of engineering at the University of Nevada, Reno, the university where I was employed at the time, invited me to team teach a course on alternative energy and to establish an interdisciplinary minor degree in Renewable Energy as well as a graduate certificate program in the College of Engineering. (Alternative energy, with some policy-designated exceptions, includes noncarbon-based energy sources, some of which may be nonrenewable sources of energy such as nuclear energy.) Ours was a highly successful partnership between a well-established electrical engineering scholar and a young political scientist. For several years, before Ted retired and I moved on to the University of Utah, we successfully (and with great enthusiasm and enjoyment) team taught energy courses to overflowing classes of interested students. In reflecting back on those years, alternative energy sources were more commonly viewed by our students as a solution to supply and security dilemmas. The students did not focus much attention on the issue of climate change and the role that nonfossil energy sources play in combating climate change.

Much has changed in the dozen or so years since the first edition. A technological revolution has led to a petroleum and natural gas bonanza. According to the U.S. Energy Information Administration (2019), the United States was the top producer of crude petroleum in 2018. Petroleum prices have declined to the $50/bbl range (in 2019 dollars), and natural gas prices have declined from over $15/MMBtu in June 2008 to less than $3/MMBtu in August 2019 (both figures in 2019 dollars). At least for the next several decades—barring unforeseen events or policy changes—the energy supply issue will likely not be the driving force behind alternative energy.

What has not changed, however, are issues related to human-caused climate change. Global warming and changes in weather patterns—and the potential for long-lasting droughts—are predicted to impact the planet in many ways, threatening the existence of human, animal, and plant species. In the twentieth century, the average temperature of the planet increased by 2°F. It sounds like a small amount, but it is a large change. As NASA's climate web page points out, the average temperature of the planet was only five to nine degrees cooler than it is today during the most recent Ice Age (NASA, 2019).

In addition to climate change, energy security remains a central concern (see Brown and Sovacool, 2001). While this book is not focused on the issue of energy security, one's attention is easily drawn to events in the Persian Gulf in 2019, Russian retaliation against Ukraine in the form of natural gas shutoffs in 2008 and 2009, the tragic events at Fukushima in Japan in 2011, and oil spills such as the one caused by the BP Deepwater Horizon in the Gulf of Mexico that began in 2010 and may still pose risks. Energy security studies focus on many dilemmas, but the aforementioned examples concentrate our attention on the fact that energy is a global issue. Markets are international, and global events—political crises, environmental disasters—shape markets. Political crises and environmental disasters shape and are shaped by political and human values in the form of policy responses and, in some cases, social movements. Our more diverse domestic energy portfolio in the United States has largely come to fruition due to the forces of politics and human values expressed through public policy and social movements. As we have learned through several decades of policy making, a diverse energy portfolio may help us overcome short- or long-term energy shortfalls and soften possible economic blows that result; maintain a steady energy supply; and combat the effects of climate change.

As we consider the move to a clean energy society and economy, there are many issues on which to reflect. In this book, I categorize these issues in terms of technical, economic, and social/political feasibility. Again, so much has changed since the first edition! Technical feasibility has improved dramatically, in large part due to the continued material science revolution, the so-called Third Industrial Revolution (Rifkin, 2011), the rise of machine learning, and next-generation simulation and fabrication processes. The economics behind many alternative energy sources has become clearer. The levelized cost of energy from alternative energy sources is becoming more affordable for consumers, particularly if one factors in the avoided social and environmental costs of not using carbon-based energy sources.

Political and social consent of alternative energy is greater today than when the first edition of this book emerged over a decade ago. For decades, national-level politics has, through wise political compromise, led to environmental regulation of air and water quality, the protection of endangered species, and the investment in alternative energy solutions. Lasting commitment to international climate change accords has not been a part of the U.S. national energy and climate change strategy. In particular, President Donald Trump's energy policies have served to roll back the clean energy agenda at the national level, spurring a response from the political left in the form of a proposed Green New Deal. Conversely, state and local alternative energy policy commitments continue to grow, particularly as the benefits of alternative energy are seen as environmentally responsible, as a source of energy security, and as good for state and local economic development.

Support for renewable energy is very high in the United States. The millennial generation and Generation Z have reached adulthood in the years since the publication of the first edition of this book. Now the largest age cohorts in the United States, millennials and Generation Z, are very supportive of renewable energy. Moreover, millennials and Generation Z demonstrate support for many of the component parts of energy proposals such as the Green New Deal. The component parts include the restructuring of government's relationship with the private economy, as well as the promotion of social justice through public policy. It very likely that the millennial generation and Generation Z values will be reflected in future social movements that shape the energy policy choices of elected representatives.

That said, rapid policy and social change are often very costly. Infrastructure costs a great deal of money. It is difficult to abandon those things in which we have already invested, even if they pose social and environmental risks and costs. Imagine if you had to walk away from your house and your car with little to no compensation simply because new policies deemed them not environmentally sound. Also, a restructuring of a multitrillion-dollar economy in a rapid fashion is likely to pose significant risks. Finally, under normal circumstances, rapid policy change might invite high levels of conflict within society and among policy makers.

With that in mind, I hope that this book sheds some light on the choices we have made in the past, the circumstances we face and opportunities we have now and in the near future, as well as the paths and policy frameworks that could guide us toward our energy policy goals. As you read and consider what you have read, I hope, too, that you see this material as informing the energy policy narrative that you and others will generate through both individual choice and collective action.

There are several people I wish to acknowledge. My parents, Raffi G. and Susan M. Simon, have always been there to support me through the writing process. My father offered quite a few tutorials on his professional field, organic chemistry, which I appreciated immensely! I was very fortunate to have Nicholas P. Lovrich, Regents Professor Emeritus, Washington State University, review my manuscript. Given his encyclopedic knowledge of public policy, I appreciated his constant encouragement and very helpful advice. I thoroughly enjoyed our conversations about alternative energy! Special thanks to the College of Social and Behavioral Science, University of Utah, for granting me a sabbatical leave so that I could develop and complete this manuscript. The manuscript might never have emerged if not for Traci Crowell, my editor at Rowman & Littlefield. I appreciate her advice and support over the last year. Thanks to those who provided reviews of the manuscript: William Lowry (Washington University of St. Louis) and Barry Rabe (University of Michigan).

Special thanks to Windustry for the use of the case study, St. Olaf College Wind Energy (www.windustry.org).

REFERENCES

Brown, M., and Sovacool, B. 2011. *Climate Change and Global Energy Security: Technology and Policy Options.* Cambridge, MA: MIT Press.

NASA. 2019. Global Climate Change. Retrieved from https://climate.nasa.gov/effects/, August 15, 2019.

Rifkin, J. 2011. *Third Industrial Revolution.* New York: Palgrave Macmillan.

Shackouls, B. 2003. *Balancing Natural Gas Policy: Fueling the Demands of a Growing Economy.* Washington, DC: National Petroleum Council.

Simmons, M. 2005. *Twilight in the Desert: The Coming Oil Shock and the World Economy.* New York: Wiley.

About the Author

★ ★ ★

CHRISTOPHER A. SIMON (PhD, 1997, Washington State University) is professor of political science and former director of the MPA program at the University of Utah. He conducts research in alternative energy policy; civic community and volunteerism; education policy; land use policy; public administration; and military sociology. He is coauthor (with David Bernell) of *The Energy Security Dilemma: US Policy and Practice* (2016), and coauthor (with Brent Steel and Nicholas Lovrich) of *State and Local Government: Sustainability in the 21st Century* (2011; 2018), and author of *Alternative Energy: Political, Economic, and Social Feasibility* (2007), *Public Policy: Preferences and Outcomes* (2007, 2010, 2017), and *To Run a School: Administrative Organization and Learning* (2001; Mandarin edition, 2005). He has published articles in *Administration & Society, American Politics Research, American Review of Public Administration, Armed Forces & Society, Assessment & Evaluation in Higher Education, Canadian Journal of Political Science, Cities, Comparative Technology Transfer & Society, Educational Research Quarterly, Energy Research & Social Science, Land Use Policy Journal, Policy Studies Journal, Journal of Political & Military Sociology: An Annual Review, Public Administration Review, Journal of Public Affairs Education, Review of Public Personnel Administration, Social Science Quarterly, and Sustainability.*

1

Why Alternative Energy and Fuels?

★ ★ ★

The twentieth century saw an unprecedented expansion in industrialization. In 1900, automobiles were not a primary means of transportation, and air travel was nonexistent. Homes were heated with wood and coal, and illuminated by tapers and whale oil rather than electricity and natural gas. Initially, industrial expansion was limited to Western countries. Today, industrial expansion is a global phenomenon of unprecedented scale. At the dawn of the third decade of the twenty-first century, China is the leading nation in gross domestic product (GDP) in terms of purchasing power parity (PPP) with the United States and India ranked second and third, respectively (World Bank, 2019). Global expansion is built on a diverse energy portfolio composed of both alternative and fossil energy. China is the leading producer of renewable energy. As of 2016, nearly 25 percent of China's electricity was generated using renewable energy sources, while less than 15 percent of U.S. electricity was produced using renewable energy (International Energy Association, 2017). China's renewable energy commitment continues to rapidly expand. In 2018, renewable energy accounted for 38.3 percent of China's installed electricity capacity (Yuanyuan, 2019). Of the top five nations in terms of GDP (PPP), Germany leads the way, generating approximately 30 percent of its electricity using renewable energy sources. Absent significant movement toward the use of renewables, and with global nuclear energy production declining in all regions except for Asia (Rising, 2018), the global expansion of energy will remain heavily dependent on finite hydrocarbon energy sources. Beyond the issue of climate change, alternative energy sources—renewables and other low or zero carbon-emitting sources of energy—reduce demand for fossil energy and simultaneously reduce the political and economic tensions related to its use (Bernell and Simon, 2016).

Energy supply and ready access to reliable energy sources, particularly those sources with high energy density, are critical to modern economic development.

1

Development is an ongoing process and is often related to the ability of individuals to exercise a whole host economic and social freedoms. The work of Brown and Mobarak (2009: 202) found that access to household electricity is related to democratization. Democracies tend to structure their energy policy incentives to favor residential consumers of electricity. Energy is needed for development to occur, and greater access to high-quality sources of energy is needed for developing nations as they seek to advance the social and political opportunities of their citizens. So-called developed nations—nevertheless, still in the process of developing and evolving—may require less energy per capita due to their capacity to innovate and become more efficient consumers of energy. A quick glance at U.S. Energy Information Administration energy projection to 2040 indicates that energy consumption for developed nations (OECD countries) is expected to remain roughly the same, while in developing nations analysts estimate a near 60 percent increase in energy consumption over the same period (U.S. Energy Information Administration, 2013). Accelerating energy demand cannot be easily met by fossil energy in the long term simply because fossil energy is in finite supply. Therefore, sustainable development must rely on energy sources that can conceivably be produced in reliably large quantities over the long term. Alternative energy sources are, therefore, the only logical choice at this time.

Another issue that arises is the nature of energy as a good. A public good is a common resource necessary for individual and collective existence that cannot be easily marketed without causing uneven distribution, deprivation, and social and economic injustice. In the United States and in many other nations, fossil energy supplies are often viewed as private goods (a commodity) rather than a pure public good. The overuse or misuse of a public good could create a tragedy of the commons—resource overuse, degradation, and depletion negatively impacting a large number of individuals (see Hardin, 1968); so, despite being viewed as a private good, fossil energy is often subject to regulation in terms of resource development, distribution, and use.

When fossil energy is viewed as readily available and affordable, it is unlikely to become the subject of large-scale public policy efforts to govern its development, distribution, and use. This is particularly the case when fossil energy costs are considered solely in terms of per-unit cost to the consumer and absent costs to society. However, when fossil energy is commonly viewed as costly and scarce, frequently it becomes the subject of intense political debate over: What are the alternatives to fossil energy, and what is the direct cost to the consumer, to society, and to the environment of these alternatives? Should its distribution and use be regulated by government?

Less than two decades ago, energy experts projected the decline of fossil energy sources due to supply limitations. The now-late Matthew Simmons (2005), energy economist and businessman, penned his well-received book *Twilight in the Desert: The Coming Saudi Oil Shock and the World Economy*. Painstakingly researched, Simmons's book arrived at the conclusion that oil supplies for the world's largest oil-producing nation at time, the Kingdom of Saudi Arabia, were on a steady path to decline. Simmons's analysis was frequently cited as further cause to pursue renewable energy sources to prepare for economic and social changes ahead.

Technology, however, has changed our perspective of hydrocarbon depletion, particularly petroleum and natural gas depletion. With the rise of hydraulic fracturing in the early twenty-first century and well-flushing technologies, previously inaccessible petroleum and natural gas resources are now more readily available, and in vast quantities that could easily meet fossil energy demand for several decades (Clemente, 2015). Interestingly enough, the enhanced oil recovery revolution that made possible the current oil boom also facilitates CO_2 underground storage—a method known as CO_2–EOR (NETL, 2010). According to the U.S. Energy Information Administration's *Annual Energy Outlook—2019,* the United States is poised to become a net energy exporter of fossil energy beginning in 2020, and will remain so through at least 2050 (U.S. Energy Information Administration, 2019). In addition to enhanced supply, technology will reduce the cost of transportation of energy resources to markets worldwide. With increased supply and greater access to fossil energy sources, it is unlikely that government will rely on the "peak oil" argument as a primary reason to pursue alternative energy resource development. There are, however, different policy narratives and strategies that can be and are being fruitfully pursued by alternative energy advocates in an effort to increase the supply and use of renewable energy.

While fossil energy is not viewed as a public good, the planet's atmosphere is viewed as such. Clean air and water, and maintaining ecological diversity, are favored public policy goals negatively impacted by the use of fossil energy. Decades of peer-reviewed academic research has led to international scientific consensus on the link between carbon emissions from fossil energy use and global climate change (NASA, 2019; IPCC, 2018). Air quality issues are linked with human health problems such as asthma and some cancers (Union of Concerned Scientists, 2016). Limited water supplies are sometimes tapped for energy extraction use, particularly for nonconventional oil and gas recovery. According to the U.S. Geological Survey (USGS), less than 1 percent of water used in the United States is used in oil and gas recovery. Hydraulic fracturing chemicals mixed with the water used in well injection could negatively impact human health as well as animal and plant species (see U.S. EPA, 2016). The use of fossil energy, therefore, produces at least some marginal social and environmental costs borne by humans and nonhuman species alike. Public policy seeks to recognize and properly distribute marginal social costs to producers and users of fossil energy. U.S. energy and environmental protection policies have focused on the production, distribution, and safe use of fossil energy.

With greater understanding of the global problems posed by fossil energy use, technological advances in alternative energy solutions present increasingly

Low Water Levels at Hoover Dam
iStock / Getty Images Plus / 4kodiak

feasible solutions. At the Rio Earth Summit in June 1992, the United States was widely criticized for being one of the leading energy polluters in the world due to its heavy reliance on fossil energy sources. Nearly three decades later, public policy changes at the state and federal levels, technological breakthroughs, and substantial private sector investment has led to a 5,000 percent increase in renewable energy consumption (Energy Information Administration, 2018). Despite a near 32 percent increase in the U.S. population between 1990 and 2018, and an approximate 82 percent increase in GDP over the same period, carbon dioxide emissions in 2017 were little more than 1 percent greater than CO_2 emissions present in 1990. To be sure, there were variations in emissions levels over the time period (U.S. EPA, 2019).

CLIMATE CHANGE AND CARBON

Carbon emissions and concentration levels in the atmosphere became a more prominent policy issue in the 1960s (Moss et al., 2010), as documented in a report by the Stanford Research Institute entitled *Sources, Abundance, and Fate of Gaseous Atmospheric Polluters* (Wiles, 2018). Environmental concerns led to the establishment of the United Nations Environment Programme, but it was not until 1988 that the Intergovernmental Panel on Climate Change (IPCC) was established. Following release of the first IPCC report showing rising atmospheric temperatures over the twentieth century, rapidly growing international concerns led to the Earth Summit in Rio de Janeiro in 1992, during which developed nations formally committed to returning to 1990 emission levels. In 1997, the Kyoto Protocol was signed by 84 signatory nations committed to an overall global reduction in carbon emissions by

2012. The United States signed the treaty in 1998, but the U.S. Senate did not vote for treaty ratification. Effective 2012, Canada withdrew from the Kyoto Protocol and Japan and Russia chose not to agree to further greenhouse gas (GHG) emission reduction targets. In 2015, the Paris Agreement, or Paris Climate Accord, committed 196 signatory nations to establishing and achieving individual national plans for reducing greenhouse gas emissions so as to keep average annual global temperature increases to below 2.0°C. The United States signed the agreement during the tenure of President Barack Obama, but the United States abandoned the agreement during the first year of the Trump administration. Despite the U.S. policy shift, the European Union (EU) member nations as well as other developed and developing nations are continuing to move forward with agreed-upon climate change policies and enhanced renewable energy development (Capros et al., 2011; Castro, 2014). The youth vote in the EU 2019 elections exhibited growing commitment to greenhouse gas emission reduction through strong support for the Green Party. It is unlikely, therefore, that EU commitments to reducing the impact of climate change through GHG emission reductions are going to fade anytime soon (Khan, 2019).

Climate change has been empirically linked to "anthropogenic emissions of carbon dioxide (CO_2), methane (CH_4), nitrous oxide (N_2O), hydrofluorocarbons (HFCs), perfluorocarbons (PFCs), sulfur hexafluoride (SF6), hydrochlorofluorocarbons (HCFCs), chlorofluorocarbons (CFCs), the aerosol precursor and the chemically active gases sulfur dioxide (SO_2), carbon monoxide (CO), nitrogen oxides (NOx), and non-methane volatile organic compounds (NMVOCs)" (IPCC, 2000: 3). By the end of the twenty-first century, the surface temperature of the Earth will likely exceed by 1.5°C the average planetary surface temperature of the mid- to late nineteenth century. In some regions, the average surface temperature will increase by more than 2.0°C. In addition to increased temperature on land as well as ocean temperature, climate change models indicate that weather patterns will change, leading to changing amounts and locations of precipitation, and increases in the number and intensity of large-scale weather events impacting human society and local/regional economies (Hsiang et al., 2017). Some regions will become wetter than normal, while other areas will become more arid. Melting ice caps in the Arctic and Antarctic regions will lead to rising ocean levels. Carbon dioxide levels in the Earth's atmosphere are absorbed by the ocean; in high concentrations, CO_2 will very likely cause increased acidification of the ocean, impacting marine life and fisheries on a vast scale.

Electric power and heat production (25 percent), agriculture and forestry (24 percent), industry (21 percent), and transportation (14 percent) are among the leading sectors in the production of global greenhouse gas emissions (US EPA, 2018). While the power production sector contributes to climate change through the combustion of fossil fuels, such as coal, natural gas, and petroleum, climate change actually negatively impacts power production, a growth area in research and a concern to policy makers (Schaeffer et al., 2012). In other words, some short-term gains actually contribute to longer-term societal and environmental challenges.

Changes in global precipitation patterns and regional droughts will result in reduced hydropower production capacity (Mukheibir, 2013) in some regions due to greatly diminished water reservoirs. Barring the development of new water reservoirs in wetter climates capable of producing hydropower in an environmentally responsible manner, an established carbon-free source of electricity generation will decline. Without sufficient alternative energy supply, fossil energy use for electricity generation will likely expand to meet electricity demand. Regional climatic changes will also impact wind speeds, impacting in turn wind energy generation. Pryor and Barhelmie (2011) conclude that wind energy in currently high-quality wind resource locations will continue to produce electricity for the next several decades, but as climate change occurs, so too will wind resource patterns. Solar photovoltaic and concentrated solar power will likewise be impacted by climate change. Increased temperatures, strong winds, blowing dust, and heat waves all have the potential to damage equipment, reduce efficiency, and destroy or damage power transmission lines. Cloudiness due to increased moisture vapor in the Earth's atmosphere reduces the power output of solar photovoltaic and concentrated solar power systems (Patt et al., 2013: 99). In terms of alternative fuels, corn ethanol will be particularly impacted by climate change. Corn plants and corn ethanol production both consume large amounts of water, and water will be less readily available if climate change occurs as anticipated; moreover, higher ambient temperatures will lead to even greater water consumption by corn producers, with lower expected yields being generated (Dominguez-Faus et al., 2013). While many renewable energy systems do not require a large land footprint, corn and algae grown for fuel production both require significant land and water resources, competing with food production and leading to unintended negative externalities (see Dale et al., 2011; Harvey and Pilgrim, 2011; Hejazi et al., 2015).

A major response to climate change comes in the form of international, national, and state/regional commitments to reducing carbon emissions. In terms of electricity generation, coal and natural gas power plants are the largest emitters of CO_2. Governmental restrictions on carbon emission into the atmosphere necessarily increase the cost of fossil energy-powered electricity generation through the purchase of carbon credits or through the cost of retrofitting plants to capture carbon. Even more restrictive, the licensing of new fossil energy power plants may be a function of political circumstance—that is, if a political majority rejects the use of fossil energy for electric power production, then plant construction will not be permitted. With a wavering commitment at the federal level due to congressional gridlock, and a lack of executive branch support from the Trump administration, it may well be that state and local commitment to carbon emission reductions and support for alternative and clean energy sources will serve as the principal loci of green solutions to climate change (Dietchman, 2017).

The use of policy tools such as government regulation and green energy mandates require significant changes in market and consumer behavior. Sellers in a market will only produce and sell a good so long as they are meeting average costs in the short term, and will exit the market at some point if greater profits can be made elsewhere. If climate change policies are too restrictive, it will likely result in a sharp reduction of the supply of electricity unless new suppliers who meet climate change policy guidelines can provide an equal or better quality good at a reasonable price. In most cases, alternative energy—particularly renewable energy—cannot meet that demand within the aforementioned parameters. Therefore, with higher energy costs, there will be a need for (a) greater efficiency in transmission and use and (b) government intervention (e.g., subsidization, energy portfolio requirements, etc.) to encourage renewable energy production and use.

Often overlooked in efforts to reduce carbon emissions is the role of nuclear energy, a form of energy that produces carbon-free electricity and does not often experience intermittency issues faced by many renewable energy systems. Greater use of nuclear as opposed to natural gas as a bridge fuel toward a renewable energy future would have the twofold impact of reducing carbon emissions and allowing additional time for technological and market maturity of renewable energy. This would lessen many of the political, economic, and social tensions likely to arise if energy supplies are curtailed or price spikes are prohibitive, and all the while benefit continued economic growth in a growing nation and world (Bauer et al., 2011).

ENERGY AND WATER

Climate change and energy security have played a prominent role in the renewable energy policy agenda (King and Gullege, 2014; Bernell and Simon, 2016; Sovacool and Brown, 2010). Less frequently discussed, but of equal if not greater significance, is the energy–water nexus. Along with arable land, access to energy and water were two of the most consequential requirements in the development of early agrarian-based human civilization. While human civilization has changed rather dramatically over the millennia, one thing most certainly has not changed: the need for ready supplies of aforementioned basic needs—in particular, arable land, energy, and water (see Sovacool and Sovacool, 2009).

In the distant past, energy and water resource needs were largely independent of each other. Water was drawn from rivers or wells either through a gravity feed process or through the use of buckets or Archimedes' screws—a mechanical device developed in antiquity to efficiently move water. Energy was gathered from surface mines in the form of coal or bitumen, animal sources (tallow or other fats), or in the form of wood from native forests or scrubland.

Technological innovation and industrialization have brought water and energy into closer proximity in the promotion of human welfare. In terms of energy for the contemporary world, hydroelectric dams are a clear representation of the energy–water nexus. Any form of electrical energy generation involving thermal energy and steam generation must be cooled using water, air, or some other cooling process in order for the thermodynamic cycle—a Rankine cycle—to maintain a cyclic process and continue to work. The fluid properties of water make it a useful medium for well injection and flushing for fossil energy extraction. As a solvent, water is very useful for cleaning equipment to remove particulates that may impede machine functions in both manufacturing and ongoing operations. Thus, water is needed to extract or produce energy, but energy is needed to extract (through pumping) and transport water resources. Without energy, water resources would not be easily available for use—we'd have to go back to carrying water in buckets, and that would not be very efficient nor would it meet the needs of a modern world.

Traditionally, many aspects of the energy–water nexus were managed at the local level, but with increased demands on both energy and water there is a growing need for federal-level policy makers to provide significant guidance in optimizing the use of natural resources, to "enhance reliability of energy and water systems," and to promote safe and responsible use of water and energy resources (Bauer et al., 2014: vi). With an estimated use of 355 billion gallons of water per day, water management is a critical policy issue in the United States (Maupin et al., 2015: 1).

Water use can be categorized as either water withdrawal or water consumption. Withdrawal means that water is removed from a source, but that a portion of the water is returned to the source and is available for other purposes. Water consumption means that the water is removed from the source and none is returned (World Economic Forum, 2010). The largest water *withdrawals* in the United States—41 percent—are for agriculture purposes. Approximately 39 percent of water withdrawals are made for the production of electric power. The remaining 20 percent of withdrawals are made for commercial, domestic, or industrial purposes. Approximately 85 percent of water *consumption* is for agricultural purposes. Eight percent of water consumption is for domestic and commercial purposes, while 4 percent of water consumption is for industrial and mining purposes. A scant 3 percent of water consumption is attributable to electric power production (Duke Energy, 2009: 9).

While energy production is associated with a significant portion of all water *withdrawals*, it is not associated with a significant portion of water *consumption*. Nevertheless, water use for all purposes must be reduced. A major reason has to do with climate change. As weather patterns change, so too will precipitation patterns. Increased aridity in some regions will lead to a decline in available water resources for hydropower facilities and for other related purposes. Arid regions may become even more arid, resulting in higher demands on electricity for water pumping from groundwater sources or desalination processing in coastal regions. Ongoing population growth will lead to growing demands for water to be used in the agricultural, commercial, and mining sectors, and for domestic use in homes and apartments.

Water treatment and transportation require energy. In a statement before the U.S. Senate's Subcommittee on Water and Power, Committee on Energy and Natural Resources, Senator Jeanne Shaheen (D-NH) noted that in the state of California "nearly 20 percent of the State's electricity and 30 percent of their natural gas consumption is used to move, treat, and heat water . . . and nearly 20 percent of the water is lost [due to seepage and pipe leaks] before the water is delivered" (Shaheen, 2012: 1–2).

In testimony before the subcommittee, Henry L. Green, president of the National Institute of Building Sciences, elaborated on the need to better manage water resources and reduce water losses. Green cited a 2009 U.S. Geological Survey report (Kenny et al., 2009) stating that "nearly two trillion gallons of water is lost annually through leaks in water pipes [20 percent of water]. This annual water loss due to seepage equates to an estimated $1 to $2 billion in lost revenue. Cost implications aside, it is estimated that a five percent reduction in water distribution leakage would save 313 million kWh of electricity . . . and avoid approximately 225,000 metric tons of CO_2 emissions annually." Beyond the electricity losses associated with water loss, there are electricity losses due to power transmission line losses coming in the form of heat generation and radiation emanation. It is estimated that more than 60 percent of electricity produced is lost before it reaches end users, either through transmission line losses or due to losses associated with power generation inefficiencies (Wirfs-Brock, 2015).

Demands on both water and energy will increase substantially in the decades ahead. According to the World Health Organization, a third of the world's population lacks appropriate quantities of water, and by 2050 nearly half will face water shortages. Energy demand will grow at a more rapid rate in the developing world than in the developed world. "The highest increases will occur in Latin America where electricity generation per capita will be four times higher than today followed by Africa and Asia, where it will almost triple" (Jain, 2010: 5). Worldwide, the demand for electricity will more than double. Due to technological advances, water consumption for electricity generation in Africa, Europe, and North America is projected to increase only slightly, while water consumption for electricity generation in Latin America and Asia is projected to nearly double "on a per capita basis" (Jain, 2010: 5). While demand for petroleum resources will decline, the demand for water resources to access nonconventional petroleum and gas will increase by nearly 80 percent (Jain, 2010). For Pacific Rim nations, water consumption is expected to increase, on average, by one-third by 2035 (Tidwell and Moreland, 2016).

Electricity generation is responsible for 41 percent of all freshwater withdrawals in the United States (Macknick et al., 2012: 1). In older plant designs, freshwater was used once to cool the plant in order to maintain an efficient operational cycle (recall the Rankine cycle mentioned earlier). Newer plant designs feature the capture of waste heat—the heat captured by the coolant—which is then used in a combined cycle power generation design. With heat energy removed, the water can be used again in the primary generation cooling process. Water consumption, usually as a result of evaporation in cooling ponds, is more than double for new generation plants than for older generation plants (Macknick et al., 2012: 6; Madden et al., 2013; Toricellini et al., 2003). That said, it is the case that some combined cycle natural gas plants are quite water- and energy-efficient.

Renewable energy systems face their own challenges in terms of water use. Solar photovoltaic and wind energy systems are by far the most water-efficient. According to a meta-analysis reported by Macknick et al. (2012), the median water use for passive solar photovoltaic systems is one gallon of water for every MWh of electricity produced. The water is used for cleaning solar photovoltaic panels to remove dust and other debris. There is no appreciable water used for wind energy electricity generation, which makes it an ideal system to produce electricity in semiarid or arid locations featuring good wind resources. Other renewable energy systems are much more water use-intense. Hydropower, for example, requires an average of 4,491 gallons of water for each MWh of electricity produced, but the water is reusable for other purposes. Biopower systems consume, on average, between 235 and 553 gallons of water per MWh of electricity produced. Concentrated solar power systems using trough or power tower consume on average between 786 and 906 gallons of water per MWh. Passive solar photovoltaic and wind energy systems place the lowest demand on water resources. At the present time, solar PV and wind energy provide slightly more than 8 percent of electricity in the United States (Dawoud et al., 2018: 2041). The remaining 92 percent of U.S. electricity generation involves significant water withdrawals and consumption.

The energy–water nexus is a complex system being placed under growing stress. The most obvious way of reducing that stress is through human behavioral change. Simply reducing energy and water consumption will result in lower demand (and supply) of energy and fewer water withdrawals and less water consumption. That might mean asking an individual to prioritize use, or abstain from use of water or electricity at certain times or on certain days. A second method of managing the energy–water nexus is through greater efficiency, providing the consumer greater benefit with either reduced or equal consumption. A good example of this is the conversion of light bulbs from incandescent bulbs to diodes, the latter producing more light while using less than one-fifth of the electricity.

While aforementioned methods rely heavily on individual consumer behavior, a third method involves collective action. Reliance solely on individual behavior poses challenges because individuals faced with limited or scarce resources are often prone to hoarding or to misuse of the resource, and therefore put other resource users at serious disadvantage (Hardin, 1968). Collective action requires us to think about our individual goals and needs in the context of societal and environmental goals and needs (Bena, 2012).

Collective action initiatives exist at the international, national, and regional levels alike. The United Nations CEO Water mandate is a corporate initiative with "more than 12,000 corporate participants and stakeholders from more than 140 countries" (UN CEO Water Mandate, 2018). The Water Resources Group 2030, which is housed within the International Finance Corporation of the World Bank, is an international organization operating in Asia, Africa, and Latin America to manage water governance and sustainability issues through the promotion of an inclusive dialogue about water use (Water Resources Group, 2030, 2018). At the federal level in the United States, water is governed by a combination of treaty obligations (international with Canada and Mexico and with recognized tribes) and a number of statutes, such as the Clean Water Act of 1972, which are enforced by the Department of the Interior, the U.S. Department of Agriculture, and the Environmental Protection Agency. Water is generally governed by access and use rights. In the arid Western United States, water is governed by prior appropriation, while in the areas of the country that have greater precipitation, water is governed by riparian rights. Water projects involving reservoirs are governed by federal or state law. Water projects may also be governed by special districts that distribute water based on availability and water rights. The water–energy nexus and water and energy use intensity will likely offer new and more conflict-ridden challenges to individuals and institutions governing water use (see Mullin, 2009). Reducing or avoiding conflict will require new methods of governing water resources, employing collaborative methods to identify individual and shared interests, challenges, and capacity to create effective resource governance, keeping in mind the need for socially and environmentally just solutions (see Weber and Khademian, 2008; Weber, 2012).

CARBON-BASED FUELS: CURRENT AND FUTURE AVAILABILITY

Carbon-based fuels are often referred to as fossil fuels. The three commonly known carbon-based fuels are coal, petroleum, and natural gas. Under intense geologic pressure and exposed to the Earth's intense core heat, decayed and decaying materials—such as diatoms—primarily from the Carboniferous Period (360–286 million years ago), formed organic compounds composed of hydrogen and carbon atoms. These hydrogen and carbon atoms are linked by chemical bonds to form hydrocarbon chains in one of two types of chemical formations (http://www.energyquest.ca.gov/story/chapter08.html, accessed April 20, 2004). Aliphatic formations are either straight or branched chains of hydrogen and carbon atoms, while aromatic formations involve something known as a benzene ring formation (see http://www.obio.com/hydrocarbon%20chains.htm, accessed April 20, 2004).

Gasoline fuel for use in cars contains a blend of liquid hydrocarbons. In order to produce gasoline or other useful products from fossil fuels, such as crude petroleum, specific carbon hydrocarbon chains—or fractions—must be separated from crude oil through "cracking"—that is, distillation. Petroleum refineries are large chemical processing plants where crude oil is "cracked," a process that reduces the molecular weight of crude oil hydrocarbons (http://www.towson.edu/~sweeting/enrich/petrolum.pdf, accessed April 20, 2004).

Following the production of lighter fractions by cracking, various fuels and other petroleum products are then separated. Gasoline is the most important and prevalent fuel produced from petroleum. Gasoline contains a mixture of liquid hydrocarbons. The amount of gasoline that can be derived from a barrel of oil is dependent on the quality of the crude petroleum. Typically, about 25 gallons of gasoline can be refined from a barrel (42 gallons) of crude petroleum. In the internal combustion engine, oxygen molecules are reacted with gasoline to convert potential energy into kinetic energy. Combustion of gasoline produces a variety of exhaust gases, primarily dioxides.

COMMON FOSSIL ENERGY SOURCES: U.S. SUPPLY AND USE

U.S. consumption of petroleum has risen steadily since 1950. Currently, the United States consumes approximately 20 million barrels of crude petroleum per day. In the 1970s, U.S. domestic petroleum production steadily declined, which led to increased reliance on petroleum imports. In the 1980s, President Ronald Reagan's energy policies led to increased petroleum production along the North Slope in Alaska. The policy impact was short-lived, however, and in the 1990s, U.S. petroleum production again declined to levels not seen since the 1940s. Technological breakthroughs and policy change led to a rapid reversal of fortunes in petroleum production, particularly in the continental United States. Since 2005, petroleum production has risen fairly steadily, with the exception of a brief period in 2015–2016. U.S. production now exceeds 10 million barrels per day, exceeding previous peak production in 1970 (figure 1.1).

One of the most common fossil fuels used in the United States is coal, which is found throughout the continental United States and is used both as a heating source and for generating electricity. Coal can used in a solid form or be made into coal gas—a highly volatile mixture of hydrogen and carbon monoxide. Coal production rose steadily between 1949 and 2008. In 2008, 1.04 billion short tons of coal were used for electricity production. Due to environmental policies enacted during the Obama administration and a rising supply of low-priced natural gas—due to hydraulic fracturing—coal consumption dropped precipitously. By 2017, U.S. coal consumption for electricity generation had dropped to 544 million short tons—approximately one-half the amount consumed only nine years earlier. In 2017, the Trump administration reversed environmental policies that regulated coal use. Nevertheless, natural gas and

Figure 1.1   Domestic Petroleum Extraction in the United States, 1900–2017 (in bbls)

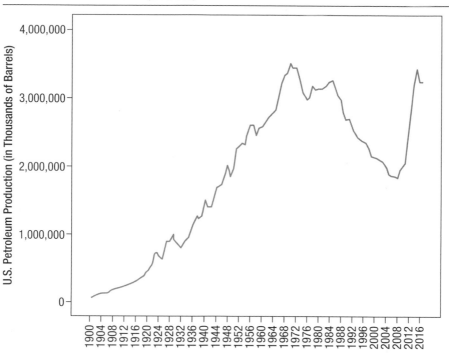

Data Source: Energy Information Administration, U.S. Department of Energy

other energy sources remain an attractive alternative to the return to coal for electricity generation due to both cost and environmental considerations—natural gas is both plentiful and relatively inexpensive and its use produces far fewer CO_2 emissions (see figure 1.2).

Natural gas consumption has increased tremendously over the last two decades. Hailed as a cleaner alternative to heating oil and coal, many homeowners and businesses converted their furnace systems to natural gas. Natural gas is primarily composed of methane gas, but may also contain small quantities of other hydrocarbon gases, such as ethane and propane. Currently, the United States extracts and markets approximately 20 trillion cubic feet of natural gas on an annual basis (figure 1.3).

According to the *U.S. Crude Oil and Natural Gas Proved Reserves, Year-End 2016,* there are 35.2 billion barrels of crude petroleum in proven reserves in the United States and U.S. protectorates. Production from petroleum reserves represents approximately 9 percent of proven reserves per year. According to the U.S. Department of Energy, Energy Information Administration, as of 2016 the United States had 341.1 trillion cubic feet of natural gas in proven reserves, which included a 16.8 trillion cubic foot increase via new field discoveries

Figure 1.2   Coal Consumption in Electricity Generation, 1949–2017 (in short tons)

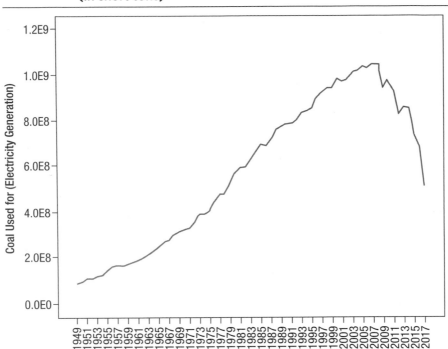

Data Source: Energy Information Administration, U.S. Department of Energy

and statistical adjustments. Production from natural gas reserves are growing at a rate 1.73 times the rate of new discoveries, and represent approximately 8 percent of proven reserves per year.

Proven reserves change on a regular basis, and do not contribute much to a broad understanding of the long-term future of fossil energy reserves. According to the U.S. Energy Information Administration (2018b):

> Technically recoverable reserves consist of *proved* reserves and unproved resources. Proved reserves of crude oil and natural gas are the estimated volumes expected to be produced, with reasonable certainty, under existing economic and operating conditions. Unproved resources of crude oil and natural gas are additional volumes estimated to be technically recoverable without consideration of economics or operating conditions, based on the application of current technology.

According to a U.S. EIA report in 2012, technically recoverable crude oil reserves are estimated to be 220.2 billion barrels. The EIA estimates that as of

Figure 1.3   Natural Gas Consumption in Electricity Generation, 1997–2017 (in mcf)

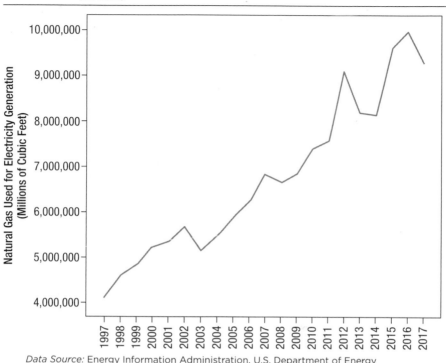

Data Source: Energy Information Administration, U.S. Department of Energy

2015, the U.S. technically recoverable natural gas reserves are 2,355 trillion cubic feet; these reserves are estimated to last for approximately eighty-six years (U.S. Energy Information Administration, 2012, 2018b).

   While the future is not known with absolutely certainty, science can tell policy makers and marketplace consumers with confidence that crude petroleum will be readily available much beyond the current century. According to British Petroleum estimates, the world's oil reserves will last for roughly fifty years (Tully, 2014). A more optimistic projection made by Rystad Energy AS, a Norwegian oil and gas service corporation, estimates that the United States has 264 billion barrels of oil remaining with a projected lifespan of seventy-seven years based on projected demand levels. Rystad also estimates that world oil remaining is 2.09 trillion barrels of oil and will last for seventy-one years (Rystad, 2016). Technological breakthroughs will likely result in more fossil energy discoveries as well as result in greater efficiency in consumption. Alternative or renewable energy source development is one method of increasing domestic energy supply for the twenty-first century and beyond.

CULTURE SHIFTS AND THE RISE OF GREEN POLITICS

Climate change and resource depletion provide impetus for pursuing these key public policy questions: Why pursue alternative energy and fuels, and why now? As a compelling "wicked" problem, energy policy in the twenty-first century requires the inclusion of a values-based discussion regarding the type of fuels and energy sources that are consistent with the political, economic, and social values important to consumers. Social values are not uniform in distribution across the country, nor are they spontaneously generated. Rather, social values evolve over time and are a function of historically grounded, often regionally specific trends (political culture) and present considerations (public opinion).

Values and beliefs shape the way societies and individuals within them respond to and create discourse around the policy issues arising from climate change and the use of alternative energy (Allo and Laureiro, 2014; Bajzeli et al., 2013; Borgstede et al., 2013; Brulle et al., 2012; Frumkin et al., 2012; Giddens, 2009; Steentjes et al., 2017; Webb, 2012; Whitmarsh and Corner, 2017; Wicker and Beckin, 2013). Costs, benefits, availability, and desirability are often evaluated through the lens of established values and prevailing beliefs. Values and belief systems tend to be fairly stable over long periods of time. That said, there have been times in which momentous events occur or circumstances arise during which values and beliefs can change far more quickly than usual.

Shifts in long-established and widely shared values and belief systems (i.e., political culture) may change substantially along intergenerational lines. The most recent example of a major intergenerational change occurred in the 1960s. In his book *Culture Shift in Advanced Industrial Society* (1990), Ronald Inglehart pointed to the baby boomer generation as substantially different from their parents' generation. Inglehart's analysis of longitudinal public opinion poll datasets supported his contention that earlier generations of Americans tended toward materialism in their beliefs and values. Materialists tend to view public policy in terms of policy impacts on their own narrowly defined economic self-interest. Materialists frequently ask government to lower their tax burden and to limit the adverse impact of social and economic maladies. Additionally, materialists call for government to fight inflation, which will negatively impact their economic well-being in the form of their standard of living. Based on Inglehart's theory, materialists' energy policy concerns lead them to focus their primary attention on readily available energy supplies and relatively low and stable per-unit prices.

The Vietnam War notwithstanding, baby boomers grew up in a period of relative luxury and surplus and with narrower income inequality than exists in present-day America (Lepore, 2015). Boomers were too young to remember the short-term post–Second World War economic recession and unemployment concerns, but the oldest among them do recall well the economic boom of the 1950s and early 1960s. Due in part to the relatively pacific socialization experiences of their youth, Inglehart argues that boomers have higher-level needs compared to their parents' generation. Basic social and economic needs were readily satisfied for many Americans during the 1950s and early 1960s, a time when boomers were in their formative youth. Absent concerns about basic needs, Inglehart argues that as postmaterialists, boomers are more concerned with higher-order life issues such as environmental justice, racial justice, and political and social equity than they are with personal economic gain and tax relief.

In terms of alternative energy policy, postmaterialists tend to view alternative energy as a method of improving the quality of life for both human as well as plant and animal species globally. Alternative energy production often costs more per kilowatt hour of electricity produced, but postmaterialists are more likely to view the increased cost as a trade-off necessary to promote and maintain global economic justice as well as a method of freeing the United States and other developed and developing nations from the yoke of foreign petroleum producers.

More particularly, boomer postmaterialists grew up during a period in which environmental policy makers were considering public policies designed to clean up the environment. As Inglehart (1990: 267–270) points out, postmaterialists worked to advance the issues of social and environmental justice in the 1960s and 1970s. Despite Reagan's efforts in the 1980s to revitalize traditional crude petroleum and nuclear energy policies, interest in alternative and renewable energy sources remained strong. Cultural values regarding the environment and the need to pursue energy independence through new methods of power generation were not abandoned, although funding for national laboratory work shifted significantly toward defense-related research (Stowsky, 1992).

GREEN POLITICS AND ENVIRONMENTAL PUBLIC INTEREST GROUPS

The political culture shift of the 1960s and 1970s led to the rise of the Greens. In European politics, the Green Party became a major force in the politics of many Western European governments. In the United States, it is more appropriate to refer to the "Green movement" since the party's direct influence is very limited within the two-party system of American politics. The Green agenda is based in environmental activism seeking to create a balanced relationship between human society and the protection of flora and fauna. Greens tend to reject the industrial capitalist society, typically arguing that industrialization created an unbalanced, unsustainable, and unjust relationship between human society and the natural environment. At the same time, Greens tend to reject the other dominant worldview of the time—namely, Marxian ideology—in large part because Marxism focused primarily on the centrality of *human* societal needs, which in practice tended to produce violations of environmental justice as occur in industrial capitalist societies. The Greens tend to share Marxism's rejection of capitalism, and embrace eco-socialism and various forms of collective action designed to advance environmental justice.

The Greens have, as part of their political agenda, the development of alternative energy policy. Petroleum and other hydrocarbon fuels are rejected by Greens because of the damage to the environment caused by carbon emissions. From their postmaterialistic perspective, Greens view zero- or low-emission renewable energy sources as representative of the true costs of energy, whereas petroleum and other hydrocarbon fuels, while initially less expensive, actually have significant hidden costs in the form of emissions that harm the environment as well as create inequalities in human society through emissions-related disease and mortality.

The Green movement is, by no means, a historical artifact. The Green Party USA is not a major political party, but its ideas about environmental justice have been embraced by some members of the Democratic Party. In 2019, U.S. Representative Alexandria Ocasio-Cortez (D-NY) introduced the "Green New Deal" into Congress. The bill represented a radical departure for business as usual, calling for the rejection of fossil energy and the speedy implementation of a clean energy economy. In Europe, the Green Party is a major political party in several countries and the EU, and it has actively and successfully promoted the Green agenda. European youth, in particular, tend to be highly supportive of the Greens. In May 2019, the Green Party won the second-most votes in Germany and the third-most votes in France during the EU legislative elections, with youthful environmental activists, such as sixteen-year-old Greta Thunberg of Sweden, demanding an accelerated public policy response to global climate change (Birnbaum et al., 2019).

A major impact of the political culture shift and the rise of Green ideology that occurred in the 1960s and 1970s can be seen in the first major statutorily derived steps toward the adoption of a clean, green energy paradigm. Emergent environmental and energy policies were given life by youthful postmaterialists who staffed agencies at the federal and state levels, working for the advancement of environmental quality through efforts to protect land, water, and air quality in a holistic manner. The dream of reduced pollutants from hydrocarbon fuels remains alive and well in the work and values of postmaterialists (Toke, 2000; Holland et al., 1996).

A secondary, but equally important, impact of the shift toward postmaterialist values can be seen in a new political and social activism that has become an increasingly acceptable method of advancing political and social causes. The 1960s and 1970s witnessed the growth of public interest groups—pressure groups dedicated to generalized societal benefits rather than to narrowly defined economic benefits for group members. Postmaterialists and public interest groups often have parallel value structures rooted in the desire to serve the collective good. In tandem, the postmaterialists' commitment to using activism as a method of promoting social and political causes, and public interest groups' sense of social responsibility, served to blunt the impact of the Reagan administration's efforts to promote energy "independence" through the enhancement of domestic fossil fuel supplies. These supplies would be created through both aggressive domestic petroleum exploration on U.S. public lands and renewed efforts to advance nuclear power production and plant construction.

The aforementioned question "why alternative energy?" is answerable on both an empirical and a normative basis. Empirically, we know well that fossil fuels are nonrenewable sources of energy, and that they are being depleted at a fairly rapid rate. There is also scientific consensus that climate change is caused by the use of fossil energy. Normatively, it is apparent that the postmaterialist view of social and economic justice leads many people to view alternative energy to be well worth the cost of promoting greater social and economic justice along with greater energy independence.

NEW ENVIRONMENTAL PARADIGM AND ALTERNATIVE ENERGY

Emerging over a decade prior to the work of Inglehart (1990), the New Environmental Paradigm (NEP) was one of the first theoretical developments to recognize the way in which individuals viewed human activity in relation to the environment. The NEP does not speak directly to the issue of alternative energy, but it does serve as a basis for understanding the historical forces that have led to the development of alternative energy policies. The paradigm requires that society and its members consider the impact of our choices on others—other individuals, other species—both now and in the future (textbox 1.1).

TEXTBOX 1.1 | The New Environmental Paradigm

1. Human beings are but one species among the many that are interdependently involved in the biotic communities that shape our social life.
2. Intricate linkages of cause and effect and feedback in the web of nature produce many unintended consequences from purposive human action.
3. The world is finite, so there are potent physical and biological limits constraining economic growth, social progress, and other societal phenomena.

Source: Catton and Dunlap, 1978: 45.

INSTITUTIONAL CHANGE AND INFLUENCE

To understand public policy, political scientists and policy analysts often look to new institutionalism—a sophisticated methodology that allows political scientists and policy analysts to study both institutional characteristics and constraints while simultaneously studying the values, opinions, and beliefs of institutional actors making decisions within particular political institutions. In this case, the institutions being addressed include: the U.S. Congress, the presidency, the federal courts, the federal bureaucracy, and parallel institutions operating at the state and local levels of government.

As an institution, Congress changes very slowly. The basic structure and rules governing the legislative process have not changed significantly in the last 230 years. Changes that have occurred in Congress tend to be related to party control of the institution, and the changing political and social values, beliefs, and opinions of congressional leaders and the memberships of the party caucuses. Over the last five decades, there have been several congressional shifts that have substantively impacted energy and environmental policy.

The U.S. general election in 1972 is most frequently associated with the infamous Watergate scandal, but for many baby boomers the election had an even more profound meaning. The 1972 election was, for many baby boomers, their first opportunity to vote—their first major opportunity to reshape the American political landscape. For many of these young postmaterialists, the election turned on issues important to their own generation of Americans. The Democratic Party retained a sizable majority in Congress, with a large freshman class composed of progressive and postmaterialist baby boomer congresspersons. The Democrats did quite well, gaining fifty-one seats in the House of Representatives and four seats in the Senate. The new progressive Democrat members of the 93rd Congress were eager to move forward with environmental and energy policies intended to regulate industry, reduce environmental pollution, and fund the advancement of renewable sources of energy to replace fossil energy.

While several landmark acts of environmental legislation had already been passed a half decade earlier, the 93rd Congress helped to preserve and expand the spirit of those laws. Within a half decade, congressional legislation led to the creation of the National Renewable Energy Laboratory (NREL). With the development of NREL, existing public and private laboratories working in the area of energy policy witnessed increased funding and an expanded charge to advance U.S. energy policy and explore new alternatives. Congressional legislation and oversight functioned to steer policy toward cleaner energy and toward improving technologies associated with renewable energy sources. Progressives were far less supportive of nuclear power as an alternative energy source. While the Democratic Congress did not act to shut down Three Mile Island following the 1979 partial meltdown of the reactor, it did investigate the event thoroughly. In so doing, it brought widespread attention to the risks associated with nuclear energy production. Thus, Congress was able to steer the energy policy agenda away from a major source of alternative energy.

Although the Republican Party regained control of the U.S. Senate in 1981, retaining control until 1987, the Democratic Party maintained its thirty-plus-year control of the House of Representatives. Divided party control of

Congress served to protect alternative energy policy from termination, although funds for these policies were severely constrained. House Democrats remained committed to the promotion of alternative energy policies. The basic values and beliefs of these congresspersons were still present both personally as well as in the spirit of nearly two decades of legislation that had emerged during the tenure of those who were once the freshman class of 1973. Nevertheless, alternative energy was not a high priority policy issue in the 1980s. Without constituent support and lacking interest group pressure, congressional attention to renewable energy waned substantially.

In the 1990s, however, Congress renewed its interest in the promotion of renewable energy. The Rio Summit and subsequent passage of the Energy Policy Act of 1992 were followed by increased congressional research and development (R & D) funding for renewable energy and energy efficiency. The overall amount of energy funding for R & D remained relatively low, with slight upward trending in the years following the terrorist attacks of September 11, 2001, with a substantial portion of the funding going to nuclear R & D and fossil energy R & D, both being heavily supported by the Republican majority at the time—next-generation nuclear and nontraditional fossil energy from hydraulic fracturing. An institution often divided along party lines, with ever-changing majorities, and comprised of members with diverse values and priorities, Congress has struggled with consistency in advancing the alternative energy agenda.

Crisis, however, often proves to be an effective method of producing policy change. In the case of Congress and energy funding, it turned out to be a combination of crisis and the highly effectively leadership of House Speaker Nancy Pelosi (D-CA) and Senate Majority Leader Harry Reid (D-NV). In the wake of the 2008 Great Recession and working closely with newly elected President Barack Obama, Congress was able to pass the American Recovery and Reinvestment Act of 2009, which more than tripled the R & D budget for the Department of Energy—funding was heavily focused on smart grid technology, energy efficiency, and renewable energy. The 2009 spike in energy R & D turned out to be a short-term bonanza, as funding levels returned to levels not much different from those of 2008 (Clark, 2018).

The evolving nature of the presidency and the priorities of individual presidents offer important insight into the issue of alternative energy. Presidents are often policy leaders, establishing national priorities and broad goals for their terms of office and for the future. President Theodore Roosevelt, for instance, demonstrated prescience when he advocated the establishment of the national park system, reserving public lands for recreational use as well as the preservation of native plant and animal species in a largely pristine environment. Other presidents have demonstrated similar concern with the preservation of the environment and the need to balance societal needs with a responsibility to be good stewards to the natural environment.

President Nixon signed major legislation—the National Environmental Policy Act of 1969 (NEPA) 42 U.S.C. 4321–4347; the Clean Air Act of 1970 (CAA) 42 U.S.C. ss/1251 et seq.; the Endangered Species Act of 1973 (ESA) 7 U.S.C. 136 & 16 U.S.C. 460; and the Occupational Safety and Health Act of 1970 (OSHA) 29 U.S.C. 651—establishing a national commitment to environmental protection. These pieces of legislation moved national energy policy toward a greater commitment to alternative energy; this was done primarily for the purpose of reducing harmful emissions resulting from the combustion of hydrocarbon fuels. President Jimmy Carter signed into law the Clean Water Act of 1977 (CWA) 33 U.S.C. ss/1251 et seq. These landmark laws reflect a growing postmaterialist values shift during this period, recognizing that the economic and social needs and desires of humans must be carefully balanced with the needs of the natural environment to assure sustainability long into the future.

In 1977, President Carter established the U.S. Department of Energy (DOE) as a cabinet-level office in the Executive Office of the President (EOP). Previously, energy issues were addressed by various federal offices with little concern for coordination. The creation of the DOE was a recognition of the need to better coordinate national energy needs with energy resource reserves and production and ongoing patterns of energy usage. The DOE conducts an annual energy policy review, determining the current status of fuel availability and use as well as coordinating external and internal research funding for the development of energy sources consistent with national and international environmental policy commitments (i.e., reduction in fuel emissions and fuel efficiency).

The Carter presidency witnessed two major crises in the operation of the nation's existing energy paradigm. First, Carter had to deal with an oil shortage resulting from a decision by the Organization of the Petroleum Exporting Countries (OPEC) to cut oil production, thus driving up prices dramatically and reducing supply for industrial and domestic commercial and household uses (e.g., trucking and private automobile use). The ensuing oil embargo demonstrated the high dependency of the United States and other industrialized nations on foreign oil supplies. If supplier nations were displeased with the United States, then organizations such as OPEC could use the oil supply as a potent diplomatic weapon to influence U.S. policy. Second, the Carter administration and the federal regulatory bureaucracy responded to the aforementioned Three Mile Island nuclear accident.

President Reagan did not actively promote renewable energy sources. Reagan did promote an alternative energy source, nuclear energy, albeit unsuccessfully. During Reagan's presidency, reduced federal funding for renewable energy substantially slowed its development. The 1980s witnessed a resurging commitment to petroleum, natural gas, and coal as primary sources of energy for the United States.

A major shift toward alternative energy development occurred during the last year of the George H. W. Bush presidency. In 1992, Congress passed the Environmental Policy Act (EPAct). Among other things, the EPAct of 1992 authorized the EPA to establish more stringent air quality standards. While President Bush did not have sufficient time in office to implement EPAct fully, the law served as an important policy shift that was quite favorable to the further development of low- or zero-emission alternative or renewable energies.

As a policy leader, President Bill Clinton established a renewed forceful commitment to environmental and alternative energy policy. As mentioned earlier, the Republican takeover of Congress in the 1994 midterm elections produced divided government and some friction over energy policy. Funding for alternative energy followed a growing budgetary commitment during the presidency of George H. W. Bush. In other words, there was some policy momentum in alternative energy established prior to Clinton's presidency. During Clinton's presidency, funding for alternative energy R & D—for the first time in nearly thirty years—reached parity on an adjusted dollar basis with funding levels of the mid-1970s.[1]

As a policy leader, Clinton, the first baby boomer elected president, astutely recognized rising postmaterialist values, the growing prominence of Green politics, and the sociological trends associated with the NEP. The Clean Cities Program, a programmatic response emerging from statutory mandates found in the EPAct of 1992, was implemented by the Clinton administration and authorized by Congress in 1993. The program was designed to develop partnerships between national, state, and local government, encouraging and rewarding state and local efforts to reduce harmful emissions and to improve air quality. As a former governor, Clinton recognized that innovative forces at the state and local level will most likely develop unique policy strategies needed to move away from the fossil fuel economy toward a twenty-first-century energy paradigm based on low- or zero-emission alternative and renewable energy sources using U.S.-originated technologies and energy management systems.

Early in his presidency, George W. Bush echoed a Reagan administration proposal to open the Arctic National Wildlife Refuge (ANWR) to petroleum and natural gas exploration. As a candidate for the presidency, Bush saw ANWR as one solution to the U.S. dependence on foreign petroleum supplies. The proposal was challenged by Democrats in Congress and by environmental public interest groups, and was opposed by a majority of the American people (ABC News, 2002). At this point, ANWR remains closed to petroleum or natural gas exploration. Following the events of September 11, 2001, however, Bush used his role as a policy leader to establish a renewed commitment to alternative energy policy development. The president proposed and Congress passed the Hydrogen Initiative. The president viewed hydrogen as a realistic fuel of the future. With the notable exception of ANWR petroleum and gas recovery, many of Bush's energy policy initiatives were incorporated into the Energy Policy Act of 2005 and the Energy Independence and Security Act of 2007.

In terms of alternative energy funding and policy initiatives, President Barack Obama was perhaps the most influential president since Jimmy Carter. The aforementioned ARRA of 2009 represented a multifold increase in funding for renewable energy policy initiatives at the federal level, with substantial funding making its way down to the state and local levels as well. Despite this tremendous increase in funding and policy initiative, President Obama's momentum toward a clean energy future—through statute and international agreement such as the Paris Climate Agreement—was greatly slowed following the assumption of power by a Republican majority in the House of Representatives in Congress in 2011. Through administrative rule-making authority, however, the Obama administration sought to limit the use of coal in power production as a method of reducing greenhouse gas emissions. Assuming office in January 2017, President Trump used his executive authority to reverse coal rules put into place during the Obama administration, and to pull the United States out of the Paris Climate Agreement. Faced with divided party control in Congress and a growing Green contingent in the Democratic congressional caucus, Trump has limited ability to move much further in reversing Obama-era energy policy.

The federal courts have played a role in the momentum shift toward alternative energy development. The changing role of the courts in legitimizing an expanded role of the national government in energy policy can be traced back to institutional changes in the 1930s. In more recent decades, the courts have reinforced the legitimacy of statutes and administrative rules governing the application of environmental policy related to the NEPA, the EPA, the CWA, and the CAA. Politics shapes administrative enforcement of regulation, and the courts have worked to steer interpretation of statutory and administrative rule compliance down a reasonable path. For instance, during the George W. Bush presidency, the EPA did not press forward with the regulation of air pollution caused by motor vehicles. A dozen U.S. states and several major cities petitioned the EPA to use its regulatory power to reduce motor vehicle greenhouse gas emissions, but their petition was repeatedly denied. Subsequently, in the case *Massachusetts et al. v. Environmental Protection Agency et al. 549 U.S. 497* (2007), the U.S. Supreme Court ruled in favor of the states, finding that the EPA did have the legal authority and responsibility to regulate greenhouse gas emissions emanating from automobiles. According to Johns (2015), the courts are overly cautious in assigning blame for greenhouse gas emissions, and even in fully recognizing climate change science, thus slowing down efforts to avoid the more damaging effects of climate change on the planet. The latter point was established in the Ninth Circuit Court of Appeals decision in *Washington Environmental Council v. Bellon* (2013).

The public bureaucracy plays a very significant role in shaping alternative-fuel development and use. Institutional changes in the public bureaucracies were a function of those bureaucracies coming into existence as a result of aforementioned legislation of the late 1960s and early 1970s. The DOE and the EPA (an independent regulatory agency) were created during a period of growing environmental awareness and rising postmaterialist values. The new agencies, whose employees are frequently advocates for environmental protection, use the power of regulation to restrict the use of hydrocarbon fuels *if* the combustion of the fuel produces unacceptable levels of emissions into the environment proven to be detrimental to human health.

In recent years, particularly during the Clinton administration, emission standards were tightened through the EPA's National Ambient Air Quality Standards (NAAQS). NAAQS emerged from the CAA of 1990, renewed. The NAAQS establish standards for ozone concentrations in the United States, in turn, shaping automobile manufacturing decisions and the development of more cleanly burning internal combustion engines (ICE). Ultimately, these NAAQS standards should lead to the greater use of alternative energy sources that produce lower levels of GHG emissions. The emission standards of NAAQS went into effect in 2010.

Regulation, however, is only one way in which public bureaucracies shape the development of alternative energy in the United States. Since the 1970s, the DOE has invested billions of dollars in alternative and renewable energy systems through the Office of Energy Efficiency and Renewable Energy (EERE). Through grants to university researchers and contracts with private sector enterprises, the EERE has brought government investment to bear on the development of renewable energy systems. Through government agencies such as EERE, research grants to universities have involved the development of demonstration projects, which typically illustrate the viability of renewable energy applications as well as identify areas where improvements can be made through either better science or better engineering. Grants have also contributed to scientific discoveries that make renewable energy less expensive and more viable for the average small business and private consumer. Additionally, DOE's national laboratories, such as the Argonne National Laboratory and the National Renewable Energy Laboratory (NREL), work with alternative energy industries to produce technologically advanced alternative energy systems. While the Argonne National Laboratory has been in existence since the 1940s, NREL emerged from the newly created DOE in the mid-1970s. Through NREL, the DOE has developed demonstration projects in many developing nations with the intent of illustrating the utility of renewable energy in suboptimal settings (textbox 1.2).

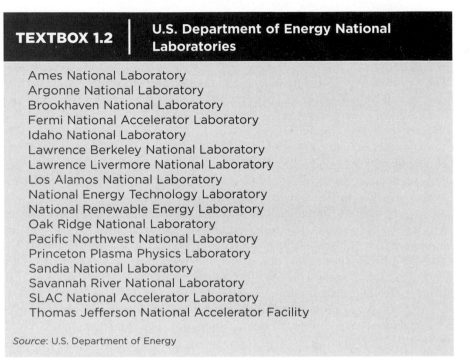

TEXTBOX 1.2 | **U.S. Department of Energy National Laboratories**

Ames National Laboratory
Argonne National Laboratory
Brookhaven National Laboratory
Fermi National Accelerator Laboratory
Idaho National Laboratory
Lawrence Berkeley National Laboratory
Lawrence Livermore National Laboratory
Los Alamos National Laboratory
National Energy Technology Laboratory
National Renewable Energy Laboratory
Oak Ridge National Laboratory
Pacific Northwest National Laboratory
Princeton Plasma Physics Laboratory
Sandia National Laboratory
Savannah River National Laboratory
SLAC National Accelerator Laboratory
Thomas Jefferson National Accelerator Facility

Source: U.S. Department of Energy

The DOE has also developed partnerships with automobile manufacturers to promote energy independence.

GLOBAL DEMANDS AND CONFLICT

Global demand for limited petroleum resources is another important explanation for the development of alternative or renewable energy resources. In the last thirty years, the world has changed dramatically. Several nations, such as China and India, which were once considered underdeveloped nations with stagnant economies, are industrializing at a rapid pace. For example, China's consumption of crude petroleum increased by 72 percent between 2008 and 2017; this accounted for approximately 23 percent of the total increase in world petroleum demand during that same time period. In 2019, developing nations accounted for 53 percent of the 101.36 million barrels of petroleum consumed every day. Developed nations, such as the United States, are consuming roughly the same volume of petroleum as they consumed forty years ago. Increased global demand may not directly impede the ability of the United States to meet its petroleum needs, but higher demand on the world supply of crude oil will likely mean higher petroleum prices.

Supply might also become more limited due to international conflict. In the past, OPEC used petroleum supplies in an attempt to shape Western foreign policy. After decades of Western, particularly British, influence over Iranian petroleum production and politics, the Iranian Revolution in 1979 led to a severe backlash. In many ways, that backlash continues to this day, with the United States using economic sanctions against a resurgent Iran for reasons related to nuclear energy and potential weaponization. While this book is not primarily focused on international politics, it is important to consider how international events—such as economic sanctions or potential military conflict—could lead to energy price spikes in the international petroleum market. While it is the case that of late a larger percentage of U.S. petroleum consumption is produced domestically, prices are determined by the global forces of supply and demand.

CHAPTER SUMMARY

There are multiple reasons why we are and should be focusing greater attention on alternative sources of energy. Society has moved, and continues to move, toward greater interest in a healthy environment for humans as well as nonhuman species. Postmaterialist values are not unique to the United States or to other developed nations—there is a growing global shift in the direction of improved quality of life for the planet as a whole. While the United States and other nations still rely heavily on fossil energy, and we are indeed fortunate to have a ready supply of energy for the near future, the world must be prepared for an eventual sunset for these finite energy sources. Climate change is an accepted scientific fact by a large portion of the U.S. and world populations. In the United States, a nation whose leadership is democratically elected, our steps toward an alternative energy future have been rather halting, with rapid progress taking place at certain times followed by periods of retrenchment and even reversal.

The question of how we achieve an alternative energy future with the time left available before certain fossil energy sources begin to decline more noticeably and climate change becomes irreversible is of central concern. Our movement must become more rapid and consistent in due course so that our citizens, businesses, industries, and governments at all levels are able to plan for a new energy future.

As noted earlier, energy and its use could be characterized as a wicked problem (Van Burren et al., 2003). Wicked problems entail issues that test the limits of human understanding, and whose costs and benefits are not well understood either by the marketplace or by government. What makes a problem "wicked"? First, wicked problems are characterized by a need for timely action in the context of high levels of information uncertainty. The validity and reliability of the information needed to take reasoned action are unclear in wicked problem situations. Second, "wicked" problems exist in a contestable policy environment where multiple actors compete with each other over both the nature of the problem and the veracity of the science being brought to bear on the problem. Finally, institutional relationships, information gathering and interpretation, and the development of policy choices are taking place at multiple nodal points in a wide network of policy actors, increasing the level of uncertainty about the nature of the "problem," about relevant information and acceptable solutions. In essence, "wicked" problems are the types of problems or circumstances that have long plagued humanity (for an earlier related discussion, see Douglas and Wildavsky, 1983). In the area of energy policy, persistent global demand growth factors (e.g., see Berk, 1981), ongoing technological development, and the increased use of network-based, collaborative processes for public policy development have made the energy policy environment more complex and more difficult to navigate politically.

Wicked problems of the twenty-first century are wide ranging and are often a function of past human choices and their externalities, or unintended consequences that emerge from such choices. Neither market nor public policy solutions are clearly defined. A good example of an externality that has become a wicked problem is the paradox of a now seemingly limitless supply of fossil energy confronted with international public policy commitments to limit its use due to the threat of global warming.

Many of the energy policy challenges can only be overcome, and the development of marketable and practical solutions can only be accomplished, through objective empiricism and the use of sound scientific and engineering knowledge. Such objective science and engineering entails the rational analysis of objects and phenomena as they exist in a measurable and describable state. Through such empirical study, science must progress rapidly in order to establish comprehension of understudied phenomena or conditions related to energy supply and efficient utilization. Other challenges, however, are most immediately related to consumer behavior and to normative visions of the world about what is right and wrong, just and unjust, and what could be improved about the conditions under which we live, the nature of our society, and the condition of the natural environment.

While empiricism is concerned with things as they *are*, normative issues are concerned with things as they *ought to* be, according to our individual and collective views of the "good" life and "good" society—questions that transcend both public policy and marketplace capitalism (see Etzioni 1988; Heilbroner 1994; Simon 2018). The wicked problems facing energy availability, distribution, and use in the twenty-first century, as has been defined through the operation of the marketplace and government policy, can only be solved in a hazy, complex, dynamic, and highly intertwined middle ground between (a) science and philosophy; (b) the private sector and government; (c) national, state, and local governmental entities; and (d) between private citizens and the corporate bodies (both governmental and private sector) providing the context for their public and private lives. As policy analysts and stakeholders, responsible citizenship will require us to develop a sound understanding of the public policy process as well as an understanding of the economic and social feasibility issues associated with alternative energy.

NOTE

1. As with earlier discussions of funding for research and development for alternative energy, I am using NREL budget data.

REFERENCES

ABC News. 2002. ANWR issue prompts a sharp political divide, *ABC News*, April 23. Retrieved from https://abcnews.go.com/images/PollingUnit/796a98%20ANWR.pdf, July 13, 2019.

Allo, M., and Loureiro, M. 2014. The role of social norms on preferences towards climate change policies: A meta-analysis. *Energy Policy* 73: 563–574.

Anderson, James. 1984. *Public Policymaking: An Introduction.* New York: Houghton Mifflin.

Bajzeli, B., Allwood, J., and Cullen, J. 2013. Designing climate change mitigation plans that add up. *Environmental Science & Technology* 47: 8062–8069.

Bauer, D., Philbrick, M., and Vallario, B. 2014. *The Water-Energy Nexus: Challenges and Opportunities.* Washington, DC: U.S. Department of Energy.

Bauer, N., Brecha,, R., and Luderer, G. 2011. Economics of nuclear power and climate change mitigation policies. *Proceedings of the National Academy of Sciences of the United States* 109(42): 16805–16810.

Bellah, Robert, Madsen, Richard, Tipton, Steve, Swidler, Ann, and Sullivan, William. 1992. *The Good Society.* New York: Knopf.

Bena, D. 2012. Testimony on water and energy use efficiency. July 25, Subcommittee on Water and Power, Committee on Energy and Natural Resources, 112th Congress (2nd Session), S. Hearing, 112–564.

Berinstein, Paul. 2001. *Alternative Energy: Facts, Statistics, and Issues.* Westport, CT: Oryx Press.

Berk, Richard A. 1981. *Water Shortage: Lessons in Conservation from the Great California Drought, 1976–1977.* Cambridge, MA: Abt Books.

Bernell, D., and Simon, C. 2016. *The Energy Security Dilemma: U.S. Policy and Practice.* New York: Routledge.

Birnbaum, M., Witte, G., and McAuley, J. 2019. European Greens surge as voters abandon old parties over climate change. *The Washington Post*, May 27. Retrieved from https://www.washingtonpost.com/world/europe/european-greens-surge-as-voters-abandon-old-parties-over-climate/2019/05/27/185be506-8085-11e9-b585-e36b16a531aa_story.html?noredirect=on&utm_term=.7500a5e15955, May 28, 2019.

Blackwood, John. 2002. *Energy Research and the Cutting Edge.* New York: Nova Science Publishers.

Borgstede, C. von, Andersson, M., and Johnsson, F. 2013. Public attitudes to climate change and carbon mitigation: Implications for energy-associated behaviors. *Energy Policy* 57: 182–193.

Brown, D., and Morbarak, A. 2009. The transforming power of democracy: Regime type and the distribution of electricity. *American Political Science Review* 103(2): 193–213.

Brulle, R., Carmichael, J., and Jenkins, J. 2012. Shifting public opinion on climate change: An empirical assessment of factors influencing concern over climate change in the U.S., 2002–2010. *Climatic Change* 114: 169–188.

Capros, P., Mantzos, Parousos, L., Tasios, N., Klassen, G., and Van Ierland, T. 2011. Analysis of the EU policy package on climate change and renewables. *Energy Policy* 39: 1476–1485.

Castro, P. 2014. *Climate Change Mitigation in Developing Countries: A Critical Assessment of the Clean Development Mechanism*. Cheltenham, UK: Edward Elgar Publishing.

Catton, Bruce, and Dunlap, Riley. 1978. Environmental sociology: A new paradigm. *The American Sociologist* 13(February): 41–49.

Chandel, M., Pratson, L., and Jackson, R. 2011. The potential impacts of climate-change policy on freshwater use in thermoelectric power generation. *Energy Policy* 39: 6234–6242.

Clark, C. 2018. *Renewable Energy R & D Funding History: A Comparison with Funding for Nuclear Energy, Fossil Energy, Energy Efficiency, and Electrical Systems R & D*, RS22858. Washington, DC: Congressional Research Service.

Clemente, Jude. 2015. U.S. oil reserves, resources, and unlimited future supply. *Forbes* April 2, https://www.forbes.com/sites/judeclemente/2015/04/02/u-s-oil-reserves-resources-and-unlimited-future-supply/#35b79a4e57e1, accessed February 27, 2018.

Dale, V., Efroymson, R., and Kline, K. 2011. The land use-climate change-energy nexus. *Landscape Ecology* 26: 755–773.

Dawoud, S., Lin, X., and Okba, M. 2018. Hybrid renewable energy optimization techniques: A review. *Renewable and Sustainable Energy Reviews* 82: 2039–2062.

Dietchman, B. 2017. *Climate and Clean Energy Policy: State Institutions and Economic Implications*. New York: Routledge.

Dominguez-Faus, R., Folberth, C., Liu, J., Jaffe, A., and Alvarez, P. 2013. Climate change would increase the water intensity of irrigated corn ethanol. *Environmental Science & Technology* 47: 6030–6037.

Douglas, Mary, and Wildavsky, Aaron. 1983. *Risk and Culture*. Berkeley, CA: University of California Press.

Duke Energy. 2009. *Sustainability Report 2008–2009*. Duke, NC: Duke Energy.

Energy Information Administration. 2017. *How Much Natural Gas Does the United States Have, and How Long Will It Last?* Washington, DC: U.S. Energy Information Administration, Accessed March 2, 2018 https://www.eia.gov/tools/faqs/ faq.php?id=58&t=8.

———. 2018. *Annual Energy Review: Total Energy*. Washington, DC: U.S. Energy Information Administration.

Etzioni, Amitai. 1988. *The Moral Dimension: Toward a New Economics*. New York: Collier-MacMillan.

Frumkin, H., Fried, L., and Moody, R. 2012. Aging, climate change, and legacy thinking. *American Journal of Public Health* 102: 1434–1438.

Giddens, A. 2009. *Politics of Climate Change*. Cambridge, UK: Polity Press.

Hardin, Garrett. 1968. The tragedy of the commons. *Science* 162: 1243–1248.

Harvey, M., and Pilgrim, S. 2011. The new competition for land: Food, energy, and climate change. *Food Policy* 36: 540–551.

Heilbroner, Robert. 1994. *21st Century Capitalism*. New York: Norton.

Hejazi, M., Voisin, N., Liu, L., Bramer, L., Fortin, D., Hathaway, J., Huang, M., Kyle, P., Leung, L., Li, H., Liu, Y., Patel, P., Pulsipher, T., Rice, J., Tesfa, T., Vernon, C., and Zhoiu, Y. 2015. 21st century United States emissions mitigation could increase water stress more than the climate change it is mitigating. *Proceedings of the National Academy of Sciences United States* 112(34): 10635–10640.

Holland, Kenneth, Morton, F., and Galligan, Brian. 1996. *Federalism and the Environment: Environmental Policymaking in Australia, Canada, and the United States*. Westport, CT: Greenwood.

Hsiang, S., Kopp, R., Jina, A., Rising, J., Delgado, M., Mohan, S., Rasmussen, D., Muir-Wood, R., Wilson, P., Oppenheimer, M., Larsen, K., and Houser, T. 2017. Estimating economic damage from climate change in the United States. *Science* 356: 1362–1369.

Inglehart, Ronald. 1990. *Culture Shift in Advanced Industrial Nations*. Princeton, NJ: Princeton University Press.

International Energy Association. 2017. Statistics: Key Electricity Trends 2016. *International Energy Agency*, April 19, https://www.iea.org/newsroom/ news/2017/ april/statistics-key-electricity-trends-2016.html, accessed February 27, 2018.

Intergovernmental Panel on Climate Change. 2000. *IPCC Special Report: Summary for Policymakers: Emissions Scenarios*. Geneva, Switzerland: IPCC.

———. 2018. *Global warming of 1.5°C. An IPCC Special Report on the impacts of global warming of 1.5°C above pre-industrial levels and related global greenhouse gas emission pathways, in the context of strengthening the global response to the threat of climate change, sustainable development, and efforts to eradicate poverty.* Geneva, Switzerland: IPCC.

Jain, C. 2010. *Water for Energy*. London: World Energy Council.

Johns, S. 2015. The roles of climate change science and standing in climate change mass: Analysis and implications. *University of Florida Journal of Law & Public Policy* 26: 243–264.

Kenny J., Barber N., Hutson S., Linsey K., Lovelace J., and Maupin M. 2009. *Estimated Use of Water in the United States in 2005*. US Geological Survey Circular vol. 1344. Reston, VA: USGS.

Khan, M. 2019. The European elections 2019—as it happened. *Financial Times*, May 26. Retrieved from https://www.ft.com/content/ea2d07f2-1ae2-3ea2-921b-2f706342bf35, May 27, 2019.

King, M., and Gullege, J. 2014. Climate change and energy security: An analysis of policy research. *Climatic Change* 123: 57–68.

Lepore, J. 2015. Richer and poorer: Accounting for inequality. *New Yorker*, March 9. Retrieved from https://www.newyorker.com/magazine/2015/03/16/richer-and-poorer, May 28, 2019.

Macknick, J., Newmark, R., Heath, G., and Hallett, K. 2012. Operational water consumption and withdrawal factors for electricity generating technologies: A review of existing literature. *Environmental Research Letters* 7: 1–10.

Madden, N., Lewis, A., and Davis, M. 2013. Thermal effluent from the power sector: An analysis of once-through cooling system impact on surface water temperature. *Environmental Research Letters* 8: 1–8.

Maupin, M., Kenny, J., Hutson, S., Lovelace, J., Barber, N., and Linsey, K. 2015. *Estimated Water Use in the United States in 2010*. Washington, DC: U.S. Geological Survey.

Mills, C. Wright. 1967. *The Sociological Imagination*. Cambridge: Oxford University Press.

Moss, R., Edmonds, J., Hibbard, K., Manning, M., Rose, S., Van Vuuren, D., Carter, T., Emori, S., Kainuma, M., Kram, T., Meehl, G., Mitchell, J., Nakicenovic, N.,

Riahi, K., Smith, S., Stouffer, R., Thomson, A., Weyant, J., and Wilbanks, T. 2010. The next generation of scenarios for climate change research and assessment. *Nature* 464: 747–756.

Mukheibir, P. 2013. Potential consequences of projected climate change impacts on hydroelectricity generation. *Climatic Change* 121: 67–78.

Mullin, M. 2009. *Governing the Tap: Special District Governance and the Local Politics of Water*. Cambridge, MA: MIT Press.

National Aeronautic and Space Administration. 2019. Scientific consensus: Earth's climate is warming. Retrieved from https://climate.nasa.gov/scientific-consensus, May 27, 2019.

National Energy Technology Laboratory. 2010. *Carbon Dioxide Enhanced Oil Recovery*. Washington, DC: National Energy Technology Laboratory, U.S. Department of Energy. Retrieved from https://www.netl.doe.gov/sites/default/files/netl-file/CO2_EOR_Primer.pdf, July 20, 2019.

Patt, A., Pfenninger, S., and Lilliestam, J. 2013. Vulnerability of solar energy infrastructure and output to climate change. *Climatic Change* 121: 93–102.

Pryor, S., and Barthelmie, R. 2011. Assessing climate change impacts on the near-term stability of the wind energy resource over the United States. *Proceedings of the National Academy of Sciences of the United States of America* 108(20): 8167–8171.

Rising, A. 2018. *World Nuclear Performance Report, 2018*. London, UK: World Nuclear Association.

Rystad Energy. 2016. Press Release: United States now holds more recoverable oil than Saudi Arabia. *Rystad Energy*, July 4, https://www. rystadenergy.com/newsevents/news/press-releases/united-states-now-holds-more-oil-reserves-than-saudi-arabia, accessed March 1, 2018.

Schaeffer, R., Szklo, A., de Lucena, A., Borba, B., Nogueria, L., Fleming, F., Troccoli, A., Harrison, M., and Boulahya, M. 2012. Energy sector vulnerability to climate change: A review. *Energy* 38: 1–12.

Shaheen, J. 2012. Water and Energy Efficiency. July 25, Subcommittee on Water and Power, Committee on Energy and Natural Resources, 112th Congress (2nd Session), Senate Hearing, 112–564.

Simmons, M. 2005. *Twilight in the Desert: The Coming Saudi Oil Shock and the World Economy*. New York: Wiley & Sons.

Simon, Christopher A. 2018. *Public Policy: Preferences and Outcomes*, 3rd Edition. New York: Routledge.

Sovacool, B., and Brown, M. 2010. Competing dimensions of energy security: An international perspective. *Annual Review of Environment and Resources* 35: 77–108.

Sovacool, B., and Sovacool, K. 2009. Identifying future electricity—water tradeoffs in the United States. *Energy Policy* 37(7): 2763–2773.

Steentjes, K., Kurz, T., Barreto, M., and Morton, T. 2017. The norms associated with climate change: Understanding social norms through acts of interpersonal activism. *Global Environmental Change* 43: 116–125.

Stowsky, J. 1992. Conversion to competitiveness: Making the most of the national labs. *The American Prospect*. Retrieved from https://prospect.org/article/conversion-competitiveness-making-most-national-labs, July 20, 2019.

Tidwell, V., and Moreland, B. 2016. Mapping water consumption for energy production around the Pacific Rim. *Environmental Research Letters* 11: 1–13.

Toke, David. 2000. *Green Politics and Neo-Liberalism*. New York: St. Martin's Press.

Toricellini, P., Long, N., and Judkoff, R. 2003. *Consumptive Water Use for U.S. Power Production*. Golden, CO: National Renewable Energy Laboratory, NREL/TP-550–33905.

Tully, A. 2014. How long will world's oil reserves last? 53 years, says BP. *The Christian Science Monitor*, July 14, https://www.csmonitor.com/Environment/Energy-Voices/2014/0714/How-long-will-world-s-oil-reserves-last-53-years-says-BP, accessed March 1, 2018.

Union of Concerned Scientists. 2016. The hidden costs of fossil fuels. *Union of Concerned Scientists*, August 30. Retrieved from https://climate.nasa.gov/scientific-consensus/, May 27, 2019.

UN CEO Water Mandate. 2018. Mission and governance. *UN Global Compact*, https://ceowatermandate.org/about/mission-governance/, accessed March 12, 2018.

U.S. Energy Information Administration. 2012. *Annual Energy Review*. Washington, DC: U.S. Energy Information Administration, https://www.eia.gov/totalenergy/data/annual/showtext.php?t=ptb040, accessed March 1, 2018.

———. 2013. Future world energy demand driven by trends in developing nations. Retrieved from https://www.eia.gov/todayinenergy/detail.php?id=14011, May 26, 2019.

———. 2018a. *U.S. Crude Oil and Natural Gas Proved Reserves, Year-End 2016*. Washington, DC: U.S. Energy Information Agency.

———. 2018b. How much natural gas does the United States have, and how long will it last? Washington, DC: U.S. Energy Information Agency, https://www.eia.gov/tools/faqs/faq.php?id=58&t=8, accessed March 1, 2018.

———. 2019. *Annual Energy Outlook—2019*. Washington, DC: U.S. Energy Information Administration, https://www.eia.gov/outlooks/aeo/pdf/aeo2019.pdf, accessed May 27, 2019.

U.S. EPA. 2016. *Hydraulic Fracturing for Oil and Gas: Impacts from the Hydraulic Fracturing Water Cycle on Drinking Water Resources in the United States (Final Report)*. Washington, DC: U.S. Environmental Protection Agency. EPA/600/R-16/236F.

———. 2018. *Global Greenhouse Gas Emissions*. Washington, DC: EPA, https://www.epa.gov/ghgemissions/global-greenhouse-gas-emissions-data, accessed March 18, 2018.

———. 2019. *Inventory of U.S. Greenhouse Gas Emissions, 1990–2017*. Washington, DC: U.S. EPA, https://www.epa.gov/sites/production/files/2019-02/documents/us-ghg-inventory-2019-main-text.pdf, accessed May 27, 2019.

Van Beuren, Ellen, Klijn, Erik-Hans, and Koppenjan, Joop. 2003. Dealing with wicked problems in networks: Analyzing and environmental debate from a network perspective. *Journal of Public Administration Research and Theory* 13(2): 193–212.

Water Resources Group 2030. 2018. Grounding Principles. *Water Resources Group 2030*, https://www.2030wrg.org/who-we-are/principles/, accessed March 10, 2018.

Webb, J. 2012. Climate change and society: The chimera of behavior change technologies. *Sociology* 46(1): 109–125.

Weber, E. 2012. Getting to resilience in a climate protected community: Early problem-solving choices, ideas, and governance philosophy. In: *Collaborative Resilience: Moving through Crisis to Opportunity*, B. E. Goldstein (Ed.). Cambridge, MA: MIT Press, 177–206.

Weber, E., and Khademian, A. 2008. Wicked problems, knowledge challenges, and collaborative capacity builders in network settings. *Public Administration Review* 68(2): 334–349.

Whitmarsh, L., and Corner, A. 2017. Tools for a new climate conversation: A mixed-methods study of language for public engagement across the political spectrum. *Global Environmental Change* 42: 122–135.

Wicker, P., and Beckin, S. 2013. Conscientious vs. ambivalent consumers: Do concerns about energy availability and climate change influence consumer behavior? *Ecological Economics* 88: 41–48.

Wiles, R. 2018. It's 50 years since climate change was first seen. Now time is running out. *Guardian*, March 15, https://www.theguardian.com/ commentisfree/2018/mar/15/50-years-climate-change-denial, accessed March 18, 2018.

Wirfs-Brock, J. 2010. Lost in transmission: How much electricity disappears between a power plant and your plug? *Inside Energy*, November 6. Retrieved from http://insideenergy.org/2015/11/06/lost-in-transmission-how-much-electricity-disappears-between-a-power-plant-and-your-plug/, July 20, 2019.

World Bank. 2019. GDP, PPP (current international $). Retrieved from https://data.worldbank.org/indicator/ny.gdp.mktp.pp.cd?most_recent_value_desc=true, July 20, 2019.

World Economic Forum. 2010. *Thirsty Energy: Water and Energy in the 21st Century.* Geneva, Switzerland: World Economic Forum.

Yuanyuan, L. 2019. China's renewable energy installed capacity grew 12 percent across all sources in 2018. *Renewable Energy World,* March 6. Retrieved from https://www.renewableenergyworld.com/articles/2019/03/chinas-renewable-energy-installed-capacity-grew-12-percent-across-all-sources-in-2018.html, May 26, 2019.

COURT CASES

Engine Manufacturers Association et al. v. South Coast Air Quality Management District et al. (2004)

Massachusetts et al. v. Environmental Protection Agency et al. 549 U.S. 497 (2007)

Washington Environmental Council v. Bellon (2013)

2

Studying Public Policy and Alternative Energy/Fuels

★　★　★

The last chapter discussed several justifications for pursuing further development of alternative energy. Climate change, growing constraints on the energy–water nexus, the changing dynamics of fossil energy, and values shifts are four interrelated and very practical explanations for the advancement of alternative energy. While fossil energy remains a significant portion of the world's energy portfolio, international scientific consensus holds that its use comes with high marginal social and environmental costs borne by the natural environment, native plant and animal species on land and in coastal waterways, deep sea fisheries, agriculture, and human health, to name but a few. Public policy, through statute and administrative rules, are the typical methods by which the United States acts to protect, regulate, and govern the use of public goods. Understanding how and why public policy exists, and how it evolves over time, is important to achieving policy goals. When former President Obama's one-time chief of staff, Rahm Emmanuel, said, "You never want a serious crisis to go to waste" (Seib, 2008), it was clear that he recognized that political opportunities for policy change more often arise at times of uncertainty than in normal times. In the wake of the 2008 financial crisis, the 2009 American Recovery and Rehabilitation Act led to major policy change for alternative energy, and for other policy areas such as health care. Understanding theories of the policy process is a critical aspect of the political and social feasibility of alternative energy innovation.

ROLES FOR PUBLIC POLICY IN ALTERNATIVE ENERGY/FUEL DEVELOPMENT

Public policy generally deals with the provision of public goods and the regulation of marginal social and environmental costs. By definition, public goods are neither *rivalrous* nor *excludable*. Alternatively, other forms of goods—such as *club goods* (e.g., toll roads) or *marketable private* goods (e.g., a privately owned residential air conditioning unit)—are generally not supplied by government, although they are frequently regulated through government policy as to their production and safe operation.

Figure 2.1 illustrates the issue of rivalry in terms of gasoline supply and demand. In this instance, gasoline demand is fairly inelastic—demand does not respond too much to issues of price (EIA, 2014), which is a function of supply and demand. If supply moves from S1 to a lower level of supply at S2, then the price for gasoline increases. Clearly, a poor person may no longer be able to afford gasoline if the price of this fuel exceeds his or her resources. Excludability means that whoever can afford the product will gain access to it; if it is beyond an individual's budget constraints, then it is not obtainable no matter how much it might be needed.

Ambient air—the air around us that we breathe—is an example of a public good. Air is so abundant that its per-unit price would be too low to be a marketable good—there would be no profit in selling this form of air! Also, air could not be excludable as it would deprive living beings of the ability to continue their existence. Frequently, government manages public goods to ensure their equitable distribution and protection of the good for current and future use (see Ostrom, 1990).

Other goods—for example, water, energy, public health—are not so easily defined in terms of their relative excludability or rivalrousness. There is a tremendous debate within public policy regarding the relative nature of goods and services provided by government. Neoclassical economists often argue that many of the goods or services provided by government are not pure public goods, but are, in fact, marketable private or semiprivate goods and, therefore, should be bought and sold by individuals freely engaged in market exchange rather

Figure 2.1   Rivalry in the Gasoline Market

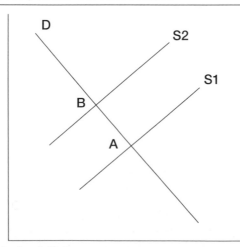

Source: Christopher A. Simon.

than distributed by government (see Hayek, 1944). Conversely, other scholars find that the use of many goods or services impacts the property or basic human rights of other individuals, necessitating government intervention through the regulation, distribution, and use of such goods or services. A good example of the latter relates to arguments made by advocates for universal national health care. The latter is a more "progressive" mindset that ties political rights and liberties to variations in economic status (see Rawls, 1971; Michelbach et al., 2003).

At various times throughout history, energy has been defined as a marketable private good, a free good, a public good, and a club good. One of the methods by which warlords or kings sought power was through private ownership of woodlands and waterways—sources of energy, water, and food. In nomadic tribal societies, clans and families migrated from location to location in search of abundant and free energy, water, and food sources—energy was viewed as both a public or free good. During the precolonial period in North America, European settlements were organized such that all residents worked cooperatively to meet individual, family, and settlement needs. For example, the miller would generate the energy needed to grind grains into flour, and the bread produced by the baker would be shared by all residents.

In colonial America, however, European settlers often faced deprivation, and in times of deprivation people are more likely to see the benefits of cooperation in order to meet their shared needs. However, as these human societies became more affluent and the supply of goods and services grew in abundance, members of society tended to look to individual market exchange as a solution to meeting most of their individual needs. Government plays a role in markets to the extent that it seeks to regulate market exchange to ensure that the process meets government standards for a well-regulated market (e.g., terms of commercial contracts are met, disputes arising among individuals are peaceably adjudicated by courts, etc.), and that goods and services exchanged meet various legal standards.

Depending upon how markets are structured, and the powers granted to government, energy goods will be viewed in particular predictable ways. When goods are in abundance and their use causes little harm to others, then decisions about their use and distribution are made at a low level and with little conflict. Conflict arises, however, when limited resources are in high demand and/or their use causes harm to others. Who gains access to the resources? Who or what is harmed through resource use, and at what cost? One way to resolve the dilemma is through market-based capitalism and a continued reliance on individual choices in market exchange. Another way to determine the distribution of goods is through public policies that distribute, redistribute, and regulate resource access and use.

Just as precolonial societies considered the balance between the individual and the collective good in managing resources, so too does public policy in a democratic society. A third way of dealing with situations of high demand and limited resources, of course, is through open conflict and plunder, which is injurious and not very desirable from the standpoint of the maintenance of the rule of law and public order. Such resolution to conflict within a community is often considered to be outside of social norms and accepted standards of interaction. Not only is such open conflict often wasteful, but when allowed to persist can erode the sense of community that can benefit all members of society.

As modern industrialized societies emerged, energy demands grew tremendously. While supply was fairly plentiful, access to supply was often a function of transportation of stored energy to cities and the distribution of the goods among consumers. Government and the private sector both played important roles in driving down the cost of transportation and storage of energy through policies relating to streets and roadways, rail line rights of way and railroads, port facilities and canals, and ultimately pipeline and transmission line development. As the prices of energy production, storage, and transportation fell to marketable levels for mass consumption, energy came to be viewed as a marketable public good. Ceteris paribus, the energy market moved toward greater inelasticity once modern economic conditions of mass production and changes in social paradigms required continuous energy consumption— and energy in very particular forms—in order to exist. Fortunately, increased supplies of energy kept prices relatively low, but given inelasticity, decreased supply could result in steep price increases (see figure 2.2).

For much of the nineteenth century and, in a practical sense, for all of the twentieth century, this model drove U.S. energy policy. With New Deal policies in the 1930s, the federal government effectively became a producer and supplier of electricity through major initiatives such as the Bonneville Power Administration (BPA) and the Tennessee Valley Authority (TVA). Rural electrification became a national priority, and state and local governments

Figure 2.2   Inelasticity of Demand

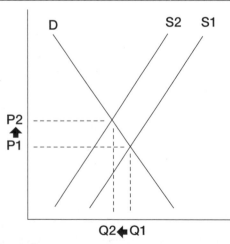

Source: Christopher A. Simon.

added their own initiatives, often working in concert with federal agencies promoting agriculture, ranching, mining, and lodging development outside of the nation's major population centers. For a substantial portion of the United States, government assumed a primary role in meeting electricity demand and reducing consumer costs by increasing the supply of cheap electricity, albeit in the enthusiasm of promoting economic growth, a good deal of ignoring of the marginal social and environmental costs of hydroelectric dams and transmission easements was being done.

At the dawn of the twenty-first century, energy supply issues—in the form of petroleum and natural gas—have been pushed off the short-term policy agenda, possibly for the next three or four decades. Advancements in technology have opened access to a significant supply of fossil energy in the form of unconventional petroleum and natural gas, and more than a century's worth of coal is available for extraction from beneath the surface of public and private lands in the United States.

The more pressing issues of today, and for most of the century ahead of us, are those pertaining to the adverse impact of energy use on climate change and the use of water in the production of energy. In the short term, the nation's energy debate now focuses on the marginal social and environmental costs of energy production. The long term requires us to consider very carefully the need for alternative replacement fuels and methods of consistent electricity generation and storage using renewable energy sources.

Marginal social and environmental costs relate to the cost borne by society and the environment from increased supply and use of a good. For example, the increased supply of gasoline leads to lower prices and greater consumption of the good. When consumers drive their cars more often, there is increased exhaust emissions in the air we breathe. In order to produce more unconventional gas and oil, drilling companies pump more freshwater and hydraulic fracturing chemicals into rock formations deep below the Earth's surface. In order to produce more ethanol, farmers till more acreage to raise corn and other feedstocks, burn more fossil fuel, and use more water. All of the previously mentioned supply activities produce negative externalities, draw heavily upon precious natural resources, and contribute to higher marginal social costs. There will always be marginal social costs—they cannot be entirely avoided, but through wise choices, the costs can be reduced significantly. Marketable alternative energy sources are one way to minimize those social costs through renewable energy and other energy sources that do not emit CO_2 or other pollutants, while simultaneously building into fossil energy use the true cost to society and the natural environment.

POLICY PROCESS

Public solutions, with some exceptions, are often slow in emerging—the result of statutory or common law requirements, public–private partnerships or government research grants, and publicly funded demonstration project funds intended to promote private investment in next-generation technology and infrastructure. It has been nearly fifty years since the first Earth Day and the dawn of a widespread social movement that led to the proenvironment and clean energy movements. Policy responses to the demand for changes in energy production, generation, and use have faced many challenges, encountering along the way, and particularly at the federal level, reversals of funding and political and social support and public attention. Elections matter, and elected officials prioritize time and resources on those policy priorities that matter most to them, their political caucuses, and their political supporters. Public investment in alternative energy sources has grown tremendously in recent decades, and alternative energy in the form of renewables now accounts for roughly a fifth of the electricity produced and consumed—approximately 17 percent of the 4,208 terawatt hours of electricity generated in the United States in 2018. If nuclear energy, an alternative energy source, is included, then the proportion of electricity generated by alternative energy in the United States is approximately 30 percent. In 2018, nuclear energy accounted for a slightly larger proportion of electricity generation than all forms of renewable energy combined, but that gap is closing quickly as renewables continue to gain a larger share of the electricity market in the United States.

Progress is being made, but what does it take to move from a policy idea to a policy innovation to a policy outcome? Progress requires both a process and a vision. When one thinks about it from the process model perspective, as discussed below, it sounds linear and simple, but please do not be deceived! It is much more complex than the simple process model would lead you to believe. Public policy making and its implementation involve numerous dynamic processes—many things happening simultaneously—often properly characterized by cycles. For instance, election cycles, public attention cycles, budget cycles, and economic cycles can all have important effects as major public policy change takes place. When that multiple intersecting cycles complexity is added to the discussion, policy analysis relies heavily on theories and frameworks to describe and explain why, in this policy process, things occur as they do. Sometimes, even, these theories and frameworks offer clues to the ways things could be done differently and, possibly, more effectively.

According to Charles O. Jones (1970), there are five major steps in the policy process: (1) agenda setting; (2) policy formation; (3) policy implementation; (4) policy evaluation; and (5) policy termination or change. In most cases, public policy does not terminate, which means that the process is cyclical rather than a linear. Consequently, there are future opportunities to advance ideas that have been rejected on their first go-around, and there is a possibility of altering existing policies to meet new policy preferences or improve upon existing policy.

Agenda Setting

Public policy has to start somewhere, and for some identifiable reason evident to policy advocates. It usually starts when people's attention is focused on a problem that, it is believed, should be solved by government action. Events and novel circumstances often play a big role in getting people's attention, but events are complex and require articulation and thick description to interpret their meaning and speculate on their cause and most likely what can be done to either prevent or change a circumstance. How an event or circumstance is understood has a lot to do with the level of priority placed on it. At the national level, the president plays a tremendous role in shaping the policy agenda through his or her unique position as the only nationally elected leader.

In the 2016 general election, Hillary Clinton was strongly committed to renewable energy and to U.S. engagement in the international efforts to combat climate change. Conversely, Donald Trump sought to reinvigorate coal mining, open pipeline access to the United States for Canadian oil transportation, and extricate the United States from the Paris Agreement, an international commitment to reduce greenhouse gas emissions. Clinton framed her description of events and circumstances around the issue of climate change and clean energy, while Trump spoke of energy independence and job creation. Congress represents the values of the nation as well as the parochial values of districts and states. Often, there are a great variety of priorities brought forth by legislators representing their districts or states, a mix of priorities that also impacts the policy agenda. Of course, the political party identification of the president and of the majority of Congress, in either or both chambers, reflects values preferences and subsequently impacts the policy agenda (see Krehbiel, 1993; Binder et al., 1999). While not overtly political, the federal judiciary is appointed by the president and confirmed by the Senate. The president is often drawn to individuals who share his or her political and social values; thus, the courts are influenced to some degree by political preferences and will shape the policy agenda accordingly (see Hulbary and Walker, 1980). For example, judges appointed by Democratic presidents in the 1950s and 1960s shaped the environmental policy agenda through court decisions. While the federal courts are being shaped by the judicial appointments of President Trump, past court decisions, through the principle of stare decisis, are not generally overturned, albeit conservative Associate Justice Clarence Thomas has signaled a willingness to do so (Stempel, 2019).

Circumstances in the domestic (Kindgon, 2003) and global (see Weatherford, 1988) social and political environment also impact the policy agenda. One of the most obvious circumstances is a crisis. The oil crisis in the 1970s led to shortages of supply and skyrocketing retail prices of gasoline and diesel in the United States. In the 1970s case, OPEC—the Organization of Petroleum Exporting Countries—cut production of oil to drive up prices and heighten profits. While other nations' citizens were used to paying high prices for fuel, domestic reaction in the United States was one of shock and dismay. Limited energy supply meant higher prices and excess energy demand that could not be met. There were angry calls for something to be done to meet the pressing energy demand. Consequently, energy policy became a prominent part of the policy agenda, with alternative energy becoming a more accepted policy solution. In the 1980s and 1990s, energy policy was a conspicuous item on the policy agenda. Efforts to promote "green" energy solutions remained in the background, often quietly explored by national energy laboratories and university-based researchers. Falling oil prices—prices that hit record lows in the late 1990s—overshadowed alternative energy policy.

In the early twenty-first century, the nation has witnessed a return to higher petroleum prices, but this time, the cost factors have been in good measure a function of things other than production decisions per se. The world economic outlook has changed in the last several decades. Nations such as India and China have among the highest GDP in the world, and are rapidly moving toward developed nation status. A middle class has formed in many non-OECD nations, which means greater demand for particular goods associated with the modern economy, such as automobiles and reliable electricity. Elevated demand for fossil energy leads to higher prices and stimulates the search for cheaper and more abundant alternatives such as renewable energy.

China is the world's largest renewable energy-generating nation. Germany has one of the strongest commitments to renewable energy in the world, setting a target goal of at least 80 percent renewable energy by 2050—shedding its reliance on fossil and nuclear energy sources. Under President Barack Obama, the United States energy policy agenda demonstrated commitment to the goals of the Paris Agreement and to heavy investment in energy efficiency and renewable energy. While some of these policies have been reversed or are losing momentum under President Trump, much support for them remains present in state and local governments across the country. This provides further evidence that policy agendas change over time in reflection of the multiple political, technological, and society cycles spoken of above.

Policy Formation

The second step in the policy process involves the formation of public policy solutions. Policy analysis occurs at this stage in the policy process; theoretically, a series of well-considered policy choices are studied and, through various deliberative political and administrative processes, policy solutions are identified for adoption. At the very least, successful policy formation requires that there is a generally accepted understanding of (a) a policy problem; (b) the target population—individuals or things to be directly benefited or whose circumstances are to be altered by public policy solutions; (c) a relatively clear sense of the costs and benefits associated with different policy solutions; and (d) the ability to link policy with desired outcomes and impacts (Simon, 2007).

A solid understanding of a policy problem is often a function of scientific theories and evidence supporting human understanding of social or physical phenomena. In the case of alternative energy, understanding the policy problem requires an assessment of social values regarding energy—reduced air emissions—as well as future demands on energy, a function of individual and collective human behavior. The target populations of energy policy range from the individual consumer and his or her energy demands to large-scale industrial users and energy producers to ecosystem needs. Understanding the target population(s) also requires an understanding of how policy will impact human behaviors and affect societal circumstances. Public policies are typically driven by the empirically guided expectation that behaviors will change and disagreeable societal circumstances will improve, the anticipated benefits that should emerge from a properly crafted and implemented public policy.

The unfortunate reality is that policy formation is often not successful in creating elegantly crafted policy plans that produce the expected outcomes at the expected costs. Frequently, the social and sometimes the physical science theories guiding policy plans are contested rather than reflect a consensus; often target populations are not clearly understood or defined; and, all too frequently, the costs and benefits of policy adoption are insufficiently measured. As Deborah Stone (1988) notes, the numerical analyses so critical to good policy formation are often politicized—in essence, numbers are assigned meaning by policy analysts, a function of a preferred set of political and social values. A good example of this dilemma can be seen in the policy debate related to the Kyoto Protocol, where there was noteworthy disagreement over the need or the potential impact of limiting greenhouse gas emissions (see LePage, 2016).

Policy Implementation

Public policy often reaches the policy agenda because there is a perceived or a real crisis that would seem to demand immediate attention. As John Kingdon has noted in *Agendas, Alternatives, and Public Policy* (2003), opportunities to establish public policy are often short-lived; the policy "window" of opportunity may open and close quite rapidly, due in some measure to short public, mass media, or policy maker attention spans. Thus, policy formation and subsequent implementation may occur with much haste and only limited knowledge on likely outcomes. In *Implementation* (1973), Jeffrey Pressman and Aaron Wildavsky catalog the challenging aspects of implementing public policy in an environment where it is expected that rapidly realized and successful policy impacts will emerge. Pressman and Wildavsky's study of the Oakland Project, a multimillion-dollar plan to revitalize the social and economic atmosphere of the California city, found that policy formulation collaboration, consistent monitoring and midcourse corrections, and consistency in key leadership roles were critical aspects of successful policy implementation.

Implementation of ill-considered plans that carry with them high hopes of success are likely to produce short-term disappointment and long-term flagging confidence in the efficacy of public institutions. In the case of alternative energy, similar disappointments arose in the 1970s, as social and physical scientists became cognizant of the competing values and perspectives within their fields of study, while public demand for the rapid implementation of an ameliorative solution to the energy crisis occasioned the need for immediate action. Alternative energy policy analysts and implementers were severely criticized in the 1980s for a lack of effective response to Reagan's fossil fuel-centered policies focused on expanded extraction activity, policies that called for significant reductions in alternative energy source development budgets (see Ahari, 1987: 589). Perceived or real policy implementation failures have been used to further buffer the claims of free market conservatives who maintain that petroleum-based energy policy is functioning well and will continue to function quite well without significant government policy intervention (Loris, 2018).

Policy Evaluation

Policy evaluation focuses primary attention on the intended and unintended impacts, outcomes, and relative (in)efficiencies of policy as it has been implemented. Most visible policy evaluation occurs at the end of a *policy cycle*, which can be defined in at least two different ways. A policy cycle commonly comes to an end every fiscal year due to the annual nature of the federal budget cycle. In deciding on how and where to fund public policy, elected leaders and administrative personnel require some evidence-based understanding of the relative success or failure of public policy as it has been implemented during the previous twelve months. In essence, evaluation plays a role in future *appropriation* decisions. A policy cycle also comes to an end when a public policy *sunsets*, a point in time usually between two and five years when Congress reviews the continued need for public policy in its present or adjusted form—that is, *reauthorization* decisions. Policy evaluation conducted at the point of reauthorization is another form of end-of-policy-cycle study and review.

Policy evaluation involves empirical review of policy processes, outcomes, and impacts on a defined target population, as well as other nontargeted individuals and phenomena of relevance. Evaluation can be either qualitative or quantitative. Qualitative evaluations tend to focus significant attention on those aspects of public policy that are not easily measured in a uniform manner. Qualitative studies are often written in narrative form, and may involve archival research or personal interviews with policy stakeholders—individuals or groups considering themselves interested in or impacted by a particular public policy. Quantitative studies employ statistics to measure the processes, outcomes, and impacts of public policy along various dimensions.

Qualitative analysis captures many of the impacts of public policy that would likely go unnoticed. Qualitative analysis can be time-consuming and costly, but the narratives captured can be well worth the effort. Using sophisticated methods of determining validity and reliability, quantitative analysis speaks to policy makers and is used in assessing costs and benefits and aligning those with public budgets. A disadvantage to overreliance on quantitative evaluation is that its very elegance and simplicity may not effectively underscore the impacts or outcomes of public policy on target populations and other stakeholders.

Policy Termination/Change

As noted above, public policies often *sunset*, requiring *reauthorization* every few years. During these periods of reauthorization, Congress and the president can make significant changes to the direction of a public policy. The Energy Policy Act (2005) is a good example of presidential and congressional reshaping of the priorities related to national-level energy policy. Additionally, public policy funding is generally decided on an annual basis. In both instances, it is in the power of elected officials—Congress and the president— to make decisions about the general direction of public policy. Agencies and programs within agencies require adequate resources to effectively implement public policy. The power to shape an agency's budget, therefore, is one of the most powerful tools available to elected officials in shaping policy change on an annual basis. Congress also has the power of *legislative oversight*, which means that agency administrators can be called before congressional committees to discuss how policy is being implemented and to receive guidance on the continuation or readjustment of policy direction (Aberbach, 1990). At all of these points, policy can be changed in small and large ways. The courts should not be left out of this discussion, particularly in the case of policy change and/or termination. The courts can have a tremendous impact on public policy implementation and can, through common law decisions, impact the direction and goals of public policy. If the federal judiciary opines that a public policy violates the U.S. Constitution, the court can effectively halt its implementation until further adjudicative deliberations are held, or even terminate it until appropriate changes are made to existing policy and agreed to by the court.

The president has tremendous power in effectively terminating or changing a policy direction. Working with a Democratically controlled Congress, President Obama used presidential power and the influence of his office to advance the American Recovery and Rehabilitation Act (ARRA), leading to a multibillion-dollar inflow for renewable energy R & D as well as efforts to remove fuel inefficient personal cars (cash for clunkers) from the roads. The ARRA also advanced efforts to increase energy efficiency. Through his power over administrative agencies and rule making, President Obama influenced the passage of EPA rules, effectively limiting the use of coal for power generation and, likewise, developing a Clean Power Plan. The disposal of coal ash, for instance, was heavily regulated under the rule structures, making coal use less economically feasible. Additionally, emissions from coal-fired power plants were subject to strict limitations so as to reduce climate-changing carbon dioxide emissions.

The Obama-era administrative rules and the Clean Power Plan, however, were quickly overturned—in effect, terminated—by the newly elected president,

The Complexities of Public Policy
iStock / Getty Images Plus / Warchi

Donald Trump. Trump's new EPA administrator, Scott Pruitt, quickly rescinded the Obama-era coal ash regulations and several other signature executive directives. The power of the president in policy termination and change has been dramatic in recent years, but the incumbent in the White House changes every four to eight years—thus future administrations are likely to move policy in new and possibly dramatically different directions.

POLICY TYPES

In his 1972 *Public Administration Review* article, "Four Systems of Politics, Policy, and Choice," Theodore Lowi developed a typology of distinct categories of public policy. Lowi argued that "policies determine politics" (Lowi, 1972: 299). In other words, policy type impacts the political choices made. Through two-dimensional analysis, Lowi studies both the probability of coercion being employed (the vertical dimension) as well as the manner in which the coercion would be focused (the horizontal dimension).

According to Lowi, coercion can best be determined through legislative intent as evidenced by statute. In the table reprinted from his now-classic journal article, Lowi argued that there were four fundamental types of public policy: constituent, distributive, regulative, and redistributive (figure 2.3).

Constituent policy has a very low likelihood of being coercive, and focuses primarily on shaping the environment in which citizen conduct occurs

Figure 2.3   Coercion, Policy, and Politics

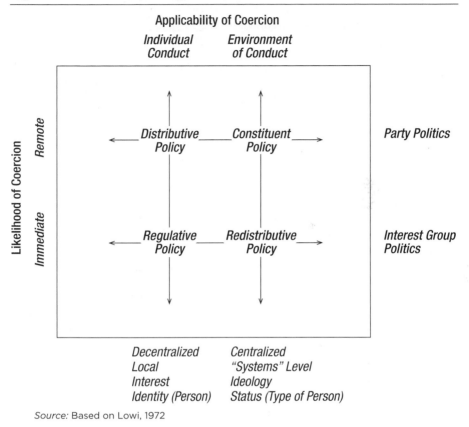

Source: Based on Lowi, 1972

(conduct is the outcome of choice). The establishment of the U.S. Department of Energy is one example of constituent policy. President Carter sought to establish himself as a principal leader in environmental and energy-related policy at a time when energy supply was of keen interest to American voters. *Redisributive* policies are similarly focused on the environment of citizen conduct, but frequently employ coercion to gain compliance. Redistributive policy involves taking resources from one group and giving resources to other groups. In terms of energy policy, one form of redistributive policy is energy tax credits for renewable energy power producers, tax credits that are intended to incentivize clean energy production and make it more competitive with fossil energy options already available in the energy market.

    Distributive policy focuses on decentralized efforts to shape individual conduct/choices, with very little likelihood of coercion. Lowi offers the nineteenth-century land grant program as an example, a policy through which significant portions of public lands in the West were deeded to individual citizens for their private use to encourage settlement of the American West. The politics surrounding distributive policy tends to center on political parties, with some political parties being more likely than others to represent a distributive policy area and to shape the manner in which that policy is formulated and implemented. Rural electrification is one example of distributive energy policy, and this program is often closely associated with Democratic president Franklin D. Roosevelt.

A fourth policy type, *regulatory policy*, tends to focus on coercive methods of shaping choice and behaviors. As an example, if a corporation such as General Motors produced automobiles that violated U.S. pollution standards, the corporation would be considered an individual violator and could be subject to legal (civil and sometimes criminal) penalties. Regulatory policy impacts individuals or groups in particular instances, and naturally these individuals or groups want to limit their exposure to penalties. One way of overcoming their dilemma is to pressure government through organized interest groups to change regulatory codes in their favor.

Government employs a combination of policy types to encourage behavioral change and choice. Energy policy does not function independently of other policy areas. Environmental regulations imposed by the EPA are one method of encouraging the use of alternative, particularly renewable, energy. Simultaneously, government uses grants, demonstration projects, production tax credits, and public land easements involving the Departments of Energy, Interior, Agriculture, and Treasury in an effort to stimulate renewable energy market development. I mention here only federal government agencies, but similar agencies at the state and local levels are also actively engaged in such regulatory activities.

BOTTOM-UP POLICY MAKING/TOP-DOWN POLICY MAKING

Policy making can occur in different ways, but one fairly simple way to think about policy making is to consider where policy ideas are first formulated and implemented (Dye, 2001). *Bottom-up* policy making focuses on policy ideas that are formulated and implemented at the local or the state level of government. Bottom-up policy frequently can be an outcome of public–private partnerships. Local–local or state–local intergovernmental partnerships and coordination are also commonly found in bottom-up policy efforts. Bottom-up policy making was promoted in the 1980s and 1990s by governors and local leaders working with for-profit and nonprofit organizations eager to make a variety of changes in their states and local communities. A former state governor, President Clinton came into office in 1993—the first baby boomer to become president of the United States. An ardent supporter of state policy innovation and a former chair of the National Governors Association, Bill Clinton found tremendous value in the "reinventing government" movement and the bottom-up domestic policy movement. Bottom-up policy has the benefit of being implemented on a small scale in states or local areas, where policy experimentation may cost less, but outcomes can be highly innovative and effective and have potential for replication elsewhere in the country. Successful policy experiments or innovations might then be implemented around the country and even at the national level (Osborne, 1990).

Top-down policy approaches are less concerned with policy experimentation and are often more generally focused on protecting the rights and liberties of all citizens. Social welfare, public health, environmental protection pollution standards, and civil rights policy areas are often considered to be examples of top-down policy areas, focused to a greater extent on national policy standards impacting all citizens, regardless of their location in the country.

Energy policy provides examples of both top-down and bottom-up policy. Carbon-based energy policy is a well-established policy area and is regulated in a top-down policy approach, although state policies have sought to go beyond federal policy in some cases. The U.S. Department of Energy (DOE) and U.S. Department of the Interior (DOI) monitor and regulate the production, processing, transportation, and use of carbon-based fossil fuels, and both cabinet-level departments have involvements with renewable energy. The Environmental Protection Agency (EPA) regulates the impact of carbon-based fuels on the environment. The Federal Energy Regulatory Commission (FERC), an independent agency attached to DOE, regulates the wholesale electricity market and interstate electricity sales. DOE, DOI, EPA, and FERC policies and regulations are applied from the national level and impact individuals and corporations regardless of location within the country.

Bottom-up and top-down policy innovation will play a large role in the future developments in alternative energy. The federal government, through grants for basic research and demonstration projects, as well as through the market regulation and access to public land and water resources, can work in tandem with state and local innovations intended to meet the clean energy needs of their residents. Federal courts and administrative law judges often become the final arbiters in disputes over resource use, often with due regard for lower court decisions at the state level that reflect the unique rules and statutes reflecting state and local values and priorities.

COLLABORATIVE POLICY MAKING

Collaborative policy making occurs on at least two levels. Within the bottom-up policy making arena, the costs of policy innovation may exceed the capacity of any single public agency's budget constraints. In order to produce tangible policy innovations at the local and the state level, government agencies frequently *collaborate* to produce mutual benefits.

Collaboration is particularly important in the development of alternative energy. Government agencies, private sector businesses, and citizens regularly identify mutual benefits. Private industry benefits from the commitment of government to alternative energy and energy-related products. Government

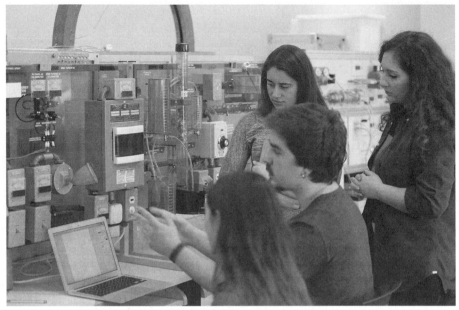

Students Collaborating in a Renewable Energy Lab
E+ / leventince

and citizens gain the benefits of clean sustainable energy source development and reduce air pollution and its related health and environmental costs. California's solar roofs initiative is a good example of the mutual benefits emergent from collaborative policy efforts (see California Solar Energy Storage Association, 2018).

As is the case with other products and services, alternative energy is given legitimacy through successful use. Building commitment to alternative energy requires that government and the private sector work in tandem to educate consumers. Many homeowners and small business owners are not fully unaware of the energy-producing potential that exists in backyards and rooftops, or through cogeneration processes. Also, individuals are unlikely to invest heavily in the search process required to determine costs and benefits associated with various forms of alternative energy. Home, farm, ranch, and business owners may also be concerned with the aesthetic costs that alternative energy might produce (e.g., noise from wind generators, glare off of solar panels, and panoramic views distorted by the physical plant of alternative energy generation). The NIMBY (Not in My Backyard!) effect can emerge when alternative energy plans move from theory to practical application. Collaborative policy making may help citizens become more aware of the costs and benefits expected to emerge from alternative energy policies. Sustainable energy paradigms for sustainable communities work best when citizens see that others are sharing in the time, cost, and commitment to building a better future. Through collaborative effort, citizens become engaged in the policy process, gain an understanding of advances in energy technology, and provide feedback to technical experts and policy makers based on their experience. Today, the public plays an active role in legitimizing technology and defining its role in their lives—the public no longer passively accepts scientific consensus or technological development without evidence of successful application in situations and circumstances similar to their own (see Manzella et al., 2019).

FEDERALISM AND ENERGY POLICY

The top-down, bottom-up, and collaborative dynamics of energy policy describe federalism at work in the United States. Rabe (2011) presents a clear discussion of the nature of federalism and energy and climate policy in the United States. He finds that from 1998 to 2007 the states played a dominant role in the development of renewable energy and climate policy. In the period 2008–2011, national policy efforts contested state domination of the clean energy and climate policy arena. Rabe (2011: 497) refers to 2008–2011 as a period of "contested federalism" in both global climate change and clean energy policy.

Writing toward the end of the President Obama's first term in office, Rabe (2011: 517) noted that "the transition from state domination to contested federalism . . . remains in a fairly early and uncertain stage." Optimistically, Rabe noted that the near decade-long period of state domination of renewable energy and climate policy—an example of bottom-up policy making and strong efforts to develop interstate climate compacts—could, with federal government capacity, serve as the basis of a national commitment to clean energy and climate policy. Given the bookend failures of the U.S. Congress to ratify the Kyoto Treaty and the Paris Agreement, however, one might conclude that the United States is drifting away from its support for clean energy. However, the U.S. Department of Energy budget commitment to alternative energy is illustrated in figure 2.4; those figures illustrate that the U.S. federal budget commitment to alternative energy remains stable overall, and even shows some moderate growth in some areas.

Many states continue to find ways to promote clean energy and climate policy through modifications in building codes, issuance of renewable energy rebates, creation of feed-in tariffs, establishment of RPS standards, and investments in the green economy as one aspect of their economic development planning (Couture and Cory, 2009; Dietchman, 2017; Lantz and Doris, 2009). According to Alagappan et al. (2011), feed-in tariffs are a particularly useful policy mechanism in increasing renewable energy capacity. Feed-in tariffs guarantee a set price for renewable energy generated and guarantee that all renewable electricity generated by the provider and put on the grid is purchased (see also EIA, 2013).

Figure 2.4   U.S. Federal Budget Commitment to Alternative Energy (2014–2019)

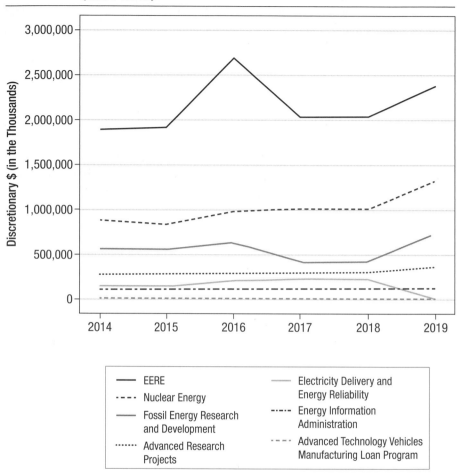

Data Source: U.S. Department of Energy

POLICY FRAMEWORKS/MODELS

The process model and policy types are foundational to understanding public policy, but the aforementioned models do not capture the truly dynamic aspects of public policy making—that is, how the process is viewed in different instances, and how the deliberative process can and does work. In the physical sciences and engineering, there are scientific laws that govern processes; in the social sciences, of which policy science is a subfield, decisional processes often depend on the use of an assortment of theories and frameworks to make political and social phenomena comprehensible.

Institutional Analysis and Development (IAD)

The IAD framework was developed by Elinor Ostrom, a world-renowned professor and Nobel Laureate (Economics). IAD is particularly useful in governing the allocation and conservation of environmental and natural resources and, by extension, energy policy. IAD could be used to overcome the marginal social environmental costs associated with energy production and use.

The IAD framework recognizes that the distribution of scarce resources occurs at the local level, and that governance of these resources—including monitoring of resource extraction—requires a commitment on the part of government, but perhaps more importantly, a commitment from the resource users themselves. By recognizing mutual benefit and agreeing to rules governing resources, it is possible to mitigate some of the costs associated with monitoring resource use—both levels and patterns of use in relation to resource availability.

IAD "examines the impacts of institutional arrangements on human behavior," relying heavily on "new institutional economics." The IAD framework links a set of institutional rules to individual choice. According to Ostrom, institutions represent

> the shared concepts used by humans in repetitive situations organized by rules, norms and strategies . . . By rules, I mean shared prescriptions (must, must not, or may) that are mutually understood and predictably enforced in particular situations by agents responsible for monitoring conduct and imposing sanctions. By norms, I mean shared prescriptions that tend to be enforced by the participants themselves through internally and externally imposed costs and inducements. By strategies, I mean the regularized plans that individuals make within the structure of incentives produced by rules, norms, and expectations of the likely behavior of others in a situation affected by relevant physical and material conditions. (Ostrom, 1999: 37)

In order for institutional decision-making to operate effectively, information quality and content must be monitored and available. Good information is the basis of good decision-making in an effective deliberative process. The "action arena" is where decisions are made by policy stakeholders. The "physical/ material conditions" of a policy setting, the "attributes of community," and extant rules governing a shared resource are critically important considerations in the deliberative process and emerging decisions (Simon, 2017).

Collective decisions made within the action arena by corporate or individual stakeholders are known as "action situations." A stakeholder's values, information processing abilities, and decision-making methods impact the courses of action taken. Stakeholders are identified and brought into the IAD process based on their interest in the management and use of a resource. Within the action arena, participant stakeholders operate within agreed-upon rules governing the action situation process, and endeavor to understand collectively what is to be acted upon and the breadth of actions to be taken within the community context. Multiple action arenas might exist within a more complex policy area.

In shared resource management action arenas, Ostrom outlines seven key concepts to be monitored:

1. The set of participants: Who and how many individuals withdraw resource units from . . . this resource system?
2. The positions: What positions exist [with regard to the various stakeholder actors]?
3. The set of allowable actions: which types of harvesting techniques are used?
4. The potential outcomes: What geographic region and what events in that region are affected by participants . . .?
5. The level of control over choice: Do appropriators [of a resource] take action on their own initiative, or do they confer with others?
6. The information available: How much information do appropriators have about the condition of the resource . . . about other appropriators' cost and benefit, . . . and about how their actions cumulate into joint outcomes?
7. The costs and benefits of actions and outcomes: How costly are various actions to each type of appropriator, and what kinds of benefits can be achieved as a result of various group outcomes? (Ostrom, 1999: 43–44)

Action arenas are generally highly dynamic. While participants strive to achieve their individual self-interest, the action arena is about achieving lasting "win-win" outcomes and about learning to achieve effective resource management outcomes for all stakeholders over the long term. Information sharing is a critical part of decision-making in the action arena. Information and information exchange is about creating shared meaning, and each stakeholder may attach different meanings to different aspects of the situation; understanding those different meanings builds collective understanding and creates opportunities for constructive compromise and effective collaboration.

The IAD process is evaluated along six dimensions:
1. Economic efficiency—do the benefits of an IAD process outweigh transaction costs associated with IAD?
2. Fiscal equivalence—are participants assuming an equitable share of the costs associated with the IAD process or are they 'free-riding?'
3. Redistributional equity—are individuals who are less well-off benefiting from the process and in the implementation of decision outcomes?
4. Accountability—are public officials—oftentimes resource managers—being held accountable to the citizenry?
5. Conformance to General Morality—are participants in the IAD process being honest brokers with one another?
6. Adaptability—Institutional rules and processes must be capable of successful change in the face of changing conditions. Resource availability changes over time as does demand. (Simon, 2017: 36–37)

Monitoring is critical in the IAD process to ensure that resources are properly managed based on the collective decisions made within the action arena.

Resource availability is frequently not static, and availability often changes depending on conditions. Water resources are a good example—under an agreement plan, it may be the case that each party has been allotted a certain amount of water to be withdrawn from a lake, but what happens if there is a drought and the lake is drying up? Monitoring helps stakeholders in an IAD process reevaluate their expectations so that the resource is well managed and not depleted. Monitoring helps in tracking the costs and benefits of various decisions, and seeks to keep transaction costs at a minimum. Monitoring also ensures that rules are followed, and that parties to an agreement are not cheating or shirking.

The IAD framework is a promising way of managing resources, and could be a beneficial mechanism in an alternative energy future. As communities begin to play a larger role in building sustainable energy systems, the IAD framework could help stakeholders—citizens, government, and private businesses—manage energy resources in ways contributing to sustainability. IAD creates opportunities to build deliberative democracy into energy policy at the community level, and to reduce the potential for serious conflict.

Multiple Streams (MS)

Ambiguity characterizes the policy process in many cases. Ambiguity means that there are multiple ways of interpreting and understanding circumstances. If one cannot describe a circumstance, it would be very difficult to identify a method of changing circumstances or, in other words, to reduce or eliminate a problem. As it turns out, many problems exist and many of them are ambiguous at first glance, and some remain ambiguous even after careful study and analysis. In the world of great ambiguity, somehow policy makers make choices nonetheless.

Policy makers are motivated to make choices for a variety of reasons, but an obvious reason might be a crisis. A crisis is a good time to make a choice because the costs of not making a choice are usually very high. If policy makers choose to do nothing, people may die or property might be destroyed. Even if the crisis does not lead to death or destruction, the fact that policy makers—our elected and appointed leaders—chose not to do anything leads some to demand change in leadership.

So, crisis often presents a good time to make decisions. As alluded to earlier, sometimes crisis gives policy makers an opportunity to adopt policies that, under more pacific circumstances, might be resisted by a major portion of the public. Think about gun control advocacy following a school shooting or mass murder event. Or, think about climate change and alternative energy policy adoption following a major climate change-related event—extended drought, a massive storm event, fossil energy price spikes, a long summer in a city with high ozone and particulate matter linked to a large number of deaths.

According to Kingdon (2003), there are three "streams" in the policy process that must converge in order for major policy initiatives to be made: the problem stream, the policy stream, and the politics stream. Problems are defined differently by different people. In the case of a crisis (or some kind of event that focuses our collective attention), it is more likely that people come to agree, at least for a short period of time, that there is a problem that needs solving by government action.

Many actors are present in the policy stream. These actors include numerous elected and appointed government officials. Elected officials at the federal level include members of Congress and the president in the form of his or her policy advisers. At the state level, it would be the state legislature and the governor's administrative team. At the local level, it might entail county commissioners, city mayors, and council members. Appointed government officials at all levels include the personal staff of elected officials, political appointees managing departments, and career civil servants.

According to Kingdon (2003), the political stream is composed of "national mood, pressure group campaigns, and administrative or legislative turnover (p. 91)." Public opinion polling is one way to gauge the national mood. The national mood changes, so polling is done on a regular basis by policy advocates seeking to either maintain or alter public policies. Sometimes, national mood is related to turnover among the elected and appointed individuals who comprise the political stream. In 2016, Donald Trump ran for office promising to change policy direction and to "build the wall" and "drain the swamp." Enough people in enough key states agreed with his ideas and elected him president. In 2018, however, voters chose to hand the reins of power in the U.S. House of Representatives back to Democrats. Clearly, some of the key actors in the political stream change regularly over time, which means that actors representing particular values and priorities may enter the stream, while other actors representing different values and priorities may exit the stream and thereby open up opportunities for policy change.

Clearly, the three streams identified by Kingdon are all highly dynamic, so it is not common for them to converge. Crises, however, can provide opportunities for the three streams to converge. Policy entrepreneurs—oftentimes, former elected/appointed officials or pressure group leaders—play a significant role in the convergence of the three streams. This convergence and the circumstances/events/crisis surrounding a policy issue are referred to as a policy "window." Windows represent brief periods in which opportunities exist for new policy solutions to be adopted. Following the adoption of a new policy solution, policy windows usually close and further innovation is foreclosed.

In the case of energy policy, the multiple streams model might help explain energy policy innovations that took place in the 1970s and 1980s when oil prices spiked and gasoline shortages occurred. During the Carter administration, the energy crisis instigated by OPEC created an opportunity for federal policy makers to fund renewable energy research and to establish the U.S. Department of Energy. In the late 1970s and early 1980s, high fuel prices along with a stagnant economy provided the Reagan administration with another rare policy window to approve greater petroleum exploration and extraction in the United States, particularly along the North Slope in Alaska.

Advocacy Coalition Framework (ACF)

The ACF highlights the substantial role of technical information in policy making. The ACF details the relationship between multiple subsystems that exist within established policy networks. "Relatively Stable Parameters" in the ACF describe political, social, and economic systems that intersect with respect to specific areas of public policy. Environmental or "External" factors in the ACF framework are variable, while the networks tend to be persistent and relatively stable in composition. Political party or governing coalitions change over time, as can sociopolitical and economic conditions. "Relatively Stable Parameters" and "External Events" can work either to facilitate or to constrain policy making.

Building off of a systems approach, environmental actors known as "policy brokers" seek to influence political systems operating within the context of particular social or economic conditions. Policy brokers, not unlike the policy entrepreneurs discussed previously, are typically former elected or appointed officials, technical experts (academics, scientists, policy analysts, political economists, think-tank researchers), bureaucrats representing agency interests, and other related purveyors of specialized technical information. Within the policy process, individuals and groups that share common agreement on problem definition, relevant technical information, and desired policy direction are likely to form networked coalitions. Through such coalitions, resources and information can be shared in a timely manner, and constraints and cleavages present in the political environment can be more easily overcome. Information is shared with elected officials in the context of establishing reasons for why policy should move in particular directions to address perceived public needs. Access to public policy makers is critical, as is establishing the perceived legitimacy of the specialized technical information commanded.

Based on their beliefs and resources, knowledge-based advocacy coalitions use various strategies to influence the decisions of government policy actors. The results of these decisions shape statutes, administrative rules, budget authorizations, agency internal allocations, and political appointments to key bureaucratic offices. The way policy is made and implemented is indirectly impacted by the activities and information shared by such coalitions, with the long-term result being the purposeful shaping of public policy outputs and impacts. The ACF model is cyclical, meaning that this process is ongoing, with outcomes and coalition formation and strength changing as values, circumstances, and public policy actors enter or exit political or administrative offices and substantial decision-making roles.

Punctuated Equilibrium (PE)

Punctuated equilibrium theory seeks to explain sudden rapid change in public policy. In ways similar to evolution in biological systems, periods of *stasis* are sometimes followed by rapid change, with the establishment of a new relatively stable set of conditions. The dramatic punctuations and rapid change episodes in natural systems are a common outcome for some forms of crisis from which recovery to a new *statis* condition is possible. In public policy, rapid change is sometimes seen in the formation of a new or greatly expanded government agency with expanded powers, large budgets, and ample staffing. While the ACF focuses attention on both macro-level and micro-level events or conditions, punctuated equilibrium theory tends to focus greater attention on macro-level analysis. As a theory element, punctuated equilibrium might be incorporated into a larger analysis using the wider lens of a policy framework, a concept that may incorporate many theories into its understanding of public policy processes.

For instance, MS and PE might aid policy analysts in identifying and explaining the significant increase in alternative energy funding made possible by the American Recovery and Rehabilitation Act of 2009, but the ACF helps in understanding the various choices made within the context of alternative energy program funding that resulted from one of the largest single-year increases in energy policy expenditures to ever take place.

Policy Diffusion

The policy diffusion model seeks to explain both policy innovation and how policy innovations migrate from their place of origin. Innovation involves identifying the development and implementation of policy solutions for either new or existing policy problems requiring more effective management. Typically, public policy diffusion relates to innovations occurring at the state and local levels, although policy innovations can develop at the national level and later spread to state and local government. Due to their close proximity to clientele, state and local government officials are often acutely aware of social problems as they arise. Policy innovation can be a function of successful advocacy by a coalition of individuals and groups pressuring policy makers, but it can also be the result of executive leadership and vision or grassroots efforts of citizen stakeholders. Good ideas can come from many sources, and have done so consistently over the course of U.S. history. Policy innovation tends to work best in states and in local communities that identify public policy problems as collective action problems necessitating public policy solutions. Innovation typically requires some timely resources in the form of some public funding sources, access to respected intellectual capital, and the presence of effective leadership.

A great deal of competition exists between states and local governments to attract citizens and businesses to their geographic location. Individuals and businesses bring with them human capital and other resources needed to make a community prosper and grow. Commercial enterprises rent properties, pay salaries, and make profits, some of which flow into government coffers to provide public services and improve the quality of life for residents.

Policy innovations can help in the effort to attract people and businesses to communities. Governments that use their tax dollars strategically and efficiently are able to provide high-quality services for lower cost. Lower costs may result in lower tax rates, making it easier for individuals to keep more of what they earn and for businesses to reinvest their earnings in both the community and in future business development.

Geography plays a big role in the area of policy innovation. When a state or local government adopts successful and highly applauded policy innovations, neighboring jurisdictions are often eager to follow suit. Regional intergovernmental organizations help spread innovative ideas from one jurisdiction to its neighbors. More importantly, adopting innovative ideas often involves adapting the innovation to meet local needs, providing opportunities to test and strengthen an innovation in various settings and in unique applications (see Fredericksen et al., 2016).

State-level renewable portfolio standards are a good example of state-level policy diffusion. While national-level policy makers have yet to establish a firm commitment to renewable energy use goals for the nation, various state governments began that process nearly three decades ago. In 1991, Iowa became the first state to adopt targets and incentives for renewable energy and its use within the state. As of 2018, RPS standards had been adopted by thirty-seven U.S. states (eight have voluntary standards) and the District of Columbia.

Narrative Policy Framework (NPF)

"A narrative is a story with a temporal sequence of events . . . unfolding in a plot . . . that is populated by dramatic moments, symbols, and archetypical characters . . . that culminates in a moral to the story" (Jones and McBeth, 2010: 329). The narrative approach is a qualitative methodology that uses a form of storytelling to explain how and why policy emerges in a particular form and the outcomes that are produced. Stories exist on three different levels: the micro-, the meso-, and the macro-levels. The micro-level story focuses on the individual as the unit of analysis. Micro-level analyses can include analysis of survey data to measure the opinions, beliefs, and values of subjects. At the meso-level, NPF focuses on coalitions of individuals. Coalitions are identified as either angels ("good") or devils ("bad"). Unlike many other theories of the policy process, the narrative approach makes room for position taking through the application of theory to policy analysis. At the macro-level, NPF views the policy narrative as it is encoded in administrative rules and statutes.

NPF takes two different approaches to building a narrative: the structuralist and the post-structuralist. Structuralists tend to use either quantitative or qualitative methodologies in constructing their narrative. Post-structuralists are more critical in their analysis, building a narrative, at times a personal account, to explain policy events from the authors' perspective.

If you are building a narrative, there are four major things you should include in it:

1. "A setting or context";
2. "A plot that introduces a temporal element (beginning, middle, end) . . . providing both the relationships between the setting and the characters, and structuring causal mechanisms";
3. "Characters who are fixers of the problem (heroes), and causers of the problem (villains), or victims (those harmed by the problem)";
4. "The moral of the story, where a policy solution is normally offered."

Jones and McBeth, 2010: 340

The content of narrative policy analysis focuses on "Belief Systems" and "Culture Theory." Belief systems focus on individual or group ideologies, while Culture Theory (CT) focuses on two distinct things: (1) Is decision-making elite-based or broad-based and majoritarian? (2) Are problems identified as individual or group concerns? Within that two-dimensional analysis, there are four categories of policy stakeholder perspective:

- *Fatalist*—nonefficacious
- *Hierarch*—all things and individuals have a place and purpose
- *Individualist*—individuals make their own choices for their own welfare
- *Egalitarian*—must consider the needs of others as well as one's own interests

Culture theory helps policy analysts understand the respective positions of key policy stakeholders and comprehend how individual or coalition values, beliefs, and opinions act to shape the policy process and determine policy outcomes.

NPF is extremely useful in policy analysis. Narrative is the basis of relating information, telling a story, and explaining social phenomena. All other policy models and frameworks discussed here require the use of narratives to describe findings, and to construct explanations of policy actor behaviors, choices, and outcomes.

Intergovernmentalism

Intergovernmentalism refers to the relationship that exists between different levels of government within a given political system. In the United States of America, intergovernmentalism refers to the federal system and the relationship between the national government and the states and local levels of government. Article VI, Clause 2 of the U.S. Constitution establishes the supremacy of the national government, and if state or local laws conflict with national law, then national law takes precedence. In practical terms, this means that the national government can create policy, at the top, and coerce lower forms of government (that is, the states and local governments) to enforce national policy priorities and standards. However, despite the Supremacy Clause, the states and local governments have created many policies that the national government has not adopted, which could very well be the subject of congressional legislation (e.g., the legalization of marijuana). In some cases, the national government adopts policies patterned after state and local policy innovations because national leaders realize that such public policy innovations are worthwhile. This is known as bottom-up policy making. Intergovernmental relationships in the U.S. federal system are quite often cooperative rather than contentious, with national, state, and local government actors finding many areas of common interest and agreement on approaches to be taken to problem management. Intergovernmental compacts and memoranda of understanding often link administrative agencies and policy domains across jurisdictional lines for the purpose of achieving common goals with shared resources and coordinated actions.

NATIVE AMERICANS, TRIBAL LANDS, AND RENEWABLE ENERGY

Native American tribal lands are rich sources of nonrenewable and renewable energy. Energy resource development offers Native American tribes opportunities for economic development as well as for promoting the sustainability of tribal lands and tribal communities. The Indian Mineral Development Act of 1982 establishes the format by which Native American mineral leasing occurs, and requires compliance with most provisions of the National Environmental Policy Act of 1970. Oil and gas leases on Native American tribal lands pose significant risks to air and water quality in situ as well as the broader regional environment. Title V of the Energy Policy Act of 2005 established the Office of Indian Energy Policy and Programs within the U.S. Department of Energy. The Department of Energy has placed a high priority on Native American energy self-determination. According to the Tribal Energy Projects Database, as of 2018 there are 283 renewable energy projects underway on Native American tribal lands.

CHAPTER SUMMARY

Renewable energy policy is a function of politics, technological development, economics, and social acceptance. Assuming that technological feasibility is a given, there are other hurdles that must be overcome. Energy as an economic good must be understood in all of its complexity. Energy is almost never a purely marketable good; in large part, this is because of the large marginal social costs associated with certain forms of energy—namely, fossil and potentially nuclear energy. There are public goods dimensions to all forms of energy and their use. Additionally, for energy policy to be effective in both the short- and long-term future, there must be a strong consumer commitment. In the case of renewable energy, this commitment is grounded in a commitment to social and environmental values and a commitment to transgenerational sustainability. Moreover, the commitment to renewable energy is not just a commitment of a consumer, but oftentimes that of a producer of renewable energy as well. Understanding how policy frameworks explain policy development is an important part of understanding the short- and long-term feasibility and commitment required to implement clean energy solutions.

REFERENCES

Aberbach, J. 1990. *Keeping a Watchful Eye: The Politics of Congressional Oversight.* Washington, DC: Brookings Institution.

Aberbach, J., and Rockman, B. 1978. Administrators' beliefs about the role of the public The case of American federal executives. *Western Political Quarterly* 31(4): 502–522.

Ahari, M. 1987. Congress, public opinion, and synfuels policy. *Political Science Quarterly* 102(4): 589–606.

Alagappan, L., Orans, R., and Woo, C. 2011. What drives renewable energy development? *Energy Policy* 39: 5099–5104.

Binder, S., Lawrence, E., and Maltzman, F. 1999. Uncovering the hidden party effect. *Journal of Politics* 61(3): 815–831.

Bowers, B. 2004. Stone age combustion. *Science News* 165(18): 276–277.

California Solar Storage Association. 2018. "The Million Solar Roofs of Energy Storage" passed California Assembly! *California Solar Storage Association*, August 29. Retrieved from https://calssa.org/press-releases/2018/8/29/the-million-solar-roofs-of-energy-storage-passed-california-assembly, June 2, 2019.

Cook, D. 2003. Spencer Abraham. *Christian Science Monitor*, September 12: 25.

Couture, T., and Cory, K. 2009. *State Clean Energy Policies Analysis (SCEPA) Project: An Analysis of Renewable Energy Feed-in Tariffs in the United States.* Golden, CO: National Renewable Energy Laboratory. NREL/TP-6A2-45551.

Dietchman, B. 2017. *Climate and Clean Energy Policy: State Institutions and Economic Implications.* New York: Routledge.

Dye, T. 2001. *Top Down Policymaking.* New York: Chatham House.

Energy Information Administration. 2013. Feed-in tariffs: A policy tool encouraging deployment of renewable electricity technologies. *Today in Energy*, May 30. Retrieved from https://www.eia.gov/todayinenergy/detail.php?id=11471, July 27, 2019.

———. 2014. Gasoline prices tend to have little effect on demand for car travel. *U.S. Energy Information Administration*, December 15. Retrieved from https://www.eia.gov/todayinenergy/detail.php?id=19191, June 2, 2019.

Fredericksen, E., Witt, S., and Nice, D. 2016. *The Politics of Intergovernmental Relations*, 3rd Edition. San Diego, CA: Birkdale Publishers.

Hayek, F. 1944. *The Road to Serfdom.* Chicago, IL: University of Chicago Press.

Houldon, R. 2004. Finding the public good: Shedding light on a bulk grid electricity card trick. *Electricity Journal* 17(9): 61–67.

Hulbary, W., and Walker, T. 1980. The Supreme Court selection process: Presidential motivations and judicial performance. *Western Political Science Quarterly* 33(2): 185–196.

Jones, Charles O. 1970. *An Introduction to the Study of Public Policy*. Belmont, CA: Wadsworth.

Jones, M. D., and McBeth, M. K. 2010. A narrative policy framework: Clear enough to be wrong? *Policy Studies Journal* 38(2): 329–353.

Lantz, E., and Doris, E. 2009. *State Clean Energy Practices: Renewable Energy Rebates*. Golden, CO: National Renewable Energy Laboratory. NREL/TP 6A2-45039.

LePage, M. 2016. Was Kyoto climate deal a success? Figures reveal mixed results. *The New Scientist*, June 14. Retrieved from https://www.newscientist.com/article/ 2093579-was-kyoto-climate-deal-a-success-figures-reveal-mixed-results/, June 2, 2019.

Kingdon, John W. 2003. *Agendas, Alternatives, and Public Policy*, 3rd Edition. New York: Longman.

Krehbiel, K. 1993. Where's the party? *British Journal of Political Science* 23(2): 235–266.

Krugman, P. 2004. A vision of power. *New York Times*, April 27: A25.

Loris, N. 2018. To improve the environment, look to the free market. *The Heritage Foundation*, March 6. Retrieved from https://www.heritage.org/ environment/ commentary/improve-the-environment-look-the-free-market, June 2, 2019.

Lowi, T. 1972. Four systems of politics, policy, and choice. *Public Administration Review* 32(4): 298–310.

Manzella, A., Allansdottir, A., and Pelizzone, A., eds. 2019. *Geothermal Energy and Society*. Cham, Switzerland: Springer.

Michelbach, P., Scott, J., Matland, R., and Bornstein, B. 2003. Doing Rawls justice: An experimental study of income distribution norms. *American Journal of Political Science*. 47(3): 524–539.

Nation's Cities Weekly. 2000. Bush and Gore address environmental, energy issues. *Nation's Cities Weekly*, October 23: 16.

Osborne, D. 1990. *Laboratories of Democracy*. Boston, MA: Harvard Business School.

Ostrom, E. 1990. *Governing the Commons: The Evolution of Institutions for Collective Action*. New York: Cambridge.

———. 1999. Institutional rational choice: An assessment of the Institutional Analysis and Development Framework. In: *Theories of the Policy Process*, Paul Sabatier (Ed.). Boulder, CO: Westview Press, 35–71.

Pressman, J., and Wildavsky, A. 1973. *Implementation: How Great Expectations in Washington Are Dashed in Oakland; Or, Why It's Amazing That Federal Programs Work at All, This Being a Saga of the Economic Development Administration as Told by Two Sympathetic Observers Who Seek to Build Morals on a Foundation of Ruined Hopes*. Berkeley, CA: University of California Press.

Rabe, B. 2011. Contested federalism and American climate policy. *Publius* 41(3): 494–521.

Rawls, J. 1971. *A Theory of Justice*. Cambridge, MA: Belknap Press.

Rochlin, C. 2004. Resource adequacy requirement, reserve margin, and the public goods argument. *Electricity Journal* 17(3): 52–59.

Seib, G. 2008. In crisis, opportunity for Obama. *The Wall Street Journal*, November 21. Retrieved from https://www.wsj.com/articles/SB122721278056345271, June 2, 2019.

Simon, C. 2007. *Public Policy: Preferences and Outcomes*. New York: Longman.

———. 2017. *Public Policy: Preferences and Outcomes*, 3rd Edition. New York: Routledge.

Stempel, J. 2019. Justice Thomas urges U.S. Supreme Court to feel free to reverse precedents. *Reuters*, June 17. Retrieved from https://www.reuters.com/article/us-usa-court-thomas/justice-thomas-urges-us-supreme-court-to-feel-free-to-reverse-precedents-idUSKCN1TI2KJ, July 13, 2019.

Stone, Deborah A. 1988. *Policy Paradox and Political Reason*. New York: Harper Collins.

Unger, R. 2004. *Mills in the Medieval Economy: England 1300–1540*. New York: Oxford University Press.

Wasserman, J. 2003. Schwarzeneggar's growth agenda may rile state's suburban builders. *Associated Press*. November 9.

Weatherford, S. 1988. The international economy as a constraint on U.S. macroeconomic policymaking. *International Organization* 42(4): 605–637.

Wilson, J. 1989. *Bureaucracy: What Government Agencies Do and Why They Do It*. New York: Basic Books

Wolfcale, J. 2005. Going solar in Kentfield. *Marin Independent Journal*, September 28: Local News.

3

Alternative Energy/Fuels as a Public Policy Innovation

★ ★ ★

The contemporary alternative energy paradigm is a combined function of governmental policy, applied science and engineering, and private sector innovation. Energy is an essential global good, and its constrained supply would adversely impact the quality of life of people and market growth on a global scale (textbox 3.1). This chapter will focus on noteworthy alternative energy and fuel supply developments dating from the early 1970s up to the present day.

DEFINING ALTERNATIVE ENERGY AND ALTERNATIVE FUELS

The federal definition of alternative energy is well summarized by former president Obama's Executive Order 13693 (2015: 15882), which reads in part:

> "alternative energy" means energy generated from technologies and approaches that advance renewable heat sources, including biomass, solar thermal, geothermal, waste heat, and renewable combined heat and power processes; combined heat and power; small modular nuclear reactor technologies; fuel cell energy systems; and energy generation, where active capture and storage of carbon dioxide emissions associated with that energy generation is verified.

E.O. 13693 focuses on building compliance with President Obama's commitment to reduce carbon emissions and facilitate increased use of alternative energy sources through coordinated actions across the elements of the federal government.

The U.S. code relates the definition of renewable energy to "energy properties." Energy properties are defined in the following manner:

> the term "energy property" means any property—(A) which is—(i) equipment which uses solar energy to generate electricity, to heat or cool (or provide hot water for use in) a structure, or to provide solar process heat, excepting

property used to generate energy for the purposes of heating a swimming pool, (ii) equipment which uses solar energy to illuminate the inside of a structure using fiber-optic distributed sunlight but only with respect to property the construction of which begins before, (iii) equipment used to produce, distribute, or use energy derived from a geothermal deposit (within the meaning of), but only, in the case of electricity generated by geothermal power, up to (but not including) the electrical transmission stage, (iv) qualified fuel cell property or qualified micro-turbine property, (v) combined heat and power system property, (vi) qualified small wind energy property, or (vii) equipment which uses the ground or ground water as a thermal energy source to heat a structure or as a thermal energy sink to cool a structure, but only with respect to property the construction of which begins before . . . (C) with respect to which depreciation (or amortization in lieu of depreciation) is allowable, and (D) which meets the performance and quality standards (if any) which—(i) have been prescribed by the Secretary by regulations (after consultation with the Secretary of Energy), and (ii) are in effect at the time of the acquisition of the property. (26 USC §48(a)(3))

TEXTBOX 3.1 | Energy versus Power … and What Is Work (W)?

These terms "energy" and "power" are often used interchangeably in everyday dialogue and thought to be the same concept. In physics, energy is defined as "the capacity to do work. Forms of energy include thermal, mechanical, electrical, and chemical. Energy may be transformed from one form into another" (EERE, 2005). Energy can be measured in a variety of ways, such as joules and British thermal units (BTUs). Power is "the rate of expenditure of energy" (Physics Forums, 2005). Power is simply expenditure of energy per unit of time (e.g., BTU/hr or BTU/sec). In everyday life, one comes across measurements of power in the form of watts or horsepower. A fuel is potential energy that can be burned and involves molecular changes that release energy.

In physics, work (W) is done when force is applied to an object that results in that object being moved. Force (F = mass × acceleration) is measured in newtons, and distance (d) is measured in meters: W = F×d. If an object is subjected to an applied force of 10 newtons and is moved 10 meters, work equals 100 newton-meters. One newton-meter equals one joule. In the case of electricity generation, consider for a moment the work accomplished in turning a near 290,000 kg industrial gas turbine generator through just one cycle.

By the way, if you calculate work (in joules) and divide it by the amount of energy needed to accomplish the work (in joules), you have calculated efficiency. Electricity generator efficiencies range between 32 and 48 percent depending upon plant type (Zactruba, 2019).

$$\eta = \frac{W(out)}{W(in)} \times 100\%$$

State-level variations in legal definitions of terms relating to alternative energy illustrate the role politics often plays in shaping the contemporary alternative energy paradigm. State energy economic interests often impact the choices available for public consideration related to the adoption of alternative energy policies. For example, in states with major coal production activity (e.g., Pennsylvania, Wyoming), it is likely that interest groups representing fossil fuel industries and environmental interests will square off toe to toe, seeking to shape the character of regulation of energy uses and production as well as the nature of redistributive policies intended to provide for cleaner energy in the future. Some redistributive policies, recall, are enacted in order to retrospectively benefit individuals and societal groups who may have had to bear heavy environmental and health costs associated with fossil fuel extraction and/or use. In some cases, different tiers or categories of "alternative energy," depending on the source's level or shades of "greenness," occasion conflict over the classification and legal definition between industry and environmental protection advocacy groups (Mandelbaum and Brown, 2004, 1).

State energy laws cover a variety of subjects, and energy policy is a major area of political conflict in many states. As discussed previously, renewable energy portfolio standards (RPS) and clean energy laws are particularly important in demonstrating a commitment to renewable energy use at the state and local level in the United States. State laws also establish green building codes, as do some county and municipal ordinances. At the federal level, Energy Star—a program sponsored by the U.S. Environmental Protection Agency—is well known as a standard for green buildings. Green buildings are water- and energy-efficient and use materials that produce only limited greenhouse gas emissions. State laws in many jurisdictions promote clean energy production, development, use, and energy efficiency through award and tax rebate programs that provide various forms of incentives to households, small businesses, farms and ranches, and local governments in the state.

Not all state energy law focuses on clean energy solutions. While Texas is one of the largest producers of renewable energy, it is also a significant producer and exporter of fossil energy. Regulatory agencies, such as the Texas Railroad Commission, oversee fossil energy production and coal mining in the state, while the Texas Land Commission oversees mineral and leasing rights to oil and gas in that very large state. Alaska, another state of vast size, is heavily dependent on the production and sale of North Slope crude petroleum. The Alaska state government accordingly focuses significant attention on liquid fossil fuel production and transportation via the Alaska pipeline and tanker ship transport, as well as the management of state oil revenues through the Alaska Permanent Fund. Wyoming produces large amounts of coal, oil, and natural gas, and a significant portion of Wyoming state law focuses on the regulation, development, and ongoing management of these resources. While this book will not discuss in great detail state energy laws, suffice it to say that states often balance interests in clean energy with interests seeking the lucrative benefits made available through fossil energy extraction within their borders.

In particular, lands that were designated by federal law as state trust lands are an important revenue stream for state and local governments seeking to meet their general fund revenue requirements for K–12 education, public safety and court operations, public employee petitions, health-care costs, and other important obligations. State trust lands are state-managed public lands whose revenue collected through private energy development leasing arrangements often generates significant funding for state government, thus reducing the tax burden on the state's citizens (see Culp et al., 2015).

State-level legislators and chief executives are expectedly quite responsive to the various energy interests and advocacy coalitions that seek to shape energy policy, particularly when the political ideology of an advocacy group or business interest parallels the elected official's values and priorities and those of their constituency. A more conservative state legislator or governor from a natural resource–based state such as Wyoming, for instance, is more likely to promote fossil energy laws and energy development than a more liberal state legislator or governor from a politically progressive state such as California or Colorado (Paul, 2019).

WHAT ARE ALTERNATIVE FUELS?

Federal law is fairly definitive when it comes to the term "alternative fuels." Alternative-fuel issues are often tied directly to their primary use, that of transportation. Federal fuels policies bring together issues related to stored energy sources and management, transportation infrastructure, and environmental quality regulations as well as federal monies to state and local governments. The federal definition of alternative fuel is found in Title 49 U.S. Code § 32901 (a)(1):

> "alternative fuel" means—(A) methanol; (B) denatured ethanol; (C) other alcohols; (D) except as provided in subsection (b) of this section, a mixture containing at least 85 percent of methanol, denatured ethanol, and other alcohols by volume with gasoline or other fuels; (E) natural gas; (F) liquefied petroleum gas; (G) hydrogen; (H) coal derived liquid fuels; (I) fuels (except alcohol) derived from biological materials; (J) electricity (including electricity from solar energy); and (K) any other fuel the Secretary of Transportation prescribes by regulation that is not substantially petroleum and that would yield substantial energy security and environmental benefits.

POLICY INNOVATION AND ALTERNATIVE ENERGY

In the 1970s, Presidents Nixon and Carter both relied on top-down approaches to initiate policy redirection away from fossil energy and toward alternative and renewable energy development (Lapp, 1973; New Republic, 1978). Conversely, President Ronald Reagan approached energy policy primarily from a free market perspective, relying heavily on marketplace solutions to energy needs and the stimulation of innovation, and focused on encouraging significant development of new sources of fossil energy extraction. During the George H. W. Bush administration, American energy policy innovation was further institutionalized through the passage of the reauthorized and amended Energy Policy Act (EPAct) in 1992. Building on the EPAct foundation, President Bill Clinton adopted a middle-ground approach to alternative energy policy, combining the power of the national government and the concentration of technical expertise in national laboratories with the bottom-up policy innovations of state and local governments and communities to produce workable, practical solutions for problems facing alternative energy production, effective storage, and efficient use. Clinton's model of sound policy development is consistent with his public commitment to a "laboratories of democracy" (Osborne 1990) approach to governance, engaging citizens at the grassroots level in the policy process to the extent possible.

In the post–September 11 policy environment, President George W. Bush signed into law the Energy Policy Act of 2005 (EPAct 2005) and the Energy Security and Independence Act of 2007 (ESIA 2007). These two laws sought to advance policy innovation at the federal, state, and local levels in promoting energy independence through the development of clean renewable fuels, the advancement of carbon capture technology through research, and the improvement of energy efficiency in the use of vehicles, the construction and operation of buildings, and the manufacturing and processing of products in the marketplace. These two laws also had the effect of encouraging the development of unconventional oil and gas supplies, resulting in a fossil energy market boom that continues to this day. Through Federal Energy Regulatory Commission (FERC) rulemaking, electricity markets and transmission was substantially altered, ultimately to the benefit of renewable energy power producers as well as other independent power producers (IPPs) (FERC, 2015). In the wake of the Great Recession, President Barack Obama signed the American Recovery and Rehabilitation Act of 2009, which provided sorely needed resources to advance renewable energy R & D and energy storage technology innovation at the local and state levels. Through the strategic placement of renewable energy-supportive political appointees, Obama fostered the development of top-down regulations to curb the use of coal in electricity generation in much of the country. Finally, Obama signed international agreements intended to demonstrate the U.S. commitment to international clean energy goals and the achievement of major reductions in climate change–causing emissions.

In this brief summary of major energy policy innovations, it is clear that carbon-emitting sources of energy have not been entirely eliminated through federal statute, yet, at the same time, several presidents and Congresses under the control of both parties have provided growing support for clean renewable energy source development and use. President Trump, however, has represented a major deviation from forty-plus years of executive leadership in U.S. energy policy innovation. While Congress continues to fund renewable energy innovation, President Trump, through his power to sign executive orders and make political appointments to agencies, has moved the United States away from international climate change agreements, rescinded Obama-era coal use limitation rules, and permitted the development of the major oil pipeline system between the United States and Canada—the Keystone Pipeline.

In studying textbox 3.2, effective innovation at the grassroots or state level requires circumspection for a reasonable chance at policy success. It is important to understand the context in which policy innovation generally occurs, the level of public support present for innovation, and the level of citizen and institutional commitment to innovation success through effective implementation.

TEXTBOX 3.2	Some Issues to Consider When Studying Policy Innovation

Environmental Factors

Is innovation driven by a real or perceived crisis?
Are policy stakeholders satisfied with the status quo?
Is the political culture of a jurisdiction conducive to policy innovation?
Are the socioeconomic conditions in a jurisdiction favorable to innovation?
Are adjacent states and local governments engaged in policy inno-vation? If so,what are the social and economic impacts of the policy innovations?

Ideology and Values

Are elected representatives supportive of policy innovations?
Are citizens supportive of policy innovation?

Adapted from: Nice (1994)

THE WAVES OF POLICY INNOVATION

Policy innovations can be divided into eight categories:[1]

- Oil Shock I/Pre-PURPA 1970s (1973–1978)
- Secondary Oil Shock Period (1979–1982)
- Resurgence of Cheap(er) Petroleum and Growth of Deregulation (1983–1999)
- Bush I: EPAct 1992 Reauthorization (1992)
- Clinton: Post-EPAct 1992 Reauthorization (1992–2005)
- Bush II: EPAct 2005 Reauthorization, ESIA 2007, FERC Order Innovations and Electricity Markets (2001–2009)

- Obama: ARRA 2009, Coal Rules, and Paris Agreement (2009–2017)
- Trump: Resurgence of Coal and Reversal of Climate Policy (2017–present)

Oil Shock I/Pre-PURPA 1970s (1973–1978)

The major state and local energy policy innovation in the century leading up to the oil shock was the creation of the public utilities commissions (PUC) across the country. The PUC model was initially established in many states in the mid- to late 1880s. Initially, PUCs regulated railroads in state and local areas and sought to stabilize suppliers and prices for railroad transportation. The PUCs sanctioned only a limited number of transportation providers and then established reasonable prices for transportation services for producers and reasonable profit margins for operators, seeking to build stability in resource provision and reliable availability.

With the advent of readily available electricity, running water, and sewage in an increasing number of cities and towns across the American landscape, PUCs extended their power to sanction energy, water, and waste disposal service providers and to set prices for goods and services provided. In many cases, the services were provided by monopolies operating under regulated franchise agreements. Prices were arguably higher than if market forces had established prices, but the logic behind the PUC price setting was that through an essentially subsidy-based pricing of energy and other utilities, local and state economic growth was more likely to occur and be sustained. The PUCs tended to be very closely aligned with utility providers, who are frequently motivated to increase profit margins by price increases. Price setting and the influence of the utilities in the PUC decision-making process led to decreased flexibility in the policy innovation process for energy as well other policy concerns—a circumstance that would prove damaging in the years following the 1973 oil shock because the PUC model assumed regular growth in energy supply.

The oil shock placed state and local policy innovators, interest groups, energy industries, and citizen stakeholders in a quandary. As noted previously, beyond a certain point, demand for energy is inelastic (see Olatubi and Zhang, 2003). One needs to drive to work and to operate electrical utilities (e.g., heater, air conditioner, washing machine) at home. Demand-side policy innovations have sought to educate citizens on methods of energy conservation. Certainly, informing citizens about turning lights off when leaving a room or keeping thermostats set at a higher temperature during summer months are not politically charged innovations. Reducing demand for energy may not have had a significant effect on energy prices because supply was tightening simultaneously. Supply-side policy innovations were a bit more contentious. The obvious point that emerges, of course, is that the post-1973 period faced a serious shortfall in the supply of oil. But one should not confuse a shortfall in oil supply with a decline in energy supply potential. Oil shocks in 1973 did not present a serious supply crisis for energy in a general sense. The oil market of 1973 represented the fuels market reaching a new equilibrium point where consumers were required to more seriously consider their economic choices. In terms of public policy, 1973 represented the beginning of a debate about the nature of energy as a good—was it a private good or a marketable public good? If it were the latter, then supply of the good should be regulated, and the nature of the good would be best dealt with in a public forum and through policy innovation and public–private partnership. The policy debate in this period was about what could be categorized as politically and socially acceptable as an energy resource, as well as cost-efficient replacement fuels for transportation and electrical energy generation due to a tightening of the petroleum supply, as well as a debate over citizen-consumer access to an increasingly essential resource.

A real or perceived crisis usually inspires some form of search process for potential solutions. Post-1973, several states and a number of major local governments began the process of identifying viable energy resources available to make up for petroleum supply shortfalls. One of the earliest efforts was made in the state of California, which had started to establish more comprehensive state energy policies in 1972 with the passage of the ambitious Miller–Warren Energy Lifeline Act (http://www.sce.com/CustomerService/ understanding Baseline/history.htm, accessed June 11, 2005). The statute directed the California Public Utilities Commission to establish rate plans that would maximize energy availability through a graduated rate structure that charged higher prices to large consumers while subsidizing the use of more limited energy users (an "'inverted' rate structure").

California energy policy encouraged the conservation of energy so as to reduce demand on constrained energy supplies. The Warren–Alquist State Energy Resources Conservation and Development Act of 1974 created a five-member commission that focused on both supply- and demand-based issues related to California's energy needs (http://www.energy.ca.gov/commission/ overview.html, accessed June 9, 2019). On the supply side, the state of California possessed a multitude of state resources that could be used to meet energy demand. Petroleum resources in California abound; the state produced well in excess of 60 percent of its in-state demand for crude petroleum. Nevertheless, oil prices are in part a function of global energy markets, constraining among other things the PUC energy model. When petroleum prices increase rapidly, its use in the generation of electricity (more common during the time-period discussed) would probably be cost-ineffective because PUCs constrain electrical energy prices. Generating firms might have chosen not to produce due to mandated price ceilings and rising marginal costs but were, regardless, contracted through PUCs to provide electricity.

One method of reducing costs for electrical energy generation is to use cheaper energy inputs in the generation process. California governor Ronald Reagan looked to nuclear power as one major source of cheaper inputs. Nuclear power was then, and remains today, a fairly controversial solution to electric energy production and supply. Environmental interest groups in particular launched an aggressive opposition to the nuclear option for meeting supply shortfalls and for reducing costs to energy producers and consumers. This observation reinforces the point made earlier that the success of innovation is always in part a function of citizen acceptance or lack thereof.

Opponents of nuclear energy proposed alternatives, seeking to gain public support and establish a new energy paradigm responding to growing environmental concerns. It was concluded that the nuclear power option was environmentally, politically, and socially untenable (see Cochran et al., 1975). Proposed energy alternatives often focused on the development of "clean" renewable energy alternatives, such as wind and solar technologies. Solar and wind energy solutions faced significant challenges. First, the technologies were, for large-scale commercial purposes, still too underdeveloped for practical application. Individual consumer use of these clean energy sources was possible but would likely not produce the energy supply needed to meet consumer demand unless demand were significantly reduced through major technological innovation, widespread behavioral change, or both. The second major problem was related to the first—namely, the cost of clean energy sources to be used for commercial purposes was, at that time, prohibitively expensive (see Cupulos, 1979: 159).

In 1977, the California Innovation Group (CIG), a local-level policy-making body operating on financial assistance from the National Science Foundation (NSF), developed a collaborative relationship with the Energy Research and Development Administration (ERDA), the latter authorized by Congress in 1974 under 42 USC 73 Ch 1 § 5811 and intended to help local and state governments respond to the 1973 energy "crisis." The CIG, composed of eight relatively prosperous California municipalities, researched energy supply options related to geothermal/coal hybrid generation projects as well as developed plans to reduce peak hour energy consumption. In their article detailing the work of the CIG, Michael Conway and Gregory Simay (1977) provide a cogent case study of policy innovation occurring in California and in a few other states in the early 1970s. They depict an active search for alternative sources of energy and the broadening of a discussion about what sources of energy would be most acceptable to consumers in terms of cost, availability, environmental stewardship, and relative safety. They note:

> Many approaches to save [and produce] energy have merit. However, to enjoy public support, they must be carried out in harmony with the total social and economic environment of the nation's cities. In particular, energy conservation and development programs must be successful when applied to cities of medium size [that is, the vast majority of cities in the United States]. (Conway and Simay, 1977: 711)

The emergent model arising during this period emphasized increased state and local dialogue about the specific energy demands and supply issues related to their state or local area's needs. The California case illustrates well the 1970s energy policy period, demonstrating the growing emphasis in energy policy networks on devolving planning and responsibility to the state and local levels where citizen engagement could take place and pilot projects could be tested out. In terms of intergovernmentalism, the federal role at the time was to help states become more aware of their relative energy self-sufficiency or vulnerability and to encourage the development of long-term planning to meet their current and future energy needs through a more diversified energy mix (see Sawyer, 1984) along with reliance on the continued and historical federal regulation of energy markets (see http://www.ferc.gov/, accessed June 9, 2019).

National energy policies in the post-1973 period continued to focus significant attention on intergovernmental solutions, although primarily employing top-down methodologies in the process. The 1973 oil shock was initially considered by an experienced price control implementer—Richard Nixon. During his naval career in the Second World War, President Nixon had spent time working in a price control office operated by the U.S. Navy. Building off of his own wartime experience, Nixon had responded to inflationary trends, which had appeared during the latter part of his first presidential term, with a price control policy innovation. His response to the oil shock differed only slightly in character. The Ford administration maintained Nixon's price control strategy, as emphasized in the Energy Production and Conservation Act

Gas Shortages
iStock / Getty Images Plus / JudiLen

of 1975, occurring in the same year as the establishment of the aforementioned ERDA. President Carter continued the price control strategies of Nixon and Ford as methods of alleviating some of the cost strain on consumers. Price controls under Presidents Nixon, Ford, and Carter, however, contributed to energy supply shortages.

To his credit, however, President Carter moved beyond price controls and took the lead in establishing a new cabinet-level response, namely, the creation of the U.S. Department of Energy. One of the intended goals of this action was to increase energy supply; more specifically, the supply of alternative energy was an intended goal. President Carter expanded energy policy into an intergovernmental response, including the use of grants and national R & D efforts to increase renewable energy supplies in the long term. Carter also sought to reduce energy demand through legislation mandating more fuel-efficient automobiles.

Large-scale coordinated intergovernmental innovation efforts—and derivative success stories—were limited in number for several reasons. First, the post-1973 period was characterized by a lack of clarity in problem definition and incomplete optional solutions identification. Second, national political priorities lacked clarity due to political turmoil at the presidential level, and the installation of the nation's first unelected president, Gerald Ford. Third, oil prices, as a then-preferred measure of the severity of the "crisis," increased only marginally until midway through the Carter presidency.

International cooperative efforts also developed during the post-1973 shock. In a study conducted in late 1970s, Bobrow and Kudrle (1979) found that international coordination of energy policy R & D was an important aspect of the global energy response to the supply shortfall. The biggest challenge to such a coordinated effort, however, was international rivalry for resources and lack of valid information on proven reserves and the quality of crude oil stocks. Perhaps equally important, the study found that comparative analysis of R & D budgets in the Western democracies of Europe and North America yielded significant per capita variation in expenditures. In other words, commitment to developing alternative and other future energy resources was not equally present, and resource development strategies, at times, diverged markedly. As a result, cooperative international policy initiatives were, at times, significantly strained (see Bobrow and Kudrle, 1979: 156).

Secondary Oil Shock Period (1979–1982)
The oil shock of 1973 leveled off in terms of impact on fuel prices, providing some sense of relief to consumers that the crisis had, at the very least, entered into a period of acceptable status quo. Prices were still high, but at least they were not getting much higher. Shortly after Jimmy Carter became president and established the U.S. Department of Energy, his administration was faced with a secondary oil shock that took place between 1978 and 1980. The price

of oil shot up nearly 90 percent, to an annual average of $21.65 per barrel in nominal dollar terms (approximately, $76.38 in 2019 dollars). The new status quo was unacceptable to many policy makers and to other energy policy stakeholders, a fact that was reflected in President Carter's low public approval ratings at that time, albeit there are several confounding factors that shaped his approval ratings (e.g., the Iran hostage crisis).

Policy of the time was influenced by the value structures of policy makers and the institutional culture, processes, and rules governing the policy process. Senior members of Congress and the bureaucracy had experienced the regulatory and distributive policies of the FDR administration, which had succeeded in alleviating the impact of the Great Depression and bringing the United States successfully through the Second World War. A new generation of policy makers—the post–Second World War generation known as the baby boomers—were introducing the green energy paradigm into the public debate. The combined effect of generational experiences, ideology, and more progressive sociopolitical value frameworks produced a new energy policy solution known as PURPA—the Public Utility Regulatory Policies Act of 1978.

PURPA represented a major national policy commitment to diversifying the nation's energy sources. The statute for the first time established national standards for energy policy—an aspect of the new policy that was particularly top-down as an innovation. While local utility regulation had historically been controlled entirely by state commissions and state governments, whose meetings were attended almost solely by power generation and transmission engineers and executives as well as commission members, PURPA opened state energy policy meetings to greater public scrutiny, public participation, and input into energy public policy. PURPA also sought to increase the level of equity being achieved in energy policy in terms of fair, nondiscriminatory energy provision and affordable pricing, and provision of emergency services to persons and families in distress.

PURPA encouraged state public utility commissions to use third-party power generators so as to increase supply and lower electricity costs (IPPs). Many of these third-party power generators had excess supply available for use at various peak or nonpeak times; using these power sources would increase energy efficiency. Numerous third-party power generators used "alternative" and/or renewable energy sources in generating electrical energy, making use of sources such as natural gas, solar, and wind power. For many of its proponents, the inclusion of public input and third-party generation established PURPA as an embodiment of cooperative federalism—a policy that recognized the value of bottom-up approaches to achieving workable policy solutions in complex areas of public policy determination (see Salisbury, 1980).

PURPA continues to be seen as an important policy initiative to recognize the need for national energy policy goals, one that opened opportunity to a wide range of electricity suppliers and that actively encouraged the provision of clean energy. The goal was to stabilize the national economy in times of energy uncertainty, and in the process to reduce the social and environmental costs of the national energy portfolio. Additionally, many aspects of PURPA reintroduced the importance of social and economic equity in the provision of electrical energy in the United States. While many aspects of PURPA were regulatory, it was viewed as only one aspect of a new energy policy paradigm that emerged in the 1970s. Many other aspects of energy policy, such as the development of national energy laboratories, were seen by proponents of PURPA at the time as distributive policies designed to help states and local governments cope with the retooling required as fossil fuel–based economies begin to shift toward alternative energy.

Concern over energy safety issues also characterized this policy period, effectively limiting the viability of nuclear energy as a future solution. The Three Mile Island incident occurred on March 28, 1979 (see Janson, 1979), resulting in nuclear radiation being vented into the atmosphere from an overheated reactor core. The resulting media attention made nuclear power a politically unpopular alternative energy source. While nuclear energy continued to play a sizable role in the U.S. energy supply, the construction of new nuclear power plants became politically unfeasible due to the image— reinforced by the media and by ecology-minded interests—of nuclear power as dangerous to individuals and to the environment. Subsequent events such as the tsunami-involved Fukushima nuclear power plant failure in Japan in 2011 have served to keep the nuclear option out of energy policy discussions.

Resurgence of Cheap(er) Petroleum and Growth of Deregulation (1983–1999)

The election of Ronald W. Reagan in 1980 occurred within one year of the "high tide" of oil prices. In 1981, crude petroleum prices reached an annual average of $66.20 per barrel—the equivalent of nearly $186 per barrel in 2019 U.S. dollars. Given the sky-high prices, energy policy was quite naturally a major issue on the policy agenda. Elected on a variety of issue positions, Reagan had campaigned on the issue of energy policy and proposed solutions at odds with many of the renewable energy and regulatory policy innovations implemented in the previous decade. As president, Reagan advanced a supply-side economic model of energy policy.

Following Reagan's inauguration in January 1981, many aspects of the alternative energy paradigm began to give way to changing economics and political values. Reagan focused on the following issues:

- "Decontrol" (Morehouse, 1981) fuel prices
- Increase access to domestic oil exploration in Alaska
- Increase access to natural gas exploration and transportation domestically
- Promote "alternative" energies, primarily nuclear energy

The logic of Reagan's model of innovation in energy policy was based on his belief in free market economic principles as the optimum solution to the energy "crisis."

Lifting price controls on petroleum was an innovation that countered the energy policy strategy of former Republican president Richard Nixon (see Smith and Phelps, 1978: 428). Certainly the academic literature and practical experience had shown that price controls have the potential to produce unintended effects on consumer behavior (see Shultz and Dam, 1977: 151; Weber and Mitchell, 1978). A price control sends a false signal to consumers about supply—consumers will likely increase consumption (from Q2 to Q3) based on an artificially lower price, resulting in ongoing supply shortfalls (see figure 3.1), contributing to economic slowdown unless the government can establish consumption limits through some form of strategic rationing plan. As can be seen in figure 3.1, at P(e), quantity of a good experiences lower demand than when price controls (Max. Price) are put into place. Price controls and rationing tend to increase government intrusion into markets, and may weaken markets supplying goods and services to consumers.

From Reagan's perspective, it was better to let price signals shape consumer choice, while simultaneously using the crisis to promote increased petroleum supplies through deregulation (fuel) and enhanced use of nuclear energy (electricity production). In the previous administration, President Carter also saw the energy crisis as an opportunity to promote renewable energy (electricity production), but it is important to recall that the energy crisis of that era was about fuel, and not about electricity.

Laws such as PURPA, while perhaps viewed as positive in terms of opening up the energy market to third-party producers, were not seen as beneficial by

Figure 3.1   Impact of Price Control on Demand

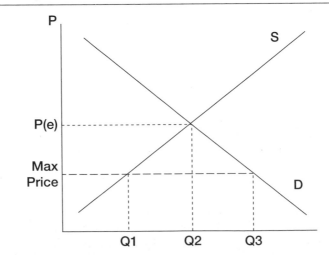

Source: Christopher A. Simon.

the Reagan administration in terms of a long-term energy solution, particularly if energy costs associated with third-party producers stood at levels far above market equilibrium price at any given point in the future. The combined effect of PUCs and PURPA would force energy providers into high-cost energy choices while simultaneously limiting prices charged to consumers, with predictable outcomes for energy producers. In the 1980s, and in the post-Reagan period of the 1990s when crude petroleum and other carbon-based energy sources stood at record low prices, the notion of paying for alternative/renewable energy supplies, such as solar or wind, was seen by its detractors as an economically undesirable effect of PURPA and its progeny, possibly leading to an electrical energy crisis on the heels of a decade-long fuels crisis. In a very general sense, PURPA's third-party-provider concept was good in theory, but perhaps too often misapplied in practice.

Third-party producers were seen by Reagan and others as being part of a long-term solution. Third-party producers would become a part of a more expansive energy market when prices made renewable energy economically feasible. In the meantime, however, there were cheaper and quite possibly simpler energy alternatives to the supply issue, as seen through the policy lens of the Reagan administration. Enhanced domestic crude petroleum exploration and extraction was a strategy seen to produce needed short-term increases in supply, and the development of the North Slope of Alaska was seen as one possible solution to the long-term supply problem.[2] President Reagan also continued to promote many of the "alternative" energy policies that he had been promoting since his governorship in California. Nuclear energy was viewed by him as a viable solution to future energy shortfalls. Given that per kW costs for nuclear energy were comparable or even lower than other forms of energy generation, and that potential liability costs had been lifted from producers' shoulders via the Price–Anderson Act (see Munson, 1979), nuclear energy was seen by many as an attractive option for electric energy supplies of the future.

During this period of fossil energy resurgence and deregulation at the national level, state policy innovation for renewable energy witnessed a growing commitment to the establishment of renewable energy targets. In 1983, the state of Iowa became the first state to adopt a renewable portfolio standard (RPS), over a dozen years before the next two states, Nevada and Massachusetts, adopted comparable state-level RPS goals in 1997. While Iowa's RPS goals required investor-owned utilities to have 105 MW of renewable generating capacity, the 1990s saw increased state commitments to RPS goals across the United States. By 1999, the states of Connecticut (1998), Maine (1999), Massachusetts (1997), New Jersey (1999), Nevada (1997), Texas (1999), and Wisconsin (1999) had all adopted RPS goals, committing their states to significant and lasting increases in the use of renewable energy in the supply of electricity. State-level energy policy advocacy and innovation efforts paralleled a policy dialogue between renewable energy advocacy coalitions and elected and appointed policy makers at the federal level, a prolonged dialogue eventually culminating in federal laws such as the EPAct 1992, EPAct 2005, and ESIA 2007.

Bush I: EPAct Reauthorization (1992)

The politics of energy policy changed a good deal in the years following the Reagan presidency. Reagan's influence was arguably so strong that a return to 1970s policy innovations was highly unlikely; nevertheless, a new energy policy paradigm featuring alternative energy began to emerge. The values of the new paradigm were shaped, in part, by PURPA as well as state-level energy policy innovations, but were also shaped by a more pragmatic so-called Third Way politics and policy. The short-lived energy crisis that occurred during the presidency of George H. W. Bush was a circumstance related to the Persian Gulf War. While theories abound about the war being about oil markets, a more objective way of viewing the conflict is that it illustrated a connection, perhaps intuitive: Middle East political stability and motivations could negatively impact the world supply of petroleum. While the annual average price of petroleum did not increase during the Persian Gulf War period, the war did cause some policy debate at the national level over the need to further diversify the nation's energy portfolio—an idea that state and local governments had promoted for years through their various bottom-up policy innovations.

A major energy policy innovation of the George H. W. Bush presidency was perhaps the least remembered aspect of his term of office—the Energy Policy Act (EPAct of 1992). Through the reauthorization process and some important amendments, national policy makers reaffirmed a now long-standing commitment to the pursuit of energy source diversification. More strongly supported than earlier laws, such as the Energy Policy and Conservation Act of 1975 (P.L. 93–163), the EPAct of 1992 established a national priority for the creation of clean *and* sustainable energy options for communities. In effect, a commitment was made to lower energy emissions, maintain cleaner air and water, and develop sustainable energy sources for the purposes of enhanced "livability" and sustainability in the broadest sense possible. The national priority being set was framed in a manner that moved the nation well beyond the price control versus free market debate and into the realm of sustainability.

The EPAct of 1992 (1993 P.L. 102–486) significantly altered rules and incentives for the energy market, setting the stage for additional energy policy innovation during the William J. Clinton and George W. Bush administrations. From a rational choice perspective, it is important to understand several key aspects of the EPAct of 1992. Many aspects of public law are to a lesser degree innovations, per se, and more frequently represent meaningful and long-lasting commitments to a policy direction and a set of core values. What follows is a brief summary of the core sections of the

EPAct of 1992 and the Clean Cities paradigm, both of which tie energy to environmental quality issues:

Energy Efficiency
Amended the *Energy and Conservation Standards for New Buildings Act of 1976* (see 42 USC §6831)[3] to include an increased emphasis on voluntary energy efficiency standards created by "consensus" among various building and heating/cooling engineering organizations (e.g., Council of American Building Officials, CABO). Federal, state, and commercial building energy efficiency codes are standards set in a manner that would either meet or exceed CABO guidelines, as reviewed by the Department of Energy. Manufactured home energy efficiency standards were raised, and the Department of Housing and Urban Development was tasked with reviewing those standards. Energy-efficient homes were encouraged through a mortgage guarantee pilot program that was tied to the National Housing Act (42 USC 12832). Amendments were made to the Public Utility Regulatory Policies Act of 1978 (16 USC 2601) encouraging energy utilities to develop comprehensive integrated energy planning; the amendments also fostered a role for small energy producers. The efficiency section also provided efficiency grants to state and local agencies and utilities involved in energy regulation and production. Finally, the efficiency section of the act encouraged the development of efficient appliances and equipment for commercial and residential use.

Natural Gas
Amended the Natural Gas Act of 1978 (15 USC 717) and emphasized the need to create a free market for natural gas and liquefied natural gas being imported into the nation.

Alternative Fuels—General
Defined alternative fuel as: "methanol, denatured ethanol, and other alcohols; mixtures containing 85 percent or more (or such other percentage, but not less than 70 percent, as determined by the Secretary, by rule, to provide for requirements relating to cold start, safety, or vehicle functions) by volume of methanol, denatured ethanol, and other alcohols with gasoline or other fuels; natural gas; liquefied petroleum gas; hydrogen; coal-derived liquid fuels; fuels (other than alcohol) derived from biological materials; electricity (including electricity from solar energy); and any other fuel the Secretary determines, by rule, is substantially not petroleum and would yield substantial energy security benefits and substantial environmental benefits." The section also clarifies that alternative-fuel vehicles are to be considered as such *if* they are manufactured as alternative-fuel vehicles, and that at least 50 percent of alternative-fuel vehicles are to come from domestic (United States and Canada) vehicle manufacturers. The federal vehicle fleet was directed to become at least 75 percent alternative fuel powered by 1999 and develop a plan for refueling sights and operations and maintenance (O & M) to be completed per manufacturer standards.

Alternative Fuels—Nonfederal Programs

Section encouraged the use of alternative-fuel vehicles for commercial and for state and local governments. The section directed the U.S. Secretary of Energy to develop and coordinate a public information campaign about the costs and benefits of alternative-fuel vehicles. The section also encouraged the states and local governments to offer tax breaks to individuals and organizations that purchase alternative-fuel vehicles. Section 410 encouraged the development of alternative-fuel bus systems in cities and states, coordinating the efforts of the U.S. Departments of Energy (DOE) and Transportation (DOT). The USDOT was also directed to provide financial assistance to states and local communities to encourage them to retrofit school buses or purchase new alternative-fuel buses with the intent of reducing air emissions; an annual $30 million budget appropriation was authorized through the EPAct 1992 for up to three years. Finally, a low-interest loan program was established for small businesses for the purchase of alternative-fuel vehicles.

Availability and Use of Replacement Fuels, Alternative Fuels, and Alternative-Fueled Private Vehicles

This section of the EPAct of 1992 effectively mandated the use of alternative-fuel vehicles for any "person"[4] involved in the production, transportation, or sale of energy. Additionally, any large consumer of petroleum energy (i.e., over 50K bbl/d) was required to use alternative energy vehicles. The section also detailed the need for the production of alternative energy, which in many cases involves agriculture (i.e., ethanol derived from corn and biodiesel from various farm-based sources), and required the DOE to monitor and seek to balance the availability and use of alternative fuels. Federal, state, local, and private fleet vehicles for persons as defined above were required to expand their alternative-fuel capacity to 70 percent of all fleet vehicles by 2006.

Electric Motor Vehicles

Defined electric vehicles as "a motor vehicle primarily powered by an electric motor drawing current from rechargeable storage batteries, fuel cells, photovoltaic arrays, or other sources of electric current and may include an electric-hybrid vehicle ["means a vehicle primarily powered by an electric motor that draws current from rechargeable storage batteries, fuel cells, or other source of electric current and also relies on a non-electric source of power"]" (Title VI §601). The EPAct of 1992 directed the DOE to request proposals for demonstration projects promising development of more effective and efficient electric vehicles. The section also encouraged collaboration of manufacturers in the development of an electric vehicle infrastructure, but sought to assuage concerns regarding the use and distribution of industries' proprietary information.

Electricity

The EPAct of 1992 maintained requirements that electricity wholesale generators receive formal Federal Energy Regulatory Commission (FERC) recognition, but the act amended the Public Utility Holding Company Act of 1935 and increased state-level power in terms of meeting PURPA alternative energy goals. The EPAct of 1992 also amended the Federal Power Act and changed interstate transmission rules so as to loosen electric wholesale generators' control of transmission lines and prevented the use of price setting to reduce access to third-party electric wholesale generators' transmission capability using already existing transmission infrastructures.

High-Level Radioactive Waste; U.S. Enrichment Corporation; Uranium Revitalization; Uranium Enrichment Health, Safety, and Environment Issues

Within the EPAct of 1992 legislation, Congress quietly loosened the regulatory process for the establishment of new nuclear power plants (*Congressional Quarterly*, 1992). "Alternative" nuclear energy was discussed in the EPAct of 1992, based on the concept of using lower-radiation reactors to generate power, while improving the safety of nuclear energy for host communities. Amending the Atomic Energy Act of 1954 (42 USC 2011 et seq.), Congress created the United States Enrichment Corporation, which was tasked with, among other things, overseeing the recycling of spent weapons-grade fissile materials for use in civilian nuclear reactors (see 102 Cong. H.R. 776 §901). While producing a significant portion of the nation's electrical power, the industry was under severe strain because of significant limitations on its ability to grow and even to maintain its existing infrastructure.

Renewable Energy

This section of the EPAct 1992 was designed to provide grant opportunities for further research, and for the development and demonstration of the practical use of renewable energy resources. The renewable energy section effectively defines renewable energies as biomass, ethanol, biofuels, photovoltaics, solar thermal, wind energy, geothermal, fuel cells, and nondefense-related superconductors.

Coal

Under §1301–1305 of the act, Congress directed that further research be conducted into the development of clean coal technology (i.e., reduced carbon emissions). Such technologies could be used to develop coal-based diesel for combustion engines, and as fuel to operate turbines in electricity generation facilities. In §1306 Congress called for further R & D of natural gas recovery from coalbeds (also in §1309). Coalbed wastes were also being used as an energy source.

Global Climate Change

Adopting the findings of a National Academy of Sciences report on global warming, Congress directed DOE to produce a "least cost energy strategy" that looks at the full range of benefits and costs associated with a variety of energy mixes (i.e., fossil fuel, alternative, and renewable energy).

Reduction of Oil Vulnerability

Under Title XX of the EPAct of 1992, Congress stated that the energy supply and the consumption of energy is an integral part of an efficient economic system. Economic performance based on foreign energy supplies increases economic vulnerability, and may lead to national security vulnerability. Additionally, greater emphasis on clean fuels will benefit the environment, and will likely improve public health.

Energy and Environment/Energy and Economic Growth

In many ways Titles XXI and XXII provide further details on various alternative and renewable energy program initiatives discussed earlier in the EPAct of 1992; a few other energy-related programs are discussed regarding strategic metals, for instance. Title XXII of the statute reaffirmed the role of alternative/renewable energy technological development as an important future growth area for the domestic economy.

Clinton: Post-EPAct 1992 Reauthorization (1992–2005)

The William J. Clinton years witnessed a period of relative tranquility in terms of crude petroleum prices. A lack of an energy "crisis" could easily have reduced a commitment to alternative energy development. What may have led to continued innovation in energy policy, however, was the particular set of core values upon which Clinton's administration was built. A young governor of the state of Arkansas at the time of PURPA's passage, Clinton had been exposed to the energy crisis and its impacts on states and local communities for most of his career. Reelected governor of Arkansas in 1982, he had served in that capacity during a decade of Reagan–Bush leadership in energy policy innovation. He remained committed to diversification of the energy portfolio, demonstrably so during his presidency, as evidenced in the dutiful implementation and full funding of the EPAct of 1992 during his terms of office.

Clinton's personal ideology focused on pragmatic solutions and thoughtful policy experimentation, utilizing to a significant degree the power of intergovernmentalism. Bill Clinton and his ecologically minded vice president, Albert Gore Jr., worked with state, local, and federal agencies to cooperatively explore "green" energy solutions designed to balance environmental and human needs. A significant difference from pre-Clinton policy innovations was the optimistic aspect of the policy innovations advanced.

In the 1970s and 1980s, U.S. energy policy generally focused on the goal of energy independence or energy sustainability. In essence, policy took on a defensive posture; in considering policy innovation, the general milieu of the energy policy debate was seemingly driven by a need to protect postindustrial, predominantly Western, economies against an uncertain energy future arising from political instability in the Middle East. Clinton and Gore saw an opportunity to build a new economy around a green energy model. For evidence of policy innovation success, they pointed to European nations such as Germany's green power infrastructure and its positive impact on that nation's economy. Additionally, academic evidence tied environment quality to improved global economies; the concepts served to reinforce the value of the Clean Cities policy innovation. As with nearly all policy innovations, however, optimism is often tempered with the need to focus on contingencies and unforeseen changing realities (see Economist, 1992: 18), but post-Clinton energy policy events have forced subsequent U.S. policy makers to focus on the need for accelerating the energy policy innovation process; whether or not the eventual outcome will be predominantly market-driven or government managed is less important than that the innovation process be maintained.

The Clinton administration emphasized presidential executive order authority rather than legislative action. In 2000, President Clinton signed E.O. 13149, which was entitled *Greening the Government through Federal Fleet and Transportation Efficiency*. The order required that federal agencies take a "leadership" role in promoting cleaner burning vehicles by reducing demand on petroleum. Clinton required federal government agencies to reduce fleet fuel demand by 20 percent, with 1999 consumption serving as a baseline. Part of this reduction could be achieved by simply reducing the distances traveled by vehicles in commercial fleets, but Clinton ordered agencies to pursue the purchase of alternative-fuel vehicles (AFVs) and more economical vehicles in terms of fuel efficiency, size, and durability in relation to use. By the end of 2005, as stated in the E.O., the majority of fuel demands by federal agency fleets were to be met by alternative fuels. Additionally, the new vehicles would need to abide by the EPA's Tier 2 standards with regard to vehicle emissions.

Key Federal Energy Regulatory Commission Orders in the 1990s

Open access transmission was first established by FERC Order 888 in 1996. The administrative rule provides suppliers of electricity equal access to energy markets. This meant that utilities that "own, control, or operate" (Greenfield, 2010: 34) interstate transmission lines cannot discriminate against IPPs. Nonpublic utilities were granted reciprocity, and are thus entitled to transmission service. Order 889 established the open access same-time information system (OASIS), which required utilities to publish real-time market data to all market participants. While Order 888 strongly encouraged open and transparent transmission planning, it did not mandate it.

FERC Order 2000 created a system of regional transmission operators (RTOs). The term "RTO" is often used interchangeably with independent system operator (ISO). There are several RTO/ISOs operating in North America that control transmission operations for the wholesale electricity markets. RTO/ISOs are most often nonprofit organizations, and they have no financial interest in market decision-making and outcomes. The core primary function of the RTO/ISO is to ensure that federal energy regulations governing energy markets are adhered to, and that the nation's transmission systems are reliable and fully operational. RTO/ISOs also ensure that electricity markets remain competitive, and that there is no discrimination in terms of either price or access. RTO/ISOs do not own the transmission grid, but they are in charge of the transmission grid in various regions insofar as the grid is a form of market. The RTO/ISOs play a key role in transmission grid planning and expansion to ensure access, reliability, security, and open access. RTO/ISOs also coordinate these activities with other regions. FERC is responsible solely for U.S. electricity markets, but RTO/ISOs overlap U.S. national borders, with some jurisdiction in both Canada and Mexico. The North American Electric Reliability Corporation's (NERC) jurisdiction overlaps the United States and the aforementioned bordering nations. Currently, there are nine regional entities (RTO/ISOs) operating under

Figure 3.2   RTO/ISOs in the United States and Canada

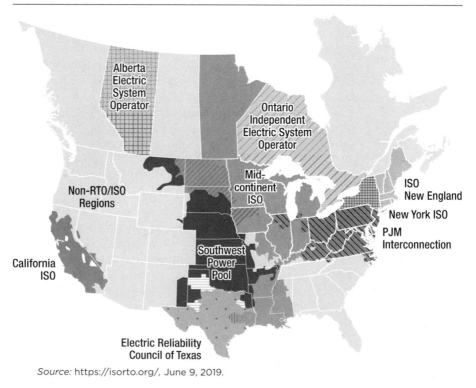

Source: https://isorto.org/, June 9, 2019.

the NERC jurisdiction (Office of Electricity Delivery and Energy Reliability, 2018) (see figure 3.2).

Bush II: EPAct 2005 Reauthorization, ESIA 2007, FERC Order Innovations, and Electricity Markets (2001–2009)

Without question, the terrorist attacks of September 11, 2001, and the subsequent military engagement in Iraq served as important motivating factors in shaping U.S. energy policy of the twenty-first century. Prior to September 11, President George W. Bush advocated the opening of the Arctic National Wildlife Refuge to further oil and gas exploration. Recognizing mixed public opinion regarding petroleum exploration in the Arctic National Wildlife Refuge (see Lazar, 2001: 1), and with a policy window opening for renewable energy following the crisis-level events surrounding 9/11, President Bush actively promoted alternative energy sources, such as hydrogen, in the period leading up to his reelection bid in 2004. The president's Hydrogen Initiative was an attempt to accelerate the movement toward a hydrogen-based infrastructure in the United States.[5]

The Bush Hydrogen Initiative built upon the foundational Clinton administration hydrogen policy innovations in substantial ways. President Bush's plan involved multiyear R & D to advance knowledge and development of hydrogen fuel and portable fuel cells. Additionally, the Initiative sought to develop a nationwide hydrogen fueling infrastructure. Safety issues for the mass production, transportation, storage, and use of hydrogen were important factors studied by federal laboratories, numerous grant-funded university scientists, and private sector R & D teams in the United States and abroad. The chart below summarizes the systematic analysis of converting an entire society constructed around carbon-based energy production and use, into a society based on hydrogen as an energy source.

Each one of these major topical areas featured in the figure below (figure 3.3) required vast amounts of research and knowledge collection before the knowledge acquired could be transformed into a series of practical policy innovations. In many ways, the Hydrogen Initiative served as a major first step in reconfiguring an entire society and economy in the new century. New codes and standards for safety and use needed to be constructed, but on the basis of sound science paired with a shared set of social and political values regarding energy policy.

In a report released in January 2003, the National Research Council (NRC) concluded that more R & D was needed before the ambitious goal of building a hydrogen-based economy could realistically be attained—quite possibly, multiple decades from the present day. Based on NRC findings, the Hydrogen Initiative is still a project quite truly in its infancy. Commitment to exploring hydrogen power saw tremendous growth in the years 2004 to 2008, but the federal budget commitment has steadily dropped since that time. In fiscal year

Figure 3.3 Hydrogen Technology and Public Policy

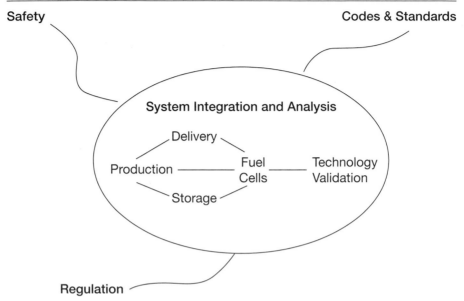

Redrawn by Christopher A. Simon, an adaptation from: http://www.eere.energy.gov/hydrogenandfuelcells/mypp/pdfs/systems_analysis.pdf, accessed June 15, 2005.

2017, the Hydrogen Initiative budget stood at a mere $122.1 million dollars, less than half of its 2008 peak.

The Hydrogen Initiative illustrates well how politics and policy priorities change and once strong commitments can wane. Nevertheless, basic science and technical knowledge gained through initiatives of this type have likely contributed to present-day policy innovations, such as collaborative efforts between Mitsubishi Hitachi Power Systems, Utah's Advanced Clean Energy Storage project, and other public and private stakeholders to build an energy storage facility with a one GW power rating. One of the energy storage technologies to be used in the facility: hydrogen fuel cells (Parnell, 2019). If storage systems of this type prove to be both technically feasible and commercially available, renewable energy would overcome one of its biggest hurdles arising from the intermittency of wind and sun, and renewable energy market dynamics would be changed dramatically on a global scale.

Energy Policy Act of 2005

The 2005 reauthorization is comprised of a series of energy policy innovations designed to meet a changing energy policy paradigm in terms of petroleum availability (i.e., innovations intended to maximize domestic petroleum and natural gas supplies), and a series of regulations to force change in energy demand structures that would lead to further development and use of AFVs as well as other forms of alternative energy.

The EPAct of 2005 changed the energy paradigm in some significant ways. A number of energy regulatory structural changes were initiated as a result of the act and remain in place. The Public Utilities Holding Company Act of 1935 (PUHCA), for instance, was not reauthorized, and its duties were transferred to the Federal Energy Regulatory Commission (FERC) and to relevant state-level administrators engaged in electric energy regulation. PURPA was reformed to make it more cost effective for new energy providers to increase their electrical energy supply capacity. The EPA clean air regulations are tightened by the EPAct of 2005. In that same vein, the act made no accommodation for a national-level renewable energy portfolio (RPF), leaving that policy innovation entirely to the voluntary implementation of RPS goals by the various states.

Alternative energy policy advocates were offered two major concessions. First, the U.S. Department of Energy remained committed through the principles of its initial authorization as well as through goals established in the EPAct 2005 to continue to conduct research and fund demonstration project development in the area of alternative energy. Second, and more specifically, the EPAct 2005 delineated a series of business and residential user tax credits for the use of alternative energy systems. The tax credits generally increased from 10 percent of initial project development costs to approximately 30 percent. Increased use of federal tax credits is indicative of a deepening commitment to the development and enhanced use of alternative energy.

In another development, conceptualization of alternative/renewable energy was broadened. First, so-called next-generation nuclear energy plants were offered incentives for more rapid development and operation. The EPAct 2005 specifically called for a demonstration project of a next-generation nuclear power plant to be developed at Idaho National Laboratories within the first quarter of the current century. The 2005 law also contained stipulations for further study and development of nuclear waste processing, and the further identification and development of nuclear waste depository sites. Second, hydropower, which was the subject of much criticism by ecologists and environmental groups for its purported impact on wildlife and plant species in the Pacific Northwest and elsewhere, was provided a major boost by a statutory commitment to the further development of hydropower energy production efficiencies. The 2005 law also made accommodations to hydropower developers, offering them a significant role in defining the conditions under which development occurred as well as defining alternative impact studies with recommended alternative solutions to deal with observed externalities (e.g., hydropower dam impact of fisheries and plant life).

The EPAct 2005 produced a strong commitment to the further development of domestic petroleum and gas as well. Energy companies were allowed to reduce their royalty payments, a change that has resulted in lower costs and greater gross (and possibly net) profit margins. Additionally, the EPAct 2005 directed the U.S. Department of Energy and affected states to conduct a thorough review of petroleum reserves, particularly offshore reserves. It is likely that increased offshore petroleum fields will be developed as a result of these studies at some point in the future. The 2005 law also committed the nation to further development of a natural gas and petroleum pipeline and refinery development. Clean coal development and equipment are offered tax incentives. Liquefied natural gas (LNG) development was advanced by the EPAct 2005 policy innovations to be managed by FERC in cooperation with the many appropriate state-level bureaucracies. Absent from the EPAct 2005 was any further discussion of the opening of the Artic National Wildlife Area to petroleum and natural gas exploration.

Energy efficiency was perhaps less of a focus of the 2005 energy law than was energy supply development. For instance, there were no new requirements for increased automobile efficiency. Yet, the EPAct 2005 did set standards for the near doubling of the ethanol supply capacity to 7.5 billion gallons by 2012. As a source of oxygenation for gasoline, ethanol has been shown to significantly reduce CO emissions in the combustion process (Schifter et al., 2001), but viewed in overall environmental and public health terms, the available research evidence indicates that corn ethanol production and use as a gasoline additive leads to a net increase in greenhouse gas emissions (Cimitile, 2009).

Energy Independence and Security Act of 2007

The EISA 2007 (P.L. 110–140) was crafted by a Democratic majority of Congress and signed into law by the Republican president George W. Bush in December 2007. As the bill's title suggests, the goal of the final legislation was to move the United States toward greater energy independence and reduced reliance on foreign suppliers in the global oil market. The final legislation focused on clean energy supplies, particularly the enhanced production of biofuels. The legislation also focused attention on energy efficiency. Perhaps the most expedient way of overcoming an energy supply issue is to simply reduce demand for a resource. The cheapest unit of energy is the unit of energy that is not needed or used. The EISA 2007 set efficiency standards for some products, such as light bulbs, commercial buildings, and automobiles. The 2007 law also established a fund for research studies on greenhouse gas emission reduction and effective carbon capture and safe storage.

The EISA 2007 set a standard of thirty-five miles per gallon for passenger and nonpassenger vehicles by model year 2020. The law gave authority to the secretary of energy and the EPA administrator to establish rules governing improved work-truck fuel efficiencies. The 2007 law also established a vehicle tire efficiency rating system and a consumer education system related to vehicle efficiency. The EISA also set stricter efficiency standards for the federal fleet of trucks and automobiles.

The federal government owns or leases over 640,000 vehicles worth an estimated $4.3 billion (GSA, 2018). Approximately 30 percent of those vehicles are operated by the U.S. Postal Service. As a large customer, the U.S. government, through federal fleet efficiency requirements, seeks to shape vehicle manufacturer design and engine efficiency standards that meet federal policy goals and standards. The 2007 law requires that the federal fleet purchases not be greenhouse gas emitters. There are some exceptions to this rule, but the law is clear that if a greenhouse gas–emitting vehicle is approved for purchase, it must meet stringent emissions standards.

Title II of EISA 2007 details biofuels policy goals. Advanced biofuel feedstock inclusions include:

(I)   Ethanol, derived from cellulose, hemicellulose, or lignin.
(II)   Ethanol derived from sugar or started (other than corn starch).
(III)   Ethanol derived from waste material, including crop residue, other vegetative waste material, animal waste, and food waste and yard waste.
(IV)   Biomass-based diesel.
(V)   Biogas (including landfill gas and sewage waste treatment gas) produced through the conversion of organic matter from renewable biomass.
(VI)   Butanol or other alcohols produced through the conversion of organic matter from renewable biomass.
(VII)   Other fuel derived from cellulosic biomass. (H.R. 6, pp. 28–29)

Renewable biomass inclusions:

(i)   Planted crops and crop residue harvested from agricultural land . . .
(ii)   Planted trees and tree residue from actively managed tree plantations on non-federal land . . . including land belonging to an Indian tribe or an Indian individual, that is held in trust by the United States . . .
(iii)   Animal waste material and animal byproducts.
(iv)   Slash and pre-commercial thinnings that are from non-federal forestlands, including forestlands belonging to an Indian tribe or an Indian individual . . . but not forests or forestlands that are ecological communities with a global or State ranking of critically imperiled, imperiled, or rare . . . old growth forest or late successional forest.
(v)   Biomass obtained from the immediate vicinity of buildings and other areas regularly occupied by people, or of public infrastructure, at risk from wildfire.
(vi)   Algae.
(vii)   Separated yard waste or food waste, including recycled cooking and trap grease.

FERC Order Innovations and Electricity Markets during Bush II

FERC Orders (2003 & 661) and Orders (2006 & 792) were intended to provide standard procedures to interconnect large and small electricity-generating facilities to the transmission grid. In terms of the former two orders, particular attention is paid to the integration of large wind energy producers and to ensure power quality. The latter rules were particularly focused on establishing fast-track procedures to integrate small power producers.

The issuance of FERC Order 890 was an effort to reinforce FERC Order 888 and 889 commitments related to nondiscriminatory transmission planning and construction. In practical terms, this means that transmission line planning and construction should not occur in such a way as to avoid interconnectivity with IPPs operating renewable energy power production facilities or other independent power facilities using natural gas or other fuel sources. The guidelines of FERC 890 create rules encouraging open planning processes providing access to a large number of community-based, governmental, industry-related, and environmental stakeholders. It also encourages the development of a dispute resolution process within the planning process where nonadversarial and interest-based collaborative approaches to getting to win-win outcomes are frequently employed.

Obama: ARRA 2009, Coal Rules, and Paris Agreement (2009–2017)

President Obama entered office in 2009 in the midst of a financial crisis. As was discussed in relation to multiple streams theory and punctuated equilibrium theory, crises often present opportunities for major policy change. It is often a setting in which an opportunity arises to identify policy directions that are not working and to change direction. In some cases it provides an opportunity to accelerate an existing policy that is likely moving in the right direction, but perhaps moving too slowly to meet the perceived needs related to the crisis at hand. The ARRA represented an opportunity to rapidly accelerate existing U.S. renewable and alternative energy policies, while international policy commitments such as the Paris Agreement represented an opportunity to show greater commitment to international efforts to counter climate change.

American Recovery and Rehabilitation Act (ARRA)

The ARRA committed over $31 billion to support renewable energy projects nationwide. Including tax incentives and other investments, President Obama claimed a greater than $90 billion investment in clean energy. The clean energy program offered grants to develop alternative-fuel vehicles, increase energy efficiency, develop smart grid technology, and develop and establish carbon capture and storage technology facilities. According to the Obama administration, "[ARRA] made the largest single investment in clean energy in history, providing more than $90 billion in strategic clean energy investments and tax incentives to promote job creation and the deployment of low-carbon technologies, and leveraging approximately $150 billion in private and other non-federal capital for clean energy investments" (Obama, 2016).

ARRA provided over $2.5 billion for renewable and alternative energy fuel R & D, which included approximately $800 million for biomass energy development. Using block grants established by the EISA of 2007, the ARRA provided over $3 billion for state, local, and tribal government to improve energy efficiency in their communities. In promoting electric vehicle development, the ARRA provided $2 billion for competitive grants to develop advanced battery manufacturing, and $400 million for advanced electric vehicle development. In order to support industry development in this area, ARRA provided $6 billion in loan guarantees.

ARRA provided $3 billion for updating the federal fleet to include more fuel-efficient and hybrid electric vehicles. Large purchases of electric vehicles of this type offer a credible commitment to industries engaged in building clean energy transportation systems and the associated infrastructure. The 2009 law also provided $300 million to retrofit diesel vehicles so that existing vehicles were more fuel efficient and produced fewer carbon emissions. In addition to direct investments, the ARRA established a series of tax credits to encourage the development and use of fuel-efficient, hybrid electric, and electric vehicles (AFDC, 2018).

Coal Rules

Built on the core principles of the Clean Air Act and the Clean Water Act, the EPA under President Obama developed three rules intended to reduce air and water pollution and related marginal social and environmental costs incurred by the use of coal in electric power production.

Disposal of Coal Combustion Residuals from Electric Utilities (2016). The rule regulates the disposal of coal ash. Power plants produced nearly 130 million tons of coal ash in 2014.[6] Coal ash is often used in the manufacture of products such as concrete, but demand for coal ash is much lower than supply, and as a result much of it is simply dumped into landfills.[7] The EPA rule was largely intended to regulate coal ash disposal in landfills and near bodies of surface water or aquifers. Soil and water pollution resulting from coal ash disposal has negative health consequences for plant and animal species, including humans.

Mercury and Air Toxics Standards (MATS). The rule sets strict standards for mercury and other toxic emissions. Coal often contains mercury and other toxic and even radioactive substances. The rule required that power plants regulate and monitor emissions for the presence of such toxic emissions. An interim final rule was established in 2012, and was challenged by many states and power utilities.[8] In the case *Michigan v. Environmental Protection Agency* 576 U.S. ___ (2015), the Supreme Court concluded that the MATS rule could not go into effect because the EPA had not determined the cost to the power industry in meeting the new air quality standards. Subsequently the U.S. Court of Appeals for the District of Columbia—the Supreme Court had remanded the case to the Court of Appeals—concluded that the MATS rule could go into effect because the EPA was in the process of completing the required cost study.

Clean Power Plan ("Carbon Pollution Emission Guidelines for Existing Stationary Sources: Electric Utility Generating Units"[9] The Clean Power Plan was developed by multiple stakeholder groups in the states, tribes, environmental groups, and power industry stakeholders. The goal is to substantially reduce carbon emissions into the atmosphere by 2030. The plan would lead to the continued reduction in the number of coal-fired power plants in operation and increase the use of natural gas–fired power plants. The power generation needed would be provided by low- and zero-emission alternative and renewable energy sources. The plan was adopted in October 2015, but the Supreme Court granted a stay in implementation in February 2016. In its statement, the Court clearly referred to the fact that EPA had continued forward with its MATS rule despite the Court's ruling in *Michigan v. Environmental Protection Agency* (2015).[10] Four days after that Supreme Court stay was issued, Associate Justice Antonin Scalia died and the Court shifted to a split 4–4 conservative–liberal membership. In April 2017, Neil Gorsuch, President Trump's nominee to fill the late Antonin Scalia's seat, was sworn in as an associate justice of the U.S. Supreme Court. While the Clean Power Plan has become a moot point due to other political dynamics, the appointment of Gorsuch means that conservative political majority has been retained—a majority often unsupportive of clean power policy.

Paris Agreement (2015)

The Paris Agreement is a landmark international climate change agreement signed by President Obama on behalf of the United States. The treaty was not ratified by the then Republican majority controlled U.S. Senate. The agreement was signed by the 197 members of the United Nations Framework Convention on Climate Change (UNFCCC). The vast majority of those 197 members have seen the agreement ratified.

A central element of the Paris Agreement is the goal of keeping climate warming to below 2°C of preindustrial-era average temperatures. It does not establish specific carbon emission mitigation targets, but signatory and acceding nations are required under the agreement to develop climate change mitigation plans and to accept the reality that some radical changes to the global and local economies must occur in order to meet mitigation goals. As the largest producers of climate change emissions, the large industrial economies party to the agreement are required to take the lead in mitigating global climate change. Under the Agreement, developed countries must commit, as a group, the equivalent of $100 billion (at a minimum) per year to finance climate mitigation efforts, said efforts to be reviewed by international governing bodies to determine the validity of claimed mitigation results.

Trump: Resurgence of Coal and Reversal of Climate Policy (2017-present)

In the 2016 general election campaign, then-candidate Donald Trump promised that, if elected, he would undo President Obama's coal-related regulations, encourage a resurgence of coal mining and use, and withdraw the United States as a signatory to the Paris Agreement. Within two months of assuming office, President Trump signed Executive Order 13783, which called upon the EPA to review the Clean Power Plan (Davenport and Rubin, 2017). In March 2018, Trump called for a review and overhaul of the coal ash rule (Dennis and Eilperin, 2018). As of spring 2018, the MATS rule was still under review by the Trump administration (Reilly, 2018; Friedman and Plumer, 2017). On June 1, 2017, President Trump announced that the United States would withdraw from the Paris Agreement (Shear, 2017).

Promoting Equity through Energy

One of the enduring themes in federal, state, and local energy policies in the twentieth and the twenty-first centuries is the goal of achieving equitable energy solutions. The exact meaning of the word "equitable" has, of course, evolved over time. In the 1930s, President Franklin Roosevelt created the blueprint for future discussions. Roosevelt's administration's energy policies focused attention on the price of energy as well as the availability of a ready supply of energy. Energy prices were relatively high prior to the Roosevelt administration, largely because the cost of developing a privately owned and operated energy infrastructure, as well as of producing energy, was exorbitant. Electric energy was available in more affluent large urban areas, which used government policy influence and incentives to aid in the establishment of an energy infrastructure. Fuels, such as gasoline, were also very expensive at the time. Automobile costs had declined as a result of mass-assembly plants developed by Henry Ford, but fuel was not cheap, nor was it always easy to access.

Roosevelt's policies, however, focused primarily on electricity infrastructure and production. Through the passage of the Rural Electrification Act of 1936, his vision was a society that would have cheap electricity and a solid infrastructure to transmit electricity. As will be discussed in subsequent chapters, hydropower was the primary method promoted by Roosevelt. With a solid electricity infrastructure, the economy would grow, and automobiles and gasoline, among other seemingly "luxury goods" of the time, would become more readily available to consumers. But electrification was the primary policy innovation used to promote equity in society and in the marketplace.

The late twentieth century brought a renewed focus on equity, but one that expanded substantially the meaning of the term. As energy policy and environmental policy issues converged, the issue of equity expanded beyond accessibility and price-related issues and began to focus instead on the impact of energy policy on the environment and on public health. In terms of environmental issues, so-called greenhouse gases became a more prominent issue in the policy equity debate. Additionally, scientific evidence has increasingly shown the impact—at times quite uneven across society—of carbon-based fuel emissions on human beings. The research evidence tends to show that children and individuals of lower socioeconomic status are disproportionately likely to be exposed to and harmed by carbon-based fuel emissions. Thus, the issue of energy policy equity remains focused on the original issues of availability and cost, but increasingly there is concern about the impact of energy use on the health and well-being of citizens and the environment. In that sense, zero-emission energy sources are more consistent with the broader definition of policy equity in relation to energy policy.

The election of President Trump challenges the momentum and direction of over fifty years of energy policy evolution. Despite recent increases in fossil energy supply, fossil energy is ultimately a limited resource. More specifically, President Trump has reversed the direction of the bipartisan policy flow and rejected international consensus on climate change and the national and international policy directions needed to mitigate the effects of climate change. Concerns about the use of fossil energy and the documented marginal social and environmental costs have been largely dismissed by the Trump administration. To that degree, the promotion of a broad definition of environmental and social equity, at least in terms of national executive leadership, is no longer a central focus of environmental and energy policy as it has been for over a half-century under the stewardship of both Democrat and Republican presidents, with the noteworthy exception of the Reagan administration when the EPA administrator Ann Gorsuch sought to roll back established environmental policy. Mrs. Gorsuch, now deceased, was the mother of Neil Gorsuch—President Trump's first appointee to the U.S. Supreme Court.

CHAPTER SUMMARY

A major shift in energy policy innovation began at the state level with the passage of the Miller–Warren Energy Lifeline Act of 1972. It was not until the 1973 oil shock that significant federal government innovation began to take form—as policy makers became increasingly aware of the need to reconsider the national energy policy paradigm that had been in place since the Public Utilities Holding Company Act of 1935. Federal policy makers in the 1970s realized the need to include state and local policy innovators, as well as private stakeholders, in the energy policy innovations of the future. An increasing supply of oil in the late 1980s and for much of the 1990s may have reduced national attention to the need to enlarge and diversify the national energy portfolio, but state-level initiatives spawned, in part, by PURPA of 1978, the EPAct of 1992, and state and local innovations led to the development of an increasingly green energy portfolio in many states and local communities. During the 1990s, the Clinton administration quietly continued to move energy policy innovation through cooperative federalism. Post 9/11, President Bush's Hydrogen Initiative, while a long-term policy innovation, represents an attempt to more rapidly move the United States into a twenty-first-century energy paradigm; however, a continued need for petroleum and other carbon-based energy sources was seen to exist as well as a likely return to a nuclear energy paradigm as evidenced by the substance of the EPAct of 2005. President

Obama's commitment to renewable energy and climate policy was renowned and broadly applauded in both the United States and internationally, but President Trump has earnestly sought to erase the energy policy innovations of his predecessor.

NOTES

1. Clearly, these categories overlap in some cases, and one could easily use a partisan approach to categorizing time periods and interpretations of those time periods. The categories are fairly general, but seem to be the optimum approach to presenting an apolitical, nonpartisan analysis of energy policy innovations.

2. It is unlikely that as free marketers, Reagan and others looked to the North Slope as a *permanent* solution to the energy crisis. Adopting principles discussed in North (1981), the free market solution was to increase short-term energy supply and to look to energy innovations in the marketplace to increase the energy supply for the future. In essence, government's role should be to promote market solutions through reduced regulation and perhaps through incentive structures. Price controls were seen as artificially spurring overconsumption of a good that was in short supply, which would likely not increase the needed lead time for new market developments. North Slope oil exploration was seen as a source or energy supply that could conceivably lengthen the lead time for new innovation, while simultaneously reducing some cost burdens on consumers. In essence, new energy supplies also reduce the inelasticity of the market and make price more responsive to consumer demand levels.

3. The Energy and Conservation and Production Act was duly reauthorized in 1998.

4. A "person" could be an organization.

5. While hydrogen-based fuel initiatives can be traced back to the Bush I administration, the more recent efforts were more fully operationalized and supported under the Hydrogen Future Act of 1996 (P.L. 104-271). This legislation further extended the legislation passed six years earlier in the form of the Spark M. Matsunaga Hydrogen Research, Development, and Demonstration Act of 1990 (P.L. 101–566). These congressional acts were indeed cautious, yet represent earnest attempts to develop the use of hydrogen as a fuel source as well as hydrogen fuel cell technology as a method of storing energy for transportation and other purposes.

6. https://www.epa.gov/coalash/coal-ash-basics#03, accessed November 28, 2016.

7. https://www.acaa-usa.org/About-Coal-Ash/A-Sustainable-Future, accessed November 28, 2016.

8. http://www.scotusblog.com/2016/02/states-seek-to-block-mercury-pollution-rule/, accessed November 28, 2016.

9. https://www.federalregister.gov/documents/2015/10/23/2015–22842/carbon-pollution-emission-guidelines-for-existing-stationary-sources-electric-utility-generating, accessed November 28, 2016.).

10. https://www.washingtonpost.com/news/volokh-conspiracy/wp/2016/02/09/supreme-court-puts-the-brakes-on-the-epas-clean-power-plan/?utm_term=.cead666eb4c4, accessed November 28, 2016.

REFERENCES

Alternative Fuels Data Center. 2018. *American Recovery and Reinvestment Act of 2009*. Washington, DC: U.S. Department of Energy. Retrieved from https://www. afdc.energy.gov/laws/arra.html, June 2, 2018.

Bobrow, D., and Kudrle, R. 1979. Energy R & D: In tepid pursuit of collective goods. *International Organization* 33(2): 149–175.

California Energy Commission. 2005. California energy commission: An overview. http://www.energy.ca.gov/commission/overview.html, accessed June 11, 2005.

Cimitile, M. 2009. Corn ethanol will not cut greenhouse gas emissions. *Scientific American*, April 20. Retrieved from https://www.scientificamerican.com/article/ethanol-not-cut-emissions/, July 21, 2019.

Climate Focus. 2015. *The Paris Agreement: Summary*. Amsterdam, Netherlands: Climate Focus. Retrieved from http://www.climatefocus.com/sites/default/files/20151228%20COP%2021%20briefing%20FIN.pdf, June 2, 2018.

Clinton, W. 2000. *Executive Order 13149: Greening the Government through Federal Fleet and Transportation Efficiency*. Washington, DC: White House.

Cochran, T., Speth, G., and Tamplin, A. 1975. A poor buy. *Environment*, 17(4): 10–18.

Congressional Quarterly. 1992. Veto cloud loomed large over 1992 floor fights. *Congressional Quarterly*, December 19, 50(50): 3854–3870.

Conway, Nicholas T., and Simay, Gregory L. 1977. Energy research and development: A partnership between federal and local government. *Public Administration Review*, 37(6): 711–713.

Culp, P., Conradi, D., and Tuell, C. 2015. *Trust Lands in the American West: A Legal Overview and Policy Assessment*. Cambridge, MA: Lincoln Institute of Land Policy.

Cupulos, M. 1979. The price of power. *National Review*, 31(5): 156–159.

Davenport, C., and Rubin, A. 2017. Trump signs executive order unwinding Obama climate policies. *New York Times*, March 28, 2017. Retrieved from https://www.nytimes.com/2017/03/28/climate/trump-executive-order-climate-change.html, June 3, 2018.

Dennis, B., and Eilperin, J. 2018. EPA moves to overhaul Obama-era safeguards on coal ash waste. *Washington Post*, March 2. Retrieved from https://www.washingtonpost.com/news/energy-environment/wp/2018/03/01/epa-moves-to-overhaul-obama-era-safeguards-on-coal-ash-waste/?utm_term=.9f12604d81ba, June 3, 2018.

Economist. 1992. Does greener mean richer? *Economist*, 325(7788): 18–19.

———. 2005. *The Institutional Origins of the Department of Energy*. Washington, DC: Department of Energy, http://www.25yearsofenergy.gov/origins.html, accessed June 13, 2005.

———. 2005. New stories: Factors for a successful renewable portfolio standard, *Renewable Energy & Energy Efficiency Partnership*. http://www.reeep.org/index.cfm?articleid=993, accessed June 8, 2005.

Energy Efficiency and Renewable Energy (EERE). 2005. Glossary of terms. http://www.eere.energy.gov/financing/glossary.html, accessed May 26, 2005.

Federal Energy Regulatory Commission. 2005. About FERC, http://www.ferc.gov, accessed June 11, 2005.

———. 2015. *Energy Market Primer: A Handbook of Energy Market Basics*. Washington, DC: Federal Energy Regulatory Commission.

Friedman, L., and Plumer, B. 2017. EPA announces repeal of major Obama-era carbon emissions rule. *New York Times,* October 10. Retrieved from https://www.nytimes.com/2017/10/09/climate/clean-power-plan.html, June 3, 2018.

General Services Administration. 2018. Vehicle Management Library: Federal Fleet Reports. https://www.gsa.gov/policy-regulations/policy/vehicle-management-policy/vehicle-management-library, accessed April 14, 2018,

Greenfield, L. 2010. *An Overview of the Federal Energy Regulatory Commission and the Federal Regulation of Public Utilities in the United States.* Washington, DC: Office of the General Counsel, Federal Regulatory Commission.

Hershey, Robert D., Jr. 1981. Can Reagan lift the cloud over nuclear energy? *New York Times,* March 8, Section 3, p. 1.

Janson, Donald. 1979. Accident at Three Mile Island nuclear power plant near Harrisburg, Pa, releases above-normal levels of radiation into atmosphere on March 28. *New York Times*, March 29, p. 1.

King, Seth S. 1981. Planning of Alaska land use and oil leases starts. *New York Times*, April 5. Section 1, p. 29.

Lapp, R. 1973. Self-sufficient by 1980? *The New Republic*, December 15, 10–12.

Lazar, K. 2001. Worlds apart. Bush, environmentalists battle over earth, wind, fire. *The Boston Herald*, March 25, p. 1.

Mandelbaum, David, and Brown, C. 2004. Pennsylvania energy alert. Baltimore, MD: Ballard, Spahr, Andrews & Ingersoll, LLP.

Morehouse, W. 1981. Gas industry battles over decontrol. *Christian Science Monitor*, May 7. Retrieved from https://www.csmonitor.com/1981/0507/050751.html, October 28, 2019.

Munson, R. 1979. Nuclear power: The price is too high. *The Nation.* 228(18): 521–539.

Neff, Shirley. 2005. Energy Policy Act of 2005: Summary. New York: Center for Energy, Marine Transportation, and Public Policy, Columbia University.

New Republic. 1978. Price and pride. *New Republic*, February 25, 5–6.

Nice, D. 1994. *Policy Innovation in State Government.* Ames, IA: Iowa State University Press.

North, D. 1981. *Structure and Change in Economic History.* New York: Norton.

Obama, B. 2016. Transforming our energy system, creating good paying jobs, and saving Americans on their energy bills. Press Release, February 25. Washington, DC: White House. Retrieved from https://obamawhitehouse.archives.gov/the-press-office/2016/02/25/fact-sheet-recovery-act-made-largest-single-investment-clean-energy, June 2, 2018.

Office of Electricity Delivery and Energy Reliability. 2018. *Annual U.S. Transmission Data Review.* Washington, DC: U.S. Department of Energy.

Olatubi, W., and Zhang, Y. 2003. A dynamic estimation of total energy demand for the Southern states. *The Review of Regional Studies* 33(2): 206–228.

Osborne, D. 1990. *Laboratories of Democracy.* Boston, MA: Harvard Business School.

Parnell, J. 2019. "World's biggest" energy storage project planned for Utah. *Forbes*, May 30. Retrieved from https://www.forbes.com/sites/johnparnell/2019/05/30/worlds-biggest-energy-storage-project-planned-for-utah/#35025975a5ed, June 9, 2019.

Paul, J. 2019. Gov. Polis signs Democrats' sweeping oil and gas bill into law, marking major shift in regulatory authority over drilling. *Colorado Sun*, April 16. Retrieved from https://coloradosun.com/2019/04/16/senate-bill-181-oil-gas-law-colorado-signed/ August 1, 2019.

Physics Forums. 2014. Energy vs. force vs. work vs. power. http://www.physicsforums. com/threads/energy-vs-force-vs-work-vs-power.768295/, November 13, 2019.

Reilly, A. 2018. Air pollution: EPA "still thinking about" Obama mercury standards— Wehrum. *E & E News*, April 19, 2018. Retrieved from https://www.eenews.net/ stories/1060079569, June 3, 2018.

Salisbury, D. 1980. Want to sell your electricity to a utility? Go ahead. *The Christian Science Monitor*, 23 December, 9.

Sawyer, Stephen. 1984. State energy conditions and policy development. *Public Administration Review*, 44(3): 205–214.

Schifter, I., Vera, M., Diaz, L., Guzman, E., Ramos, F., and Lopez-Salinas, E. 2001. Environmental implications on the oxygenation of gasoline with ethanol in the metropolitan area of Mexico City. *Environmental Science and Technology*. 35(24): 4957–4960.

Shear, M. 2017. Trump will withdraw U.S. from Paris Climate Agreement. *New York Times*, June 1, 2017. Retrieved from https://www.nytimes.com/2017/06/01/climate/trump-paris-climate-agreement.html, June 3, 2018.

Shultz, George P., and Dam, Kenneth W. 1977. Reflections on wage and price controls. *Industrial and Labor Relations Review*, 30(2): 139–151.

Smith, Rodney, and Phelps, Charles. 1978. The subtle impact of price controls on domestic oil production. *American Economic Review*, 68(2): 428–433.

Southern California Edison. 2005. Understanding baseline—Baseline facts: History and background. http://www.sce.com/CustomerService/understandingBaseline/ history. htm, accessed June 11, 2005.

U.S. Congress. 1993. Energy Policy Act of 1992. 102 Congress. H.R. 776 P.L. 102–486.

U.S. Department of Energy. 2005. The institutional origins of the Department of Energy. http://www.25yearsofenergy.gov/origins.html, accessed June 13, 2005.

Weber, Arnold R., and Mitchell, Daniel J. 1978. Further reflections on wage controls: Comment. *Industrial and Labor Relations Review*, 31(2): 149–158.

Zactruba, J. 2019. The efficiency of power plants of different types. *Bright Hub Engineering*. Retrieved from https://www.brighthubengineering.com/power-plants/ 72369-compare-the-efficiency-of-different-power-plants/, July 21, 2019.

4

Solar Energy

★ ★ ★

In 1994, in the wake of the EPAct of 1992, the U.S. Department of Energy began requiring the Energy Information Agency (now named the Energy Information Administration) to collect annual data on the manufacture and use of renewable energy equipment, such as solar photovoltaic panels (see EIA, 2003). Solar energy production in the United States increased by nearly 1,540 percent in the fifteen-year time period between 2004 and 2018 (see figure 4.1). Despite this very rapid growth, solar energy produced less than 1 percent of all energy consumed in the United States in 2018. In large part, this is due to the natural gas revolution that produced nearly 85 percent of the marginal increase in electricity production between 2017 and 2018—in total, renewable energy production growth accounted for slightly less than 10 percent of that marginal production increase.[1] Nevertheless, solar energy is likely to increase significantly its productive capacity in the future. This will be particularly the case if advancements in renewable energy storage capacity technology becomes cost effective and it is rapidly commercialized.

WHAT IS SOLAR ENERGY? HOW DOES IT WORK?

Solar power is perhaps the oldest form of energy utilized by human beings. At a very basic level, the sun provides thermal energy or heat, a type of energy that is very important for agriculture and plant growth and ocean-based resources. The sun plays a significant role in weather patterns and the snow, rain, and wind that contribute mightily to the water supply. These same weather patterns produce the winds harnessed by wind farms. Photosynthesis relies on the sun to grow our food and to grow, too, the wood products we use for construction and for the heat of wood fires. Fossil energy—in the form of coal, petroleum, and natural gas—can be traced back in one way or another to energy provided by the sun. In many ways, fossil energy is a form of stored solar energy. While we already benefit from the sun's energy in many ways,

Figure 4.1   Solar PV and Solar Thermal Electricity Production (2009–2018)

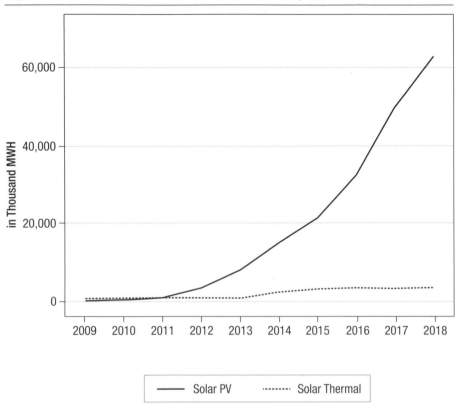

Data Source: Energy Information Administration

developments in solar energy technology have made it possible to capture a fraction of the 430 quintillion joules of energy from the sun that reach the Earth *every hour*. For comparison purposes, humankind uses 410 quintillion joules of energy *every year* (Harrington, 2015).

In the 1860s, French mathematician Auguste Mouchout created the first thermal solar-powered steam engine. Mouchout, and later Englishman William Adams, devised methods by which solar radiation could be concentrated on tanks of water. Solar radiation would heat the water, creating steam power. In the 1870s, American John Ericsson created the first solar trough, which was a long parabolic device that focused solar radiation onto a pipe carrying an efficient thermal absorbing liquid, usually water or oil, that would absorb and transport solar thermal energy used to generate steam to spin turbines for the generation of electrical energy. Solar thermal energy continued to evolve as the primary form of solar power research experimentation until the 1910s (http://www.solarenergy.com/info_history.html, accessed June 17, 2005).

Electrochemical applications of solar energy were pioneered by French physicist Alexandre Bequerel (Lenardic, 2005). In thermal solar processes, capturing energy from light seems rather simple, as described in the previous paragraph. In electrochemical processes, however, the energy contained in light is used directly to generate an electric current. While Becquerel and other late-nineteenth-century scientists observed the impact of illumination on electrochemical phenomena, it was not until Albert Einstein's work in 1904 that the photovoltaic effect was more fully understood in the scientific community. Einstein theorized about the dual nature of light as both a particle and a wave. The particle aspect of light is known as a photon—properly understood as a small but powerful bundle of energy (see Würfel, 2005).

It is one thing to use illumination to change the nature of an electrochemical process; it is quite another thing to make photons create a source of controlled electrical energy. Silicon photovoltaic cells absorb solar radiation—the energy of photons—and direct the movement of electrons in a controlled pattern to produce electrical voltage and current—the core elements of electrical power. The material that absorbs photons in most photovoltaic cells is a known semiconductor substance, such as silicon (Si).

SILICON-BASED PHOTOVOLTAIC CELLS

The most commonly available solar cells on the market today are Si-based cells. I will discuss other types of cells, but because of their prevalence, it is important to start off the discussion with Si-based photovoltaic cells. Of particular importance to Si-based photovoltaic (PV) systems is the reduction of unwanted impurities in the silicon material, and to create a uniform crystal structure. Silicon is a highly desirable material because it can be manufactured by known industrial processes into a controlled and pure crystalline form. Monocrystalline silicon is a premium material because the crystal formations are uniform and free of impurities, which makes the substance very efficient at absorbing energy from photons. Polycrystalline silicon is also a semiconductor, but it has a much lower level of efficiency for absorbing energy from photons. Silicon can be cut into very thin translucent wafers that effectively absorb photons. A standard silicon-based multicrystalline photovoltaic cell varies between 150 and 325 micrometers in thickness (see Tool et al., 2002).

Manufacturers introduce a very small amount of impurity into the silicon crystal so the silicon can build a charge while irradiated by solar energy. N-Type picks up extra electrons and is negatively charged. Silicon can also be charged "positive" (P-Type), which means that the materials need extra electrons. N-Type silicon has phosphorus added to it, while P-Type silicon has boron added.[2] The process of making the silicon N-or P-Type is called doping in the world of materials science. P-type and N-type silicon are placed adjacent to one another, but separated by a silicon oxide insulating layer that prevents electrons from moving directly between the two silicon media. With the introduction of solar energy, the silicon cell develops an electrical charge and current. The electrons are then forced to travel through an electrical circuit, one that directs the electrons through some form of electrical mechanical device, such as a water pump, which uses the electrical energy, or into a storage location. Electrical energy can be stored in a battery for later use when the solar radiation is no longer present (figure 4.2).

Photovoltaic systems using monocrystalline silicon were first developed in the 1940s, but the cost of producing Si-based photovoltaic cells was prohibitive. In the 1950s and 1960s, photovoltaic technology was used in the space industry to provide electric power to satellites and other space travel–related system applications.

Solar thermal energy remains an important part of solar power technological development and use, particularly in residential and small commercial applications. The load requirements for well-designed energy efficient homes are much lower than earlier construction because of high-tech insulation and low-energy requirement equipment such as high-efficiency hot water heaters, dishwashers, and laundry machines. Better insulated doors and windows are also featured in energy-efficient construction. Additionally, proper site location and structural consideration can make solar energy a better choice, simply because of reduced electric lighting requirements and the solar thermal benefits resulting from more efficient home design.

Several technical and economic issues are addressed in the following sections, issues that serve as important information about the current feasibility

Figure 4.2 Schematic of an Si-Based Solar Cell

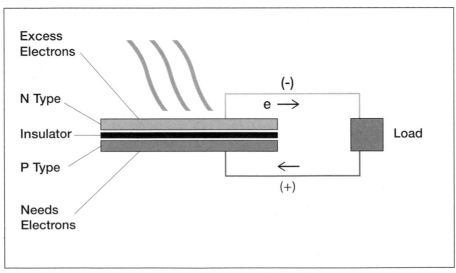

Courtesy of the author

of solar energy and its future growth potential. Understanding current technical and economic issues will produce better energy choices that properly incorporate solar energy systems.

TECHNICAL FEASIBILITY OF SOLAR PHOTOVOLTAICS

Technical issues often relate to the development of efficient and effective energy collection devices for photovoltaic cells and cell housing. As shown in the diagram above, it is necessary to have wires connected to solar cells to collect electrons that are freed from the N-Type material due to exposure to photons emitted by the sun. While silicon has many benefits, one of its great strengths is simultaneously one of its greatest weaknesses, namely, its status as a semiconductive material. Semiconductors are not very effective or efficient in creating an electrical current because their atomic structure is such that their electrons are fairly stable. Electrons trying to move through the outer shell of the silicon atom are not really able to do that very effectively. Therefore, a metal grid of collectors is constructed to overlay the photovoltaic cell to collect electrons.

Collector grids block cell exposure to photons, which means that a small portion of the cell is not producing electrical current. Even a small amount of shading can significantly reduce photovoltaic cell efficiency. Collector grids are composed of highly conductive metal able to effectively transport electrons through very thin wires capable of retaining structural integrity with limited shading. In order to meet the necessary standards of functionality, metal conductor grids may require expensive materials and manufacturing processes. Other alternatives to dealing with metal grid impacts on cell efficiencies include embedding the metal grid in grooves along the cell surface. A technique known as photolithography is used to literally "paint" the metal grid onto the surface of PV cells. A commonly used material for collector grids has been tin oxide (SnO_2). The advantage to certain grid materials is that they are nearly transparent and do not shade the surface of the silicon materials where electrons are being freed from N-type material. The most ideal materials are nearly transparent yet retain sufficient integrity to remain in their proper place despite exposure to temperature extremes and varying solar radiation patterns.[3]

Nanotechnologists anticipate the construction of ever cheaper and more efficient photovoltaic cells as advances in materials science continue at a rapid pace. The components of these next-generation efficient cells are so small that it is necessary to construct the cells on a nearly atom-by-atom basis, a hallmark of the nanotechnology revolution taking place in contemporary high-tech manufacturing. As mentioned previously, photolithography is an important part of modern solar cell construction, but advances in nanotechnology also promise greatly improved solar efficiencies. Since light is composed of many different frequencies, it is necessary to efficiently capture photons over the entire light spectrum. These variations in frequency require correspondingly different N-type materials used in the solar cell, but will also require newly emerging techniques of making these spectral frequencies into useful electrical energy for different system load requirements.

Third-generation solar PV (SPV) technologies are both confronting the challenges associated with photon capture over a broader range of the light spectrum and employing materials other than silicon as an energy-absorbing material. Perovskite solar cells (PSC) are the fastest-advancing next-generation solar cells, reaching efficiency levels in the 18–25 percent range depending on materials and configuration (see Ahn et al., 2015; Green et al., 2015: 3; Mesquita et al. 2018; Tong et al., 2019). Perovskites are materials with a crystal structure that is the same as calcium titanium oxide ($CaTiO_3$). Perovskite cells have a wide band gap and are able to capture energy from sunlight. Perovskites are cheap and easy to produce, thus reducing the material costs of solar photovoltaics, while simultaneously boosting collection cell efficiencies (Snaith, 2013). Experiments with dye-sensitized solar cells (DSCs) are technically feasible and offer a low-cost method of increasing light absorption in solar cells, although the materials in dye-sensitized cells are subject to degradation due to heat (see Nazeeruddin et al., 2011). Ultrathin organic and polymer solar cells (OPSCs) are currently in rather early stages of R & D (see Kaltenbrunner et al., 2012). Organic and polymer solar cells are comprised of carbon-based semiconductor materials that can maintain their plasticity (see Lipomi et al., 2011). According to Zhou et al. (2012: 607), polymer solar cells have an efficiency rating of nearly 10 percent (Jørgensen et al., 2012). Material scientists are developing various semiconductor materials with the goal of increasing the frequency range of light absorption taking place in solar cells. The cells are usually printed as a liquid that will increase production speed and at a low cost. The cells have a relatively low efficiency rating in the range of 2–10 percent, but the ability to produce large quantities of these solar cells at a low price may prove a deciding factor in meeting very strong market demand (see Cai et al., 2010).

The types of third-generation photovoltaic system advances should not be thought of as independent of one another. For example, PSCs and OPSCs can be dye sensitized to increase solar energy absorption so as to improve their photovoltaic efficiency rates. PSCs, DSCs, and OPSCs are all part of a family of third-generation solar cells known as *thin film*. There are other thin film photovoltaics that fit within the same family, and these are discussed below.

Thin film photovoltaic technology has been a continually evolving concept since photovoltaic systems were developed in earnest in the mid-twentieth century. The concept behind a thin film system is to create ultrathin cell compositions (e.g., collector components of ~500 nanometers to 200 microns in thickness). Thin film efficiencies are a function of film architecture (e.g., semiconductor scaffolding, porous films, and hole transfer material factors), material usage, and fabrication. Commonly available thin film photovoltaic systems are made of amorphous silicon (a-Si) and cadmium telluride (CdTe).

Thin Film Solar Array
iStock / Getty Images Plus / Airubon

There is a growing commercial interest in copper iridium gallium selenide (CIGS) and gallium arsenide (GaAs) thin films.

Problems that arise for thin film technologies relate to durability and susceptibility to environmental impacts. All solar systems are exposed to high levels of solar radiation, high temperatures, wind, dust, water, and other contaminants or corrosives, but thin films, given their very fragile nature, are more likely to be easily destroyed by adverse environmental conditions. Moisture and oxygen can lead to thin film degradation. In the case of PSCs, the cells often contain lead in their composition, which could pose environmental costs (Mesquita, 2018: 2472). Due to the very thin structure of thin film technologies and the efforts to reduce glass protective plating requirements for systems of this type,[4] the direct environmental exposure of thin films makes the product much more likely to delaminate and to fail in operation (see McMahon, 2004). Technical research has focused on combining solar thermal and photovoltaic systems to, in essence, cool solar panels and thus increase efficiencies, while simultaneously reducing the negative impact of intense heat on materials and component integrity (see Tripanagnostopoulos et al., 2005).[5]

The management of thermal effects on solar PV cells is particularly acute for concentrator solar PV (CPV), which has the potential to increase PV outputs and efficiency (record efficiencies between 41 and 46 percent), thus reducing the number of solar cells and land area needed to generate electricity. Fresnel lens are used to concentrate sunlight on CPV cells. Without cooling, the CPV cells will be damaged or destroyed by the high temperature of the concentrated sunlight. The high temperature will also reduce the efficiency of CPV (Wiesenfarth et al., 2017).

Efficiency ratings for solar photovoltaic systems improved quite steadily over the 1990s, and have continued to improve in the early twenty-first century. Efficiency rating improvements are in large measure a function of continued R & D in photovoltaics. Monocrystalline silicon cells have produced well-documented efficiency ratings of nearly 15–18 percent, while polycrystalline and thin film studies have produced efficiency ratings of 13–16 percent and 6–12 percent, respectively (Keane, 2014: 95).

According to *PR Newswire* (2019), the prospect for continued improvement in photovoltaic cell efficiency remains viable, with perovskite cells, for instance, reaching 40 percent efficiency. With dye sensitization, it is possible that cell efficiencies will rise even further. Nevertheless, material issues, degradation rates, and efficiency ratings in photovoltaic cells will likely have a significant impact on the economics of solar power increasing its role in producing energy supplies for the twenty-first century. As thin film systems become cheaper due to reduced material costs in fabrication (e.g., low-cost conductive materials for collectors), the eventual micro-manufacturing of solar photovoltaic technology (Pique et al., 2016: 7–8) will likely produce a market boom.

TECHNICAL FEASIBILITY OF SOLAR THERMAL

Solar thermal is technically feasible in both residential and commercial settings. In residential settings, solar thermal energy is usually used to heat water. Solar hot water heaters and solar thermal systems for heating swimming pools and providing hot water in the home are typical uses of solar thermal energy in residential settings. A solar hot water heater uses the energy of the sun to heat water for domestic use, reducing or eliminating the use of natural gas or electricity to heat water. A secondary fluid is circulated through copper tubes on a roof-mounted panel with good sun exposure. The fluid travels through a heat exchanger unit where the high temperature of the fluid is transferred to water traveling through a secondary tube in the heat exchanger unit. The hot water is then stored in a hot water heater until needed. Water heating systems for swimming pools are built on similar principles, but usually involve direct heating of the pool water through copper tubes mounted on rooftop panels with good sun exposure.

Commercial solar thermal systems are used to heat fluids involving a similar heat exchange process as described above. The heat exchange is often used to heat water either for direct use or for the production of steam to power turbines for electricity generation. Most typically, these commercial systems are forms of concentrated solar power (CSP), but nonconcentrated solar thermal applications are feasible (see Islam and Morimoto, 2018). The systems noted here typically use a system of mirrors and reflectors to concentrate sunlight to heat a fluid that is then used to heat water and create steam used to power a turbine to generate electricity.

Solar troughs concentrate solar energy from the sun onto fluid-filled pipes located at the trough's focal point. Temperatures of the fluid, typically an oil, reach 400°C (752°F)—for comparison purposes, recall that at sea level water boils at 100°C. The oil circulating through the pipes is used to heat water in a heat exchange unit to produce steam. The steam is used to power a turbine to produce electricity. The steam is then cooled, and the liquid water is recirculated into the heat exchange unit.

Solar power towers involve a stationary tower unit and an array of flat mirrors that can be moved; these are known as heliostats. The tower unit sits in the middle of the array, and can be of variable heights, typically 500–600 feet tall. Atop the tower is a salt chamber. The mirrors are adjusted such that sunlight is directed at the salt at the top of the solar tower. The concentrated solar energy heats the salt to over 560°C (over 1,000°F), turning the salt into a molten form. The molten salt is then fed into a tank at the base of the solar tower where it can be stored until needed for electric power production. Typically, the storage tank can maintain the salt in a molten state for up to sixteen hours. When used for electricity production, the molten salt enters a heat exchanging unit, transferring the heat from the molten salt to water, which then becomes superheated steam. The steam is directed at a turbine generator, which produces electricity. The steam is then cooled to a liquid form, which then reenters the heat exchanging unit to continue the cycle (see Collado and Guallar, 2019).

Similar to solar troughs and solar towers, solar parabolic dish systems concentrate sunlight onto a focal point. The focal point is typically within the concavity of the mirrored parabolic dish. At the focal point, the sun's energy is approximately a thousand times greater than what you might experience when you feel the sunlight on your skin on a hot day. At the focal point, different types of systems can be used to capture the energy of the sun. Solar photovoltaic cells can be installed at the focal point and directly convert the sun's energy into electricity. Another option involves the installation of a Stirling engine at the focal point. A Stirling engine converts thermal energy into mechanical energy in the form of a spinning flywheel. The flywheel would be part of a generating system to convert the mechanical energy of the Stirling engine into electrical energy (see Barreto and Canhoto, 2017).

The steam-driven turbine systems described previously (i.e., power tower and solar trough designs) are known as closed systems, but they still require water to operate, and replacement water is required due to inevitable water loss through evaporation. The Stirling engine turbine system does not require water. A Stirling engine relies on heat to push a piston driving a fly wheel through a half-phase of a cycle, and relies on air cooling for the piston to return to its starting position—the second half-phase of a cycle.

A technical solution to the issues facing dish-CSP is addressed by the Luter system (see Garcia-Ortiz et al., 2018). In a Luter system, the focal point in a dish-CSP unit contains a reflective mirror that concentrates and reflects solar energy toward an aperture at the mirror's axis and onto the hot end of a Stirling engine, or onto a circulating heat-absorbing fluid that transfers thermal energy to the Stirling engine, located outside of the parabolic mirror. There are two benefits to this approach. First, the Stirling engine suffers from lower levels of heat exposure and degradation. Second, the Stirling engine is cooler and more easily serviced due to greater accessibility.

There are advantages and disadvantages to steam-driven systems and Stirling engine systems. The notable advantage to the Stirling engine turbine system is that CSP systems operating in an arid climate do not require ready access to water resources. One disadvantage of Stirling engine CSP systems is that the heat generated by concentrated solar energy can easily damage and destroy some system components. Another problem experienced by dish-Stirling systems is misalignment. If the Stirling motor is not directly in the focal point of the dish, significant losses of system efficiency will result.

A Power Tower in Nevada
E+ / Mlenny

A Parabolic Dish
iStock / Getty Images Plus / smodj

Additionally, the Stirling engine can, itself, cause inefficiency due to shading of the parabolic dish. The advantage to CSP systems relying on steam to operate electricity-generating turbine systems is that there is greater power potential. A disadvantage to CSP systems such as solar troughs and solar towers is their use of water and the vast acreage (see Ong et al., 2013) required for physical plant facilities. A particular disadvantage for solar towers of concern to environmentalists is their potential impact on wildlife. Birds that fly through the solar rays directed from the heliostat (mirrors) array to the salt tower are killed by the extreme heat; they have been seen to catch fire and explode in flight (see Sahagun, 2016).

ECONOMICS OF SOLAR POWER

The economics of solar power can be divided in at least three subtopics. First, what type of economic infrastructure currently exists for solar power? What are the historic costs of solar energy systems, and in which direction are costs trending? Second, solar power should be studied to determine its feasibility as a replacement energy source, reducing the need for carbon-based energy sources. How does $/kWh for solar energy compare with carbon-based energy sources, and what are the future prospects for $/kWh? A related question is, how does solar energy as a replacement reduce economic and social costs associated with carbon-based energy systems? A third question centers around economic development opportunities associated with the advancement of a solar energy paradigm. Do solar energy systems have the capacity to create job opportunities?

These three sets of questions become quite important when one considers the sustainable community model undergirding much of the alternative/renewable energy paradigm. A sustainable community involves a great deal more than a clean environment built on a sustainable, possibly "green" energy paradigm. Citizens in all communities also need a green economic and commercial base providing them with some form of economic opportunity. The full vision of sustainability requires a setting in which environmentally safe products and services are produced and sold in a responsible and socially/environmentally just form of exchange, often made available through an equitable sharing-oriented economy (Sundararajan, 2016).

Current Solar PV Energy Economic Infrastructure and Levelized Cost of Electricity

The Energy Information Administration, U.S. Department of Energy, is a recognized data source regarding energy production and consumption in the United States. Its most recent published data indicate that, in 2018, U.S energy consumption was approximately 101.237 quadrillion British thermal units (BTUs);[6] according to the EIA report, approximately 0.951 quadrillion BTUs, or about 0.9 percent of the energy consumed, was created using solar power (EIA, 2018a). For use in the production of commercial electricity, solar energy consumption increased from 76 GWh in 2008 to 49,688 GWh in 2017 (EIA, 2018b). Solar thermal energy net production rose from 788 GWh in 2008 to 3,269 GWh in 2017. Despite witnessing such tremendous growth during the Obama administration, due in large part to the credible commitments provided by national, state, and local governments, solar energy remains greatly underutilized given that solar energy is a major potential replacement energy source for the future.

Generally, solar energy production and consumption occur in high solar radiation areas of the nation. Climatologically, the southern Pacific Coast area and the inland southwestern United States are prime locations for the location of solar energy systems (NREL, 2019). Residential use of solar photovoltaic and thermal systems is largely dependent on solar radiation patterns at particular locations. State and federal incentives for the use of alternative/ renewable energy systems play a substantial role in the economic choice to purchase and utilize residential solar energy systems, which also impacts IPPs seeking to capitalize from zero-emission energy production.

All available evidence indicates that solar power is rapidly enlarging its share of the energy supply in the United States. "Since 2008, U.S. installations have grown seventeen-fold from 1.2 gigawatt (GW) to an estimated 30 GW today . . . enough capacity to power the equivalent of 5.7 million average American homes" (EERE, 2018). In particular, one energy-producing sector that is showing a sizable increase in solar energy use is represented by the approximate 6,696 percent growth in solar energy production by IPPs taking place between 2006 and 2016—from 493 GWh to 33,502 GWh (EIA, 2017; EIA, 2019). Paralleling this increase in solar energy production by IPPs, evidence indicates that solar system manufacturing and generating capacity is holding steady despite growth in natural gas-based electricity generation capacity (SEIA, 2019).

Approximately 13.5 million peak kWh photovoltaic modules were shipped by domestic manufacturers in 2016. Of that total, nearly 12.8 million of the peak kWh modules shipped in the United States were imported from other countries. "Peak kWh" in this case means that the total number of photovoltaic modules shipped had the capacity to produce 13.5 million kW on an hourly basis during peak solar photovoltaic performance, under optimum solar radiation conditions. In 2016, the United States produced domestically only about 1.1 million (or 8 percent) of the peak kWh modules shipped to domestic users. Approximately 2.7 million modules shipped were manufactured and imported from the People's Republic of China. Over 3.7 million (30 percent) of the modules shipped were manufactured in and imported from Malaysia. Other nations from which the United States imported solar panels included South Korea, Thailand, Vietnam, and India. The total value of the module shipments in 2016 alone was $9.7 billion, with a vast majority of that revenue going to overseas manufacturers from which the United States imported the solar photovoltaic modules (EIA, 2018c). The number of domestic solar industry companies reporting in the EIA63B survey has declined due to industry consolidation "and changes to the strategic planning of companies in the U.S. solar photovoltaic (PV) industry." In 2012, the year featuring the peak number of active companies, there were 122 PV companies in the United States employing 17,487 full-time equivalent employees. By 2016, that number had declined to 53 PV companies in the United States employing only 6,021 full-time equivalent employees. While there were 57 PV manufacturing companies in the United States in 2012, there were only 22 PV manufacturing companies in the United States in 2016.

Figure 4.3 indicates that U.S. demand for solar panels has increased dramatically since 2010, while prices per peak kW have dropped from $2.22 per kW to $0.75 in constant 2018 dollars. While demand for solar photovoltaic cells has increased, prices for solar modules and cells decreased between 2010 and 2015, a fact that is partially a function of the numerous technical advances discussed previously. The average price per kW did not change substantially between 2015 and 2016, indicating a likely leveling in pricing for the foreseeable future. The fabrication of PV systems has declined in large part because of the increased capacity to mass-produce the technology. Figure 4.3 indicates the price of a peak load watt of energy produced by a solar photovoltaic system.

According to the Solar Energy Industries Association, there are nearly 59 GW of installed solar photovoltaic capacity in the United States. The solar

Figure 4.3 Domestic Photovoltaic Manufacturing Activities and Prices, United States (2010–2016)

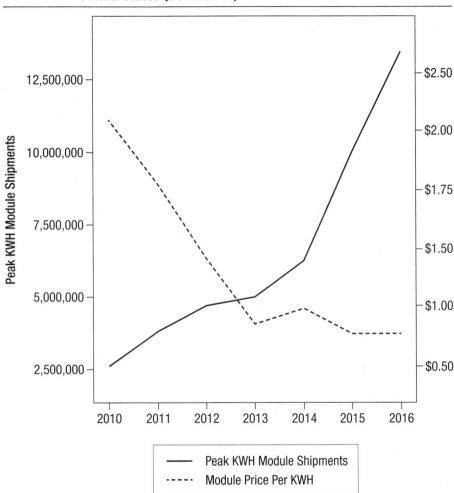

Data Source: Energy Information Agency 2018. *Solar Photovoltaic Cell/Module Shipments Report.* Washington, DC: U.S. Energy Information Agency. Retrieved from https://www.eia.gov/renewable/annual/ solar_photo/archive/2014/, accessed July 12, 2018.

market grew at its fastest quarterly pace in the first quarter of 2018. This growth was fueled by market uncertainty due to a 30 percent tariff on imported solar panels imposed by the Trump administration. With supply and cost uncertainty, several utility-scale solar photovoltaic projects were completed in the first quarter of 2018 (Eckhouse et al., 2018).

The total system levelized cost of electricity generated from solar photovoltaic energy was approximately 6.3 cents per kWh. This figure compares to a conventional combined cycle natural gas–generating system that produces electricity at a levelized system cost of 5.01 cents per kWh. Purely in terms of levelized system costs of electricity, a conventional natural gas power plant generates electricity that costs roughly 21 percent less than solar photovoltaic systems. However, the economics change if tax credits are factored into the equation. The current tax credit for solar PV production is 13.3 cents per kWh. Factoring in the production tax credit, the levelized cost of solar PV electricity is 4.99 cents per kWh, which is 0.4 percent less than electricity produced by conventional combined cycle natural gas power plants (see Solar Industries Association, 2019).

ECONOMICS OF SOLAR THERMAL— CONCENTRATED SOLAR POWER

Concentrated solar power systems in the United States are currently located in seven U.S. states: Arizona, California, Colorado, Florida, Hawaii, Nevada, and Utah. According to the National Renewable Energy Laboratory (NREL), California has the largest CSP capacity with fourteen solar thermal energy projects producing approximately 2.3 terawatt hours (TWh) of electricity per year as of 2017 (NREL, 2018b).

Currently, the largest CSP project in the United States is Ivanpah Solar Electric Generating System located at Primm, NV, a town forty-four miles southwest of Las Vegas on the Nevada–California state line. The 377 MW Ivanpah facility broke ground in October 2010 and was operational in January 2014. The facility cost $2.2 billion and created 1,896 construction job-years. Approximately ninety full-time employees conduct operation and maintenance activities. BrightSource Energy received $1.6 billion in federal loan guarantees as an incentive to construct the 3,500-acre power tower facility. The facility anticipates producing 1.08 TWh of electricity per year.

At this moment, the largest concentrated solar plant in the world is the 580 MW Noor Complex Solar Plant in Morocco, which is expected to provide electricity to one million people (Parke and Giles, 2018). By 2030, it is anticipated that Dubai, in the United Arab Emirates, will set a record with a new 5,000 MW facility—over thirteen times the size of Ivanpah. "Once complete . . . [the Dubai plant] is expected to reduce 6.5 million tons of carbon emissions per year. A typical coal plant produces around 3.5 million tons of CO_2 per year" (Dvorsky, 2016).

One of the biggest economic challenges facing concentrated solar power is the system levelized cost of electricity. The average cost of electricity produced by CSP systems in the United States is 16.5 cents per kWh, with a range of 14.5 to 18.8 cents per kWh. On average, tax credits bring the cost of CSP-generated electricity down to 12.7 cents per kWh, which is about 1.7 times higher per kWh than solar PV factoring in a production tax credit.

ECONOMIC DEVELOPMENT IMPACTS

Economic development impacts and the magnitude of impacts is largely case-specific. In a 2013 report titled *Spurring Local Economic Development with Clean Energy Investments:Lessons from the Field*, the Energy Efficiency and Renewable Energy (EERE, 2013) Office of the U.S. Department of Energy provided a number of case studies of solar PV investment impacts at the local level. There are a variety of potential benefits that emerge for any investment in renewable or clean energy sources. Construction jobs are part of the initial investment and exist as long as the project is being built. For commercial utility-grade solar installations, construction jobs may abruptly come to an end, but in the case of residential and commercial solar PV, construction jobs may continue to exist as long as there is a market demand for solar PV installation.

After the construction phase of a utility grade solar PV field, a certain number of permanent jobs will be created to handle the operations and maintenance of the solar PV system. The same is likely true for residential solar PV, although many of the operations and maintenance tasks associated with residential solar PV installations are likely to be handled either by home or business owners or contract electricians familiar with solar PV systems. In addition to these direct service jobs, the employment related to the training and education of electricians and service personnel is growing at U.S. community and technical colleges where solar commercial and residential systems are in operation.

Increased employment as a result of solar PV installation will likely result in increased demand for goods and services in the community, which has the potential to attract new businesses to communities and sustain existing business growth. In the case of residential solar PV that is net metered, it means that the homeowner or resident sells their PV solar energy to the power company, reducing the consumer's electric bill. In the case of commercial solar PV, local businesses using net metering can expand and/or be more profitable through ongoing energy cost savings.

Local environmental impacts lead to other noteworthy economic benefits. Air quality impacts from reduced use of fossil energy for electricity production translate into health benefits and reduced health costs closely associated with air pollution, particularly pulmonary illnesses in youth with chronic conditions and older adults experiencing diminished lung capacity. Additionally, good air quality and the use of clean energy in a community can be used to favorably brand a community and to attract residents and businesses with this selling point. The use of solar PV also reduces the water demand in a community. Fossil energy–based electricity generation is normally quite water intensive.

In energy savings alone, EERE estimates an average multiplier effect of 2.2 for municipalities with populations of 50,000 or more individuals. In other words, for every dollar saved in conventional electricity demand, there is an estimated \$2.20 benefit to the local community in money kept within the local community (see also Hughes, 2003).

CASE STUDY—RIFLE, COLORADO: USING SOLAR ENERGY TO POWER MUNICIPAL WATER AND SEWER SYSTEMS

"Background—Rifle is a municipality in Garfield County, Colorado, in the heart of the Rocky Mountains. It is a small city, with an area totaling just over four square miles and a population under 10,000. While it has been a regional center for the cattle ranching industry, it also has a lengthy history of hosting a major energy economy. At the New Rifle Mill, two miles south of the city, the Union Carbide Corporation (UCC) produced uranium and vanadium concentrates, and processed uranium ore from 1958 to 1970. The city then experienced the oil shale boom and bust of the 1970s and 1980s. UCC's uranium was sold to the Atomic Energy Commission (AEC), and the vanadium was delivered to the commercial market for use in steel and other products.

"While the AEC terminated its last contract with UCC in 1970, the Mill continued to produce uranium for the commercial market until 1972, and produced vanadium concentrate until 1984. During these years, about 2.5 million tons of radioactive tailings were accumulated at the site, and the groundwater was contaminated with uranium, vanadium, arsenic, molybdenum, nitrate, and selenium.

"In 1978, Congress passed the Uranium Mill Tailings Radiation Control Act that required the U.S. Department of Energy to clean up 24 inactive uranium ore processing properties, including New Rifle. After the plant closed, the State of Colorado acquired the 130-acre Mill site in 1988. Encapsulation of the waste radioactive materials began in the spring of 1992 and was completed in 1996, but the site remained idle under state ownership.

"In 2004, the State transferred the property to the City of Rifle, providing the opportunity for the exercise of local initiative. The following year, the City Council adopted Rifle's Economic Opportunities Assessment that re-defined the city as an 'Energy Village.' In pursuit of its new energy identity, the city sought out private sector partners for innovative projects. Rifle subsequently partnered with SunEdison, LLC on two solar energy projects that utilized the old UCC site.

"In December 2008, the city began construction of a wastewater reclamation facility, and SunEdison began the first installation—a 1.72 MW Direct Current (DC) solar PV system, on 12 acres of the property to provide the power needed to operate the plant. Nearby, SunEdison installed the second project—an additional 0.60 MW DC PV solar system, which provides 100 percent of the power needed to pump drinking water from the Colorado River for local residents. SunEdison—not the City of Rifle—financed, constructed, maintains, and monitors both solar power systems.

"The Results—Over the first 20 years of power generation, the two systems will replace more than 76,000 tons of carbon dioxide that would have been emitted by electricity production from fossil fuels. But this environmental benefit is not the only reason why Rifle partnered with SunEdison. Important economic advantages have accrued from these solar projects for the community.

"First and foremost, the City is saving money on its energy bills. Under a 20-year power purchase agreement (PPA), SunEdison will sell power to Rifle at a fixed rate per kilowatt-hour that is below what the city had been paying for its electricity. The savings to the city will likely go up over time, as the fixed rate is compared to the historical trend of rising fossil fuel energy costs. Unlike traditional economic development programs that often rely on businesses or residents to take advantage of incentives, the City's direct control over these projects guaranteed that there would be economic payback.

"Further, the success of the PV projects has encouraged other local land and business owners to pursue their own systems, which has improved their economic well-being. And although job creation was not the primary goal of this work, SunEdison's ongoing maintenance of its PV facilities in the area has added to local employment.

"The initial partnership with SunEdison has also positioned the City to pursue other energy initiatives. The PV projects have served as anchors for Rifle's new Energy Innovation Center—an industrial complex that promotes energy firms that use renewable bio-based materials to produce products and energy. The Center is already home to a new processing plant operated by a local college that is piloting conversion of easily grown mountain crops into biobutanol that can fuel traditional gasoline engines. Eventually, the Center hopes to become a highly visible showcase for other economically implementable alternative power sources, and plans also include a bio-based research and visitor center, an energy feedstock storage area, and gathering space for renewable energy conferences. The Center is helping to create green jobs for local residents, and to foster innovation and entrepreneurial opportunity and/or pilot testing. All of these projects and the sectoral clustering serve as marketing and branding tools, facilitating the emergence of Rifle as a model for a clean energy local economy" (EERE, 2013: 11–12).

The Jobs and Economic Development Impact (JEDI) model system developed by the National Renewable Energy Laboratory (NREL) provides a good conceptual resource for understanding the economic impacts of concentrated solar power development. Based on a generic JEDI simulation for a 100 MW concentrated solar power system located in California, it is estimated that local economic impacts would produce 2,613 jobs having a total impact (earnings and value added impact) of approximately $610.3 million. As far as an annual postconstruction local economic impact, a total of ninety-seven full-time equivalent jobs and approximately $14.83 million in new local economic purchasing power (in 2018 dollars) can be expected (NREL, 2018c).

FEDERAL SOLAR ENERGY TECHNOLOGIES PROGRAM

With natural gas supplies projected to last for about ninety years (EIA, 2018), it is unlikely that solar energy will come to dominate the U.S. electric energy portfolio in the near future. Currently, solar PV and CSP provide approximately 2 percent of grid-quality electricity. As some point, however, a replacement energy source must be found to match the energy demands currently placed on hydrocarbon sources. It is better to have multiple supply options available rather than only a handful, and it is better to have well-developed options rather than unproven alternatives. In the postindustrial Third Way political and economic environment, U.S. energy policy history indicates that the responsibility falls on government *and* the private sector work together to pursue a seamless transition to a new energy paradigm, continuously monitoring energy needs in relation to energy supply options. In the U.S. system of governance, federal, state, and local efforts are required to coordinate public policy—in this case, alternative/renewable energy policy.

At the federal level, one program seeking to promote continued research into ever more efficient solar energy systems is the Solar Energy Technology Program (SETO). The program's goals are as follows:

- Supports early-stage research and development to improve affordability, reliability, and performance of solar technologies on the grid.
- Invests in innovative research efforts that securely integrate more solar into the grid, enhance the use and storage of solar energy, and lower solar electricity costs.
- Strategically [address] critical research gaps, ensuring the solar industry has the technological foundations necessary to continue growth and preserve American energy choice, independence, and security. (Quoted from https://www.energy.gov/eere/solar/about-solar-energy-technologies-office, accessed July 14, 2018)

According to the program's analysis, solar energy costs have declined significantly but still remain above the cost of hydrocarbon energy sources. Projections indicate that cost will remain either slightly higher than or at parity with carbon-based fuel costs for quite some time, assuming that current carbon-based electricity generation systems maintain current price levels.

SETO seeks to streamline market processes to advance solar energy potential in the near future. Program leaders intend to use a systematic approach to R & D in the solar industry and to promote the use of solar energy by commercial enterprises as a form of supplemental energy for factories and offices. The program also expects to coordinate and/or monitor the solar industry in various manufacturing and retail subsectors, ranging from "materials" and "component" manufacturing to "applications" and "markets" (see https://www.energy.gov/eere/solar/about-solar-energy-technologies-office, accessed July 14, 2018). University and private industry partnerships with the Solar Energy Technologies Office are encouraged through grant opportunities and collaborative research and development contracts.

SETO operates through five subprograms:

- Photovoltaics: "The photovoltaics subprogram works with industry, academia, national laboratories, and other government agencies to advance solar PV. This team supports research and development to aggressively advance PV technology by improving efficiency, energy yield, reliability and lowering manufacturing costs. The office's PV portfolio spans work from early-stage solar cell research through technology commercialization, including work on materials, processes, and device structure and characterization techniques."
- Concentrating Solar Thermal Power: "The concentrating solar thermal power (CSP) subprogram supports the development of novel CSP technologies that will help to lower cost, increase efficiency, and provide more reliable performance when compared to current technologies. These projects demonstrate new concepts in the collector, receiver, thermal storage, heat transfer fluids, and power cycle subsystems, as well as technologies that will lower operations and management costs. The CSP subprogram is most interested in transformative concepts with the potential to break through existing performance barriers, such as efficiency and temperature limitations."
- Systems Integration: "The systems integration subprogram works to enable the widespread deployment of safe, reliable, and cost effective solar energy on the nation's electricity grid by addressing the associated technical challenges and regulatory requirements. The systems integration team focuses on the research and development of cost effective technologies and solutions that enable the sustainable and holistic integration of hundreds of gigawatts of solar generation onto the power grid."
- Soft Costs: "The soft costs subprogram works to develop strategies and solutions that directly reduce the costs and barriers to solar access and deployment. It supports leaders at the local level in developing innovative strategies and solutions that make going solar faster, cheaper, and easier. DOE-funded programs build networks to support the development and diffusion of proven and effective programs that establish clear pathways for sustainable solar deployment across the U.S."
- Technology to Market: "The technology to market subprogram—also known as Innovations in Manufacturing Competitiveness—investigates and validates groundbreaking, early-stage technology, software, and business models to strengthen early-stage concepts and move them toward readiness for greater private sector investment and scale-up to commercialization. Technology to market targets two significant funding gaps: funding of initial proof of concept and the pre-commercial stage. The subprogram funds projects that address innovations in solar, energy grid, technology performance, supply chain, and manufacturing."

(Quoted from https://www.energy.gov/eere/solar/about-solar-energy-technologies-office, accessed July 14, 2018)

The SETO 2018 budget request was approximately $69.7 million for FY 2018, constituting approximately 11 percent of the budget for the Office of Energy Efficiency and Renewable Energy. In comparison to the 2017 annualized continuing resolution budget, EERE and SETO will experience a 69.3 percent budget cut. In terms of national political priorities, this major reduction in funding would indicate that the EERE and the SETO programs are not a high priority in national energy policy under the Trump administration (https://www.energy.gov/cfo/downloads/ fy-2018-budget-justification, accessed July 14, 2018).

The SETO (and EERE) budget cut is not a function of program failures. In fact, SETO has been a highly successful program by virtually all accounts. Perhaps its greatest accomplishment was its SunShot Initiative. First launched in 2011, the SunShot Initiative established the ambitious goal of making solar electricity cost-competitive with conventional sources of electricity. The SunShot Initiative report concludes that if Initiative recommendations are followed, it is possible that over a quarter (27 percent) of the U.S. electricity demand could be met by solar by 2050.

SunShot focused on systems integration, technology development, and markets. In terms of systems integration, SunShot identified the need to increase grid-flexibility options in integrating solar electricity onto the grid, as well as the use of high-capacity inverter technology and smart grid systems to manage load. SunShot worked closely with the FERC to improve the interconnection of solar from small generators to the energy grid. SunShot financially supported efforts to use machine learning technology to better forecast solar radiation patterns. The 2011 report recommends continued investment in advanced science and technology R & D to drive down system costs and increase efficiency. In the area of technological development, SunShot created the Foundational Program to Advance Cell Efficiency (F-PACE) to encourage the development and commercialization of high-efficiency solar cells, some of which were referenced earlier in this chapter. SunShot also funded research for high-efficiency heat transfer technology to be used in CSP applications.

Finally, SunShot sought to financially help small solar technology start-up companies working with promising technologies. According to SunShot, for every dollar of public investment, $22 in private investment follow-on funding occurred, leading to the creation of thousands of jobs in the solar industry (SETO, 2016: 8). In terms of market-enabling efforts, SunShot facilitated efforts to bring together key stakeholders in an effort to standardize interconnection methods and facilitate permitting. The program sought to reduce per-unit costs through group purchasing of solar technology. SunShot also helped local energy cooperatives by offering preset solar engineering designs for solar PV systems, thus reducing costs in system development and reducing time to installation and use.

Despite having to cope with tremendous budget cuts to solar energy programs operated through the Office of Energy Efficiency and Renewable Energy, the federal government's investment and production tax credits—at least for the time being—remain in place. Future presidents and national legislative majorities may find value in renewing public investment in this area of high proven potential for the provision of clean energy.

MAJOR FEDERAL SOLAR INCENTIVES

Federal laws and regulations related to solar PV and solar thermal energy can be divided into commercial incentives and personal incentives.

Commercial Incentives

The Solar Investment Tax Credit (ITC) is one of the major policy instruments used to encourage the development of solar energy in the United States. The investment tax credit was extended by the Bipartisan Budget Act of 2018 (P.L. 115–123). Currently, the solar tax credit allows for tax deduction claims up to 30 percent of the cost of a solar PV system in the tax year in which it begins operation. Solar PV systems that begin construction by the end of December 2019 can claim a 30 percent deduction. The proportion deducted will scale down accordingly, as shown in table 4.1.

Other tax stipulations required that the system must be used by individuals or corporate entities subject to U.S. income tax; the system must be operated in the United States or U.S. territories; it must be new equipment; and it must not be used for heating swimming pools. Allowable expenses related to the system include the solar PV panels, installations costs and related equipment, and energy storage devices. When making a federal tax claim on your annual taxes, after the solar PV system has been installed and is operational, use IRS Form 3468. According to the IRS, it will take an estimated thirty hours to learn the basis of the law, follow IRS form instructions, and complete the form.

Created under the Energy Policy Act of 1992, the corporate production tax credit (PTC) for renewable energy production faces challenges in the years ahead. In terms of solar PV and solar thermal systems, the PTC applies only to systems that commenced construction before January 1, 2018, and applies only to the first ten years of operation. The PTC is inflation adjusted and currently is $0.023/kWh. There is no maximum on the PTC rebate. It was renewed in the Bipartisan Budget Act of 2018. Future electoral outcomes at the federal level

Table 4.1   Federal Commercial Solar Tax Credits

Commence Construction by	Claimed Deduction of System Cost
December 31, 2020	26 percent
December 31, 2021	22 percent
December 31, 2022, and after	10 percent

will likely shape the future of the PTC. The IRS paperwork to be consulted for the PTC are IRS Form 8835 ("Renewable Energy Production Credit") and IRS Form 3800 ("General Business Tax Credit").

When the PTC and ITC were both in place for solar PV and solar thermal systems installed prior to January 1, 2018, commercial operators could only file for PTC or ITC, but not both (see Bolinger et al., 2009; Pfahl, 2010). At the moment, that issue is easily resolved for solar PV and solar thermal systems commencing operations after January 1, 2018, as the ITC remains, but the PTC no longer applies. The downside to this outcome is that demand for solar PV and solar thermal may decline as the ITC for solar PV and solar thermal declines and as PTC for existing systems begins to sunset in the decade ahead.

Personal Tax Incentives for Solar PV and Solar Thermal

Under the Bipartisan Budget Act of 2018, personal tax credits remain in place for small residential solar PV and for solar thermal (a solar hot water heater). The system must be used by a U.S. residence, but does not have to be the taxpayer's primary residence. All costs associated with installation and equipment are considered "costs" when the system is installed and becomes operational. The amount that can be deducted is based on when the system begins service (see 26 USC §136). See table 4.2.

Table 4.2   Solar PV and Solar Thermal

System in Service by	Tax Credit
December 31, 2019	30 percent
After December 31, 2019, but before January 1, 2021	26 percent
After December 21, 2020, but before January 1, 2022	22 percent

Note: Other requirements for eligibility can be found at: programs.desireusa.org/system/program/detail/1235, accessed July 16, 2018.

Notice, this differs from commercial ITCs, which are based on when project construction commences. Under the personal tax credit, there is no maximum deduction. While solar PV systems are not required to provide a certain percentage of the homeowner's primary electrical load, solar thermal (solar hot water heaters) must provide at least half the hot water used in the residence. In addition to ITC and PTC, the federal government also provides financial incentives or subsidies for customers of public utilities who meet eligibility requirements to help finance solar PV.

STATE AND LOCAL EFFORTS

State and local efforts are often grounded on renewable energy portfolio standards (RPS), which establish green energy consumption targets, as well as loan and tax incentive-based programs focusing specifically on solar energy use. RPSs shape markets by creating new incentives and constraints, ultimately shaping consumer behavior in the energy market. Tax incentive policies steer policy makers and citizens toward new types of energy purchase decisions.

The top five states in terms of total solar energy capacity are (Levin, 2018)

- California (17.3 MW)
- North Carolina (3.3 MW)
- Arizona (3.0 MW)
- Nevada (2.1 MW)
- New Jersey (1.9 MW)

California

With over five times the solar capacity of any other U.S. state, the state of California leads the nation in the purchasing of solar energy systems. With the passage of the Solar Rights Act (SRA) of 1978, California demonstrated an early commitment to solar energy development and to the promotion of the use of solar power. The SRA prevented homeowners associations (HOAs) from imposing limits on the use of solar energy systems by residents of an HOA. Subsequent laws provide for solar easements for homeowners whose solar panels are shaded by shrubs and trees on adjacent properties. California has also adopted a renewable portfolio standard mandating that by 2030, 50 percent of electricity used in the state must be from renewable energy sources (CPUC Code §399.11). Property tax incentives are offered to energy producers (CA Civil Code §801.5) through 2024. Under the California Revenue and Taxation Code, property tax assessments are not levied on state-approved solar energy systems. Additionally, the state offers a variety of Supplemental Energy Payments (SEPs) to alternative/renewable energy producers who receive below-market prices for energy sales to utilities; the SEP brings total energy payments up to market prices for energy sold to electricity consumers.

With a growing portion of electricity produced in California coming from renewable energy sources (27 percent), such as solar PV and solar thermal (10 percent), the state legislature acted in a timely manner to prevent market distortion. California State Senate Bill SB 2 (Statutes of 2011, Chapter 1) mandates that the California Energy Commission (CES) "establish a limitation for each electrical corporation on the procurement expenditures for all eligible renewable energy resources used to comply with the [State] renewable portfolio standard." SB 2 was followed up with a 2015 bill, SB 350 (Statutes of 2015 Chapter 547), which further emphasized the need to set supplemental energy payments for renewable energy at a per kWh level that prevents market distortion. In addition to SEP incentives, California's net metering regulation allows for 100 percent of (in this instance) solar electricity produced by a commercial, residential, nonprofit, or state/federal government entity (in California) to be sold on the grid and receive credit on their power bills (with the sole exception of the Los Angeles Department of Water and Power). In 2016, the California Public Utility Commission (CPUC) placed limits on the amount of credit small producers (10 kW systems and smaller) could receive for their system output (CPUC, 2016).

Honolulu, Hawai'i

As of 2017, San Diego was the number one city in the United States in terms of solar PV capacity, and Honolulu was the number one city in the United States in terms of solar PV capacity per capita (Bradford et al., 2017). Honolulu solar development is a clear recognition of the unique challenges faced by a major city in an island state with limited access to fossil energy needed for power generation. Perhaps more importantly, Honolulu and Hawai'i, in a more general sense, are seeking energy solutions that are green, reduce water consumption, and prevent water and air quality degradation. Honolulu residents pay nearly three times more for their electricity compared to the average customer in the rest of the United States. On a state-by-state basis, the average household electricity customer in the United States pays 13.57 cents per kWh, whereas the average customer in Hawai'i pays 32.05 cents per kWh (EIA, 2018e). As the largest city and state capital, Honolulu is leading the way toward the statewide renewable energy portfolio goal of 100 percent renewable energy by 2045. Honolulu benefits largely from state policy initiatives rather than simply local-level efforts. The state solar rights law follows the same guidelines as those set forth in California's state law. The state of Hawai'i also has commercial and residential tax credits of up to 35 percent of qualified system costs for solar thermal (solar hot water heaters) and solar PV systems up to a set maximum incentive, which varies depending upon technology (see State of Hawai'i, Department of Taxation, 2012, HRS §235-12.5).

While the state of Hawai'i began permitting net metering in 2001, that policy changed in 2015 when net metering came to an end. The main power company in the island-chain state—Hawai'i Electric Company—had claimed repeatedly that the power grid could not handle the surge in electricity production taking place during the daytime hours. In addition to ending the net metering benefit, the state also limited the number of qualified projects that can export surplus power to the grid, as well as the amount electricity exported. The result has been a sharp decline in solar installations and a shrinking of the solar PV and solar thermal industry in Hawai'i, particularly on the island of Oahu where Honolulu is located (Wesoff, 2018).

CHAPTER SUMMARY

Solar energy policy relies heavily on consumer awareness of a product, its benefits and its costs. Despite citizen/consumer benefit structures that have been put in place through public policy innovations, citizens' energy choices are increasingly moving in the direction of solar energy. Full understanding of the increasingly seamless technological interface of solar energy systems, and residential and commercial energy demand may not be fully understood by potential consumers. The technology behind solar energy policy is conceptually solid, and continues to improve as efficiency ratings approach 40 percent, which means that smaller systems are effectively meeting load demands. The economics behind solar energy also remain quite solid, with national, state, and local government incentives in place as well as the growing presence of a substantial domestic solar energy system production infrastructure. As fossil energy prices continue to rise, citizens/consumers are likely to increasingly find that costs for solar energy alternatives may be a viable solution to meet their energy needs and a significant way in which individuals can contribute to community sustainability.

NOTES

1. Data from https://www.eia.gov/totalenergy/data/monthly/pdf/sec1_7.pdf, June 10, 2019.

2. The first photovoltaics developed at Bell Laboratories used boron substrates (see Green 2000, 443).

3. Source: https://www.energy.gov/eere/solar/solar-energy-technologies-office, June 10, 2019.

4. In a typical comparative solar cell study, Fanney et al. (2002: 2) employed 6mm glass plating, which reduces collector efficiencies but protects solar cells from damage. Fanney et al. found that the conversion efficiency controlling for cell area was highest for monocrystalline cells, ranging from 10.5 percent to 12.5 percent. Thin film cell efficiency ranged from 4.8 percent to 6.9 percent. The efficiencies reported illustrate the variations in cell efficiencies probably related to the methodology of study and local conditions of study. Amphorous silicon can be used in thin film cells. Unlike crystalline formation, amphorous silicon can be produced by super-heating silicon and then rapidly cooling it in thin sheets. Crystalline formations are more likely to establish collector points based on uniformity of doped silicon, but crystalline formations—particularly monocrystalline silicon—is more expensive to produce. Material development and use is, at least partially, a function of economic trade-offs.

5. Other types of materials are being actively explored by solar technology researchers. One type of material that will be of future interest to manufacturers and users of solar energy is found in the plants that surround us: chlorophyll. Material scientists have explored the value of chlorophyll as a material for collecting electricity in a solar cell and have produced evidence of success. Yun et al. (2005) created a chlorophyll-based solar cell with a conversion efficiency of 1.48 percent. As a material, chlorophyll is abundant. With continued technical development, it could be a technically efficient and effective method of collecting energy for meeting electrical energy load demands. The technical achievement is consistent with other research being conducted in materials science, applied physics, and electrical engineering that have successfully advanced the solar energy paradigm beyond crystalline silicon.

6. To provide some perspective, one BTU is the amount of energy required to raise one pound of water 1°F. Dry wood contains 7,000 BTUs of potential energy per pound (see http://bbq.about.com/od/gasgrills/g/gbtu.htm, accessed June 21, 2005).

REFERENCES

Abraham, M. 2005. Engineers pioneer affordable alternative energy resources—solar cells made of everyday plastic. *News Center: Henry Samueli School of Engineering and Applied Science, UCLA,* October 10. http://www.engineer.ucla.edu/news/2005/plasticsolarcells.html, accessed March 11, 2006.

Ahn, N., Son, D., Jang, I., Kang, S., Choi, M., and Park, N. 2015. Highly reproducible Perovskite solar cells with average efficiency of 18.3% and best efficiency of 19.7% fabricated via Lewis base adduct of lead (II) iodide. *Journal of the American Chemical Society* 137: 8696–8699.

Barreto, G., and Canhoto, P. 2017. Modelling a Stirling engine with parabolic dish for thermal to electric conversion of solar energy. *Energy Conversion & Management* 132: 119–135.

Bolinger, M., Wiser, R., Corey, K., and James, T. 2009. PTC, ITC, or cash grant? An analysis of the choice facing renewable power projects in the United States. *Ernest Orlando Lawrence Berkeley National Laboratory,* LBNL-1642E/NREL/TP-6A2-45359. Retrieved from https://www.nrel.gov/docs/fy09osti/45359.pdf, July 16, 2018.

Bradford, A., Weissman, G., Sargent, R., and Fanshaw, B. 2017. *Shining Cities 2017: How Smart Local Policies Are Expanding Solar Power in America.* Denver, CO: Environment America Research and Policy Center. Retrieved from https://environmentamerica.org/sites/environment/files/cpn/AMN-033117-REPORT/shining-cities-2017.html, July 17, 2018.

Cai, W., Gong, X., and Cao, Y. 2010. Polymer solar cells: Recent development and possible routes for improvement in the performance. *Solar Energy Materials and Solar Cells* 94: 114–127.

California Public Utilities Commission. 2016. Decision 16-04-020: Decision adopting net energy metering bill credit estimation methodology for generating facilities paired with small storage devices, April 28. San Francisco, CA: CPUC.

Campbell, B., and Pape, A. 1999. *Economic Development from Renewable Energy: Yukon Opportunities.* Drayton Valley, Alberta, Canada: The Pembina Institute.

Cascade Solar Consulting. 2005. Solar Starter Guide. http://www.cascadesolar.com/ssguide.pdf, accessed June 23, 2005.

Collado, F., and Guallar, J. 2019. Quick design of regular heliostat fields for commercial solar tower power plants. *Energy* 178: 115–125.

Day Star Technologies. 2004. Products, http://www.abanet.org/media/faqjury.html, accessed June 20, 2005.

Dvorsky, G. 2016. Dubai is building the world's largest concentrated solar power plant. *Gizmodo,* June 6. Retrieved from https://gizmodo.com/dubai-is-building-the-worlds-largest-concentrated-solar-1780781150, July 13, 2018.

Eckhouse, B., Natter, A., and Martin, C. 2018. President Trump slaps tariffs on solar panels in major blow to renewable energy. *Time,* January 22. Retrieved from https://time.com/5113472/donald-trump-solar-panel-tariff/, July 22, 2019.

Energy Efficiency and Renewable Energy. 2005. Electrical Contracts. http://www.eere.energy.gov/solar/electrical_contacts.html, accessed June 17, 2005.

———. 2013. Spurring local economic development with clean energy investments: lessons from the field. Washington, DC: Energy Efficiency and Renewable Energy. Retrieved from https://www.energy.gov/sites/prod/files/2014/05/f15/clean_energy_investment_cases.pdf, July 14, 2018.

————. 2018. *Solar Energy in the United States*. Retrieved from https://www.energy. gov/eere/solarpoweringamerica/solar-energy-united-states, July 9, 2018.

Energy Information Administration. 2003. *Renewable Energy Annual*. Washington, DC: U.S. Department of Energy, http://www.eia.doe.gov/cneaf/solar.renewables/ page/rea_data/rea_sum.html, accessed June 17, 2005.

————. 2017. *Electric Power Annual*. Retrieved from https://www.eia.gov/electricity/ annual/, July 9, 2018.

————. 2018a. *Total Energy*. Washington, DC: U.S. Department of Energy. Retrieved from https://www.eia.gov/totalenergy/, July 9, 2018.

————. 2018b. *Electric Power Monthly—April, 2018*. Retrieved from https://www.eia. gov/electricity/monthly/epm_table_grapher.php?t=epmt_ 1_01_a, July 9, 2018.

————. 2018c. *Solar Photovoltaic Cell/Module Shipments Report*. Retrieved from https:// www.eia.gov/renewable/annual/solar_photo/, July 10, 2018.

————. 2018d. *Gas Explained: How Much Natural Gas Is Left*. Retrieved from https:// www.eia.gov/energyexplained/index.php? page=natural_gas_reserves, July 14, 2018.

————. 2018e. *Rankings: Average Retail Price of Electricity to Residential Sector, March 2018 (cents/kWh)* http://www.eia.gov/electricity/monthly, November 13, 2019.

————. 2019. EIA forecasts renewable will be the fastest growing source of electricity generation. *Energy Information Administration*, January 18. Retrieved from https://www.eia.gov/todayinenergy/detail.php?id =38053, June 10, 2019.

Fanney, A., Dougherty, B., and Davis, M. 2002. Performance and characterization of building integrated photovoltaic panels. *Proceedings of the 28th Annual IEEE Photovoltaic Specialists Conference*. May 20–24, New Orleans, LA.

Garcia-Ortiz, J., Gonzalez, I., and Gonzalez, C. 2018. Luter system a new approach to CSP energy diversification. *Renewable and Sustainable Energy Reviews* 82: 2106–2111.

Green, M. 2000. Silicon solar cells: At the crossroads. *Progress in Photovoltaics: Research and Applications* 8: 443–450.

Green, M., Emery, K., Hishikawa, Y., Warta, W., and Dunlop, E. 2015. Solar cell efficiency tables (version 45). *Progress in Photovoltaics: Research and Applications* 23: 1–9.

Han, D. 1998. *Experimental Study of the Factors Governing the Staebler-Wronski Photodegradation Effect in a-Si: H Solar Cells*. Golden, CO: National Renewable Energy Laboratory.

Harrington, R. 2015. This incredible fact should get you psyched about solar power. *Business Insider*, September 29. Retrieved from https://www. businessinsider.com/ this-is-the-potential-of-solar-power-2015–9, July 21, 2019.

Honolulu Electric Company 2005. Honolulu Solar Roofs Initiative Loan Program. http://www.heco.com, accessed June 23, 2005.

Hughes, D. 2003. Policy uses of economic multiplier and impact analysis. *Choices* 2: 25–29.

Islam, M., and Morimoto, T. 2018. Advances in low to medium temperature non-concentrating solar thermal technology. *Renewable and Sustainable Energy Reviews* 82: 2066–2093.

Jørgensen, M., Norrman, K., Gevorgyan, S., Thomholt, T., Andreasen, B., and Krebs, F. 2012. Stability of polymer solar cells. *Advanced Materials* 24: 580–612.

Kaltenbrunner, M., White, M., Glowacki, E., Sekitani, T., Someya, T., Sariciftci, S., and Bauer, S. 2012. Ultrathin and lightweight organic solar cells with high flexibility. *Nature Communications* 3.770.19.1038/ncomms1772: 1–7.

Kazmerski, L., and Broussard, K. 2004. *Solar Photovoltaic Hydrogen: The Technologies and Their Place in Our Roadmaps and Energy Economics*. Prepared for the 19th Annual European PV Solar Energy Conference and Exhibition. Golden, CO: National Renewable Energy Laboratory, August. NREL/CP-520–36401.

Keane, J. 2014. *Pico-solar Electric Systems: The Earthscan Expert Guide to the Technology and Emerging Market*. New York: Routledge.

Lenardic, Denis. 2005. A walk through time. PV Resources.com, http://www.pvresources.com/en/history.php, accessed June 18, 2005.

Levin, A. 2018. A state-by-state view of U.S. renewable energy in 2017. *Solar Industry Magazine*, March 1. Retrieved from https://solarindustrymag.com/state-state-view-u-s-renewable-energy-2017/, July 17, 2018.

Lipomi, D., Tee, B., Vosgueritchian, M., and Bao, Z. 2011. Stretchable organic solar cells. *Advanced Materials* 23: 1771–1775.

Maui Electric Company. 2005. Welcome to Maui Electric! http://www.mauielectric.com/ MECO/page/, accessed June 23, 2005.

McMahon, T. J. 2004. Accelerated testing and failure of thin-film PV modules. *Progress in Photovoltaics: Research and Applications* 12, 235–248.

Mesquita, I., Andrade, L., & Mendes, A. 2018. Perovskite solar cells: Materials, configurations, and stability. *Renewable and Sustainable Energy Reviews* 82: 2471–2489.

National Renewable Energy Laboratory (NREL). 2018a. *Solar Maps*. Retrieved from https://www.nrel.gov/gis/solar.html, accessed July 9, 2018.

———. 2018b. *Concentrating Solar Projects in the United States*. Golden, CO: NREL. Retrieved from https://www.nrel.gov/csp/solarpaces/by_country_detail.cfm/country=US%20(%22_self%22), July 13, 2018.

———. 2018c. *JEDI Concentrating Solar Power Model*. Golden, CO: NREL. Retrieved from https://www.nrel.gov/analysis/ jedi/csp.html, July 14, 2018.

———. 2019. *Solar Maps*. Retrieved from https://www.nrel.gov/gis/solar.html, October 28, 2019.

Nazeeruddin, M., Baranoff, E., and Grätzel, M. 2011. Dye-sensitized solar cells: A brief overview. *Solar Energy* 85: 1172–1178.

Ong, S., Campbell, C, Denholm, P., Margolis, R., and Heath, G. 2013. *Land Use Requirements for Solar Power Plants in the United States*, NREL/TP-6A20-56290. Golden, CO: National Renewable Energy Laboratory. Retrieved from https://www.nrel.gov/docs/fy13osti/56290.pdf, June 10, 2019.

Parke, P., and Giles, C. 2018. Morocco's megawatt solar plant powers up. *CNN*, May 17. Retrieved from https://www.cnn.com/2016/02/08/africa/ouarzazate-morocco-solar-plant/index.html, July 13, 2018.

Pfahl, G. 2010. ITC or PTC for your renewable energy project? *Renewable Energy World*, July 19. Retrieved from https://www.renewableenergyworld.com/articles/2010/07/itc-or-ptc-for-your-renewable-energy-project.html, July 16, 2018.

Pique, A., Auyeung, R., Kim, H., Charipar, N., and Mathews, S. 2016. Laser 3D micro-manufacturing. *Journal of Physics D: Applied Physics* 49: 1–24.

Riches, Derrick. 2005. BTU. http://bbq.about.com/od/gasgrills/g/gbtu.htm, accessed June 21, 2005.

Sahagun, L. 2016. This Mojave Desert solar plant kills 6,000 birds a year. Here's why that won't change any time soon. *Los Angeles Times*, September 2. Retrieved from https://www.latimes.com/local/california/la-me-solar-bird-deaths-20160831-snap-story.html, July 22, 2019.

Schwer, R., and Riddel, M. 2004. *The Potential Economic Impact of Constructing and Operating Solar Power Generation Facilities in Nevada*. NREL/SR-550–35037. Golden, CO: National Renewable Energy Laboratories.

Smith, Charles. 1995. History of solar energy: Revisiting solar power's past, Solarenergy, http://www.solarenergy.com/info_history.html, accessed June 17, 2005 [see also Smith 1995, Solar Power, in *Technology Review*].

Snaith, H. 2013. Perovskites: The emergence of a new era of low-cost, high efficiency solar cells. *The Journal of Physical Chemistry Letters* 4: 3623–3630.

Solar Energy Industries Association. 2019. Solar market insight report: 2018 year in review. *Solar Energy Industries Association*, Retrieved from https://www.seia.org/research-resources/solar-market-insight-report-2018-year-review, June 10, 2019.

Solar Energy Technologies Office. 2016. On the path to SunShot: Executive summary. Retrieved from https://www.energy.gov/sites/prod/files/2016/05/f31/OTPSS%20-%20Executive%20Summary-508.pdf, July 14, 2018.

Solar Industries Association. 2019. Solar Industry Research Data. Retrieved from https://www.seia.org/solar-industry-research-data, July 22, 2019.

State of Hawai'i, Department of Taxation. 2012. *Renewable Energy Technologies Income Tax Credit (RETITC)-HRS §235-12.5*. Honolulu, HI: Department of Taxation. Retrieved from http://tax.hawaii.gov/geninfo/renewable/, July 17, 2018.

Sundararajan, A. 2016. *The Sharing Economy: The End of Employment and the Rise of Crowd-Based Capitalism*. Cambridge, MA: MIT Press.

Tong, J., Song, Z., Kim, D., Chen, X., Chen, C., Palmstrom, A., Ndione, P., Reese, M., Dunfield, S., Reid, O., Liu, J., Zhang, F., Harvey, S., Li, Z., Christensen, S., Teeter, G., Zhao, D., Al-Jassim, M., Van Hest, M., Beard, M., Shaheen, S., Berry, J., Yan, Y., and Zhu, K. 2019. Carrier lifetimes of >1 μs in Sn-Pb perovskites enable efficient all-perovskite tandem solar cells. *Science* 364(6439): 475–479.

Tool, C., Burgers, A., Manshanden, P., Weeber, A., and van Straaten, B. 2002. Influence of wafer thickness on the performance of multicrystalline Si solar cells: An experimental study. *Progress in Photovoltaics: Research and Applications* 10: 279–291.

Tripanagnostopoulos, Y., Soutliotis, M, Battisti, R., and Corrado, A. 2005. Energy, cost and LCA results of PV and Hybrid PV/T solar systems. *Progress in Photovoltaics: Research and Applications* 13, 235–250.

U.S. Department of Energy. 1996. The jobs connection: Energy use and local economic development. *Tomorrow's Energy Today for Cities and Counties*. Washington, DC: U.S. Department of Energy.

Wesoff, E. 2018. Rooftop solar in Oahu crashes with loss of net metering, lack of self-supply installs. *Green Tech Media*, February 7. Retrieved from https://www.greentechmedia.com/articles/read/rooftop-solar-in-hawaii-crashes-with-loss-of-net-metering-lack-self-supply#gs.cH_P2jc, July 17, 2018.

Wiesenfarth, M., Philipps, S., Bett, A., Horowitz, K., and Kurtz, S. 2017. *Current Status of Concentrator Photovoltaic (CPV) Technology*. Golden, CO: National Renewable Energy Laboratory.

Würfel, P. 2005. *Physics of Solar Cells: From Principles to New Concepts*. Berlin, Germany: Wiley-VCH.

Yun, J., Jung, H., Kim, S., Han, E., Vaithianathan, V., and Jenekhe, S. 2005. Chlorophyll-layer-inserted poly(3-hexyl-thiophene) solar cell having a high light-to-current conversion efficiency of up to 1.48%. *Applied Physics Letters* 87(2): 12–14.

Zheng, Guang Fu, Wenham, Stuart R., and Green, Martin A. 1998. Short communication: 17.6% efficient multilayer thin-film silicon solar cells deposited on heavily doped silicon substrates. *Progress in Photovoltaics: Research and Applications* 4(5): 369–373.

Zhou, H., Yang, L., and You, W. 2012. Rational design of high performance conjugated polymers for organic solar cells. *Macromolecules* 45: 607–632.

5

Wind Energy

★ ★ ★

Wind energy is one of the oldest forms of energy used by humankind. Today, wind energy is a critical part of the renewable energy paradigm and is primarily used to generate electricity. In the 1970s and early 1980s there was tremendous growth in R & D funding for wind energy in the United States, as suppliers and consumers sought an expansion of the energy supply base (Wind Energy Technologies Office, 2019). The cost of wind energy is declining due, in large part, to improved siting technology; better wind blade control and structure; and advancements in turbine technology. While U.S. energy policy featured a reduced commitment to wind energy development during the late 1980s, that commitment has experienced a clear resurgence in the years following the passage of the EPAct 1992. Internationally, China, India, and several Western European nations have made significant progress in the development of wind energy technology. Currently, China has 168 GW installed wind energy capacity, while the United States has more than 84 GW of wind energy capacity with four U.S. states—Iowa, Kansas, Oklahoma, and South Dakota—accounting for more than 30 percent of state electricity demand being met by wind energy (Hill, 2018). According to the American Wind Energy Association, by the end of the third quarter of 2017 the United States had a wind energy capacity of 84,944 MW. To illustrate the tremendous growth in wind energy capacity, the United States had 4,147 MW capacity in 2001—meaning that there has been an approximate increase of 1,950 percent in wind energy capacity in fewer than twenty years (AWEA, 2018) (figure 5.1).

WHAT IS WIND POWER? HOW DOES IT WORK?

Nearly 7,000 years ago in the Middle East and Egypt, wind energy was used extensively to operate mills to grind grains. In the United States, windmills were used well into the twentieth century to operate mills and to pump groundwater, but these structures were largely replaced by steam and electrical power. The

Figure 5.1   Wind Electricity Production (2009–2018)

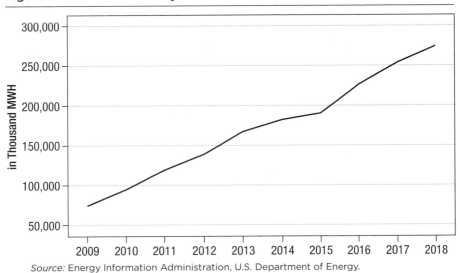

Source: Energy Information Administration, U.S. Department of Energy.

Rural Electrification Act of 1936 (7 USC 31) provided relatively cheap, reliable, and abundant hydroelectricity to many rural areas, making wind generation an inferior energy generation system for the modern age (figures 5.2 and 5.3).

Figure 5.2   Wind System Design

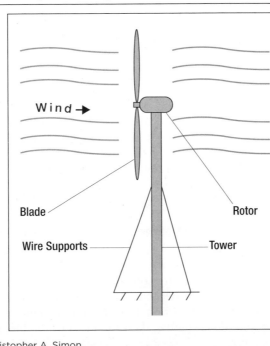

Source: Christopher A. Simon.

Figure 5.3 Wind Turbine Blades

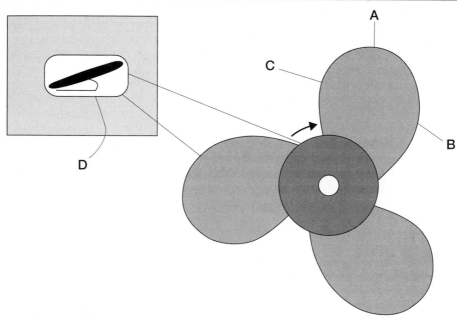

Courtesy of the author

Wind power systems have at least three major structural components: propeller blades, rotors, and support towers. Blades for wind power systems operate on the same principles used to construct blades for propeller-driven aircraft and for ships' propellers.

Important parts of a propeller:

- blade tip (A): the very end of a propeller blade. Blade tip to center of rotor is one way to measure blade length. While the entire blade may be revolving twenty times per minute, the blade tip, due to the length of the blade, might be moving at the speed of 150 mph.
- leading edge (B): the part of the blade with which the wind first comes into contact.
- trailing edge (C): the part of the blade with which the wind is last in contact.
- pitch (D): the angle at which the blade sits, as measured by the imaginary perpendicular line in relation to the wind. Blade pitch depends upon the strength of the wind in sustained wind speed as well in terms of wind gust speed. When the angle (D) becomes larger, then the pitch of the blade is considered deeper, which is typical in wind systems operating in areas with high sustained winds and/or high speed wind gusts. When the angle (D) is smaller, then the pitch of the blade is considered

more shallow, which is often the case when sustained wind speeds are much slower and/or wind gusts are much lighter.

The rotor is the central feature of the blade assembly. At the rotor juncture, blades are attached to the wind power system. Within the rotor assembly, at least two different control and power takeoff processes occur. First, blade pitch control exists within the rotor unit, allowing system operators to adjust pitch depending upon wind speed. Pitch can be controlled automatically in response to variable wind speeds. Second, the rotor assembly contains a system of gears that mechanically increase the rotation speed of the electrical generator or other power takeoff system—the *nacelle*. The nacelle also houses a generator for the production of electricity. Due to the system of gears involved, rotation speeds within the generator unit may reach 1,800 rpm (see U.S. Department of Energy, 2018).

Within the nacelle, generated power fed onto the electrical grid must match the 60 hertz (or cycles per second) of conventional power systems in the United States. In contemporary wind power generation, power takeoff is usually in the form of alternating current (AC). Even in light winds, properly designed propeller blades, often constructed from strong lightweight materials (e.g., aluminum, carbon fiber or fiber glass) maintained at an optimum pitch, are capable of generating significant amounts of electricity.

Wind energy towers are particularly important in the energy generation process. Tower height is often a function of the length of propeller blades

Inside the Nacelle of a Wind Turbine—Gearbox, Axle, and Generator
iStock / Getty Images Plus / CreativeNature_nl

and the size of rotor assembly. Additionally, wind speed analyses at various points above ground level may reveal optimum wind speed conditions and tower height. Propeller blade length must be properly sized and pitched so that efficient wind speeds are captured by wind generation systems, while simultaneously minimizing the impact of wind velocity and turbulence on tower and other wind turbine physical plant harmonics and load (see Preciado et al., 2015). The height of modern wind turbine towers is typically between 200 and 300 feet, and towers are more than ten feet in diameter. Towers are either solid metal structures or feature a lattice design. Towers are well anchored into the ground, and the strength of the anchoring depends on tower size and wind speeds at the generating site. Tower footings may be as much thirty feet deep, composed of steel rebar and hundreds of tons of concrete (National Wind Watch, 2018). Cable support wires may be used to assist in supporting the tower and prevent torsion forces from causing any damaging sway motion. Large-scale wind turbines are assembled on-site, and generally weigh between 160 and 350 tons. According to National Wind Watch, the average large-scale wind turbine requires fifty acres of land per megawatt capacity.

TECHNICAL FEASIBILITY OF WIND POWER SYSTEMS

Depending on site location, wind power is highly feasible because of tremendous technological advancements made in this area. Technological developments discussed in this section will focus attention on materials-related achievements, which have increased the feasibility of wind energy systems placement in a variety of locations. Additionally, the chapter will discuss location decisions that are increasingly well informed because of new wind tracking data systems.

Advancements in materials science have positively impacted virtually all aspects of basic wind energy design, placement, and operations. Propeller technology continues to evolve due to material developments and generation system refinements; this is in part a function of the wider use of wind energy, both domestically and globally. For example, approximately 90 percent of propeller cost is related to materials used in fabrication (Froese, 2017). Different locations require that flexible energy systems meet site-specific requirements. For instance, in locations with very strong winds or particularly high wind gust regions, systems must be designed to resist propeller and tower damage while simultaneously maintaining high levels of efficiency in adequately meeting load requirements. Material fatigue needs to be considered as well. Due to technological developments, wind energy systems can be footed in the ocean with propellers and rotor assemblies placed just above ocean level. In an ocean or sea-air environment, proper materials must be used to resist the corrosive impact of salt water; in desert climates, materials must withstand the impact of intense heat, dry air, and the frequent presence of airborne particulates. Finally, low-wind environments require the use of lightweight materials that will more easily capture the force of the wind and produce usable electrical energy, requiring the use of both lightweight materials and strong bonding adhesives in system fabrication. In other words, turbine design and material use are not uniform across wind energy applications. Materials, project designs, and fabrication processes must be in line with the conditions under which the system operates and must be cost effective.

Early propeller systems were constructed from wood or lightweight metals, such as aluminum. In some instances early on, aircraft propellers were used in wind energy systems. Wooden propellers can be used, although they pose many problems, such as cracking as well as material decomposition due to moisture and degradation from contact with airborne particulate matter and other environmental conditions. Additionally, wooden propellers may be heavy, thus requiring stronger sustained winds for operation. Lighter weight materials—such as aluminum or carbon fiber—may experience fewer problems with decomposition and operate on a wider range of wind speeds.

Early propellers were also "fixed" at a particular pitch. Fixed propellers effectively reduce the range of usable winds for power generation. Light winds might not produce enough revolutions to operate rotors. Conversely, heavier winds might actually result in very high RPMs, resulting in damage to blades, wind turbines, and towers alike.

Load reduction has become a significant issue because wind turbine systems have become larger and their propeller blades longer. Wind does not contact wind turbine systems in a constant flow perpendicular to the blade rotation pattern. "As the turbine blade sweeps around the 'rotor disc,' it experiences

One Propeller Blade on a Semi Truck
iStock / Getty Images Plus / milehightraveler

changes in wind speed and direction as a result of wind shear, tower shadow, yaw misalignment and turbulence. As rotor sizes increase with respect to the typical sizes of turbulent eddies, the importance of turbulent wind speed variations across the rotor disc becomes greater" (Bossanyi, 2003: 119). In order to reduce load on wind turbine systems and reduce the likelihood of system damage, wind energy researchers have developed "intelligent control systems" (Bossanyi, 2003: 119) designed to model asymmetric loads impacting wind turbines, and made automated adjustments to blade pitch on an individual blade basis, turbine direction in relation to the wind flow, and system braking. A complicating factor in wind modeling is the impact of wind turbine wakes on other turbines operating in wind farms. Wind wakes cause wind turbulence and increase wind shear effects and "roughness" (Crespo et al., 1999: 3).

Propeller engineering has addressed some of the aforementioned issues by creating stronger and lighter weight propellers using new generation materials and twenty-first-century production technologies. Contemporary production technologies make use of computer simulation to test system designs based on design specifications and multiple simulated events or conditions. Simulation makes it possible for system optimization to occur before fabrication even begins.

Propellers can be constructed out of hollow balsa wood frames, with well-engineered internal support framing to prevent torque (or twisting) due to wind force impact. Balsa frames are covered with fiberglass to further strengthen the propeller, and lightweight (yet durable), leading edge caps are designed to prevent fiberglass wear or propeller destruction due to impact with flying objects (e.g., birds). With computer wind simulations, it is possible to more efficiently place leading edge caps to effectively protect propellers from damage while reducing material weight. Computer technology also helps engineers more effectively reduce unwanted wind drag on the propeller system. While drag is critical for the propeller to spin, drag may also lead to decreased propeller rotation, thus negatively impacting energy production (see Mohamed, 2004).

Engineers are experimenting with the use of carbon fibers as a coating to be combined with fiberglass or used as a protective and strengthening layer over balsa wood framing. The logic behind the use of carbon fibers is twofold: (a) carbon fibers are lighter weight than fiberglass and its gel coating and (b) carbon fibers are more resilient than fiberglass. Recent studies have shown that carbon fiber propellers exhibit some very promising results, and may reduce replacement and/or operation and maintenance costs for system propellers. However, engineers indicate that continued work is needed to reduce the rates of "flexural, compressive, and fatigue failure" (Swolfs, 2017: 1; see Veers et al., 2003).

Jackson et al. (2005) conducted extensive research comparing the effectiveness of fiberglass and carbon fiber propeller blades, controlling for blade thickness, length, internal propeller stud support, and chord dimensions. Their studies found that increased internal supports reduce the required thickness of fiberglass or carbon fiber lamination; reduced thickness translates into reduced weight and material costs in blade manufacturing. Jackson et al. (2005) also studied the impact of various fiberglass and carbon fiber blades, controlling for the aforementioned characteristics, under clean and dirty blade conditions to compare power curves. Blade condition had noticeable impacts on longer blades operating under windy conditions.

Advances in technology have also made it possible for propeller pitch to be adjusted automatically, depending upon wind speed, so as to increase system energy production. This means that propellers must be connected to a rotor in a manner that prevents detachment, yet permits pitch adjustment while the wind turbine is in operation. Studies have found that propeller fasteners (typically, bolts) must be designed such that torque specifications are met, but that costs are constrained. Some forms of blade attachment—for example, fiberglass/metal hybrid t-bolts—may be less expensive yet equally effective. Systematic materials analysis is conducted to relate costs to required wind energy system specifications (see Jackson et al., 2005a).

Rotor size and design—that is, two- or three-blade design—in relation to wind speed is another important factor in maximizing energy production. The rotor assembly is composed of the propeller blades and motor unit rotated by the impact of wind force on the blades. Rotors on many commercial-grade wind turbines are between 40 and 120 meters in diameter, with rated power production ranging between 0.6 MW and 4.2 MW. The impact of wind on these rotors varies, ranging from 312 W per meter squared of wind force to nearly 500 W per meter squared of wind force (Jackson et al., 2005b). Rotor size is positively related to power production and may reduce the need for larger generators within the rotor assembly (see Jackson et al., 2005b). Researchers have found that the tailoring of wind turbine parameters (e.g., rotor and generator size) to load demands creates greater system efficiency, reduces costs, and increases power generation revenues. Technology is increasingly making it possible for wind turbine peak production periods to match peak load demand through proper turbine placement.

Griffin (2001) found that rotor sizes are pushing the limits of current wind energy system materials. As blades become larger, some exceeding sixty meters (197 feet) in length, blade materials and blade tip caps must be made thicker, thus increasing blade weight. Heavier blade materials translate into more wear on rotor assemblies, and require taller and heavier support towers. In order to maintain system efficiency, lighter weight materials must be developed as wind energy systems scale up in size and number of units. In a study conducted by Fingersh et al. (2006), cost curves for advanced lightweight materials used for blades—using fiberglass and carbon fiber—demonstrated significant cost reduction for wind energy systems. The strength of the next-generation materials overcame blade length limitations and reduced rotor wear. As noted in Malcolm and Hansen (2003: 12), the optimum wind tip speed/wind speed ratio is between 7.5 and 8.0.

Larger and cheaper wind energy systems require more than simply identifying next-generation materials. New tools and manufacturing processes must be developed to fabricate the systems. Thus, the path toward increased use of wind energy systems, particularly large wind energy systems, will require continued commitment to R & D and engineering assessments. New Age materials will only come to fruition with increased availability of financial, technical, and human resources needed to support this development.

At times, new materials and system design are at odds with one another, and a new synthesis on the interaction of design and materials must occur. In his holistic analysis of wind systems, Ahlstrom (2005) pointed to these types of challenges. For example, the lighter and more flexible materials that are now used in the construction of towers and blades may actually decrease system efficiency. Flexibility in construction may reduce costs and the impact of wind on equipment failure, but it can also lead to reduced energy generation. There is an interaction effect of blade design and other critical parts of wind turbine systems. Effective designs cannot deal with the individual parts in isolation, but must consider the whole, requiring the use of computer simulation analysis to isolate the dynamic qualities of wind turbines under different operating conditions and to determine optimum system design and capacity for in-operation adjustment. Simply put, "A wind turbine is a complex system working in a complex environment. It is composed of subsystems working in a tightly coupled way" (Diveux et al., 2001: 153).

John Conti-Ramsden and Kirsten Dyer (2015) concur with earlier authors on the need to meld the discussion of design, material innovation, and changing demand. Wind energy system costs are driven by demand for longer blades that will increase unit electricity production as well as the siting issues in often "hostile locations" plagued by extreme temperatures, frequent and potentially destructive storm events, and the corrosive impacts of salt water on offshore systems. The use of lightweight materials and thermoplastics are highlighted by Conti-Ramsden and Dyer (2015) as two currently employed material solutions to wind energy system challenges, but the authors conclude that the material and design solutions for future demand remain in the planning stages or have yet to be conceived. The left leg cannot run if the right leg is walking.

We are now nearly two decades into the twenty-first century. Technology has changed tremendously with advances coming in the form of a material science revolution, continued government and private sector enthusiasm and support for wind energy, and advancements in computing technology that have revolutionized both the manufacture and the operation of wind turbine technology. Does wind energy still face the upward limits in potential described by scholars in the early part of the twenty-first century?

In addressing this issue, Wiser et al. (2018) published the results of an expert elicitation survey of 163 experts in wind energy technology, policy, and economics. The article was published in the prestigious journal *Nature Energy*. Wiser and his colleagues found that experts were very optimistic about continued reduction in the future costs of wind energy. The "median scenario experts anticipate [indicates a] 24–30% reduction [in the levelized cost of wind generated electricity] by 2030, and 35–41% reductions by 2050. While many factors that are offered by way of explanation for these anticipated cost reductions will be discussed later in the chapter, the important point to be made here is that experts anticipate that the most significant factor in reducing costs will be associated with "capacity factor," meaning that cost reduction will predominantly be driven by continued technological innovations in materials science, computing, manufacturing, and turbine technology, all leading to increased efficiency and production levels.

Wiser et al. conclude that "experts apparently believe that the recent history of rising costs is likely to be reversed eventually as the [wind energy] market matures. Whether these views are prescient or are instead overly optimistic, influenced by motivational or other biases, will be known only in hindsight" (2018: 5). Expert optimism may be driven by evidence that learning rates in wind energy technology and capital expense reduction methods have been nearly twice as fast as anticipated (Wiser et al., 2018: 6).

Beyond the complexities associated with individual wind energy systems, there is the larger issue of how many wind systems should be deployed at any given generation site. In a study conducted in Scandinavia, Holttinen (2005) found that increasing the number of turbines in a single location does not necessarily improve the ability of wind systems to meet peak load demand. Rather, more turbines in a single location produces greater variation in wind energy production—variation roughly translates into greater uncertainty about the ability of wind generation at a particular site to meet demand. Through a longitudinal study of hourly wind power variations, Holttinen (2005) found that smoothing energy generation, thus reducing variation in expected wind energy production, is best accomplished through greater geographical diversity in wind turbine siting. Single-site wind energy production methodologies are held captive by variations in wind speed; hence, energy production level variability leads to potentially unmodeled costs that must be borne by wind energy producers due to reliance on back-up generation and its associated costs. Reliability issues can trigger a regulatory response from organizations implementing FERC and/or from state energy policy regulators (see Hibbard et al., 2017). Conversely, multiple wind energy production sites take advantage of the variability that naturally exists in wind speeds over a large geographical area. Additionally, a smaller number of wind turbines at any given energy production site reduces their "footprint."

Other technological solutions to wind speed variation and its impact on wind energy production are those of energy storage and selective release on demand. Energy storage generally means battery storage, although there are other ways of storing wind energy (for example, pumped hydro and compressed air). Oversizing wind turbines to meet both live-time peak load demand as well as storage needs in anticipation of intermittency issues is a consideration.

In small wind energy systems, Paatero and Lund (2005) found that energy storage reduced power fluctuations by 10 percent, simply by using a small 3kWh storage device.

Wind energy turbines are increasingly being sited in a variety of locations, including in coastal waterways and in mountainous terrain. The advantage of using these out-of-the-way locations is that they are out and away from areas where their presence would be contested. Placed in locations that are not close to homes and businesses, wind turbines are less likely to be opposed by property owners who are concerned about visual and noise pollution. A major technical difficulty in placing the turbines in these locations, beyond the initial construction issues, is the availability of wind data for proper siting. Wind pattern variations along coastal waters may be difficult to measure and predict with reliability. The confluence of wind and ocean currents along with water temperatures can impact wind patterns considerably. Similar problems plague wind energy development in mountainous locations, which are often impacted by wind following ravines and winds incident to large air temperature variations.

Technology has made it possible for wind engineers to overcome many of the obstacles faced by nonconventional wind energy sites. In Hasager et al. (2005), the authors identify four major remote sensing technologies employed in measuring wind patterns for offshore wind farm siting and development:

- passive microwave
- scatterometers
- radar altimeters
- synthetic aperature radar (SAR)

In all cases, the systems are not active methods of measuring wind speed. Analog systems usually involved a rotating device and the analysis of revolutions per second to measure wind speed. Passive wind speed measurement evaluates other dynamics related to wind speed without directly measuring the wind itself. Passive microwave, for instance, can be used to measure the impact of wind on a "wind driven ocean surface" from several different measurement points. A data matrix is created to determine speed of wind and direction of wind currents (see Piepmeier and Hass, 2002). Scatterometers use satellite tracking to measure movement in small waves along ocean surfaces; using known mathematical algorithms for wave movement and wind speed, it is possible to determine wind speeds at different locations.

Altimeters measure pressure changes associated with changes in altitude or high or low pressure fronts moving about in a particular area. Measurements of variations in atmospheric pressures in a particular area can be applied to a predictive mathematical algorithm that would allow a wind turbine to respond to changing conditions in real time.

Imaging SAR has frequently been used to measure the topography of various locations on the Earth's surface. Radar signals are directed at the target location, and Doppler returns are measured to determine image topography. When used to measure the topography of ocean currents and small wind-waves, some of the radar signal energy becomes "backscattered"—in other words, the signal return measured has been scattered across the surface being studied. Empirical analysis of backscatter is used to measure instantaneous wind speed along the ocean's surface. Hasager et al. (2005) found that imaging SAR was a valuable method of measuring wind speeds over the ocean where other forms of wind speed measurement are not readily available.

High-altitude mountain locations also face wind direction and strength analysis challenges. Western regions of the United States are characterized by high-altitude mountain areas, many of which have excellent wind resources. Internationally, Turkey and countries located in the Central Asia region have high-altitude mountain areas with significant proven wind energy capacity. As with ocean wind resources, mountain wind resources require high-tech approaches to analyzing reoccurring wind patterns. Several programs have been developed to measure surface temperature and wind patterns, controlling for topographical characteristics (see Eidsvik et al., 2005, 2004). Understanding turbulent air flows around mountains is a critical part of understanding wind energy turbine placement in mountainous regions. Turbulence studies in fluid dynamics have demonstrated that air currents and water currents share many similar dynamic characteristics (see Belcher and Hunt, 1998). Modeling of wind patterns for turbine siting is becoming increasingly feasible, a fact that

Offshore Wind and a Transfer Vessel
E+ / CharlieChesvick

will increase opportunities for remote wind farm locations and increased energy production—assuming that existing transmission lines are accessible. Where they are not, transmission right-of-ways need to be granted and line installation must be completed in an economically and environmentally sound manner.

LiDar is one of the newest technological breakthroughs in wind sensing and wind pattern modeling. Lidar technology was first developed in the 1960s, and it has been used in many applications for mapping and measuring rates of change, such as the measurement of ocean floor geology and forest terrain. In wind energy applications, Lidar reflects laser beams off of airborne particulate matter to gauge wind speed and wind patterns. Lidar systems can be mounted directly to a wind turbine system to provide real-time data on wind patterns, allowing for automatic turbine direction and blade angle adjustments for maximum system efficiency. Modeling wind gusts allows wind turbine systems to anticipate and adjust so as to avoid system damage.

ECONOMIC FEASIBILITY OF WIND POWER SYSTEMS

The economic feasibility of wind power has improved due to technological advancement in wind energy systems and the development of increasingly lighter and stronger materials. Economic efficiencies are also improved by the presence of growing demand for wind energy systems. Initial costs on a per-unit basis decline as more units are produced. This assumes, of course, that a large number of devices of a similar type are manufactured using standard production techniques and tools. However, as wind systems become more prevalent, there will likely be greater variation in local wind conditions and terrain, potentially impacting efficiencies in wind energy production. To overcome efficiency limitations, wind energy system producers will need to adapt to more varied demands, meaning that fewer wind systems of any particular type will be produced. Accordingly, production costs for any particular wind energy system will be spread over fewer units produced, resulting in higher per-unit costs.

In some cases, wind energy system manufacturing will involve a process of original equipment manufacturing (OEM) production to meet local wind energy site conditions. This would likely be the case in some sea- or mountain-based wind energy systems. Market forces, government incentives, and/or regulations will likely shape wind energy system producers' choices to produce as well as price levels for items produced. Price will impact demand. As market demand expands, tools and materials will become more numerous as well as multiple fabrication processes will arise, thus potentially reducing costs for a wider demand. An early study found that "blade mass and costs scale as near-cubic of rotor diameter" (Griffin, 2001: ii).

As noted in table 5.1—data based on Griffin's 2001 study of materials costs associated with different sized wind energy systems—the costs for larger wind energy systems scale up quite rapidly because of the increased need

Table 5.1   Blade Mass and Cost of Rotors

Raidus (m)	Rating (kW)	Areas (m²)	Mass (kg)		Average Cost per Blade			Rotor Costs	
			Blade	Root	Fixed	Prod.	Total	S/kW	S/MWh/yr
23.3	750	66.3	1577	111	$115	$19,100	$19,215	$76.9	$25.1
32.9	1500	132.6	4292	243	$520	$51,850	$52,370	$104.7	$31.4
38.0	2000	176.8	6528	336	$970	$79,230	$80,200	$120.3	$34.9
40.8	2300	203.3	8010	388	$1,320	$97,495	$98,815	$128.9	$36.6
46.6	3000	265.2	11,783	515	$2,350	$144,910	$147,260	$147.3	$40.8
53.8	4000	353.6	17,961	681	$4,405	$224,395	$228,800	$171.6	$46.0
60.2	5000	442.0	24,869	851	$7,180	$316,590	$323,770	$194.3	$50.8

for stronger systems to respond to wind impacts. While energy production increases with longer blades, blade mass and blade costs increase at an even faster rate. Rotor costs do not increase appreciably in relation to the size of a wind energy system.

The mass (in kg) of the blade and root assembly (the portion of the blade that attaches to the turbines in the rotor assembly) increases quite substantially as the power rating (in kW) increases. While the power rating increases by approximately fivefold in the chart above, the combined mass of the blade and root increases by fourteenfold. In other words, system materials tend to increase nonlinearly, as do blade costs, as a function of power rating. Smaller systems tend to be more efficient than larger systems. While some time has passed since Griffin (2001), the basic dilemma remains a critical aspect of wind energy economics. The economic feasibility of large-scale wind power systems, therefore, will largely depend on the ability of materials science and engineering to construct larger, lighter weight blades, lightweight and higher-speed rotors, and taller towers using site-tailored wind turbine designs at reduced manufacturing costs (see Ashwill, 2009; see also Wiser et al., 2016a, 2016b). As Chen et al. (2018) conclude, turbine costs are a function of turbine-rated wind speed and access to turbine optimum wind speed siting.

The cost of wind energy in an optimum wind scenario of 12 m/s will produce energy at approximately five cents per kWh, which is competitive with the costs of conventional power generation. The caveat to this price estimation, however, is that it assumes that the optimum wind is sustained on a twenty-four-hour basis, which is generally not possible. For grid power generation, this poses a smaller problem, since other forms of power generation can take over when wind energy systems are not actively meeting load demands. Stand-alone wind power systems, however, will require appreciable extra capacity to produce surplus energy to be stored in batteries or other energy storage systems. The surplus stored power can be used to meet load demand during periods when wind energy systems are not actively meeting load. A wind farm requires some form of housing for power storage devices, such as batteries. Servicing storage devices, buildings, and additional wind turbines will require staffing as well as the costs of disposing of retired storage devices, which may contain environmentally harmful substances, such as acid and lead. These requirements will add a substantial cost to the relatively optimistic 5¢/kWh.

Cost reductions in wind energy are eagerly pursued through the aforementioned materials science, engineering, and manufacturing breakthroughs leading to larger and cheaper wind energy systems. Tower height has become a key issue in wind turbine systems, as wind speeds are more consistent for taller towered systems (see Chen et al., 2018; Lantz et al., 2019). The goal is to reduce the cost of energy produced to somewhere between three and four cents per kWh, a cost that would make wind energy cheaper than fossil energy even without factoring in the marginal social and environmental costs associated with fossil energy.

The National Renewable Energy Laboratory (NREL) produces an annual report on the cost of wind energy. Stehly et al. (2017) have determined turbine capital, balance of system (BOS), and operations and maintenance (O & M) costs of wind energy systems. Three system scenarios are analyzed in their analysis—a land-based 2.16 MW system; a 4.71 MW fixed-bottom offshore wind energy system; and a 4.71 MW floating offshore system. The systems are assumed to be operating in Class 3 winds.

The land-based project is assumed to be a wind farm of ninety-three wind turbines with a 200 MW wind plant capacity operating at 1,500 feet above sea level. The land-based scenario assumes no catastrophic events impacting operations and maintenance costs, and it is assumed to have a twenty-five-year project lifespan. The fixed-bottom offshore and floating offshore project scenarios are located in the North Atlantic, in waters between thirty and one hundred meters deep, with each project having 128 turbines with a plant capacity of 600 MW. The fixed offshore systems are assumed to be built on a monopile, while the floating systems are assumed to be semisubmersible. The projects' lifespan is twenty years.

For land-based systems, over 67 percent of capital expenditure involves turbine capital costs, nearly half of which relates to the cost of the nacelle module—nacelle assembly, drivetrain, electrical assembly, and yaw (table 5.2). The nacelle module cost is estimated to be $1.14 million. The rotor module—composed of the blades, pitch, and hub assembly costs an estimated $654,000, while the tower is estimated to cost $518,000. The BOS costs are estimated to be $786,000, of which the electrical infrastructure is nearly half of that cost—an estimated $352,000. Other significant BOS costs include the footing or foundation (est. $140,000); site access and staging (est. $108,000); and assembly and installation (est. $104,000). Finance-related costs—construction financing and contingency funds—are estimated

Table 5.2 Land-Based Wind Turbine Scenario (2.16 MW Turbine)

	$/kW	CapEx	
Rotor Module	303	$654,480.00	19.06%
Blades	193	$416,880.00	12.14%
Pitch assembly	64	$138,240.00	4.03%
Hub assembly	46	$99,360.00	2.89%
Nacelle module	527	$1,138,320.00	33.14%
Nacelle structural assembly	105	$226,800.00	6.60%
Drivetrain assembly	205	$442,800.00	12.89%
Nacelle electrical assembly	185	$399,600.00	11.64%
Yaw assembly	32	$69,120.00	2.01%
Tower module	240	$518,400.00	15.09%
Turbine capital cost	1,071	$2,313,360.00	67.36%
Development cost	18	$38,880.00	1.13%
Engineering management	20	$43,200.00	1.26%
Foundation	65	$140,400.00	4.09%
Site access and staging	50	$108,000.00	3.14%
Assembly and installation	48	$103,680.00	3.02%
Electrical infrastructure	163	$352,080.00	10.25%
Balance of system	364	$786,240.00	22.89%
Construction financing cost	60	$129,600.00	3.77%
Contingency fund	95	$205,200.00	5.97%
Financial costs	155	$334,800.00	9.75%
Total capital expenditures	1,590	$3,434,400.00	100.00%
		$319,399,200.00	
Operations	15.2	$32,832.00	
Land lease cost	8.1	$17,496.00	
Maintenance	28.4	$61,344.00	
OpEx	51.7	$111,672.00	
Net annual energy production	3,588 MWh		
LCOE		$0.049–0.052/ kWh	

Data Source: Stehly et al., 2017

to be approximately 10 percent of total capital expenditures—approximately $335 million. The total capital expenditure for each land-based turbine in the scenario is estimated to be $3.43 million, which means that a ninety-three-turbine wind farm capital cost will be $319.4 million. Operating expenditures (O & M and land lease costs) are estimated to be $111.7 thousand per turbine per year. Given the wind and finance scenarios modeled, the levelized cost of energy (LCOE) for land-based wind in the scenario is estimated to range from $0.049 to $0.052 per kWh.

In the fixed-bottom offshore scenario, the most significant turbine costs were assembly and installation (approx. $4.1 million), and construction costs for the substructure and foundation (approx. $3.01 million) (table 5.3). While

Table 5.3   Fixed-Bottom Offshore Turbine Scenario (4.71 MW Turbine)

	$/kW	CapEx
Turbine Costs		
Development costs	66	$310,860.00
Engineering management	71	$334,410.00
Substructure and foundation	639	$3,009,690.00
Site access, staging, port	21	$98,910.00
Electrical infrastructure	411	$1,935,810.00
Assembly and installation	872	$4,107,120.00
Plant commissioning	36	$169,560.00
Turbine Cap Cost Total	2,115	$9,961,650.00
Balance of system		
Insurance during const.	42	$197,820.00
Decommissioning bond	222	$1,045,620.00
Construction financing	294	$1,384,740.00
Contingency	307	$1,445,970.00
BOS Total	2,115	$9,961,650.00
Financial Costs Total	959	$4,516,890.00
Total Capital Expenditures	4,579	$21,567,090.00
Operations	158	$744,180.00
Net annual energy production	3,650 MWh	
LCOE	$0.173/kWh	

Data Source: Stehly et al., 2017

turbine capital costs were over 67 percent of the total capital cost of land-based systems, turbine capital costs are estimated to be slightly less than half the cost of fixed-bottom offshore wind turbines. BOS costs are estimated to be equal to turbine capital costs—approximately, $9.96 million. BOS costs include insurance costs, construction financing, decommissioning bonding, and contingency funds. Financial costs are more than ten times higher than the land-based wind energy scenario, and annual operations costs are also significantly higher for fixed-bottom offshore wind energy. The LCOE of fixed-bottom wind energy in the scenario is estimated to be $0.173 per kWh, which is triple the cost of land-based wind energy in the scenario.

The floating offshore wind energy scenario is by far the most expensive in terms of capital costs: approximately $30.1 million per 4.71 MW wind turbine installed or nearly forty percent more expensive than fixed-bottom offshore wind energy systems. Substructure and foundation costs for floating offshore wind systems are slightly more than one-third of the total capital cost of floating offshore wind energy systems. BOS costs in a floating wind energy system are much greater than turbine costs. Turbine costs are estimated to be $7.1 million, while BOS costs are estimated to be $18.3 million, which is largely due to the tremendous substructure and foundation costs incurred with floating offshore wind energy. The LCOE of floating wind energy in the scenario is $0.207 per kWh (table 5.4).

According to a 2017 U.S. Department of Energy report, wind energy installations have experienced tremendous growth in recent years. The report found that 7,017 MW of wind energy capacity were installed in 2017, "bringing the total utility-scale wind capacity to nearly 89 GW" (Wiser and Bollinger, 2018).

POLITICAL AND SOCIAL FEASIBILITY OF WIND ENERGY

Recent public opinion polls regarding wind energy indicate strong support. A Pew Research Center poll, "The Politics of Climate," conducted in May–June 2016, found that 83 percent of U.S. adults are in favor of the United States building more wind turbine farms (Funk and Kennedy, 2016). The authors of the report further found that support for wind energy and other renewables was strongly bipartisan, but that support was strongest among adults 18–49 years old. Approximately 83 percent of U.S. adults polled were in favor of wind turbine farms, while only 14 percent were against wind farms. By comparison, approximately 46 percent of survey respondents were in favor of offshore oil drilling, nuclear power, fracking, or coal mining. The evidence clearly points in the direction of strong majoritarian support for wind energy.

While public support is important in shaping energy policy futures, business interest and trade association advocacy play a very important role in keeping policy issues on the political agenda. Organized coalitions comprised

Table 5.4   Floating Offshore Turbine Scenario (4.71 MW Turbine)

		$/kW	CapEx
Turbine Costs		1,505	$7,088,550.00
	Development costs	66	$310,860.00
	Engineering management	140	$659,400.00
	Substructure and foundation	2,174	$10,239,540.00
	Site access, staging, port	35	$164,850.00
	Electrical infrastructure	693	$3,264,030.00
	Assembly and installation	721	$3,395,910.00
	Plant commissioning	53	$249,630.00
Balance of system		3,881	$18,279,510.00
	Insurance during const.	64	$301,440.00
	Decommissioning bond	76	$357,960.00
	Construction financing	410	$1,931,100.00
	Contingency	447	$2,105,370.00
Financial Costs Total		997	$4,695,870.00
Total Capital Expenditures		6,383	$30,063,930.00
Operations		93	$438,030.00
Net annual energy productions		3,636 MWh	
LCOE		$0.207/kWh	

of key stakeholders—business, academic, legal, and concerned members of the public—work together in crafting and advancing policy agendas that offer clean energy alternatives in opposition to fossil and nuclear energy interests who are simultaneously seeking to advance their own policy priorities.

A trade association, the American Wind Energy Association (AWEA), is one of the largest organized wind energy interests in the United States. In 2017–2018, it was the second-largest alternative energy lobbying organization in Washington, DC, second only to Poet LLC—a major biofuels manufacturer. In 2017–2018, the AWEA contributed $214,035 to senators and members of Congress. In that same time period, the AWEA spent $290,000 on direct lobbying efforts, a substantial amount but a far cry from their 2009 high of $4.37 million.

Putting things into a broader perspective, the top political contributor in the energy sector is Koch Industries, which spent nearly $8 million in

2017–2018 on political contributions, all of which went to Republicans or conservative groups. The top twenty political contributors from the energy industry at the national level in 2017–2018 were from electricity utilities and the oil and gas industries. The only mixed energy contributor was NextEra energy ($2,075,538), an estimated $45.5 billion wholesale electricity provider with an energy portfolio that includes substantial investments in wind and solar energy (OpenSecrets.org, 2018). On average, the AWEA's lobbying activities and political contributions have declined significantly since 2009. In that year, the alternative energy stakes were quite high due to the passage of the American Recovery and Reinvestment Act (P.L. 111–5), a statute that authorized nearly $90 billion for clean energy investment, leading to a thirtyfold increase in wind energy development in the United States (White House, 2016). The wind energy sector is indeed growing, but principally on its own accord, and it is becoming lean in terms of direct lobby and political contribution efforts at the national level.

The Trump administration has a mixed perception of wind energy support, with one source referring to Trump energy policy as "manic" (Harder and Swan, 2018). Harder and Swan (2018) claim that "Trump has a visceral hatred of wind turbines . . . [Trump thinks that wind turbines] are terrible returns on investment that blight coastlines and obstruct views." Nevertheless, the authors point out that President Trump's Interior Department is working in a bipartisan manner with state governments to lease offshore waters in the Northeast, making it easier for offshore wind energy development. Based on unnamed sources, the authors conclude that President Trump's policy on energy reflects an interest in telling various constituencies what they want to hear, and that President Trump is given to a "not in my backyard" view of wind energy that impacts scenic views important to his interests (Rathi, 2018).

An article from the *Denver Post* by Steve LeBlanc (2018) may help in more fully understanding the Trump administration approach to wind energy. The article points to President Trump's stated goal of "energy dominance." The term "energy dominance" means, in this case, the capacity to be both energy independent and capable of exporting energy to other nations for the broader purpose of exercising international political and economic influence. Within that broad energy policy paradigm, President Trump's support for fossil energy as well as renewable energy, such as wind and hydropower, is comprehensible, particularly given that concern for climate change is not what undergirds President Trump's energy and environment philosophy (LeBlanc, 2018).

While President Trump has publicly praised the coal and fracking industries, he remains particularly supportive of wind energy development as part of his plan to promote "energy dominance." According to former U.S. Secretary of the Interior Ryan Zinke, "'On designated federal lands and off-shore, [the policy goal is to provide] an equal opportunity for all sources of responsible energy development, from fossil fuels to the full range of renewables'" (LeBlanc, 2018).

Wind energy is drawing strong bipartisan support at the national, state, and local levels. Public support is high, but there are claims that not in my backyard (NIMBY) forces offer "pockets of opposition to wind farms and . . . community 'acceptance'" (Marshall, 2017). Citing Rand and Hoen (2017), Christine Marshall notes that NIMBY is not an accurate description of local-level resistance to wind energy. Public support for wind energy is not shaped so much by NIMBY issues, but is rather shaped by public perception of basic fairness in the development stage of wind energy systems. There is evidence that local public stakeholders need to feel that their concerns about wind energy are dealt with in a manner that builds public trust. Public opposition has been effectively dealt with through inclusive processes that build trust and result in better implementation. While environmental concerns are important, community stakeholders are also eager to realize sustained benefits through the economic development brought by wind energy projects.

TEXTBOX 5.1 | St. Olaf Wind Turbine Case Study

For decades, Saint Olaf College [Northfield, Minnesota] has been thinking carefully about its energy consumption and impacts on the environment. On September 19, 2006, a 1.65 megawatt turbine became a symbol of its commitment to sustainability.

Pete Sandberg, the man who spearheaded the college's effort to erect its own turbine, came to St. Olaf in the 1980s and currently serves as assistant vice president for facilities. Since he arrived at St. Olaf, Sandberg has been involved in numerous efforts to reduce the college's impact on the environment. As early as the 1980s, St. Olaf considered restoring its land to the condition it was in before European settlement. Long before the current level of concern about climate change, Sandberg and his colleagues realized that sequestering carbon in the soil and vegetation would be an added benefit of this conservation and restoration initiative.

AN INDEPENDENT GRID

In the 1990s, St. Olaf took proactive steps to upgrade its electrical supply and distribution system. In 1999, the college installed three diesel generators, which can produce up to 4.2 megawatts of electricity. St. Olaf also upgraded its internal electrical distribution system to a 13.8kV line that loops through campus in an underground tunnel. Thanks to these investments, St. Olaf can provide electricity to almost all of its buildings even in the event of a blackout. The ability to do so allows the college to qualify as an interruptible customer, and to take advantage of lower rates from its electric utility, Xcel Energy. As a result, the college saves about $150,000 annually on its electricity costs. In addition to benefiting from lower energy bills, these investments later played a key role in helping St. Olaf optimize the use of its own wind turbine.

THE SEED WAS PLANTED

In the early 2000s, St. Olaf began to explore a future for wind energy on its campus, and the idea of installing a wind turbine grew out of both conviction and practicality. At the time, the college was in the early stages of planning a new 100,000-square-foot science center that would consume a significant amount of electricity. Despite pursuing LEED certification and maximizing energy efficiency, Sandberg and staff had been left to wonder how they might further reduce the operating cost impact of adding this new building to the campus grid. On-site renewable generation emerged as a potential alternative to buying more electricity from Xcel.

Plans for the wind turbine gained momentum in 2003. That spring, Honor the Earth and the Indigo Girls came to St. Olaf to launch a national tour aiming to raise money and create a groundswell of awareness and support for wind projects on Native American lands. The event also generated interest among students to begin exploring how they might sustainably harness wind energy on their campus. Little did they know, Sandberg was already one step ahead, having passed on to the administration an initial proposal to construct four wind turbines at St. Olaf.

GETTING THE MONEY AND THE MACHINE

Planning for the wind turbine began in earnest when Sandberg applied to the Xcel Energy Renewable Development Fund in response to their second request for proposals in 2004. While St. Olaf ultimately received funding, this proved to be a mixed blessing. While the college waited for the Public Utilities Commission to approve their grant contract, the federal government renewed the production tax credit, which unleashed a burst of wind energy development activity. As a result of the high demand and tight supply circumstances prevailing at the time, what Sandberg originally projected to be a $1.9 million project rose to over $2.5 million. Undeterred, St. Olaf gladly accepted the $1.5 million grant and paid upfront for the remaining costs out of its capital operating budget.

THE ECONOMIC BENEFITS

St. Olaf worked with Windlogics, a wind resource assessment company, and determined a feasible site less than a quarter of a mile northwest of campus. The proximity made it economically feasible to connect the wind turbine to the campus's internal distribution loop, a direct connection that paid off in a major way. By interconnecting with the campus grid, St. Olaf is able to consume the wind-generated electricity on-site and therefore reduce their energy imports from Xcel. The school only sells excess wind energy to Xcel at night and during break periods, when campus demand is low.

This arrangement translates into a significant financial advantage. Instead of selling their entire production to Xcel for the standard small wind tariff of 3.3 cents/kWh, St. Olaf reduces its purchases from Xcel, which are set at a rate of 6.2 cents/kWh. As a result, the school is able to save about $250,000 per year on electricity bills. Since this dwarfs the $36,000 in operation and maintenance that the school pays in its service contract for the turbine, St. Olaf expects to recuperate its initial capital investment four to five years after the turbine blades began to spin.

BUMPS IN THE ROAD

The road to acquiring their own turbine has not been without surprises or setbacks. While awaiting a decision from the Renewable Development Fund, not only did the project's capital costs spike, but the company from which St. Olaf originally planned to purchase a turbine, NEG Micon, was acquired by Vestas. Consequently, the school had to reenter negotiations with Vestas and ultimately sign a more expensive service contract.

Accepting the grant set limits on St. Olaf in other ways, too. One of the conditions required St. Olaf to pass all environmental attributes of the wind energy, sometimes called green tags or renewable energy credits, to Xcel. Furthermore, St. Olaf was also not eligible for the Minnesota Renewable Energy Production Incentive, which ceased accepting new applicants in 2005. A final surprise came after the turbine went up and production numbers failed to meet the projections. Initial estimates projected 6 million kWh of energy would flow from the turbine each year, but annual figures to date have averaged about 4.5 million kWh, roughly a quarter of the school's yearly electricity consumption. Luckily, though, this underperformance has not significantly impacted the financial viability of the project, which remains on-schedule to pay for itself by 2011.

Overall, Pete Sandberg considers the St. Olaf wind turbine an unequivocal success. It stands tall as a source of pride for the school and a highly visible symbol of the college's commitment to the environment. The wind turbine also offers learning opportunities for professors to incorporate into their courses. Sandberg is regularly called upon to give tours to groups who come to learn about wind energy from the greater Northfield area and beyond. Indeed, St. Olaf serves as a model for many other campuses around the country that contact Sandberg to learn how they might replicate his success.

Although St. Olaf currently has no plans to add another turbine, the one they already have is not likely to fade into oblivion. The campus plans to transform the site of the turbine into a living model of sustainability. Student groups will practice organic agriculture on some of the surrounding farmland, and nearby a new building covered in solar panels will house art studios and produce enough electricity to meet on-site needs and feed excess energy into the St. Olaf grid.

Source: Special thanks to Windustry for the use of the case study, St. Olaf College Wind Energy, http://www.windustry.org/resources/st-olaf-wind-turbine-case-study, accessed July 22, 2019.

CHAPTER SUMMARY

Wind energy capacity in the United States is substantial. The technical feasibility of wind energy development is a function of the materials, engineering, and product fabrication capable of meeting the various wind patterns and environmental factors to be conquered. Large-scale wind turbines are limited by current material strengths and costs. In some cases, that might not pose a problem because there is evidence that less powerful turbines might have higher performance ratings (see Thompson, 2018). Economic feasibility is a function of capital costs and operations and maintenance expenses. As wind energy explores increasingly challenging environments, such as high-altitude mountainous regions as well as coastal area ocean siting locations, the technical feasibility that allows for wind energy development impacts the costs associated with establishing a wind farm. Political feasibility at the national level is steady, thanks in large part to bipartisan commitments. State and local commitment to wind energy is often a function of good faith policy making and implementation efforts that positively engage community stakeholders and contribute to long-term economic development.

REFERENCES

Ahlstrom, A. 2005. Influence of wind turbine flexibility on loads and power production. *Wind Energy* 9(3): 237–249.

Ashwill, T. 2009. Materials and innovations for large blade structures: Research opportunities in wind energy technology. *50th AIAA/ASCE/AHS/ASC Structures, Structural Dynamics, and Materials Conference*, AIAA 2009–2407.

American Wind Energy Association. 2018. Wind energy facts at a glance. Washington, DC: AWEA. Retrieved from https://www.awea.org/wind-energy-facts-at-a-glance, August 20, 2018.

Belcher, S., and Hunt, J. 1998. Turbulent flow over hills and waves. *Annual Review of Fluid Mechanics* 38: 507–538.

Bossanyi, E. 2003. Individual blade pitch control for load reduction. *Wind Energy* 6: 119–128.

Chen, J., Wang, F., and Stelson, K. 2018. A mathematical approach to minimizing the cost of energy for large utility wind turbines. *Applied Energy* 228: 1413–1422.

Conti-Ramsden, J., and Dyer, K. 2015. Materials innovations for more efficient wind turbines. *Renewable Energy Focus*, September 21. Retrieved from http://www.renewableenergyfocus.com/view/42937/materials-innovations-for-more-efficient-wind-turbines/, October 9, 2018.

Crespo, A., Hernandez, J., and Frandsen, S. 1999. Survey of modeling methods for wind turbine wakes and wind farms. *Wind Energy* 2: 1–24.

Diveux, T., Sebastian, P., Bernard, D., and Pulgali, J. 2001. Horizontal axis wind turbine systems: Optimization using genetic algorithms. *Wind Energy* 4: 151–171.

Flowers, L. T., and Dougherty P. J. 2002. *Wind Powering America: Goals, Approaches, Perspectives, and Prospects*. NREL/CP-500-32097. Golden, CO: National Renewable Energy Laboratory.

Kanpur, Chandra. 2005. On what principle does an altimeter work? *Times of India*, May 28, http://timesofindia.indiatimes.com/articleshow/1125635.cms, accessed July 3, 2005.

Eidsvik, A. 2005. A system for wind power estimation in mountainous terrain: Prediction of Askervein Hill data. *Wind Energy* 8: 237–249.

Eidsvik, K., Holstad, A., Lie, I., and Utnes, T. 2004. A prediction system for local wind variations in mountainous terrain. *Boundary-Layer Meteorology* 112(3): 557–586.

Elliott, D., and Schwartz, M. 1993. Wind Energy Potential in the United States, http://www.nrel.gov/wind/wind_potential.html. Accessed November 27, 2005.

Elliott, D., and Schwartz, M. 2005. *Development and Validation of High-Resolution State Wind Resource Maps for the United States*, NREL/TP-500–38127. Golden, CO: National Renewable Energy Laboratory.

Energy Center of Wisconsin. 2005. Parts of a Turbine, http://www.ecw.org/windpower/cat2a.html, accessed June 30, 2005.

European Space Agency. 2005. Scatterometer Design, http://earth.esa.int/rootcollection/eeo4.10075/scatt_design.html, accessed July 3, 2005.

Fingersh, L., Hand, M., and Laxson, A. 2006. *Wind Turbine Design Cost and Scaling Model*. Golden, CO: National Renewable Energy Laboratory.

Froese, M. 2017. How are blade materials and manufacturing changing to keep up with larger turbines? *Wind Power Engineering*, January 4. Retrieved from https://www.windpowerengineering.com/business-news-projects/blade-materials-manufacturing-changing-keep-larger-turbines/, October 1, 2018.

Funk, C., and Kennedy, B. 2016. The politics of climate. *Pew Research Center*, October 4. Retrieved from http://www.pewinternet.org/2016/10/04/the-politics-of-climate/, October 15, 2018.

Griffin, Dayton A. 2001. *Wind PACT Turbine Design Scaling Studies Technical Area 1—Composite Blades for 80- to 120-Meter Rotor*. NREL/SR-500–29492. Golden, CO: National Renewable Energy Laboratory.

Harder, A., and Swan, J. 2018. Trump's manic energy policy. *Axios*. Retrieved from https://www.axios.com/donald-trump-energy-policy-wind-power-hydroelectric-7d54680b-5a1d-41f0-9be7-700ff0f6a0c6.html, October 15, 2018.

Hasager, C, Nielsen, M., Astrup, R. Barthelmie, E. Dellwik, N., Jenson, B., Jorgenson, S. Pryor, C., Rathmann, O., and Furevik, B. 2005. Offshore wind resource estimation from satellite SAR wind field maps. *Wind Energy* 8(4): 403–419.

Hibbard, P., Tierney, S., and Franklin, K. 2017. *Electricity Markets, Reliability, and the Evolving U.S. Power System*. New York: Analysis Group. Retrieved from https://www.analysisgroup.com/globalassets/uploadedfiles/content/insights/publishing/ag_markets_reliability_final_june_2017.pdf, June 11, 2019.

Hill, J. 2018. US wind energy now supplies more than 30% in four states. *Clean Technica*, April 18. Retrieved from https://cleantechnica.com/2018/04/18/us-wind-energy-now-supplies-more-than-30-in-four-states/, August 19, 2018.

Holttinen, Hannele. 2005. Hourly wind power variations in the Nordic countries. *Wind Energy* 8: 173–195.

Jackson, K. J., Van Dam, C. P., and Yen-Nakafuji, D. 2005b. Wind turbine generator trends for site-specific tailoring. *Wind Energy* 8(4): 443–455.

Jackson, K. J., Zuteck, M. D., Van Dam, C. P., Standish, K. J., and Berry D. 2005a. Innovative design approaches for large wind turbine blades. *Wind Energy* 8: 141–171.

Lantz, E., Roberts, O., Nunemaker, J., DeMeo, E., Dykes, K., and Scott, G. 2019. Increasing wind turbine heights: Opportunities and challenges. *National Renewable Energy Laboratories,* NREL/TP-5000–73629. Retrieved from https://www.energy.gov/sites/prod/files/2019/05/f63/73629.pdf, June 11, 2019.

Larsen, T., Madsen, H., and Thomsen, K. 2005. Active load reduction using individual pitch, based on local blade flow measurements. *Wind Energy* 8: 67–80.

LeBlanc, S. 2018. Donald Trump likes coal, but that doesn't mean he's hostile to wind. The Trump administration is looking to renewable energy sources to help create "energy dominance." *Denver Post*, April 23. Retrieved from https://www.denverpost.com/2018/04/23/donald-trump-stance-wind-power/, August 19, 2018.

Malcolm, D., and Hansen, A. 2003. *WindPACT Turbine Rotor Design, Specific Rating Study*, NREL/SR-500–34794. Golden, CO: National Renewable Energy Laboratory.

Marshall, C. 2017. Renewable energy: What makes people dislike wind? It's not NIMBY. *E&E News*, June 29. Retrieved from https://www.eenews.net/stories/1060056815, October 16, 2018.

Mohamed, M. 2004. 3D woven carbon-glass hybrid wind turbine blades. Presentation at Wind Turbine Blade Workshop. Sponsored by Sandia National Laboratories, http://www.sandia.gov/wind/2004BladeWorkshopPDFs/MansourMohamed.pdf, accessed March 13, 2006.

National Wind Watch. 2018. How Big Is a Wind Turbine? Retrieved from https://www.wind-watch.org/publication/nwwpub-size.pdf, August 20, 2018.

OpenSecrets. 2018. Energy/Natural Resources. Washington, DC: The Center for Responsive Politics. Retrieved from https://www.opensecrets.org/industries/indus.php?Ind=E, October 16, 2018.

Paatero, Jukka, and Lund, Peter D. 2005. Effective energy storage on variations in wind power. *Wind Energy* 8(4): 421–441.

Piepmeier, J., and Hass, J. 2002. "Ultra-low power digital correlator for passive microwave polarimetry," Moscow, ID: Center for Advanced Microelectronics and Biomolecular Research, http:/www2.cambr.uidaho.edu/hips/ulp_polarimetry_correlator.pdf, accessed July 3, 2005.

Pinard, Jean-Paul, Benoit, Robert, and Yu, Wei. 2005. *A WEST Wind Climate Simulation of the Mountainous Yukon*. Montreal, Canada: Environment Canada, http://collaboration.cmc.ec.gc.ca/science/rpn/ publications/pdf/paperyukon_19_04_05. pdf, accessed July 4, 2005.

Preciado, V., Madrigal, M., Muljadi, E., and Gevorgian, V. 2015. Harmonics of a wind power plant. *National Renewable Energy Laboratory*. Retrieved from https://www.nrel.gov/docs/fy15osti/63588.pdf, August 19, 2018.

Rand, J., and Hoen, B. 2017. Thirty years of North American wind energy acceptance research: What have we learned? *Energy Research & Social Science* 29: 135–148.

Rathi, A. 2018. The wind farm Donald Trump tried to block is now complete. *Quartz* May 29. Retrieved from https://qz.com/1291269/the-scottish-wind-farm-donald-trump-tried-to-block-is-now-complete/, October 15, 2018.

Stehly, T., Heimiller, D., and Scott, G. 2017. *2016 Cost of Wind Energy Review*. Golden, CO: NREL. NREL/TP-6A20-70363.

Swolfs, Y. 2017. Perspective for fibre-hybrid composites in wind energy applications. *Materials* 10(11): 1–17. https://www.windpowerengineering.com/business-news-projects/blade-materials-manufacturing-changing-keep-larger-turbines/.

Thompson, A. 2018. U.S. wind turbines are getting less powerful—and that's a good thing. *Popular Mechanics*, September 14. Retrieved from https://www.popularmechanics.com/science/energy/a23120126/us-wind-turbines-are-getting-less-powerfuland-thats-a-good-thing/, October 16, 2018.

U.S. Department of Energy. 2018. The inside of a wind turbine. *Office of Energy Efficiency and Renewable Energy*, August 19. Retrieved from https://www.energy.gov/eere/wind/inside-wind-turbine-0, August 19, 2018.

Veers, P., Ashwill, T., Sutherland, H., Laird, D., and Lobitz, D. 2003. Trends in the design, manufacture and evaluation of wind turbine blades. *Wind Energy* 6: 245–259.

White House. 2016. Fact Sheet: The Recovery Act made the single largest investment in clean energy in history, driving the deployment of clean energy, promoting energy efficiency, and supporting manufacturing. February 25. Washington, DC: White House. Retrieved from https://obamawhitehouse.archives.gov/the-press-office/2016/02/25/fact-sheet-recovery-act-made-largest-single-investment-clean-energy, October 16, 2018.

Wind Energy Technologies Office. 2019. *Wind Energy Technologies Office Budget History*. Retrieved from https://www.energy.gov/eere/wind/wind-energy-technologies-office-budget, July 22, 2019.

Wiser, R., Jenni, K., Seel, J., Baker, E., Hand, M., Lantz, E., and Smith, A. 2016a. Expert elicitation survey on future wind energy costs. *Nature Energy* 1(16135): 1–8.

Wiser, R., Hand, M., Seel, J., and Paulos, B. 2016b. Reducing wind energy costs through increased size: Is the sky the limit? *Berkeley Lab: Electricity Markets & Policy Group*, November. Retrieved from https://emp.lbl.gov/sites/all/files/scaling_turbines.pdf, July 13, 2019.

Wiser, R., and Bollinger, M. 2018. *2017 Wind Technologies Market Report*. Washington, DC: Wind Energy Technologies Office, U.S. Department of Energy. Retrieved from https://www.energy.gov/sites/prod/files/2018/08/f54/2017_wind_technologies_market_report_8.15.18.v2.pdf, October 15, 2018.

6

Geothermal Energy

★ ★ ★

Geothermal energy presents remarkable potential for global clean energy production (Ghose, 2004; Li et al., 2015). As an energy source, it relies on the Earth's heat without altering the Earth's core temperature. In the United States, the highest-quality geothermal energy resources exist domestically in the Southwest, but usable "grades" of geothermal resources can be found scattered throughout the entire nation (U.S. Department of Energy, 2018) (figure 6.1).

WHAT IS GEOTHERMAL ENERGY? HOW DOES IT WORK?

The Earth's mantle is composed of superheated iron and other elements. In some locations, this superheated material rises into the Earth's crust, and thus

Figure 6.1   Geothermal Electricity Production (2009–2018)

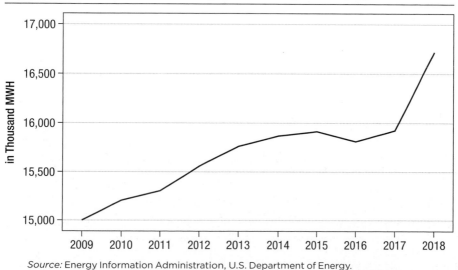

Source: Energy Information Administration, U.S. Department of Energy.

comes closer to deep Earth groundwater supplies, which often contain high concentrations of dissolved gases, minerals, and heavy metals in solution. Wells are drilled in areas of accessible geothermal activity, and the superheated water known as *brine* is extracted from deep Earth reservoirs. In its superheated state, the brine can reach the surface in the form of superheated steam and, in a closed-loop system, can be used to power turbines directly. If the brine resource is not superheated, it can still exchange its thermal energy to other heat-conductive substances. In the latter case, a closed system allows the brine resource to transfer its energy to other low boiling point materials. The low boiling point materials in the secondary stage system are used to operate high efficiency turbines, which in turn generate electrical energy. Because it is a closed system, the brine extracted from the geothermal wells is never contaminated by surface use. The brine resource is then reinjected into deep-Earth wells in close proximity to the extraction well (figure 6.2).

CASE STUDY—CALIFORNIA JOB GROWTH AND GEOTHERMAL DEVELOPMENT

"California's new Renewables Portfolio Standard (RPS) is expected to create very substantial growth in economic activity and job creation within

Figure 6.2   Flash Steam Power Plant

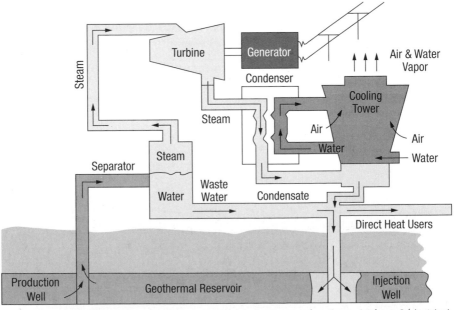

Source: http://coloradogeologicalsurvey.org/energy-resources/geothermal-2/uses-2/electrical-generation/, accessed October 23, 2018

the geothermal industry. The RPS was set at 20 percent renewables in 2017. If California energy companies satisfy 50 percent of RPS-required renewable energy growth with geothermal energy, they will develop 1,680 MW of geothermal power capacity over the next 14 years.

> According to the Geothermal Energy Association, California has the potential to boost output from existing plants in the near term by 300 to 600 MW, and can develop up to 1,000 MW at known but undeveloped reserves at each of three locations—the Salton Sea, northern California, and The Geysers area north of San Francisco—for a total of 3,600 MW that can be practically developed with today's technology. The Geothermal Resources Council lists 20 California-based geothermal energy development and service companies. Three of the world's biggest geothermal power companies are located in California. These businesses should benefit from this growth also. Assuming that just 30 percent of manufacturing activity associated with California geothermal energy development occurs in-state, full realization of the targets in the California RPS would result in [an estimated 61,060 person/years of employment] . . .
>
> Development and use of a domestic energy resource such as geothermal energy brings with it a multitude of economic and employment benefits. These economic benefits, such as the multiplier effect, are greatly extended within the local domestic economy when development of a domestic energy resource is realized. Many of the jobs created occur in rural areas where economic development initiatives are frequently overlooked. Growth in the energy production sector of the economy will occur, and the character of the energy resources developed will have significant economic and employment repercussions for the United States. In turn, this growth will have a positive impact on the environment. (EERE, 2005b: 13)

According to the Department of Energy map displayed below, geothermal resources above 200°C are classified as high-grade geothermal resources. Geothermal resource temperatures can be as high as 700°C. High-grade geothermal resources are abundant in the American West. Medium-grade resources (150–200°C) are located primarily in the West and Southwest, while low-grade resources (100–150°C) are found throughout the United States (figure 6.3).

SAFETY, ENVIRONMENTAL DAMAGE, AND EMISSION-RELATED ISSUES: GEOTHERMAL ENERGY

Potentially, use of a geothermal energy resource can lead to environmental damage and the production of quite harmful airborne emissions, but such problems can be minimized through the use of a closed-loop system as described in the previous section. A closed-loop system withdraws, uses, and reinjects brine, maintaining it within the confines of piping while on the Earth's surface. No geothermal brine is composed exclusively of pure water. H_2S and other

Figure 6.3 U.S. Geothermal Provinces

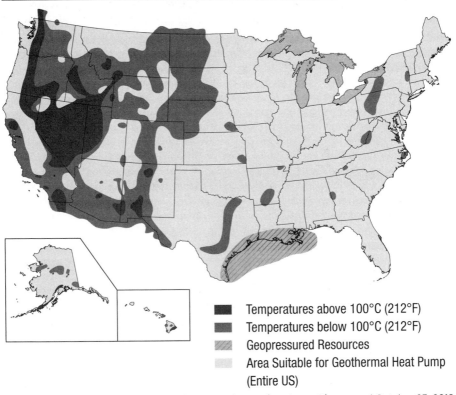

	Temperatures above 100°C (212°F)
	Temperatures below 100°C (212°F)
	Geopressured Resources
	Area Suitable for Geothermal Heat Pump (Entire US)

Source: https://geology.utah.gov/resources/energy/geothermal/, accessed October 23, 2018

dissolved gases in the brine must be trapped in the brine extraction process to prevent health risks and environmental damage; this can be accomplished through the use of a closed-loop system. If an open-loop system is used, then brine has contact with surface soils and air, possibly releasing any of several sources of contamination:

- hydrogen sulfide (H_2S)
- NH_3 (ammonia)
- CH_4 (methane)
- CO_2 (carbon dioxide)
- toxic sludge containing sulfur (S), vanadium (V), arsenic (As), mercury (Hg), nickel (Ni), and so on (see: Norman and Moore, 1999; Finster et al., 2015).

Soil and air contamination—such as sulfur dioxide (SO_2), which causes acid rain—are particularly problematic when resource development occurs on public lands. Assuming proper system management occurs, it is possible to maintain a small human technology "footprint" for geothermal resource extraction and use, thus reducing harmful effects on the environment and minimizing risk to public health (Union of Concerned Scientists, 2018).

TECHNICAL FEASIBILITY OF GEOTHERMAL ENERGY

Geothermal energy can be tapped and developed for use in a variety of ways. In some cases, geothermal energy is used to generate electricity. In such cases, the technical feasibility of the energy resource is measured in kilowatts (kW_e) or megawatts (MW_e). In other instances, the geothermal resource is used as a source of thermal energy and is measured in kilowatts (kW_t) or megawatts (MW_t). Four widely used types of geothermal technology will be discussed here: heat pumps, direct-use, flash steam power, and binary steam power (the two former technologies are thermal, while the two latter technologies are primarily used to generate electricity).

Heat Pumps

Although in use since the 1940s, this well-established technology experienced a surge in consumer interest in the 1970s. Heat pumps have become the most popular geothermal technology in the United States (Lund, 2003: 414), and have great potential for reducing thermal heating costs through large-scale system design (see Bujakowski and Barbacki, 2004; Phetteplace, 2007). Heat pump use declined sharply due to the housing market contraction and economic crisis of 2006–2008. The decline in heat pump use at that time also coincides with the prevalence of cheap natural gas in the wake of the hydraulic fracturing revolution. In recent years, however, heat pump use has again been increasing due to consumer demand for clean energy alternatives (Fialka, 2019).

Due to regulatory requirements for energy efficiency, energy costs, and consumer preferences, heat pump market penetration increased dramatically during the Obama presidency, with over 40 percent of new housing containing heat pump technology (Lapsa et al., 2017: 4). As with other forms of renewable energy discussed thus far, heat pump usage is largely dependent on the intersection of geography and geology—more specifically, on subsurface geology at a specified site and home design considerations (Roman, 2004).

Heat pumps can be relatively simple devices involving a well, piping, and a conventional circulatory pump. For commercial building heating purposes, the completed geothermal well must have ground or water temperatures that are satisfactory to meeting the heating needs of a building. A piping system is lowered into the well and chemicals such as antifreeze are put into the closed-loop system (see Zhao, 2004). Optimally, there must be no leakage of the heat transfer substance in the piping system into the well's water and surrounding soil resources. A pump at the surface level moves the heated liquid through the closed piping system, and building air is heated by transferring heat to or from the geothermal resource. For instance, in the winter months, cooler air is displaced by the transfer of geothermal heat energy to the building's air flow system. Conversely, in the summer months, heat in the building's air can be transferred to the antifreeze or other chemicals in the geothermal piping and pumped into the ground, thus cooling a building's interior climate (see Bloomquist, 2000).

While such closed-loop systems described above are a typically used option, some systems support an open-loop process. In open-loop systems, water resources, from either surface or well water, are circulated directly through the geothermal heat pump system. Open systems are only practical when there is access to a large water resource and assuming that the water resource meets water quality standards. For example, water with elevated sulfur content can pose serious health hazards.

Heat pump technology has advanced substantially due to in part to waste heat capture and use. In the cooling phase of a Rankine cycle—a thermodynamic model of a heat engine—waste heat exits the generation process. In more advanced heat pump systems, the waste heat is captured and used in a secondary energy generation process. The reuse of waste heat to generate either thermal or electrical energy increases the efficiency of heat pump technology.

Other Forms of Direct Use

Heat pumps represent one the largest direct-uses of geothermal energy, but there are a variety of other forms of direct-use mentioned below. Direct-use of geothermal resources worldwide has grown rapidly in recent years, and will continue to accelerate in growth for the foreseeable future (see IEA, 2018). In 2017, global direct-use of geothermal energy was approximately 544.9 PJ of energy. Currently, nearly 75 percent of geothermal direct-use is done by China. Combined, China and Turkey account for approximately 80 percent of geothermal direct-use globally. The United States accounts for only 11.8 J, which is approximately 2.1 percent of worldwide direct-use (figure 6.4).

Fish farming and greenhouses are two increasingly common direct-uses of geothermal resources, with typical resource temperatures being 150°C and below (Demirbas et al., 2004; Van Nguyen et al., 2015). According to Lund (2003), the largest concentration of aquaculture fish farming in the United States is in the Imperial Valley in Southern California. Over one million tons of bass, tilapia, and catfish are raised on an annual basis in about a dozen geofarms. Alligators are also raised in Imperial Valley commercial geofarm facilities, and the meat and skins harvested are used for food products and apparel.

Advanced farming practices are often made possible by the use of geothermal energy. Geothermal energy is frequently used in hothouse farm operations. In shopping for produce at a grocery store, it is likely that one will come across hydroponically raised tomatoes and other fruits and vegetables. Hydroponics requires raising plants in warm water, which is often accomplished

Figure 6.4   Geothermal Use, 2017

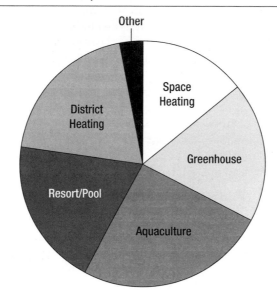

Data Source: Snyder et al., 2017: 3

with direct-use geothermal water. Geothermal heat resources are also used in produce dehydration facilities—for example, dried fruits, vegetables, herbs, and spices. Geothermal energy technology makes it technically feasible to grow and process a variety of crops throughout the United States (see Office of Energy Efficiency and Renewable Energy, 2018).

While the United States has abundant arable farmland in temperate climates, the technical feasibility of geothermal greenhouses is especially valuable in nations where weather and soil are less conducive to crop production. The geography of Turkey, for instance, is quite mountainous and the soil and climate have historically made farming challenging. In a burgeoning society, food resources must keep up with the ever-growing need for long-term sustainability. Demand for energy has inspired significant energy search processes to maximize the use of the country's geothermal resource potential. Turkey has increased its geothermal greenhouse acreage from near zero to over 100 hectares (approximately 247 English system acres). Greenhouse acreage must be thought of differently than standard cropland, since it is farmed much more intensively and often on a year-round basis. The warmer and more humid greenhouse conditions also allow for optimum crop growth and reduced time to harvest. This means that more food can be produced in a shorter amount of time because of direct-use geothermal agriculture technology (Melikoglu, 2017).

Geothermal energy technology is also readily used in the nonfood and leisure/tourism industry. Nonfood industries, such as flower growers, use geothermal aquaculture to produce houseplants and flowers for floral arrangements. Tree seedlings are developed in geothermal tree farm operations in several Western states, according to the EERE (2005a). Resort complexes make use of geothermal energy to create spas and maintain heated swimming pools. In the arid desert southwest, new citizens are often attracted to the hot climate, but are likely also to be attracted to warm water in swimming pools and spas, the use of which makes life in the desert regions fun.

Geothermal deep direct-use operations have become a focus of U.S. Department of Energy technology development grants (EERE, 2017). Direct use of geothermal energy reduces some capital costs of heat exchanger units and heat-conductive secondary fluids. Aquaculture and agriculture applications are typical examples of direct use. Technologically, it is possible to maintain geothermal aquaculture, agriculture, and deep direct-use operations so long as geothermal wells are maintained and water temperature managed so that plant growth rates are enhanced. Well water levels must either be managed through reinjection of surface water, or through careful water withdrawal plans. It is important, however, to realize that direct-use of geothermal resources remains under close study by scientists, determining its availability and seeking to specify the best methods and practices for protecting the resource.

Flash Steam Power

High-quality geothermal resources (i.e., very high temperatures and consistent geothermal water availability) typically emerge from geothermal wellheads as superheated steam. The steam in question can be piped directly into turbine systems for the generation of electricity. Power takeoff from the turbines is subject to signal management (see Köse, 2005: 69). After steam has been used to operate the turbine, it can be used to operate secondary or even tertiary stage flash steam turbines (Selek-Murathan et al., 2008). When the resource is no longer capable of operating turbine systems, it exits the turbine chamber and is cooled in a condensing system to the point where it becomes a liquid. The liquid in question is then reinjected into the geothermal reservoir through a secondary well outlet (DOE, 2018; DOE, 2003: 9).

Reinjected water is cooler than the geothermal brine in the reservoir. The cooler water resource has the potential to reduce the average temperature of the geothermal reservoir unless the reservoir gains energy at a rate faster than the rate at which energy is being lost through cooling. Geothermal scientists have been exploring the impact of reinjected water on the geothermal resource in at least two ways. First, scientists have studied the flow patterns of reinjected water. Second, scientists have studied the reservoir temperature recovery time of geothermal resources being used for direct-use and power generation (see Aliyu and Chen, 2017).

In a study conducted on Italian geothermal reservoirs, scientists used a 3-D numerical model of a geothermal plant reservoir to determine the sustainability of the reservoir given various reservoir temperature, pressure, and flow rates.

The study found that reinjected water can indeed lower the average temperature in a geothermal reservoir. The study found that locating the reinjection well 2km from the production well would maintain the quality of the reservoir and plant sustainability for fifty years at a flow rate of 1,050 tons/hour (277,380 gallons/hour) (Volpi et al., 2018). As was found in an earlier Japanese study, the cooler reinjected water mixes with hotter geothermal brine resources and potentially can reduce the quality of the resource if flow rate into the plant and reinjection rate and quality are not managed correctly (Kumagai et al., 2004). Resource quality reduction, however, has more to do with deep Earth geology surrounding geothermal reservoirs than return flow injection of cooled water. If the geothermal reservoir is in close proximity to magma veins extending from the Earth's mantle into the Earth's crust, then the impact on geothermal resources might be negligible.

A secondary issue relates to the availability of adequate geothermal water resources. As water is drawn for direct-use or electricity generation, brine in geothermal reservoirs may become depleted through evaporation losses. The disposal of treated waste water in the reinjection process has become commonplace in California's Imperial Valley direct-use geothermal projects. In Northern California, The Geysers, the only dry steam geothermal reservoir in use in the United States and the "world's largest single source of geothermal power"[1] (DOE, 2018), geothermal electricity generation projects are using treated waste water from nearby cities, such as Santa Rosa, California, for reinjection. Known as the Southeast Geysers Effluent Recycling Project (SEGEP), waste water is transported from California towns and cities such as Clear Lake, Lower Lake, and Middleton to The Geysers project field and injected into geothermal reservoirs (Calpine, 2018). Despite having passed through waste water treatment, there is some danger that the waste water might contaminate geothermal reservoirs. The contamination concern is heightened by evidence of impurities in the geothermal brine. Pryfogle et al. found that impurities in geothermal water provided the nutrition and warmth necessary for bacterial growth, resulting in a biofilm that formed on equipment (DOE, 2003: 174). Regulatory guidance exists to help manage the possibility of harmful bacterial contamination. In 1978, the Environmental Protection Agency produced a report on managing water reinjection quality through the use of bactericides (EPA, 1978).

Despite attempts to monitor geothermal reservoir movement and water levels, The Geysers geothermal electrical generation projects illustrate the long-term problem of heavy use of geothermal resources. Lund (2003: 410) reported that power generation was declining quite rapidly, but the rate of decline has been stabilized by the SEGEP injection plan. Goyal and Conant (2010) found that The Geysers was experiencing a 3 percent annual decline in steam production, which was less than the decline estimated without a reinjection plan (i.e., SEGEP). The Geysers produces almost 6 percent of California's total system power (California Energy Commission, 2019).

Binary Systems

The binary geothermal energy system is an alternative method of utilizing geothermal resources. Hot water is drawn up from a geothermal reservoir and is then run through a heat exchanger where the heat from the geothermal resource is transferred to substances with a low boiling point. The time required for efficient heat transfer must be carefully determined (see Nowak and Stachel, 2005). Typically, organic materials such as pentane (C_5H_{12}) or butane (C_4H_{10}) are used in binary systems for the heat transfer medium. Pentane and butane have low boiling temperatures (−36.1°C and −1°C, respectively). Even a low-grade geothermal resource contains sufficient thermal energy to raise pentane or butane above their respective boiling points. The superheated pentane or butane is then directed against a turbine generator for electricity production. Following use, the pentane or butane goes through a condenser to be cooled back to a liquid form, and then returned to the heat exchange unit to be converted back into steam in the generation cycle (Wicker, 2005). The cooled geothermal brine is then reinjected into the reservoir.

As with a flash steam process, the binary system is a closed system. In other words, geothermal water is never exposed to the surface atmosphere. Most importantly, the binary system does not mix geothermal water with the low-boiling point chemicals running through the heat exchange unit. Often, binary systems rely on lower quality geothermal resources that do not arrive at the surface in the form of steam; the geothermal water can be more easily reinjected. In the long run, this means that binary systems will be less likely to reduce the quality of the geothermal reservoir. Improved turbine technologies and the use of high-quality heat transfer, such as iso-butane, in the turbine operation process produces higher production efficiencies than have been found in flash steam systems.

Technology has made it possible for geophysicists to more accurately identify geothermal potential in geographic regions worldwide. Increased use of geothermal may mean decreased demand for fossil energy. For example, at its present rate of growth, India would have to more than double coal production by 2035 to meet the needs of the population and industry (*The Economic Times*, 2017). The resulting carbon monoxide, carbon dioxide, sulfur, nitrogen oxides, and particulate emissions would produce significant amounts of air and water pollution. Indian carbon dioxide emissions reached 1.8 GT in 2016 with a projected annual increase of slightly more than 6 percent during average economic growth conditions (see Andrew, 2018). Geothermal energy in India is a potential method of reducing carbon-based emissions (Sivasakthivel et al., 2014; Ghose, 2004).

As with India, Poland is a developing nation experiencing rapid growth. Between 2000 and 2017, Polish GDP rose by 205 percent. In the modern world, economic growth requires energy. In Poland, coal is the primary fuel in electrical energy production—53 percent of fuel used in the generation process, compared with a world average of 37 percent (OECD, 2016). While coal is readily available in Poland, geothermal energy could meet the nation's energy demands, reducing carbon-based emissions. Geothermal resources have been more fully explored in Poland since the fall of the Iron Curtain and the introduction of Western geophysical technology. The Southern Poland region along the Carpathian Mountain Range features high-quality geothermal resources. Polish geothermal resources in the region could potentially make the nation an energy exporter in Europe (see Sowizdzal, 2018; Bujakowski and Barbacki, 2004).

Technical developments have also led to the standardization of geothermal power plants and systems. Well development (see Garcia-Valladares et al., 2006), well casing (see Thomas, 2003),[2] turbine system corrosion resistance strategies

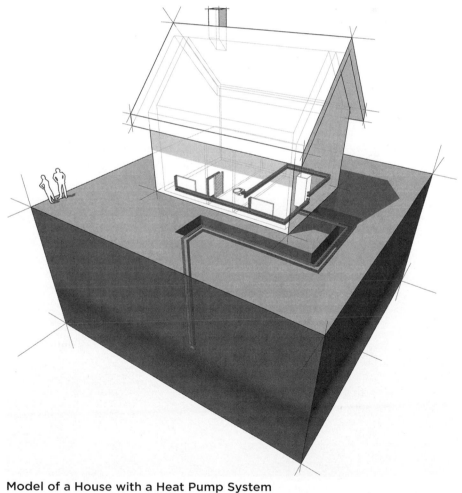

Model of a House with a Heat Pump System
iStock / Getty Images Plus / valigursky

(see Kubiak and Urquiza-Betran, 2002), and operations and maintenance have become standardized. Turbine systems do not have to be developed on-site; rather, the systems are now produced using standardized technology and are self-contained "turn-key" units capable of being easily transported to the geothermal site for ready use. Technical support is widely available for geothermal systems. Fortunately, energy systems wherever they might be are capable of being monitored globally via satellite data collection and Internet communication technology.

Technical feasibility is, however, ultimately a function of the continued quality and quantity of existing geothermal resources. While it is possible that overuse of geothermal resources will reduce the quality of known reservoirs, new developments in 3-D imaging have increased our understanding of geothermal reservoir flows and the impact of geothermal energy development on those flows. Energy scientists and developers now have a much better understanding of temperature differences across reservoirs and can optimize energy systems, monitor the rate of flow in and out of the reservoir, and manage pressure levels as well as accurately document the energy production taking place.

Much of what has been discussed above relates to conventional geothermal energy systems that use superheated steam or brine found deep within the Earth as a primary source of energy. However, the focus of geothermal energy has been increasingly moving toward enhanced geothermal systems (EGS). EGS uses some of the same technology breakthroughs that were discussed previously in terms of reservoir management, but goes several steps further. EGS seeks to

Drilling a Geothermal Well (Casings in Foreground)
iStock / Getty Images Plus / Rgtimeline

access hot dry subsurface rock (HDR) formations that are fractured before a geothermal fluid is injected for heat transfer. One of the potential downsides to EGS is the potential for micro-earthquakes resulting from fracturing hot rock. Fluid is circulated through a system of extraction and reinjection similar to conventional geothermal energy systems. EGS systems are largely possible to due to substantial public and private investment in drilling technology (EERE, 2018a; EERE, 2018b).

Technology is making it easier and more cost effective to manage geothermal reservoirs. Machine learning technology is used in the R & D stage for geothermal systems. Machine learning technology can be used to mine large datasets to identify optimum locations for siting geothermal production wells. Machine learning technology can also use real-time data on reservoir quality, facilitating more efficient system management and energy production (EERE, 2018c). Water use in the fracking of subsurface hot rock is an environmental concern. Next-generation technology aims to use foams and other substances to fracture rock formations without the use of water. In many cases, geothermal power is used to produce baseload electricity, but technological developments bring geothermal energy systems into the realm of energy storage. Heat pumps work on a similar principle—storing heat energy in the Earth and withdrawing it when needed.

In some areas of the country large-scale geothermal energy storage could be used to increase power grid reliability and enhance energy security. Furthermore, as we are becoming increasingly adept at accessing geothermal energy on the

Geothermal Energy Plant in Niland, California
iStock / Getty Images Plus / AvailableLight

A Steam Turbine Condenser
iStock / Getty Images Plus / imantsu

Earth, it is entirely possible that geothermal energy will be a key source of energy in any future space colonization efforts—other celestial bodies also contain subsurface thermal energy reservoirs (see Dorminey, 2016).

ECONOMICS OF GEOTHERMAL ENERGY

Economic calculations for geothermal power vary substantially among sources. Estimated costs are a function of the quality of the geothermal resource (reservoir flow rate and pressure, and geological fractures), location, demand level (related to wholesale price of electricity), type of energy use (i.e., electrical or thermal uses), and project development (see Tester et al., 1994: 119). Daniilidis et al. (2017) found that load factors (i.e., flow rates and resource quality) were the single most important consideration shaping perceptions of the techno-economic feasibility of geothermal energy. High-quality resources whose development is less costly are reflected in lower LCOE. Conversely, geothermal resources that are more difficult to access and develop will result in higher costs per unit of electricity.

One approach to dealing with resource quality, particularly resource quality variation in a single reservoir region, is known as cycling. Cycling limits continual use of any single geothermal resource. Cycling relies on the use of multiple technologies and power generation scenarios to maximize the economic benefits and at the same time protect geothermal resources for future productive uses (see Bloomfield, 2002).

Access to detailed geothermal development costs is limited due to their proprietary nature. Companies do not often share the detailed cost analysis behind plant development and operations due to concerns about divulging valuable information to competitors. Therefore, here I rely on a number of reports to piece together a picture of the costs and benefits associated with commercial-grade geothermal energy projects. Reported here are generic cost estimates, and the range of costs are due to various factors that shape geothermal energy plant development. According to Daniilidis et al. (2017), there are four general factors that shape commercial geothermal plant development: Operations, Geology, Technologies, and Well Factors.

Operational factors relate to flow rate and temperature of a geothermal resource. If a resource is of lower quality (i.e., medium or low brine temperature), this impacts operational system design. Lower quality brine resource might mean the use of a binary system as opposed to a flash steam system. As noted earlier, plant operations may have to rely on cycling to maintain the pressure and temperature of a geothermal resource, reducing system efficiency in the process. Geology plays a big role in operational efficiency as geology has a direct impact on well drilling costs and well depth for resource access as well as system pressure and flow. EGS systems require the fracturing of subsurface geological formations and the injection of fluids for heat transfer. Technological factors that shape system efficiency are often related to turbine efficiency, effective heat transfer, electrical system costs and quality control, and transmission/network costs. Finally, well factors include well exploration, drilling, and well-casing costs. Other factors not directly noted in Daniilidis et al. (2017) are land leasing costs, water rights costs, energy performance certificate costs (costs of having system registered for energy efficiency standards), labor costs (variable) and other regulatory costs; also, subsidies and incentives (may offset costs). In the United States, subsidies and incentives include production tax credits.

In 2017, Lazard, a financial and asset management firm with corporate headquarters in Bermuda, produced a report on the levelized cost of electricity across a broad spectrum of fossil and renewable energy resources. The report offers some insight into the types and ranges of costs being estimated for commercial geothermal energy development. For a 20 to 50 MW capacity geothermal plant (80–85% capacity factor), total capital costs range from $4,000 to $6,400/kW. Total capital costs include siting, design, well exploration and drilling, construction, permitting, and transmission tie-ins (rights of way and construction costs). Under this scenario, capital costs range from $80 to $320 million.

The U.S. Department of Energy offers a much lower capital cost estimate of $2,500/kW for commercial geothermal plants (U.S. Department of Energy, 2018). Lazard (2017) estimates variable operations and maintenance costs range from $30 to $40/MWh, which is 1.5 to 3.0 times higher than U.S.

Department of Energy (2018) estimates of between $10 and $30/MWh. Lazard (2017) estimates that construction time for a facility is thirty-six months, and facility life is estimated at twenty-five years. Lazard (2017) estimates that LCOE is between $77 and $117/MWh, with other estimates reporting LCOE ranging from $50 to $113/MWh (ThinkGeoenergy, 2018).

With EGS and increased system efficiencies, the U.S. Department of Energy estimates that the capital costs of commercial geothermal (capacity factor 91%) will decrease to $2,830/MW installed with a levelized O & M (annual) of $1,350/MWh. Under the U.S. Department of Energy scenario, the LCOE for geothermal would be $43/MWh—with a $2.8/MWh tax credit, the cost would slip to $40.3/MWh. If the Department of Energy estimates are correct, geothermal would become the second cheapest form of electricity by 2022—onshore wind is estimated to cost $37/MWh (U.S. Energy Information Administration, 2018).

Geothermal well costs are significant. According to Lukawski et al. (2014), well costs for oil and gas wells—the comparison group used for estimation—are approximately $587/foot for a 9,000-foot production well. Shevenell (2012) demonstrated that production and injection well costs vary substantially across sites, ranging from approximately $263,000 to $4.4 million per well, and that costs per foot ranged from $771 to nearly $3,827/ft (in 2018 dollars) (Shevenell, 2012).

Geothermal energy used by individual homeowners often comes in the form of heat pump technology. Heat pump technology uses existing heating and cooling ducts, reducing installation costs. According to a Canadian analysis, the use of geothermal heat pump technology can reduce the capital costs associated with home energy use by as much as 50 percent (U.S. Department of Energy, 2019a). Additionally, the associated energy production costs can be as little as one-fourth the costs associated with traditional fossil energy–based heating and cooling systems.

According to a study conducted by Goldberg et al. (2018), homeowners who use heating oil or propane to heat their homes are the most likely to see energy cost savings by incorporating a heat pump into their heating system. Switching from propane to a heat pump is estimated to save $1,462 annually in heating costs, while switching from oil to a heat pump is estimated to save $255 annually. Homeowners using natural gas for heating would not save money from switching to a heat pump, but would likely reduce their carbon footprint. Incorporating a heat pump into a cooling system could reduce energy costs $50–$200 per year. The payback time for heat pump installation is between nine and twenty-five years, depending upon the type of fossil energy system being replaced by the heat pump system. Depending upon heat pump brand, an installed heat pump system generally costs between $4,500 and $8,500 (2018) installed (Heat Pump Price Guides, 2019).

Geothermal energy currently benefits from federal corporate and individual tax credits. The federal corporate tax credit is a 10 percent rebate for corporate

Rotor of a Turbine
iStock / Getty Images Plus / photosoup

investment in geothermal energy systems (U.S. Department of Energy, 2019b). The Bipartisan Budget Act of 2018 resulted in the reinstatement of personal tax credits for fuel cells and small wind and geothermal heat pumps. The 2019 rebate amount is 30 percent, which can be applied to both materials and labor costs for residential systems. The rebate percentage will step down in future years—in 2022, the tax credit will be 22 percent (U.S. Department of Energy, 2019c).

FEDERAL GEOTHERMAL ENERGY PROGRAMMING

Federal involvement in geothermal energy is focused on three major areas: (1) direct and externally funded R & D programs; (2) the monitoring of geothermal energy demand, supply, and cost; and (3) intergovernmental and public–private partnerships. Federal programs are designed to promote geothermal energy development through a well-regulated and efficient market environment (see also Office of Energy Efficiency, 2018). In the United States, the federal government monitors the use or misuse of geothermal resources so as to maintain resource quality and availability. Through the three-pronged approach just noted, the federal government seeks to minimize its role in the development of geothermal energy resources, but at the same time maintain a major role in promoting the growth of geothermal energy. Energy policy in the area of geothermal resources is often intended to shape public–private institutional arrangements, leading to greater energy independence and the promoting of public health through clean energy usage.

Since 1971, the U.S. Department of Energy and related organizations have actively pursued ambitious domestic geothermal R & D projects (U.S. Department of Energy, 2018). The new millennium has witnessed many developments in geothermal energy. The U.S. Department of Energy Geothermal Technologies Office (GTO) emphasizes EGS as a next-generation approach to geothermal resource development. The GTO places emphasis on improved drilling technology and subsurface mapping of geothermal resources using LiDAR. The GTO has also built an initiative to enhance peer review of geothermal system design, bringing together Department of Energy bureaucrats, researchers, and industry research and design specialists in a collaborative effort to advance a sound science of geothermal energy systems. The U.S. Department of Energy also seeks to advance small business development in geothermal energy and also issues calls for proposals for competitive research and demonstration project grant funding.

According to the U.S. Energy Information Agency (2011), the relatively slow growth of geothermal generating capacity can be attributed to six major factors:

> "Technology costs"—EGS, which would access much deeper geothermal resources relying on "hot rock" and water injection rather than existing superheated steam and hot water reservoirs, are more expensive than current conventional geothermal plants
>
> "Location"—the economics of geothermal requires that plants be located at specific site with access to high temperature subsurface water resources.
>
> "Transmission access"—the highest-quality conventional geothermal resources are in the western United States, often in areas with limited transmission line access.
>
> "Completion lead times"—according to the EIA, geothermal facility development takes four to eight years, which is a much longer time than it takes to develop wind farms or solar fields.
>
> "Risk"—as noted earlier, water resources and reservoir management requires that geothermal development must proceed with due caution so as to not deplete the geothermal resource at specific sites.

Geothermal energy production has witnessed modest growth in net electricity generation over the last two decades of 21.7 percent between 2001 and 2018, growing to 16,728.45 thousand MWH (U.S. EIA, 2019).

The geothermal industry, university researchers, elected officials, and the U.S. Department of Energy bureaucracy act as an advocacy coalition that seeks to promote geothermal energy as a solution, and to maintain geothermal as a significant market player with the hopes of future growth through enhanced energy technology and improved economics through greater certainty of energy resource availability and better access through drilling technology development.

U.S. DOE is also seeking to improve geothermal energy economics by tying drilling for energy resources to mining for rare earth metals, which are an important potential by-product found in tailings from the well drilling process. In recent years, the United States has become heavily reliant on China for its supply of rare earth metals, sparking publicly expressed concerns (see Johnson and Seligman, 2019).

STATE AND LOCAL EFFORTS

State and local government R & D efforts are often financed by private development money or federal research grant money. Some states—Maine, for example—offer a matching fund program for renewable resource projects, such as geothermal projects related to specific public institution or community needs—for example, the University of Maine, the Maine Maritime Academy, and community renewable energy demonstration projects. Most states use a system of tax credits as incentives for private development of geothermal and other renewable energy resource projects.

Renewable portfolio standards at the state level create a market for "green energy"—a market that is increasingly global in scope (see Goken et al., 2004: 442)—requiring the enhanced use of green energy (zero- or low-emission-produced energy). Tax incentives for geothermal thermal projects, such as heat pumps, are quite common. Additionally, public utility commissions and power companies offer green energy generation incentives for renewable energy providers, such as commercial and small production geothermal energy generators. These incentives often come in the form of property tax credits or net metering programs that pay green energy producers for their zero- or low-emissions energy. Green tag programs and free market trading possibilities are additional incentives that exist at the state and local levels and are used by utilities and businesses to meet green energy requirements (see Victor, 1998).

Some of the highest-quality geothermal resources in the United States exist in California, Oregon, Washington, Arizona, Nevada, and Utah. Lower-grade geothermal resources exist throughout the United States. Enhanced geothermal systems hold the promise of greater access to deep energy resources throughout the United States, often located in pockets of high-quality subsurface heat resources at relatively shallow depths. Unlike wind and solar energy, geothermal is largely invisible to the public, as the resource is subterranean and the footprint for energy production equipment has become compact and nonintrusive. Since the passage of State Assembly Bill 1905 in 1981, which promoted the development of geothermal resources, California has developed geothermal direct-use and electrical generation facilities scattered in numerous cities and towns throughout the state (www.energy.ca.gov/geothermal/, accessed July 31, 2005). Similarly, Hawai'i Electric Light Company and its industry partners have tapped the subterranean heat of the island state's volcanoes to produce steam to power turbine generators. Geothermal power plants in Nevada produce over 3 million MWH of electricity on an annual basis. Geothermal accounts for just over 52 percent of renewable energy generation in the state of Nevada. The state of Nevada RPS requires 25 percent of electricity by 2025 to be produced by renewable energy—in 2017, the state was producing 41 percent of electricity using renewables (Sandoval and Dykema, 2017). Utah is the number three geothermal power producer, with 48 MW of installed capacity—a distant third when compared with California (2,732 MW) and Nevada (517 MW). Geothermal is in the early stages of development in Utah, with significant upward growth foreseen in the near future (O'Donoghue, 2013). Utah has hopes for a $140 million federally funded project through the U.S. Department's FORGE program to use fracking technology to extract pockets of heat to create steam to run turbines for electricity generation (Canham, 2018).

CHAPTER SUMMARY

Geothermal energy sources in the United States are ubiquitous, but are of varying levels of quality. Of minimal impact to resources, geothermal heat pumps are of growing interest to homeowners and commercial building managers. Heat pumps can significantly reduce the costs of heating a home or office building. Using higher-quality geothermal resources, thermal systems are capable of producing large quantities of energy for use in the operation of private business enterprises, homes, and office spaces. Geothermal electric systems are capable of generating power to be sold by power companies as green energy; additionally, independent green energy power producers (e.g., geothermal energy power producers) can receive green tags, certifying their green energy production capacity. Such green tags are sold on the open market to commercial power producers who can use them to document a claim that green energy is part of their energy portfolio, hence meeting green energy production requirements.

The future of geothermal energy is a function of the ability of technical experts to locate high-quality geothermal resources and effectively utilize them without depleting the resource in the process. The economics of geothermal energy production are for the most part straightforward. Geothermal energy costs are competitive with other energy sources. However, without proper understanding of a specific geothermal site, it is possible for geothermal to become cost ineffective over time. Understanding and management of a geothermal energy source is a critical aspect of developing a sustainable resource.

The political and social feasibility of geothermal energy requires continued investment in geothermal advances, such as the FORGE program that uses fracking technology to access subsurface heat resources, deep Earth mapping of geothermal resource potential, and efforts to expand the pool of geothermal energy producers through efforts to grow small business development in the geothermal industrial sector. Some limits on social feasibility might occur if the perceived risk of the aforementioned shallow earthquakes that occur in proximity to some geothermal production facilities is misunderstood, or if the public is not properly educated about such risk factors. Also, as with nearly any form of renewable energy facility located in remote regions, the environmental, cultural, and property rights issues offer opportunities for differences of opinion and for conflict to arise.

NOTES

1. Dry steam resources are very rare except in deep earth geothermal processes. The resource is accessed through wells between 7,000 and 10,000 feet deep. The high temperature resource is brought to the surface as steam and is used to operate turbine generators. In a hot water or flash steam system, the resource is brought to the surface as hot water and then through lowering pressure of resource, the water flashes into steam used to operate turbine generators for electricity.

2. Thomas (2003) discusses the use of titanium as a well casing material due to its ability to resist the corrosive capacity of certain geothermal brines.

REFERENCES

Aliyu, M., and Chen, H. 2017. Sensitivity analysis of deep geothermal reservoir: Effect of reservoir parameters on production temperature. *Energy* 129: 101–113.

Andrew, R. 2018. India's CO_2 emissions grew by an estimated 4.6% in 2017, despite a turbulent year for its economy. *Carbon Brief*, March 28. Retrieved from https://www.carbonbrief.org/guest-post-why-indias-co2-emissions-grew-strongly-in-2017, December 11, 2018.

Bloomfield, K., and Mines, G. 2002. Predicting future performance from reservoir management cycling. *Transactions*, September 22–25, volume 26.

Bloomquist, R. 2000. Geothermal heat pumps: Five plus decades of experience in the United States. *Proceedings World Geothermal Congress*, 3373–3378.

Brown, B. 2001. Klamath Falls geothermal district heating system flow and energy metering. *GHC Bulletin*, June, 10–11.

Bujakowski, W., and Barbacki, A. 2004. Potential for geothermal development in southern Poland. *Geothermics* 33: 383–395.

California Energy Commission. 2019. California geothermal energy statistics and data. Sacramento, CA: California Energy Commission. Retrieved from https://www.energy.ca.gov/almanac/renewables_data/geothermal/, June 14, 2019.

Calpine. 2018. The water story. Houston, TX: Calpine Corporation. Retrieved from http://geysers.com/water, December 11, 2018.

Canham, M. 2018. Utah will launch a major geothermal experiment with $140 million in federal energy grants. *Salt Lake Tribune*, June 14. Retrieved from https://www.sltrib.com/news/2018/06/14/utah-will-launch-a-major-geothermal-experiment-with-140-million-in-federal-energy-grants/, January 2, 2019.

Daniilidis, A., Alpsoy, B., and Herber, R. 2017. Impact of technical and economic uncertainties on the economic performance of a deep geothermal heat system. *Renewable Energy* 114: 805–816.

Database of State Incentives for Renewable Energy. 2005. Business Energy Tax Credit, http://www.dsireusa.org/library/includes/incentivesearch.cfm?Incentive_Code =US02F&Search=Technology&techno=geothermalelectric&currentpageid=2. Accessed July 31, 2005.

Demĭrbaş, Ayhan, Şahin-Demĭrbaş, Ayşe, and Demĭrbaş, A. Hilal. 2004. Turkey's natural gas, hydropower, and geothermal energy policies. *Energy Sources* 26: 247–248.

Dorminey, B. 2016. Why geothermal energy will be key to Mars colonization. *Forbes*, September 30. Retrieved from https://www.forbes.com/sites/brucedorminey/2016/09/30/why-geothermal-energy-will-be-key-to-mars-colonization/#638885744b25, June 14, 2019.

Economic Times. 2017. India's energy consumption to grow faster than major economies. *The Economic Times/India Times*, January 27. Retrieved from https://economictimes.indiatimes.com/industry/energy/oil-gas/indias-energy-consump-tion-to-grow-faster-than-major-economies/articleshow/56800587.cms, December 11, 2018.

Energy Efficiency and Renewable Energy (EERE). 2005a. Direct-use of geothermal energy. http://www.eere.energy.gov/geothermal/directuse.html. Accessed November 27, 2005.

———. 2005b. *Buried Treasure: The Environmental, Economic, and Employment Benefits of Geothermal Energy*. Washington, DC: U.S. Department of Energy, Geothermal Technologies Program.

———. 2017. Energy department announces up to $4 million for geothermal deep direct-use feasibility studies. June 30. Washington, DC: U.S. Department of Energy. Retrieved from https://www.energy.gov/eere/articles/energy-department-announces-4-million-geothermal-deep-direct-use-feasibility-studies, October 29, 2018.

———. 2018a. EERE success story: University of Oklahoma scientists crack the case wide open for enhanced geothermal systems, December 7. Washington, DC: U.S. Department of Energy. Retrieved from https://www.energy.gov/eere/success-stories/articles/eere-success-story-university-oklahoma-scientists-crack-case-wide-open https://www.energy.gov/eere/success-stories/articles/eere-success-story-university-oklahoma-scientists-crack-case-wide-open, December 11, 2018.

———. 2018b. Energy Department announces $11.4 million in new projects to advance efficient drilling for geothermal energy, October 9. Washington, DC: U.S. Department of Energy. Retrieved from https://www.energy.gov/articles/energy-department-announces-114-million-new-projects-advance-efficient-drilling-geo-thermal, December 11, 2018.

———. 2018c. Energy Department announces $3.6 million in machine learning for geothermal energy, July 19. Washington, DC: U.S. Department of Energy. Retrieved from https://www.energy.gov/eere/articles/energy-department-announces-36-mil-lion-machine-learning-geothermal-energy, December 11, 2018.

Fialka, J. 2019. Heat pumps gain traction as renewable energy grows: A switch from natural-gas-powered home heating and cooling could be cheaper and reduce carbon emissions. *Scientific American*, April 17. Retrieved from https://www.scientificamerican.com/article/heat-pumps-gain-traction-as-renewable-energy-grows/, June 14, 2019.

Finster, M., Clark, C., Schroeder, J., and Martino, L. 2015. Geothermal produced fluids: Characteristics, treatment technologies. *Renewable and Sustainable Energy Reviews* 50: 952–966.

Fridleifson, I. 2003. Status of geothermal energy amongst the world's energy sources. *Geothermics* 32: 379–388.

———. 2005. Geothermal energy amongst the world's energy sources. *Proceedings: World Geothermal Congress*, April 24–29, 1–5.

Garcia-Valladares, O., Sanchez-Upton, P., and Santoyo, E. 2006. Numerical modeling of flow processes inside geothermal wells: An approach for predicting production characteristics with uncertainties. *Energy Conversion & Management* 47(11/12): 1621–1643.

Gelegenis, J. 2004. Rapid estimation of geothermal coverage by district-heating systems. *Applied Energy* 80: 401–426.

Ghose, M. 2004. Environmentally sustainable supplies of energy with specific reference to geothermal energy. *Energy Sources* 26: 531–539.

Goken, G., Ozturk, H., and Hepbasli, A. 2004. Geothermal fields suitable for power generation. *Energy Sources* 26: 411–451.

Goldberg, D., Malone, E., Kallay, J., Takahashi, K. 2018. *Switching on the Savings: A Heat Pump Cost Effectiveness Study*. Cambridge, MA: Synapse Energy Economics. Retrieved from http://www.synapse-energy.com/about-us/blog/switch-savings-heat-pump-cost-effectiveness-study, January 1, 2019.

Goyal, K., and Conant, T. 2010. Performance history of The Geysers steam field, California, USA. *Geothermics* 39: 321–328.

Heat Pump Price Guides. 2019. Heat pump price comparison guides. Retrieved from https://www.heatpumppriceguides.com/, January 1, 2019.

International Energy Agency. 2018. Geothermal energy. Paris, France: International Energy Agency. Retrieved from https://www.iea.org/topics/renewables/geothermal/, October 29, 2018.

Johnson, K., and Seligman, K. 2019. How China could shut down America's defenses: Advanced U.S. weapons are almost entirely reliant on rare-earth materials only made in China—and they could be a casualty of the trade war. *Foreign Policy*, June 11. Retrieved from https://foreignpolicy.com/ 2019/06/11/how-china-could-shut-down-americas-defenses-rare-earth/, June 14, 2019.

Kaygusuz, K., and Kaygusuz, A. 2004. Geothermal energy in Turkey: The sustainable future. *Renewable and Sustainable Energy Reviews* 8: 545–563.

Köse, R. 2005. Research on the generation of electricity from greenhouse resources in Simav region, Turkey. *Renewable Energy* 30: 67–79.

Kubiak, J., and Urquiza-Betran, G. 2002. Simulation of the effect of scale deposition on a geothermal turbine. *Geothermics* 31(5): 545–562.

Kumagai, N., Tanaka, T., and Kitao, K. 2004. Characterization of geothermal fluid flows at Sumikawa geothermal area, Japan, using two types of tracers and an improved multi-path model. *Geothermics* 33: 257–275.

Lapsa, M., Khowailed, G., Sikes, K., and Baxter, V. 2017. The U.S. residential heat pump market, a decade after "The Crisis." 12th IEA Heat Pump Conference. Retrieved from http://hpc2017.org/wp-content/uploads/2017/05/O.2.1.2-The-U.S.-Residential-Heat-Pump-Market-a-Decade-after-The-Crisis-and-Regional-Report-North-America.pdf, October 24, 2018.

Lazard. 2017. *Lazard's Levelized Cost of Energy Analysis Version 11.0*. Bermuda: Lazard.

Li, K., Bian, H. Liu, C., Zhang, D., and Yang, Y. 2015. Comparison of geothermal with solar and wind power generation systems. *Renewable and Sustainable Energy Reviews* 42: 1464–1474.

Lukawski, M., Anderson, B., Augustine, C., Capuano, L., Beckers, K., Livesay, B., and Tester, J. 2014. Cost analysis of oil, gas, and geothermal well drilling. *Journal of Petroleum Science and Engineering* 118: 1–14.

Lund, J., and Boyd, T. 2000. Geothermal direct-use in the United States. *Geo-Heat Center Bulletin*, Klamath Falls, OR: Geo-Heat Center, 21(1).

Lund, John W. 2003. The USA Geothermal Country Update. *Geothermics* 32: 409–418.

Melikoglu, M. 2017. Geothermal energy in Turkey and around the world: A review of the literature and an analysis based on Turkey's Vision 2023 energy targets. *Renewable and Sustainable Energy Reviews* 76: 485–492.

Norman, D., and Moore, J. 1999. Methane and excess N_2 and Ar in geothermal fluid inclusions. Proceedings: 23rd Workshop in Geothermal Reservoir Engineering, Stanford University, Stanford, California. Retrieved from https://pangea.stanford.edu/ERE/pdf/IGAstandard/SGW/1999/Norman.pdf, October 24, 2018.

Nowak, W., and Stachel, A. 2005. Assessment of operation of an underground closed-loop geothermal heat exchanger. *Journal of Engineering Physics and Thermophysics* 78(1): 136–143.

O'Donaghue, A. 2013. Utah no. 3 in the country for geothermal power. *Deseret News*, February 26. Retrieved from https://www.deseretnews.com/article/865574271/Utah-No-3-in-the-country-for-geothermal-power.html, January 2, 2019.

Office of Energy Efficiency and Renewable Energy. 2018. *2017 Annual Report: Geothermal Technologies Office*. Washington, DC: U.S. Department of Energy. Retrieved from https://www.energy.gov/sites/prod/files/2018/01/f47/GTO%202017%20Annual%20Report.pdf, January 1, 2019.

Organization of Economic Cooperation and Development. 2016. *Fossil Fuel Country Note: Poland*. Paris, France: OECD. Retrieved from file :///C :/Users/u0722430/Downloads/POL_Country_Brief_05SEP2016-cou_feedback.pdf, December 11, 2018.

Ozgener, O., and Kocer, G. 2004. Geothermal heating applications. *Energy Sources* 26: 353–360.

Phetteplace, G. 2007. Geothermal heat pumps. *Journal of Energy Engineering* 133(1): 32–38.

Podger, P. 2003. Geysers wastewater project begins an uphill run today. *San Francisco Chronicle*, December 3, A23.

Prasad, G., Swidenbank, E., and Hogg, B. 1999. A novel performance monitoring strategy for economical thermal power plant operation. *IEEE Transactions on Energy Conversion* 14(3): 802–809.

Raghuvanshi, S., Chandra, A., and Raghav, A. 2006. Carbon dioxide emissions from coal based power generation in India. *Energy Conversion & Management* 47(4): 427–441.

Roman, H. 2004. The Earth can heat our homes. *Power & Energy*. www.techdirections.com, accessed March 19, 2006.

Rozen, K., and Olejniczak, P. 2005. Poland's coal-based power generation: Will pressure create diamonds? *World Power* 2005: 1–5.

Rybach, L. 2003. Geothermal energy: Sustainability and the environment. *Geothermics* 32: 463–470.

Sandoval, B., and Dykema, A. 2017. *Status of Energy Report—2017*. Carson City, NV: Governor's Energy Office, State of Nevada. Retrieved from http://energy.nv.gov/uploadedFiles/energynvgov/content/About/2017%20SOE%20v10.4%20(High%20Res).pdf, January 2, 2019.

Selek-Murathan, A., Murathan, A., and Demirbas, A. 2008. Electricity production from geothermal sources by using double-stage flash system. *Energy Sources Part A: Recovery, Utilization & Environmental Effects* 30(20): 1884–1889.

Serpen, U. 2004. Hydrogeological investigations on Balçova geothermal system in Turkey. *Geothermics* 33: 309–355.

Shevenell, L. 2012. The estimated costs as a function of depth of geothermal development wells drilled in Nevada. *GRC Transactions* 36: 121–128.

Sivasakthivel, T., Murugesan, K., and Sahoo, P. 2014. A study on energy and CO_2 saving potential of ground source heat pump system in India. *Renewable & Sustainable Energy Reviews* 32: 278–293.

Snyder, D., Beckers, K., and Young, K. 2017. Update on geothermal direct-use installations in the United States. *Proceedings: 42nd Workshop on Geothermal Reservoir Engineering*, Stanford University, Stanford, CA. SGP-TR-212.

Sowizdzal, A. 2018. Geothermal resources in Poland: Overview of the current state of knowledge. *Renewable & Sustainable Energy Reviews* 82: 4020–4027.

Tester, J., Herzog, H., Chen, Z., Potter, R., and Frank, M. 1994. Prospects for universal geothermal energy from heat mining. *Science & Global Security* 5: 99–121.

ThinkGeoenergy. 2018. New report by IRENA shows competitiveness of geothermal based on LCOE. *ThinkGeoenergy*, Retrieved from http://www.thinkgeoenergy. com/new-report-by-irena-shows-competitiveness-of-geothermal-based-on-lcoe/, December 12, 2018.

Thomas, R. 2003. Titanium in the geothermal industry. *Geothermics* 32(4–6): 679–687.

Union of Concerned Scientists. 2005. Environmental impacts of renewable energy technologies. http://www.ucsusa.org/clean_energy/renewable_energy_basics/environmental-impacts-of-renewable-energy-technologies.html, accessed November 27, 2005.

———. 2018. Environmental impacts of geothermal energy. Retrieved from https://www.ucsusa.org/clean_energy/our-energy-choices/ renewable-energy/environmental-impacts-geothermal-energy.html#.W9CxS9VKjX5, October 24, 2018.

U.S. Department of Energy (DOE). 2001. *Federal Geothermal Research Program Update Fiscal Year 2000*. Washington, DC: U.S. Department of Energy, Office of Wind and Geothermal Technologies.

———. 2003. *Federal Geothermal Research Program Update*, DOE/NE-ID-11147. Washington, DC: U.S. Department of Energy.

———. 2018. *Geothermal Basics*. Washington, DC: U.S. Department of Energy. Retrieved from https://www.energy.gov/eere/geothermal/geothermal-basics, October 23, 2018.

———. 2019a. *Heat Pump Systems*. Washington, DC: U.S. Department of Energy. Retrieved from https://www.energy.gov/energysaver/ heat-and-cool/heat-pump-systems, January 1, 2019.

———. 2019b. *Business Energy Investment Tax Credit (ITC)*. Washington, DC: U.S. Department of Energy. Retrieved from https://www.energy.gov/savings/business-energy- investment-tax-credit-itc, January 1, 2019.

———. 2019c. *Residential Renewable Energy Tax Credit*. Washington, DC: U.S. Department of Energy. Retrieved from https://www.energy.gov/savings/residential-renewable-energy-tax-credit, January 1, 2019.

U.S. Energy Information Administration. 2011. U.S. has large geothermal resources, but recent growth is slower than wind or solar. *Today in Energy*, November 18. Retrieved from https://www.eia.gov/todayinenergy/detail.php?id=3970, July 13, 2019.

———. 2018. *Levelized Cost and Levelized Cost of New Generation Resources in the Annual Energy Outlook 2018*. Washington, DC: U.S. Energy Information Administration. Retrieved from https://www.eia.gov/outlooks/aeo/pdf/electricity_generation.pdf, December 12, 2018.

———. 2019. *Electricity Data Browser*. Retrieved from https://www.eia.gov/electricity/data/browser, July 13, 2019.

U.S. Environmental Protection Agency. 1978. *Pollution Control Guidance for Geothermal Energy Development*. Washington, DC: EPA

Van Nguyen, M., Arason, S., Gissurarson M., and Pálsson, P. G. 2015. Uses of geothermal energy in food and agriculture: Opportunities for developing countries. Rome, Italy: Food and Agriculture Organization, United Nations. Retrieved from http://www.fao.org/3/a-i4233e.pdf, June 14, 2019.

Victor, D. 1998. Green markets. *Ecology* 79(6): 2210–2211.

Vimmerstedt, L. 1999. Opportunities for small geothermal power projects. *GHC Bulletin*, June, 27–29.

Volpi, G., Margri, F., Colucci, F., Fisher, T., DeCaro, M., and Crosta, G. 2018. Modeling highly buoyant flows in the Castel Giorgio: Torre Alfina deep geothermal reservoir. *Geofluids* 18: 1–21.

Wicker, K. 2005. Geothermal: Hotter than ever. *Power* 149(1): 40–44.

World Energy Council. 2005. *Geothermal Energy*. London, UK: World Energy Council, http://www.worldenergy.org/wec-geis/publications/reports/ser/geo/geo.asp, Accessed July 17, 2005.

Zhao, L. 2004. Experimental evaluation of a non-azeotropic working fluid for geothermal heat pump system. *Energy Conversion and Management* 45: 1369–1378.

7

New Century Fuels and Their Uses

★ ★ ★

Energy storage is an important part of the current and future energy infrastructure. New forms of energy storage, such as the use of ultra-capacitors, in conjunction with batteries (see Gao and Lu, 2018; Ashtiani et al., 2006), will become more readily available in the future. At the present time, however, batteries and fuels are the most common elements in the energy storage paradigm. Advances in battery technology have been quite dramatic because of much technical research and the effective commercialization of numerous breakthroughs on materials, storage methods, and increased discharge capacities (see Service, 2018; Park et al., 2015; Jacoby, 2006). Through programs such as the National Renewable Energy Laboratory's Vehicle Technologies Office and the Batteries and Electrification R&D Program, the U.S. Department of Energy has vigorously pursued next-generation battery R & D. Battery research, however, is only one dimension of the energy future.

A new fuel paradigm is a critical part of the energy future. A useful fuel is one that can be effectively stored and, in a stored setting, is accessible for use on demand. Coal was once a very large portion of our fuel paradigm, prominently used for cooking, heating, industrial applications, transportation, and for the generation of electricity. It now represents a shrinking proportion of the nation's fuel paradigm—in 2001, 52 percent of electricity produced in the United States was generated using coal, but as of 2019, less than 38 percent of the nation's electricity is generated with coal, with more reductions likely in the future. Heavy reliance on petroleum for transportation fuel is well known and understood. Price factors, supply forecasts, and concerns with fuel emissions have moved the energy paradigm toward increased diversity in both fuel type and source. Natural gas, for instance, has risen to prominence, and alternative fuel development is rising fast. Knowledge of the status of the fuel paradigm and potential is an important aspect of understanding energy policy and energy sustainability in communities of the future. Electrical energy storage in fuels and in batteries are both important in overcoming the intermittency problems posed by alternative energy sources, such as wind and solar energy.

FUEL AS A CONCEPT

A fuel is a form of stored energy that is typically expended (generally, through combustion) to release energy. The ability to access and harness a fuel is the critical first step in making it a useful source of energy for human society. In everyday life, most individuals do not actively consider the near-miraculous nature of fuel understood as stored energy, or the very high energy densities (J/m^3) of petroleum, natural gas, and other fossil energy fuel sources that are still in wide use today, compared with the very low energy densities of renewable energy (see table 7.1). An alternative energy source, nuclear energy, has extremely high energy density. It is conjecture, of course, but it is possible that human society has become so used to high-density energy sources, in particular fossil fuel sources, that the average person believes that all fuel sources are equally of high quality. That, however, is not remotely the case (see Shellenberger, 2019).

Accessible fuel sources, in particular those with high energy density, have been a central concern to humanity since the discovery of fire in prehistoric times. Many traditional sources of fuel discovered and used by human societies thousands of years ago are still widely used to heat homes and offices, and to generate electricity. Wood is probably the earliest known form of fuel in human society.[1] Another traditionally used fuel still in wide use today is crude petroleum, sometimes found in the form of a thick tar called bitumen.

Table 7.1 Energy Density

Source	Joules per Cubic Meter
Solar	0.0000015
Geothermal	0.05
Wind at 10 mph (5m/s)	7
Tidal water	0.5–50
Human	1,000
Oil	45,000,000,000
Gasoline	10,000,000,000
Natural gas	40,000,000
Coal	22,500,000,000 – 33,750,000,000
Fat (food)	30,000,000
Nuclear	1,500,000,000,000,000

Source: (Layton 2008: 441–442)

Over the past 200 years, technological developments have made energy sources more accessible and methods of production have been streamlined. Economically, it became possible to extract, process, and store large quantities of fuel at a reasonable cost. Fuel sources became much more accessible to consumers, commercial and private alike. Revolutionary new exploration, extraction, and refining developments in the petroleum industry and the development of large-scale coal mining in the United States and in other developed nations were critical preconditions to the development of modern and highly sophisticated militaries; the construction of factories; the growth of cities; and the provision of electrical energy to millions of consumers. In fact, large quantities of reasonably priced stored energy in the form of fuel has become an essential good in modern society (Pront-van Brommel, 2016; Podobnik, 2006).

In the twentieth century, it was widely believed a permanent energy solution was found in the form of fossil energy, but optimism about fossil energy began to decline in the 1970s and continues today. First, the advent of oil crises demonstrated that reasonably priced accessible fuel sources are not "a given"; as with nearly every other good or service in modern society, fuels are a commodity with prices driven by forces of supply and demand. For various reasons, the price of petroleum declined during the 1980s and 1990s, which may have closed policy windows for renewable energy—albeit, for a short time. World energy demand has grown greatly, partly because of

LNG Storage
iStock / Getty Images Plus / CreativeNature_nl

rapid economic development in nations such as China and India. The price of fossil fuel sources would be increasing dramatically if it were not for dramatic technological advancements in hydraulic fracturing and drilling technology, developments that have increased the supply of petroleum and natural gas markedly. At least for the time being, fuel supply is less of a concern, while the growing marginal social and environmental costs, in the form of carbon emissions, are of great concern (Flower, 2019). Public perceptions of the fuel sources used for well over a century have changed, and while we continue to rely on fossil energy quite heavily, there is growing demand for clean alternative sources of energy (Groom, 2017). We are beyond doubt moving toward a lower energy density energy paradigm that will require society to make some tough choices about energy consumption (see Wilson, 2013).

The culture shift and environmental movement in the 1960s and 1970s brought increased awareness of the pollution produced by the use of traditional fuels such as wood, petroleum, and coal. In all three cases, the use of these energy sources produces quite harmful effects relating to the Earth's climate and its plant and animal species. Critics of the fossil fuel paradigm argue that the total costs—to include marginal social and environmental costs—of using traditional fuels outweigh the economic and social benefits produced. The political and social divide on political, environmental, and social costs is particularly acute at the current time, with President Trump referring to climate change as a "hoax" (Flowers, 2019), while progressive politicians, academics, and citizen groups point to strong scientific evidence of likely irreversible climate damage caused by the widespread use of fossil fuels.

Alternative fuels are best viewed as an attempt to respond to both climate change realities and changing consumer values. Alternative fuel source development will expand the supply of energy available for sale in the marketplace. Basic economics dictates that increased demand shaped by consumer values will likely bring more suppliers into the marketplace. Competitive markets lead to lower prices for consumers. In terms of climate change, increased demand for alternative fuels will lead to reduced emissions into the atmosphere associated with climate change.

At the federal level, a move to develop clean fuels was first driven by early environmental policies, such as the Clean Air Act of 1970 and the Energy Policy and Conservation Act of 1975, which established emissions and fuel economy standards for motor vehicles (CAFE standards). Later laws, such as the EPAct of 1992, the EPAct of 2005, the EISA of 2007, and the ARRA of 2009, both raised environmental standards for motor vehicles as well as encouraged the development of alternative-fuel motor vehicles (AFVs). Through policy innovation at the U.S. state level, several states offer noteworthy incentives for the purchase of AFVs and offer incentives to retrofit existing motor vehicles for alternative-fuel usage.

NATURAL GAS

Natural gas is not normally considered to be an alternative fuel, because oftentimes "alternative" is misunderstood to mean "renewable" or "green." Natural gas is a hydrocarbon composed primarily of methane and propane, but under U.S. federal statute, it is an alternative fuel that produces far fewer GHG emissions than do conventional fuels such as gasoline and diesel (see 42 U.S. Code 13211). Natural gas was first used in Britain in the late eighteenth century for both commercial and residential purposes. The U.S. natural gas industry began to take form in the early nineteenth century, with well-digging and gas pipeline developments following the discovery of abundant sources. In 1859, Edwin Drake, who dug the first successful oil well in Titusville, Pennsylvania, piped natural gas from the wellhead to a local community for residential and commercial purposes. As a source of illumination, natural gas was eventually superseded by the incandescent light bulb, invented by Thomas Edison in 1878. Nevertheless, natural gas assumed and maintained other useful purposes as a source of thermal energy. With technological developments in efficient pipeline transportation (for example, advanced welding techniques that made pipelines less leak prone), natural gas was considered a low-risk fuel source and demand for it rose over time. Following the passage of the Natural Gas Act of 1938, federal rules in addition to state regulations governing the natural gas industry were promulgated by Congress and are enforced by the FERC (table 7.2).

The natural gas industry was partially deregulated in the 1980s and 1990s so as to encourage further development of natural gas resources. Natural gas's relatively low level of emissions and low price remained major selling points. In the early years of the twenty-first century, domestic supply was curtailed by high demand on the existing proven reserves and reduced access to natural gas exploration on public lands. For a time, the excess demand led to increased importation of natural gas. For transportation purposes, the gas is cooled and stored in a liquefied form—liquefied natural gas (LNG). In the early twenty-first century, only six major U.S. ports were capable of handling

Table 7.2 Natural Gas Consumption

Methane	70-90%
Propane	0-20%
Carbon Dioxide	0-8%
Oxygen	0-0.2%
Nitrogen	0-5%
Hydrogen sulfide	0-5%
Rare gases	trace

LNG off-loading from transport ships, a fact that reduced supply accessibility.[2] One major LNG port facility area was located along the Texas and Louisiana Gulf Coast region—an area hit hard by Hurricane Katrina (see Parfomak, 2003: CRS-4–CRS-5), causing some concern about the security of the natural gas supply.

By 2005, domestic natural gas production had reached a low of 18 trillion cubic feet of production annually. Through tax credit incentives, public–private partnerships to advance drilling and extraction technology, and the maturity of hydraulic fracturing processes, U.S. domestic "tight" oil and gas were accessed in large quantities and at substantial profit in several areas, including North Dakota and Pennsylvania. By 2017, dry natural gas production had increased by over 50 percent to 27.3 trillion cubic feet. Through existing environmental regulation, the Obama administration sought to limit the growth of oil and gas extraction on public lands, but the Trump administration put fears of environmental damage aside and reversed Obama's course of action, accelerating the process of oil and natural gas field exploration, development, and production on public lands (Fears, 2018).

Uses for natural gas are expanding beyond the traditional thermal energy market. In compressed form, natural gas is used to operate internal combustion engines and produces fewer emissions than gasoline on a per-BTU basis. In response to tightened emissions standards, some cities have adopted natural gas as a primary fuel for mass transit operations (Gaul and Young, 2003: 12). Natural gas is now the leading fuel source used for U.S. electricity generation, surpassing coal in 2015–2016 (Energy Information Administration, 2018c).

Natural gas is a traditional fuel source of growing importance to the U.S. fuel paradigm. While some emissions reductions can be achieved through the use of natural gas, there are two factors that limit its long-term place in the fuel paradigm. First, natural gas is not renewable. At some point, availability will fall off and prices will rise significantly. As it is, current demand has been largely met and exceeded by increased natural gas supply, leading to a substantial decline in wellhead prices—from $10.79/tcf in July, 2008 to an average $2.31/tcf in July 2019, representing a 78.59 percent drop in natural gas prices.

Second, the exploration of natural gas is technically feasible, but is not always political/socially acceptable. Under the Trump administration, environmental rules are being relaxed substantially, and natural gas exploration is highly encouraged, but the political future of natural gas is likely to be curtailed by Democratic majorities in Congress and future more progressively minded presidents. Extraction of coal bed methane involves continued resource extraction in the form of virgin coal, or the reclamation of older mines, which may pose safety risks—again, both plans face forms of political and social opposition. In the long run, other clean fuel paradigms will be pursued.

OTHER ALTERNATIVE FUELS

Clean Diesel

As mentioned earlier, the large-scale use of clean diesel is driven by energy and environmental regulation, which requires a significant reduction in sulfur emissions, specifically, a 95 percent reduction in sulfur dioxide emissions from diesel vehicles. In response to regulation, clean diesel is an industry response to meeting new environmental regulations (see HP Innovations, 2005).

While next-generation diesel engine systems are being produced to burn fuel more efficiently and with reduced emissions (see Ehrenman, 2005), existing vehicle fleets require retrofitting. In 2005, the EPA provided $1.6 million in grants for retrofitting projects (see Pollution Engineering, 2005). Furthermore, in 2018 the EPA announced $2 million in competitive grants to help Native American tribes clean up diesel engines being used on U.S. Native American reservations across the country (Air Quality & Climate Change, 2018). In several states, such as California, Washington, and Oregon (http://www.hydrogencomponents.com/hythane.html, accessed August 14, 2005), clean diesel retrofit programs provide tax credits to owners who retrofit their farm vehicles. Research on clean diesel has demonstrated that approximately 90 percent of the harmful emissions from traditional diesel engines can be eliminated through clean diesel retrofitting and the sequestration of particulates and the use of fumigation to control NOx emissions (Jankowski and Kowalski, 2018; http://www.energy.ca.gov/afvs/clean_diesel.html, accessed August 14, 2005).

Biodiesel

Clean diesel research programs also focus on the development of a product known as biodiesel. The fuel is made from virgin oils (or previously used cooking oils) produced from plant seeds such as canola and soybeans, and also from animal fats. Biodiesel development is driven by public–private partnerships, often involving the U.S. Department of Energy, Office of Energy Efficiency and Renewable Energy, and the U.S. Department of Agriculture.

In the production of biodiesel, the oil and/or fats are purified and water is removed. The triglycerides present are separated and purified through a process known as transesterification (Alvarez et al., 2010; Meher et al., 2006). Two products that result from transesterification are methyl esters (biodiesel) and glycerin (used for other products such as soaps and cleaners). It has been shown that blending traditional diesel with biodiesel significantly reduces emissions due to the absorption characteristics of chemical compounds found in biodiesel (Bakeas et al., 2011; Durán et al., 2006). Blends of biodiesel with diesel fuel are typically 5 to 20 percent biodiesel. B-100 is a product comprised entirely of biodiesel. There is evidence that diesel engine operating parameters need to be adjusted when using biofuel blends or B-100—for example, engine timing and compression ratios require adjustment. There is also evidence of short-term problems with engine operation, such as "carbon deposition, lubricating oil dilution, piston ring sticking, and injector nozzle choking" can occur with some frequency (Patel et al., 2016: 41) (figure 7.1).

The emissions reductions gained from the use of biodiesel are significant. Using B-100, it is possible to reduce carbon emissions of diesel vehicles by as much as 78.45 percent. A study conducted in Brazil demonstrated a 3.9 percent decrease in CO_2 vehicle emissions from the use of B-5, and a 15.7 percent decrease in emissions from the use of B-20 in diesel engines (Coronado et al., 2009: 210).

Ethanol

Under the EPAct of 1992, a blend of 85 percent ethanol and 15 percent gasoline (E85) is considered an alternative fuel. Ethanol is made from sugar feedstock—often field corn or sugar cane. After the feedstock is harvested, it is ground up

Figure 7.1   U.S. B-100 Production and Consumption (2001–2018)

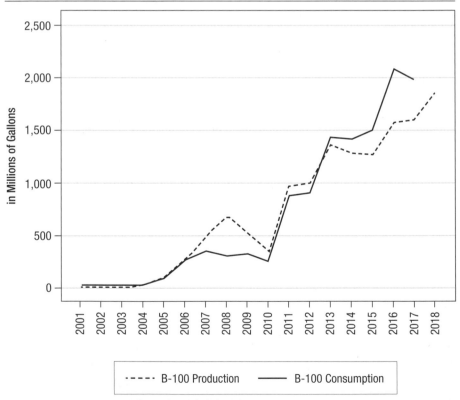

Data Source: Energy Information Administration

and the sugar is separated. The sugar is then used as a food supply for microbes (yeasts). One by-product produced from microbial digestion is ethanol.

One problem with using corn, sugar cane, and similar high sugar content feedstocks in the production of ethanol fuel is that these feedstocks are part of the human food chain. When food is diverted to fuel production, then there is real potential for food price increases; rising food prices have both domestic and international implications. While most, but not all, Americans have access to basic foodstuffs, food security is a real problem in many other parts of the world. Increased food prices and reduced supply has its largest impact on developing nations (Jianping et al., 2014). While the connection between biofuels and food prices has been pointed out as cause for concern, there remains disagreement about the degree to which biofuels have an adverse impact upon food prices (see Araujo Encisco et al., 2016). With respect to food insecurity, this problem has been linked to public health crises as well as political and social unrest (Krzyminiewska, 2013).

Ethanol production that does not use food as a feedstock is likely a more socially responsible method of producing alternative fuels. Cellulosic sugars found in crop waste, wood waste, or from products such as switch grass and green algae are alternative sources of food for the microbes used in ethanol production (Biello, 2008; Rapier, 2018). Cellulosic sugars are more expensive to process than sugars from corn or sugar cane, but the benefit is that sources of cellulosic sugars are not part of the human food supply. Crop waste, wood waste, and related sources of cellulosic sugars are often in large supply in both urban and rural settings (Woodson and Jablonowski, 2008) (figure 7.2).

Figure 7.2   U.S. Ethanol Production (1981–2018)

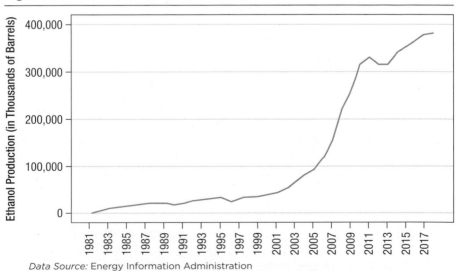

Data Source: Energy Information Administration

Ethanol raises the level of oxygen in gasoline when used as a blended fuel. Higher oxygen levels contribute to higher performance of the fuel and reduce air-borne emissions, as required by the amended Clean Air Act of 1990. Most gasoline blended in the United States is E10—that is, 10 percent of a gallon of gasoline is composed of ethanol (Energy Information Administration, 2019). When blended in this form, E10 is not considered to be an alternative fuel, but rather serves to reduce the overall use of petroleum-based fossil energy. Blends higher than 10 percent during the summer months are considered by the EPA to be harmful to the environment as the emissions contain a higher amount of particulates than is contained in unblended gasoline. Politics, however, appears to be reshaping the regulation of ethanol blends. The Trump administration is seeking to end the 10 percent restriction and allow fuel blends to increase to E15 during the summer months. One reason for this decision is higher demand for ethanol and resulting profits for farmers who raise feedstock and ethanol production facilities that blend and market fuels (Wald, 2018).

A study conducted by Argonne National Laboratories found that the use of E10 (corn ethanol) reduced greenhouse gas emissions by approximately 5 percent. The use of E25 and E40, under research conditions, produced an additional 10 and 15 percent reduction in GHGs, respectively. Using corn stover (cellulosic ethanol using the leaves and stalks of corn plants) results in much more significant reductions in GHGs because the whole plant is being used more efficiently. E40 made using corn stover results in a near 30 percent reduction in GHGs compared to E10 (corn ethanol) serving as a baseline (Han et al., 2015). U.S. farmers currently produce nearly all of the ethanol consumed domestically. In 2018, domestic production of ethanol was approximately 382.4 million barrels of ethanol (Energy Information Administration, 2017a).

While ethanol is one method of oxygenating gasoline, another substance known as methyl tertiary-butyl ether (MTBE) can also used for oxygenation. MTBE can be produced in large quantities at a relatively low price; however, MTBE has been linked to groundwater and soil contamination—an undesirable aspect of the fuel additive. For this reason the state of California phased out use of MTBE between 1999 and 2002, and much of the rest of the nation has followed California's lead in this regard (Energy Information Administration, 2018a). By 2006, twenty-three states had banned MTBE, and it is no longer used domestically; it remains an export product from the United States to some Latin American countries (Energy Information Administration, 2018a).

THE HYDROGEN INITIATIVE

In his 2003 State of the Union address, President George W. Bush announced a $1.2 billion initiative to develop a hydrogen-based economy. According to the Bush White House, hydrogen fuel cells were "a proven technology."

Ethanol Biorefinery Plant
E+ / BanksPhotos

The proponents of the initiative contended that the technical and economic uncertainties related to the use of hydrogen in fuel cells will be overcome through efforts to lower the cost of hydrogen and fuel cells, as well as developing better methods of storage of hydrogen-based fuels. The initiative intended to link the hydrogen economy to President Bush's "Freedom Car" initiative, a program that established the goal of U.S. energy independence by 2020. The Bush Hydrogen Initiative maintained that the development of the hydrogen economy will reduce air pollution and greenhouse gas emissions by "more than 500 million metric tons of carbon equivalent each year by 2040" (White House, 2003).

The Bush plan was broadly criticized as being built on false promises and without full recognition of the difficulties facing the development of a hydrogen economy (Hoffman and Harkin, 2003). Many difficulties facing alternative energy policy in the United States may have been made worse because of a lack of commitment to previous policy goals and overreliance on fossil fuel and existing energy infrastructure (see Jaskow, 2003; Jorgneson, 1981; see Mattoon, 2002). By contrast, a more consistent European commitment to "green" energy and environmental standards (see Dunn and Flavin, 2002) has produced more coherent energy policy results in the EU (see Miller et al., 2002; Fuel Cells Bulletin, 2018).

Nevertheless, proponents of the hydrogen initiative such as Jeremy Rifkin (2002, 2003) concluded that a hydrogen-based economy will come

Hydrogen Fuel Cell for an AFV
iStock / Getty Images Plus / 4P_Wei

to fruition (see also Lakely, 2003). International momentum does exist to promote hydrogen fuel cells as a key component in efforts to reduce GHG emissions, as evidenced by some initiatives launched by the World Economic Forum, Davos, Switzerland (Dincer and Acar, 2018), which link hydrogen fuel cell technology with smart energy innovations. Japan has a growing commitment to hydrogen fuel cell transportation applications. Located in Aichi Prefecture, a factory unit owned by the Toyota Motor Corporation produces about ten hydrogen fuel cell vehicles per day. As more nations urgently pass climate change legislation to reduce GHG emissions, it is likely that demand for such hydrogen fuel cell vehicles will increase. Certainly, as an island nation and importer of energy, Japan would benefit from greater energy independence and reduced reliance on the international petroleum market (see Phillips, 2019).

HYDROGEN AND FUEL CELLS

Technical Feasibility Issues

The major advantage to the hydrogen fuel cell is its efficiency in producing electricity. Hydrogen fuel cell development can be traced to studies conducted by Sir William Grove in 1839, whose early work was later refined by Francis Bacon in 1932 (Francis, 2002: 34; Ketelaar, 1993). The basic idea behind the fuel cell is that pure hydrogen is isolated from oxygen molecules within a fuel cell system. In a fuel cell, an anode attracts the electrons—thus forming H$^+$ ions—particles that are then free to travel though electric circuits. The cathode, or positive end of the fuel cell, distributes oxygen molecules along its surface. A proton exchange membrane (PEM) dividing the fuel cell anode and cathode allows H$^+$ ions to travel freely to the cathode, but restricts the passage of electrons, which are then forced through electric circuits. A catalyst composed of platinum powder facilitates the combination of the H$^+$ ions, O$_2$ molecules, and the electrons traveling to the cathode; the resulting combination is H$_2$O, or pure water.

Pure hydrogen is a highly explosive gas commonly broadly thought to be dangerous. The evidence for the gas's explosive qualities is mixed, however (Vaitheeswaran, 2004). In its favor, hydrogen is an odorless gas and is not harmful to humans except in very high concentrations. The gas also rises and disperses into the atmosphere very quickly, which reduces its threat in outdoor applications. Hydrogen gas also has a high burn/explosive velocity, which means that while it burns, it does so very quickly and is therefore less explosive as a concentrated gas (see Tran et al., 2018; Rigas and Sklavounos, 2005). Based on these positive qualities of hydrogen, many technical proponents of hydrogen fuel cell vehicles argue that it is a safe energy source for vehicle use and for energy storage.

However, technically minded critics point to several areas of concern with regard to hydrogen fuel cell vehicles. First, hydrogen fuel cells have the potential to run on very high voltages. Exposure to voltages of greater than 50V can cause heart failure—some fuel cell vehicles run on 350+V, which increases the risk of electrocution (Hennessey and Nguyen, 2014; College of the Desert, 2001). A second area of concern is the inability to rapidly detect failures in the fuel cell. Tanrioven and Alam (2005) assessed the reliability of grid-connected PEM fuel cell (PEMFC) power plants. While not a transportation system, PEMFC systems require auxiliary power generation systems to maintain generation capability due to periodic system failures. PEMFC system operations are adversely impacted by hours of operation and age of system; failure rates become much higher after eight years of operation. Temperature variation impacts in winter months also adversely impact PEMFC systems to a small degree (Tanrioven and Alam, 2005: 277). One method of detecting fuel cell failures and reducing the impact of failures on equipment and continued system operation through back-up power is through the use of fault tolerant switches (Guilbert et al., 2016). Alternatively, PEMFC systems can be used as auxiliary power in case of failure of a primary power system reliant on fossil or other sources of alternative energy in both road vehicle and aircraft operations (see Stratonova et al., 2003; Guida and Minutillo, 2017).

The production and storage of hydrogen are additional areas of potential technical problems and conflicting conclusions. Hydrogen is the most abundant element in the universe, but it is clearly not easy to produce and store for use in energy systems. On Earth, hydrogen is not found in its elemental state, but rather forms chemical bonds with other elements. All petroleum-based products contain hydrogen, but the energy inputs required to remove or "strip" hydrogen are extremely high and result in carbon emissions. The hydrogen for fuel cell use will be "clean" energy, but any carbon-based source material used to produce the hydrogen in this scenario must also be considered.

Green power approaches are a second method of producing hydrogen. In essence, hydrogen would be obtained from water through a process known as electrolysis. The use of fossil fuels to run electrolysis plants would make little sense economically because, in essence, there would be a huge loss of energy in the hydrogen production process—that is, more energy would be lost to create hydrogen gas than would be produced from the resulting hydrogen gas used in fuel cell vehicles or for other uses. Therefore, the use of wind, solar, or geothermal energy to produce electricity to be used to power an electrolyzer for the production of hydrogen is the basis of the "green" power approach to producing a net reduction in GHG emissions while simultaneously "producing" a valuable fuel.

Several issues must be addressed in the "green" power model. First, the model requires a huge capital investment in alternative energy production systems. Since the first edition of this book was published in 2007, wind turbine prices have fallen more than 50 percent (Hirtenstein, 2018). Photovoltaic technology is in a period of transition, but system prices have come down appreciably in the last ten years (Energy Information Administration, 2018b). The operations and maintenance costs associated with wind and solar systems vary based on location, climatic conditions, and character of use. Depending upon site location of a renewable energy system and a hydrogen gas production facility, electricity generated by the "green" energy systems could conceivably store electricity on the power grid or, alternatively, store electricity in batteries. Deep cycle lead acid batteries were commonly used a decade ago, but lithium-ion batteries are seen as a better technology. Lithium-ion batteries now command 80 percent of the large battery storage market (EIA, 2018d, 1), but they have their own environmental issues. Polytetrafluoroethylene, an ozone-depleting chemical, is used in the production of lithium-ion batteries (Vandepaer et al., 2017). Pumped hydro or compressed air could be alternative ways of storing "green" electrons needed to power an electrolyzer.

In the green power model described above, battery storage is intended to overcome the intermittency issues associated with solar and wind energy for an off-grid hydrogen production facility. That assumption might not be realistic because the power grid exists, electrons are electrons, and the electricity market purchases electricity from many power producers. But, for the sake of argument, let us assume that in a grid-connected model for hydrogen production using electrolysis to generate hydrogen, the producer still insists that the electricity used comes from zero-carbon emission sources. In order to accomplish this goal, the hydrogen producer would have to either have dedicated transmission lines from an alternative generating source, or would have to purchase green tags to account for any carbon-based electricity generated and used by the hydrogen production facility.

The most common method of storing hydrogen is in gaseous, liquid form. Gaseous hydrogen is stored in tanks under great pressure. Because hydrogen is the smallest element, it is tends to be an "escape artist" and there is the potential for fuel losses in both storage and transportation. Storage tanks must be heavily lined with lead sheathing to reduce gas losses. Another method of storing hydrogen is in a supercooled or liquid form. The process of liquefying hydrogen is very expensive because of the tremendous pressure required and the need for maintaining a supercooled state to avoid tank rupture. Solid hydrogen is actually a gaseous state in which the hydrogen molecules bond with metal hydride filigrees constructed within tanks (Rueda et al., 2018; Zuttel, 2003). In its bonded state, hydrogen must be returned to a free gaseous state for use in a fuel cell. On a final note, the storage of hydrogen is further hampered by the gas's ability to weaken metal structures, which may cause gas losses as well as pose public and workplace safety issues.

Overcoming the energy storage issues surrounding intermittent solar and wind energy "naturally," geothermal energy can be used to produce electricity for the production of hydrogen. The southwestern region of the United States holds some of the greatest promise for geothermal development. In terms of social and environmental costs, "[g]eothermal plants emit about 5% of the carbon dioxide 1% of the sulfur dioxide, and less than 1% of the nitrous oxide emitted by a coal-fired plant of equal size, and certain types of geothermal plant produce near-zero emissions" (Holm et al., 2012: 2).

Economic Feasibility Issues

The cost and benefits of producing hydrogen are reflected in the wide range of estimated production costs involved using energy sources ranging from biogas pyrolysis to nuclear energy. The cheapest method of producing hydrogen listed below is through biogas pyrolysis—not the electrolyzer process discussed earlier. The pyrolysis process involves the burning of household wastes, waste wood, agricultural by-products, and other waste materials in "waste to energy" plants. Biogas pyrolysis involves the emission of carbon into the atmosphere (assuming it is not captured and sequestered), but the feedstock is from waste materials. Some feedstock needs to be chemically treated prior to pyrolysis, and different feedstocks have different energy contents (see Skodras et al., 2006). Steam reforming gasification, which often involves the pyrolysis of everyday waste products—such as household and commercial garbage—is the most expensive method of producing hydrogen gas. In the steam reforming process, syngas is produced and hydrogen is then stripped from the syngas product. The price of feedstock, energy density, and carbon emissions, along with processing costs, are significant factors in the price of the hydrogen produced (Salkuyeh et al., 2018). In terms of solar and wind energy sources, concentrated solar power is one of the most expensive methods of producing H_2 ($9.12/kg), and even with low wind energy costs, the price per kg of H_2 produced is quite high ($5.30–5.80/kg H_2). Arguably, solar and wind energy costs, while high, involve near-zero carbon emissions and thus minimal marginal social costs compared to the burning of waste products via pyrolysis, although the latter (with carbon capture and sequestration) results in an estimated $2.41/kg H_2. Nuclear energy is another zero-carbon emission fuel yielding an estimated $3.00/kg H_2, not factoring in the high capital costs of nuclear energy if the process involved building new reactors and, likewise, not factoring in the costs of disposing of nuclear waste (table 7.3).

Hydrogen used in fuel cell applications is a method of storing energy for later generation of electricity or for combustion purposes (e.g., Hythane™ or related products). For purposes of electricity production in electric vehicle applications, the market price of hydrogen was $13.99/kg in 2018, which is the equivalent of $5.60 per gallon of gasoline (California Fuel Cell Partnership, 2019). While the fuel price is higher, hydrogen-powered vehicles are more efficient than gasoline-powered vehicles—the cost per mile to operate a hydrogen-powered vehicle is approximately 8 percent lower than equivalent gasoline-powered vehicles. The added benefit is that hydrogen is a renewable energy source. Depending upon the fuel source used in fuel production, it is also carbon neutral, which translates into lower social and environmental costs.

In terms of bulk energy storage, hydrogen is unlikely to become an optimum solution. According to a key report prepared by Deloitte (2015), hydrogen for bulk energy storage is anticipated to become a part of the bulk energy storage framework within the next two years, but will be only a moderate part of energy storage planning through 2030. Compressed air storage is likely to be the most prominent player in the bulk energy storage market, while lithium ion

Table 7.3   Hydrogen Production Costs by Energy Source

Energy Source	Cost/kg H_2
Biogas pyrolysis (Peng et al., 2017: 193)	$0.91–$1.52
Steam reforming (Peng et al., 2017: 193)	$1.78
with CCS	$2.41
gasification	$9.17
electrolysis	$7.75
CSP electrolysis (Mohammadi and Mehrpooya, 2018)	$9.12
Biomass feedstock ($30/ton) (Salkuyeh et al., 2018)	$1.38
Wind energy (~ $0.08/kwh) (Moshin et al., 2018)	$5.30–5.80
Nuclear (Antony et al., 2012)	$3.00
Geothermal Energy (Yilmaz, 2017)	$1.08–$1.15

and advanced lead-acid batteries are predicted to be the major part of ancillary energy storage (Deloitte, 2015).

OTHER TYPES OF FUEL CELLS CURRENTLY IN USE AND/OR DEVELOPMENT

Alkaline Fuel Cells (AFC)

AFCs were developed in the 1960s and used aboard spacecraft in the Apollo missions as a key source of power. AFCs are also used aboard Space Shuttle vehicles. Given the energy "creation" process, an ACF can also produce potable water, which is a valuable asset in space flight. The inputs into an ACF fuel cell are H_2 and O_2. The former input occurs on the anode end of the fuel cell, while the latter is on the cathode end of the fuel cell. It should be noted that both of these materials are potential fire hazards; therefore, the AFC must be carefully managed to protect against possible accidents.

The electrolytic material between the anode and the cathode portion of the fuel cell is composed of potassium hydroxide (KOH). Potassium is part of the alkalai earth metals family of elements and has a tendency to give up an electron needed by an OH-molecule, thus forming an ionic chemical bond. Visualizing the electrolytic material, one would likely see it in the form of a white flaky material called caustic potash or lye. The material is easily dissolved in water, and it gives off tremendous heat when that occurs—this means that it has exothermic qualities. Potassium hydroxide also "likes" to absorb CO_2, which would effectively destroy its value as an electrolyte in the AFC fuel cell. The system must be closed so as to prevent CO_2 from corrupting the fuel cell. Note: this is much easier to do in outer space than in terrestrial applications.

In essence, at the anode end, covalently bonded hydrogen molecules are attracted to the hydroxyl ions in the electrolyte, producing water and four free electrons. The electrons travel to the cathode side of the fuel cell via the electrical circuits (where they can be used as an energy source). At the cathode end of the fuel cell, the electrons chemically interact with oxygen molecules and water molecules, producing four hydroxyl ions (OH-), which are then drawn into the electrolytic portion of the fuel cell: the cycle begins anew and repeats (see Mugerwa and Blomen, 1993; http://www.fctec.com, accessed August 13, 2005).

Direct Methanol Fuel Cells (DMFC)

DMFCs were first developed in the 1990s and operate similarly to standard hydrogen fuel cells. At the anode end of the cell, liquid methanol is introduced to pure water, producing CO_2 gas, hydrogen ions, and electrons. The hydrogen ions travel through the electrolyte, but the electrons are forced to travel through an electrical circuit to react, on the cathode end of the fuel cell, with oxygen and the hydrogen ions to form water. DMFCs remain in development stages, with relatively low efficiency rates at the present time (< 10%). The polymer materials required for the process are a bit more expensive because they must be sturdier in the chemical reaction process than the thinner platinum used in PEM hydrogen fuel cells; this makes the DMFC option more expensive currently. It is hoped that with continued materials science research and engineering development, DMFCs can eventually be used to power automobiles and trucks and be used in other consumer products.

Molten Carbonate Fuel Cells (MCFC)

MCFCs were first developed in the 1950s by two Dutch scientists, G. H. J. Broers and J. A. A. Ketelaar (see account: http://www.fossil.energy.gov/programs/ powersystems/ fuelcells/fuelcells_moltencarb.html, accessed August 14, 2005). In the 1960s, scientists at Texas Instruments developed small-scale (i.e., 100W– 1kW) MCFCs for the U.S. Army. Following the oil shocks of the late 1960s and early 1970s, the U.S. Department of Energy formed cooperative relationships with several private sector enterprises (e.g., FuelCell Energy) to promote research, development, and pilot production of MCFCs. According to the Office of Fuel Energy in the U.S. Department of Energy, FuelCell Energy MCFC units currently "are operating at 42 installations nationwide" (http://www.fossil.energy.gov/ programs/ powersystems/fuelcells/fuelcells_moltencarb.html, accessed August 14, 2005).

MCFCs require tremendous energy inputs to operate. As the name of the fuel cell would imply, the process requires melting an electrolytic material known as lithium potassium carbonate salts, requiring temperatures at or exceeding 1,200°F. In a molten state, the electrolyte is able to attract ions that are passed between the anode and the cathode. The MCFC fuel cell anode input is hydrogen (H_2), which interacts with the molten electrolyte to produce water, carbon dioxide, and two free electrons that travel through electrical circuitry (available for use as a source of power) to the cathode. The inputs at the cathode are oxygen (O_2) and carbon dioxide (CO_2). The carbon dioxide produced by the anode reaction can be recaptured and become an input for the cathode, as CO_2 levels need to be replenished in the electrolyte due to the loss of carbon dioxide at the anode end chemical reaction (Anahara, 1993).

The MCFC requires and produces tremendous thermal energy. The extremely high temperature operation means that chemical compounds of which the fuel is comprised move quite freely and allow the efficiency of electricity production to be very high. If the thermal energy used and produced in the MCFC fuel cell is recaptured, and is used to keep the fuel cell process operating, the production overall efficiency of the MCFC fuel cell "can be as high as 85%" (See http://www. fossil.energy.gov/programs/powersystems/fuelcells/ fuelcells_moltencarb.html;http:// www.fossil.energy.gov/programs/ powersystems/ fuelcells/fuelcells _moltencarb.html, accessed August 14, 2005).

A major disadvantage of MCFC cells is that the very high temperature at which they operate restricts the variety of their applications—for instance, it would not be safe in most residential applications (http://www.visionengineer. com/env/mc.shtml, accessed August 14, 2005). Another disadvantage of MCFCs is that high temperature production units have a tendency toward corrosion and resultant system failure; thus, the operation and maintenance of MCFC units is likely to be relatively expensive (http://www.corrosion-doctors.org/FuelCell/mcfc. htm, accessed August 14, 2005).

One major advantage of MCFCs is that the system does not require the expensive platinum catalysts used in other fuel cell systems; the Office of Fossil Energy reports that relatively inexpensive nickel catalysts are sufficient for MCFC units (http://www.fossil.energy.gov/programs/powersystems/fuelcells/fuelcells_ moltenc arb.html, accessed August 14, 2005). According to Roberge (2005):

> If built in low numbers, MCFCs are likely to cost around $3000/kW. If costs can be reduced to $1500/kW, which would require order commitments to support high-volume manufacturing, these systems could find significant utility markets for distributed generation in grid-support applications.

Phosphoric Acid Fuel Cells (PAFC)

PAFCs were first developed in the 1960s and 1970s. The basic design of a PAFC is not dissimilar from that of the other fuel cells discussed. The fuel cell operates at optimum levels at temperatures ranging between 300°F and 400°F. As with other fuel cell systems, PACFs usually use platinum catalysts at both the anode and the cathode. Hydrogen is the input at the anode. Hydrogen ions migrate through the phosphoric acid electrolyte, while the freed hydrogen electrons travel through electrical circuits to perform useful work. The input at the cathode is oxygen, which can be ambient air from the atmosphere. Experiments have shown that the carbon dioxide in ambient air will be tolerated by an SOFC up to a certain concentration level. The output at the cathode is pure water (Van den Broek, 1993).

The operating efficiency of PAFCs is approximately 40 percent, but if used in a "cogeneration" system—such as heat input sources coming from excess heat generation at fossil fuel fired energy plants—the efficiency rate achieved can be as high as 85 percent (http://www.fctec.com/fctec_types_pafc.asp, accessed August 14, 2005). One of the advantages of PAFCs is that they are very useful in small-scale applications, such as homes and commercial enterprises. Running at cooler temperatures, PAFCs are safer systems to operate. Nevertheless, the price of a PAFC is still quite substantial, and would likely require incentive programs to make the systems affordable to the average homeowner or business. According to the Office of Fossil Energy, U.S. Department of Energy, the typical PAFC costs between $4,000 and $4,500 per kW plant size.

Solid Oxide Fuel Cells (SOFC)

SOFCs were first developed in the 1930s by Swiss scientists. Despite many developmental problems discovered by European and Russian scientists in the 1940s and 1950s, SOFC research was not discontinued. In the early 1960s, the Westinghouse Corporation conducted additional research on the development of a viable SOFC system.

SOFC systems run at very high temperatures (approximately 1,800°F). The electrolytic portion of the SOFC is composed of a series of thin tubes. The tubes often resemble a compact diskette in terms of their thickness (http://chemelab. ucsd.edu/ fuelcell/soxide.htm, August 14, 2005), and are often hollow, allowing air to flow through the tube. Along the outer portion of the inside of the tube a solid oxide compound is used. The studies conducted by Westinghouse noted above used zirconium oxide and calcium oxide. The chemical reactions that occur may require methane as an input on the anode portion and ambient air as an input at the cathode, although oxygen molecules are the primary reactive elements needed. The process produces carbon dioxide and water as outputs, as well as substantial electrical power (http://chemelab.ucsd.edu/fuelcell/ soxide.htm, accessed August 14, 2005). Other systems may use pure hydrogen gas an anode input, producing only pure water and electricity as an output. One significant advantage to the SOFC is that a ceramic-type tubing can be used, which is more resistant to corrosion problems brought on by the extreme operational temperatures (see also Murugesamoorthi et al., 1993).

APPLICATIONS FOR NEXT-GENERATION ALTERNATIVE FUELS, FUEL CELLS

Applications for alternative fuels—beyond the natural gas paradigm—have been primarily initiated by government regulations and clean air benchmarks in domestic regulations and in international agreements such as the Kyoto Treaty.[3] Briefly discussed earlier, ethanol (manufactured from corn) is a form of alternative fuel that can be used in gasoline-powered engines. Ethanol has been a subsidized energy product (U.S. Department of Energy, 2019) for several decades, and has been touted as a clean renewable energy source of the future. Clean diesel and biodiesel blend applications are of immediate importance in alternative fuel development. The Environmental Protection Agency has developed a reduced sulfur rule for diesel requiring a 95 percent reduction in sulfur emissions for trucks produced in the 2007 model year and beyond (U.S. Environmental Protection Agency, 2019; Milbourn, 2001).

Transportation

Transportation is one of the largest consumption sectors in the fuel market. According to the Energy Information Agency, U.S. Department of Energy, over 46 percent of petroleum demanded in the U.S. market is sold and used in the form of gasoline, and approximately 71 percent of petroleum is used for transportation (U.S. Energy Information Administration, 2019b). Of some note, given the exceptionally high petroleum prices in nominal terms in the current market, petroleum demand has not substantially declined. The mobility and sustainability of the modern society is imperative; therefore, safe, reliable, and effective fuel alternatives must be researched and developed for application in transportation.

While the natural gas model has become more prevalent, another simple transition involving next-generation fuel would involve a clean diesel vehicle. In other words, clean diesel engines would replace the current generation of internal combustion gasoline engines, in part driven by the aforementioned EPA standards. Of the two requisites outlined by many proponents of alternative fuel, clean diesel addressed only one issue: namely, the issue of air, water, and soil impacts from fuel emissions. It would not, however, move the fuel paradigm beyond reliance on fossil fuels.

Alternative fuels such as hydrogen for fuel cells are also being developed for large-scale use. Hydrogen fuel cells are being developed in mass transit bus systems, and are currently either used or tested in many metropolitan areas in Europe, Canada, the United States and elsewhere. Hydrogen fuel cells have demonstrated their capacity to produce the large quantities of power needed to move a bus at an efficient speed (see Eudy and Post, 2019).

Light-duty utility vehicles face the primary problem of trying to gain access to a refueling site. The infrastructure for hydrogen refueling is being developed, but projections for a refueling infrastructure and vehicle development envision market growth in the 2020s and beyond. If states, such as California, are to meet their GHG emission targets, getting people into zero-emission (ZEV) or low-emission vehicles and out of their gas and diesel cars and trucks is a good strategy. A multistate *State ZEV Programs Memorandum of Understanding* was agreed to by seven states, including California (EIA, 2017c), seeking to promote and accelerate market growth in zero-emission vehicles through rebates and tax incentives for consumers and financial penalties for vehicle manufacturers that do not meet required sales levels of zero-emission vehicles (EIA, 2017c: 2). California's goal is to have at minimum 3.3 million zero-emission vehicles on the road by 2025.

In a 2005 study of transportation and fuel cell technology, niche transportation units are growing in popularity. Niche transportation units are not primary vehicle systems, but are an important first step in the development of affordable, reliable, and easily refueled personal and mass transportation.

In the 1960s, the market demand for fuel cells tended toward the development of scooter transportation, forklifts, and various forms of marine/submarine applications (Adamson, 2005: 2). What is particularly interesting is that while NASA has used fuel cells in spacecraft, a survey of niche market demand demonstrates that aerospace applications have never been a significantly large portion of the niche fuel cell transportation market. In recent years, market growth in fuel cells has concentrated heavily on stationary and transportation applications.

The domestic fuel cell market has been consolidated and is experiencing tighter profit margins due to international competition and basic material costs for fuel cell fabrication. Fuel cell manufacturers are developing partnerships and are receiving federal grants to develop a range of "proof of concept" demonstration projects. Internationally, fuel cell markets are growing rapidly in places such as Japan, which seeks to reduce its reliance on petroleum imports and to reduce GHG emissions. China and the European Union are also making great strides in fuel cell technology and product development and marketing. Japanese, Korean, and European car companies are all manufacturing fuel cell electric cars. U.S. heavy-duty truck manufacturers are working with the U.S. Department of Energy to build heavy-duty semitrucks powered by fuel cells. Fuel cell manufacturers are also partnering with governments in Europe to develop fuel cell–powered rail demonstration projects. Airlines, such as EasyJet, are using fuel cells to power aircraft during taxiing to reduce both carbon fuel use and GHG emissions (see Curtin and Gangi, 2017).

At the moment, the fuel cell market demand is still developing, likely due, in part, to changing governmental regulations and incentives reflecting sustainability concerns. Without government regulations and incentives, market growth is likely to be hampered by high pilot system costs. Fuel cell personal vehicles are significantly more expensive than similar vehicles powered by fossil fuel. The argument in favor of fuel cell vehicles, however, is that base price does not factor into the social and environmental costs of using fossil energy. However, the contrarian argument is that fuel cell and electric vehicles reduce GHG emissions only if the energy inputs into fuel cell or electric vehicles are low- or zero-emission sources (see Lesser, 2018).

Electric vehicles are another alternative to gasoline- and diesel-powered motor vehicles. Electricity produced by alternative and renewable energy sources—natural gas, nuclear, wind, solar, geothermal, biofuels, and others—are low- or zero-emission alternatives to powering vehicles using gasoline or clean diesel. California is a strong proponent of moving to an electric or hybrid electric vehicles scenario where approximately half of the one million light-duty electric vehicles are in use (Myers, 2019). Nevertheless, overall demand for electric vehicles has been trending downward in the United States in recent years (U.S. Energy Information Administration, 2018d).

Military Applications

Fuels and fuel cells are two distinct issues in military applications. As a fuel source, alternative fuels are being explored with vigor. Fuel standards and supply chain issues pose the biggest challenges for large-scale military application. In the mid-1990s, the U.S. Department of Defense moved to a uniform fuel for use in military aircraft, land vehicles, and for other military purposes. The fuel and its variations fall under the general title of "JP-8." When discussing alternative fuels for military applications, alternative fuels must meet high standards of purity, must meet the needs of multiple vehicle types and purposes, and must be available in large and regular supply.

This is not to say, however, that the military is resistant to fuel research and to exploring applications through research and demonstration projects—it is open to new game-changing innovations. Under Title III of the Defense Procurement Act of 1950, the military seeks ways of developing strategic materials and supplies needed for defense purposes. In conjunction with the U.S. Department of Agriculture's efforts to demonstrate a strong commitment to alternative fuels, the U.S. Department of Defense is testing out and incorporating alternative fuels into its fuel supply chain infrastructure on a regular basis (see U.S. GAO, 2015).

In terms of fuel cells, the military is experimenting with fuel cell applications that may, one day, be used on the battlefield. Applications include power systems for drones, autonomous submersibles, light duty vehicles, and power systems for soldiers' field equipment. The issues of fuel cell size, weight, reliability, and durability are important considerations for any future large-scale defense procurements (Magnuson, 2017).

Residential

Residential uses for alternative fuels often focus on residences seeking methods of storing green energy that has been produced by the homeowner. Green energy can be net metered, and sold back to the power grid in many locations.[4] There are instances when a net metering option is neither available nor desirable, however. For instance, a family or an individual homeowner may live on a farm or ranch some distance from power lines and may wish to store energy for his or her future use. A traditional method of storing energy in these circumstances is using lead-acid batteries, but traditional batteries of this type are not environmentally friendly and require special venting, regular maintenance, and periodic replacement. Energy could also be stored in the form of hydrogen, produced through the same method described earlier, but on a much smaller scale.

Commercial

Businesses that manufacture and sell products and services often own factories or retail spaces. As noted earlier, auxiliary power units are one of the fastest-growing areas for fuel cell technology demand. Commercial enterprises, particularly those featuring multiple production units, require easily transportable and highly reliable energy sources. Fuel cell technology, once improved and pretested, can easily provide such benefits.

CHAPTER SUMMARY

This chapter has focused on a handful of fuels and fuel systems that are either currently being employed or are in developmental stages, or are available in limited supply for special pilot testing. It has also provided up-to-date information on ethanol, the most recognizable next-generation fuel used today. It is generally found in the fuel used by automobiles driven by millions of Americans. Biodiesel is also a prominent next-generation fuel used by many commercial and government automobile fleets. As a form of energy storage, hydrogen is becoming more prominent in the United States, although refueling station development lags and the price of hydrogen per gallon of gasoline equivalent remains high, particularly if hydrogen is produced using clean energy such as wind or solar power. Hydrogen fuel cell systems are likely to play a fairly minor role in storing grid-quality electricity compared to pumped hydro storage, compressed air storage, and lithium ion batteries. Fuel cell markets are shaped to a large extent by government policy initiatives in areas such as defense, energy, and transportation. A large-scale move toward a hydrogen-powered transportation infrastructure is unlikely to occur before the 2020–2030 time period, at least according to private sector market analysis (see Kelly-Detwiler, 2019; California Air Resources Board, 2018: xi; Taibi et al., 2018: 13). The cost of materials used in hydrogen fuel cells, such as platinum membrane materials, and hydrogen storage—in liquid, gaseous, or "solid" form—is high and "loss" hurdles remain substantial.

NOTES

1. In proportion to other fuel sources, wood has declined in use. Proportionally, coal use peaked in the early twentieth century and has declined in use (Podonik 2006: 5).

2. Parfomak (2003) indicates that seven additional LNG off-loading sites are pending approval by the U.S. government.

3. The United States is not a signatory to the treaty, but the goals upon which it is grounded have been offered tacit, albeit qualified, support from former presidents George W. Bush and Barack H. Obama. As president, Donald Trump has not been particularly clear in his level of support for Kyoto, but was clear in his rejection of the Paris Agreement.

4. This form of energy production and net metering of surplus energy is part of the distributed energy production paradigm.

REFERENCES

Adamson, K. 2005. Fuel Cell Today Market Survey: Niche Transport (Part I). *Fuel Cell Today*, www.fuelcelltoday.com, accessed August 11, 2005.

Air Quality & Climate Change. 2018. EPA announces $2 million grant competition for tribes to help clean up diesel engines. *Air Quality & Climate Change* 52(2): 21.

Alvarez, M., Segarra, A., Contreras, S., Sueiras, J., Medina, F., and Figueras, F. 2010. Enhanced use of renewable resources: Transesterification of glycerol catalyzed by hydrotalcite-like compounds. *Chemical Engineering Journal* 161(3): 340–345.

Anahara, R. 1993. Research, development, and demonstration of molten carbonate fuel cell systems, in Blomen, L. and Mugerwa, M., eds. *Fuel Cell Systems*. New York: Plenum Press, 271–343.

Antony, A., Maheshwari, N., and Rao, A. 2012. A generic methodology to evaluate economics of hydrogen production using energy from nuclear power plants. *International Journal of Hydrogen Energy* 42: 25813–25823.

Araujo Encisco, A., Rene, S., Fellman, T., Perez Dominguez, I., and Santini, F. 2016. Abolishing biofuel policies: Possible impacts on agricultural price levels, price variability and global food security. *Food Policy* 61: 9–26.

Ashtiani, C., Wright, R., and Hunt, G. 2006. Ultracapacitors for automobile applications. *Journal of Power Sources*, 154(2): 561–566.

Bakeas, E., Karavalakis, G., and Stournas, S. 2011. Biodiesel emissions profile in modern diesel vehicles. Part I: Effect of biodiesel origin on the criteria of emissions. *Science of the Total Environment* 409(9): 1670–1676.

Baker, A., and Jollie, D. 2005. Fuel Cell Market Survey: Military Applications. *Fuel Cell Today*, www.fuelcelltoday.com, accessed August 11, 2005.

Biello, D. 2008. Grass makes better ethanol than corn does. *Scientific American*, January 8. Retrieved from https://www.scientificamerican.com/article/grass-makes-better-ethanol-than-corn/, June 18, 2019.

Blomen, L., and Mugerwa, M., eds. 1993. *Fuel Cell Systems*. New York: Plenum Press.

California Air Resources Board. 2018. *2018 Annual Evaluation of Fuel Cell Electric Vehicle Deployment & Hydrogen Fuel Station Network Development*. Sacramento, CA: California Air Resources Board. Retrieved from https://ww3.arb.ca.gov/msprog/zevprog/ab8/ab8_report_2018_print.pdf, July 11, 2019.

California Fuel Cell Partnership. 2019. Cost to refill. Sacramento, CA: California Fuel Cell Partnership. Retrieved from https://cafcp.org/content/cost-refill, January 19, 2019.

Claycomb, J., Brazdeikis, A., Le, M. Yarbrough, R., Gogoshin, G., and Miller, J. 2003. Nondestructive testing of PEM fuel cells, *IEEE Transactions on Applied Superconductivity*. 13(2): 211–214.

College of the Desert 2001. Module 6: Fuel cell engine safety. http://www.eere.energy.gov/hydrogenandfuelcells/tech_validation/pdfs/fcm06r0.pdf. Accessed November 27, 2005.

Coronado, C., de Carvalho, J., and Silveira, J. 2009. Biodiesel CO_2 emissions: A comparison with the main fuels in the Brazilian market. *Fuel Processing Technology* 90(2): 204–211.

Curtin, S., and Gangi, J. 2017. Fuel cell technologies market report 2016. Washington, DC: Office of Energy Efficiency and Renewable Energy, U.S Department of Energy. Retrieved from https://www.energy.gov/sites/prod/files/2017/10/f37/fcto_2016_market_report.pdf, July 11, 2019.

Deloitte. 2015. *Energy Storage: Tracking the Technologies that Will Transform the Power Sector*. New York: Deloitte Consulting LLC. Retrieved from https://www2.deloitte.com/content/dam/Deloitte/us/Documents/energy-resources/us-er-energy-storage-tracking-technologies-transform-power-sector.pdf, January 19, 2019.

Devine, M., O'Connor, B., Ellis, T., Rogers, T., Wright, S., and Manwell, J. 2003. Massachusetts Wind Energy Predevelopment Support Program and Feasibility Study for Marblehead, Massachusetts. Amherst, MA: Renewable Energy Research Lab, University of Massachusetts. See report and key set of studies at: http://www.ceere.org/rerl/publications/reports/WEPS_and_Marblehead_Wind_Feasibility_AWEA03.pdf. Accessed November 27, 2005.

Dincer, I., and Acar, C. 2018. Smart energy solutions with hydrogen options. *International Journal of Hydrogen Economy* 43(18): 8579–8599.

DiPardo, J. 2002. *Outlook for Biomass Ethanol Production and Demand* [working paper last modified July 30, 2002]. http://www.eia.doe.gov/oiaf/analysispaper/ biomass.html. Accessed March 29, 2006.

Dunn, S., and Flavin, C. 2002. The climate change agenda: From Rio to Jo'burg and beyond. *International Journal of Technology Management & Sustainable Development* 1(2): 87–111.

Durán, A., Monteagudo, J., Armas, O., and Hernández, J. 2006. Scrubbing effect on diesel particulate matter from transesterified waste oils blends. *Fuel*, 85(7/8): 923–928.

Ehrenhman, G. 2005. Cleaner fuel economy. *Mechanical Engineering* 127(5): 12–14.

Energy Information Agency 2005. Petroleum Products, http://www.eia.doe.gov/ neic/infosheets/petroleumproducts.htm, accessed August 8, 2005.

Energy Information Administration. 2017a. Petroleum and other liquids. Retrieved from https://www.eia.gov/dnav/pet/pet_sum_snd_a_EPOOXE_mbbl_a_cur.htm, January 11, 2019.

———. 2017b. U.S. fuel ethanol production continues to grow in 2017. *Energy Information Administration*, July 21. Retrieved from https://www.eia.gov/todayinenergy/detail. php?id=32152, January 11, 2019.

———. 2017c. Analysis of the effect of zero-emission vehicle policies: State level incentives and the California zero-emission vehicle regulations. *Energy Information Administration*, September. Retrieved from https://www.eia.gov/analysis/studies/ transportation/zeroemissions/pdf/zero_emissions.pdf, July 11, 2019.

———. 2018a. The United States continues to export MTBE, mainly to Mexico, Chile, and Venezuela. *Today in Energy*, July 13. Retrieved from https://www.eia.gov/ todayinenergy/detail.php?id=36614, January 11, 2019.

———. 2018b. Solar photovoltaic costs are declining, but estimates vary across sources. *Today in Energy*, March 21. Retrieved from https://www.eia.gov/todayinenergy/ detail.php?id=35432, January 13, 2019.

———. 2018c. EIA forecasts natural gas to remain primary energy source for electricity generation, *Today in Energy*, January 22. Retrieved from https://www.eia. gov/todayinenergy/ detail.php?id=34612#, June 14, 2019.

———. 2018d. U.S. battery storage: Market trends. Washington, DC: Energy Information Administration, U.S. Department of Energy. Retrieved from https://www.eia.gov/analysis/studies/electricity/batterystorage/pdf/battery_storage.pdf, July 15, 2019.

———. 2019. How much ethanol is in gasoline, and how does it affect fuel economy? *Energy Information Administration*, May 14. Retrieved from https://www.eia.gov/ tools/faqs/faq.php?id=27&t=10, June 17, 2019.

Eudy, L., and Post, M. 2019. *Fuel Cell Buses in U.S. Transit Fleets: Current Status 2018.* Golden, CO: National Renewable Energy Laboratory. Retrieved from https://www. nrel.gov/docs/fy19osti/72208.pdf, July 11, 2019.

FCTec. 2005. Fuel Cell Basics. *Fuel Cell Technologies*, http://www.fctec.com/fctec_about. asp, accessed August 14, 2005.

Fears, D. 2018. Trump administration tears down regulations to speed drilling on public land. *The Washington Post*, February 1. Retrieved from https://www.washingtonpost. com/news/energy-environment/wp/2018/02/01/trump-administration-tears-down-regulations-to-speed-drilling-on-public-land/?noredirect=on&utm_ term=.17147ac56381, January 8, 2019.

Flower, K. 2019. After three years of decline, carbon emissions rose sharply in the U.S. in 2018. *CNN* January 8. Retrieved from https://www.cnn.com/2019/01/08/politics/us-carbon-emissions-rise-2018/index.html, January 8, 2019.

Francis, M. 2002. Modeling: driving fuel cells. *Materials Today* 5(5): 34–39.

Fuel Cells Bulletin. 2018. European hydrogen initiative aims to maximize potential of sustainable hydrogen technology. *Fuel Cells Bulletin* 2018(9): 1.

Gao, Z., and Lu, Q. 2018. Using the combination of batteries and ultra-capacitors to improve the performance and flexibility for energy storage systems. *IEEJ Transactions on Electrical and Electronic Engineering* 13: 1362–1371.

Garvison, P. 2003. Solar Markets and Storage. *Systems-Driven Approach for Solar Applications of Energy Storage.* Washington, DC: U.S. Department of Energy, 13–14.

Gaul, D., and Young, L. 2003. U.S. LNG markets and uses. *Energy Information Administration, Office of Oil and Gas,* January, http://ww.eia.doe.gov/pub/oil_gas/natural_gas/feature_articles/2003/lng/lng2003.pdf, accessed March 20, 2006.

Groom, N. 2017. America's hungriest wind and solar power users: Big companies, *Reuters* June 20. Retrieved from https://www.reuters.com/article/us-usa-companies-renewables-analysis/americas-hungriest-wind-and-solar-power-users-big-companies-idUSKBN19C0E0, June 14, 2019.

Guida, D., and Minutillo, M. 2017. Design methodology for a PEM fuel cell power system in a more electrical aircraft. *Applied Energy* 192: 446–456.

Guilbert, D., N'Diaye, A., Gaillard, A., and Djerdir, A. 2016. Fuel cell systems reliability and availability enhancement by developing a fast and efficient power switch open-circuit fault detection algorithm in interlaced DC/DC boost converter typologies. *International Journal of Hydrogen Energy* 41: 15505–15517.

Han, J., Elgowainy, A., and Wang, M. 2015. *Well-to-wheels greenhouse gas emissions analysis of high-octane fuels with various market shares and ethanol blending levels* ANL/ESD-15/10. Argonne, IL: Argonne National Laboratory.

Han, J., Ryu, J., and Lee, I. 2013. Multi-objective optimization design of hydrogen infrastructures simultaneously considering economic cost, safety and CO_2 emission. *Chemical Engineering Research and Design* 91: 1427–1439.

Hennessey, B., and Nguyen, N. 2014. Status of NHTSA's hydrogen and fuel cell vehicle safety research program. *U.S. Department of Energy*. Retrieved from https://www.energy.gov/sites/prod/files/2014/03/f12/07-0046-O.pdf, June 18, 2019.

Herzik, E., Simon, C., Marks, S. 2004. Economic Feasibility—Life Cycle Cost Study: Regional Transportation Commission, Hydrogen Fuel Project. Reno, NV: T3/University of Nevada.

Hirtenstein, A. 2018. Wind turbine manufacturers hit turbulence as machine prices fall. *Bloomberg*, November 11. Retrieved from https://www.bloomberg.com/news/articles/2018-11-12/wind-turbine-manufacturers-hit-turbulence-as-machine-prices-fall, January 13, 2019.

Hoffmann, P. and Harkin, T. 2003. *Tomorrow's Energy: Hydrogen, Fuel Cells, and the Prospects of a Cleaner Planet*. Boston, MA: MIT Press.

Holm, A., Jennejohn, D., and Blodgett, L. 2012. *Geothermal Energy and Greenhouse Gas Emissions*. Baltimore, MD: Geothermal Energy Association.

HP Innovation. 2005. Process converts oil sands bitumen into low-sulfur distillates. *Hydrocarbon Processing* 84(7): 30.

Jacoby, M. 2006. Boost for battery performance. *Chemical & Engineering News* 84(8): 10.

Jankowski, A., and Kowalski, M. 2018. Alternative fuel in the combustion process of combustion engines. *Journal of Konbin* 48(1): 55–81.

Jaskow, P. 2003. Energy policies and their consequences after 25 years, *The Energy Journal* 24(4): 17–49.

Jianping, G., Yalin, L., and Suminori, T. 2014. Non-grain fuel ethanol expansion and its effects on food security: A computable general equilibrium analysis for China. *Energy* 65: 346–356.

Jorgensen, J. 1981. Social impact assessments and energy developments. *Policy Studies Review* 1(1): 66–86.

Kelly-Detwiler, P. 2019. Plug Power CEO: Soon fuel cells will be everywhere, really. *Forbes*, July 8. Retrieved from https://www.forbes.com/sites/peterdetwiler/ 2019/ 07/08/plug-powers-ceo-a-brighter-outlook-for-a-broader-application-of-fuel-cells/ #84851e17b0d1, July 11, 2019.

Kennedy, R. 2005. *Ethanol Market Outlook for California*, CEC-600-2005-037. Sacramento, CA: California Energy Commission.

Ketelaar, J. 1993. "History," in Blomen, L. and Mugerwa, M., eds. *Fuel Cell Systems*. New York: Plenum Press, pp 19–36.

Krzyminiewska, G. 2013. Food crisis versus threats to the world's social and economic stability. *Economic Science for Rural Development Conference Proceedings* 31, 16–19.

Lakely, J. 2003. Abraham outlines plans for hydrogen fuel, Canadian oil, *The Washington Times*. November 17, A11.

Langreth, R., and Fritz, S. 1994. Hydrogen + natural gas=hythane. *Popular Science* 244(3): 34–35.

Layton, B. 2008. A comparison of energy densities of prevalent energy sources in units of joules per cubic meter. *International Journal of Green Energy* 5: 438–455.

Lesser, J. 2018. Are electric cars worse for the environment? *Politico*, March 15. Retrieved from https://www.politico.com/agenda/story/2018/05/15/are-electric-cars-worse-for-the-environment-000660, July 11, 2019.

Maack, M., and Skulason, J. 2006. Implementing the hydrogen economy. *Journal of Cleaner Production* 14(1): 52–64.

Magnuson, S. 2017. Fuel cells fail to make inroads with the military. *National Defense*, June, 35–37.

Mattoon, R. 2002. The electricity system at the crossroads. *Society*, November/ December: 64–79.

Meher, L.,Vidya-Sagar, D., and Naik, S. 2006. Technical aspects of biodiesel production by transesterification—a review. *Renewable and Sustainable Energy Reviews* 10(3): 248–268.

Milbourn, C. 2001. EPA Gives the Green Light on Diesel-Sulfur Rule. February 28, United States Environmental Protection Agency. http://yosemite.epa.gov/ opa/ admpress.nsf/b1ab9f485b098972852562e7004dc686/0237f756e256922c85256a 010072e4f6?OpenDocument, accessed August 12, 2005.

Miller, S., Bhushan, B., and Ball, J. 2002. A global report: Europe launches hydrogen initiative. *Wall Street Journal*, October 16.

Mohammadi, A., and Mehrpooya, M. 2018. Techno-economic analysis of hydrogen production by solid oxide electrolyzer coupled with dish collector. *Energy Conversion and Management* 173: 167–178.

Moore, L., Malcynski, L., Strachan, J., and Post, H. 2003. Lifecycle Cost Assessment of Fielded Photovoltaic Systems, *NCPV and Solar Program Review Meeting—National Renewable Energy Laboratories*. NREL/CD-520–33586, 416–418.

Moritsugu, K. 2002. Hydrogen fuel cell technology remains many years in future, *Pittsburgh Post-Gazette Journal*, January 13, A10.

Moshin, M., Rasheed, A., and Saidur, R. 2018. Economic viability and production capacity of wind generated renewable hydrogen. *International Journal of Hydrogen Energy* 43: 2621–2630.

Mugerwa, M., and Blomen, L. 1993. Research, development, and demonstration of alkaline fuel cell systems, in Blomen, L. and Mugerwa, M., eds. *Fuel Cell Systems*. New York: Plenum Press, 531–564.

Murugesamoorthi, K., Srinivasan, S., and Appleby, A. 1993. Research, development, and demonstration of solid polymer fuel cell systems, in Blomen, L. and Mugerwa, M., eds. *Fuel Cell Systems*. New York: Plenum Press, 465–492.

Myers, A. 2019. 4 U.S. electric vehicle trends to watch in 2019, *Forbes*, January 2. Retrieved from https://www.forbes.com/sites/energyinnovation/2019/01/02/4-u-s-electric-vehicle-trends-to-watch-in-2019/#6bb420e15a3c, June 19, 2019.

Nijkamp, P., and Pepping, G. 1998. A meta-analytical evaluation of sustainable city initiatives. *Urban Studies* 35(9): 1481–1500.

Parfomak, P. 2003. *Liquefied Natural Gas (LNG) Infrastructure Security: Background and Issues for Congress*, CRS Order Code RL32073. Washington, DC: Congressional Research Service.

Park, M., Kim, J., Kim, Y., Choi, N., and Kim, J. 2015. Recent advances in rechargeable magnesium battery technology: A review of the field's current status and prospects. *Israel Journal of Chemistry* 55: 570–585.

Patel, P., Lakdawala, A., Chourasia, S., and Patel, R. 2016. Bio fuels for compression ignition engine: A review on engine performance, emission, and life cycle analysis. *Renewable and Sustainable Energy Reviews* 65: 24–43.

Peng, K., Morrow, G., Xiaolei, Z., and Tipeng, W. 2017. Systematic comparison of hydrogen production from fossil fuels and biomass resources. *International Journal of Agricultural and Biological Engineering* 10(6): 192–200.

Penner, S. 2006. Steps toward the hydrogen economy. *Energy* 31: 33–43.

Perez, P. 2005. Ethanol in California. *Platts Ethanol Finance & Investment Conference*, May 25–26, 2005.

Phillips, S. 2019. Japan is betting big on the future of hydrogen cars, *National Public Radio*, March 18. Retrieved from https://www.npr.org/2019/03/18/700877189/japan-is-betting-big-on-the-future-of-hydrogen-cars, June 17, 2019.

Podobnik, B. 2006. *Global Energy Shifts: Fostering Sustainability in a Turbulent Age*. Philadelphia, PA: Temple University Press.

Pollution Engineering. 2005. EPA retrofits diesel engines. *Pollution Engineering*, April: 10–11.

Portney, K. 2002. Taking sustainable cities seriously: A comparative analysis of twenty four US cities. *Local Environment* 7(4): 363–380.

Pront-van Brommel, S. 2016. A reasonable price for electricity. *Journal of Consumer Policy* 39(2): 141–158.

Pryor, T., and Wilmot, N. 2001. *The Effect of PV Array Size and Battery Size on the Economics of PV/Diesel/Battery Hybrid RAPS Systems*. Murdoch, WA: Murdoch University Energy Research Institute.

Rapier, R. 2018. Algal Biofuels dead? "Not so fast," says Algal Biofuel researcher. *Forbes*, November 2. Retrieved from https://www.forbes.com/sites/rrapier/2018/11/02/algal-biofuels-dead-not-so-fast-says-algal-biofuel-researcher/#3377aca356c4, June 18, 2019.

Reeves, A. 2003. *Wind Energy for Electric Power: A REPP Issue Brief.* Washington, DC: Renewable Energy Policy Project.

Rifkin, J. 2003. Thinking big: The forever fuel: The new hydrogen economy will not only eliminate our dependence on foreign oil, it will turn our automobiles into power plants, *The Boston Globe*, February, D12.

Rifkin, J. 2002. *The Hydrogen Economy: The Creation of the Worldwide Energy Web and the Redistribution of Power on Earth.* New York: Putnam.

Rigas, F., and Sklavounos, S. 2005. Evaluation of hazards associated with hydrogen storage facilities. *International Journal of Hydrogen Energy* 30(13/14): 1501–1510.

Roberge, P. R. 2005. Molten Carbonate Fuel Cells [MCFCs]. *CorrosionDoctors.Org*, http://www.corrosion-doctors.org/FuelCell/mcfc.htm, accessed August 14, 2005.

Rueda, M., Sanz-Moral, L., and Martin, A. 2018. Innovative methods to enhance the properties of solid hydrogen storage materials based on hydrides through nanoconfinement: A review. *Journal of Supercritical Fluids* 141: 198–217.

Salkuyeh, Y., Saville, B., and MacLean, H. 2018. Techno-economic analysis and life cycle assessment of hydrogen gasification production from different biomass gasification processes. *International Journal of Hydrogen Energy* 43: 9514–9528.

Schroeder, W. 2002. Clear thinking about the hydrogen economy, *Connecticut Law Tribune*, December 20, p. 5.

Service, R. 2018. Advances in flow batteries promise cheap backup power: Upstart technology could enable widespread adoption of renewables. *Science* 362(6414): 508–509.

Shellenberger, M. 2019. We shouldn't be surprised renewables make energy expensive since that's always been the Greens' goal. *Forbes*, May 27. Retrieved from https://www.forbes.com/sites/michaelshellenberger/2019/05/27/we-shouldnt-be-surprised-renewables-make-energy-expensive-since-thats-always-been-the-greens-goal/#66d5ccac4e6d, August 14, 2019.

Sierens, R., and Rosseel, E. 2000. Variable composition hydrogen/natural gas mixtures for increased energy efficiency and decreased emissions. *Journal of Engineering for Gas Turbines & Power* 122(1): 135–140.

Skodras, G., Grammelis, P., Basinas, P., Kakaras, E., and Sakellaropoulos, G. 2006. Pyrolysis and combustion characteristics of biomass and waste-derived feedstock. *Industrial & Engineering Chemical Research* 45: 3791–3799.

Smithsonian Institute. 2005. Collecting the History of Fuel Cells. *Smithsonian National Museum of American History.* http://americanhistory.si.edu/fuelcells/index.htm, accessed August 14, 2005.

Staka, C. 2002. Local energy policy and smart growth. *Local Environment* 7(4): 453–458.

Stratonova, M., Lasher, S., and Carlson, E. 2003. Assessment of fuel cell auxiliary power systems for on-road transportation applications. Washington, DC: Energy Efficiency and Renewable Energy, U.S. Department of Energy. Retrieved from https://www1.eere.energy.gov/hydrogenandfuelcells/pdfs/ivf4_lasher.pdf, June 18, 2019.

Stone, D. 1988. *Policy Paradox and Political Reason.* New York: Harper Collins.

Taibi, E., Miranda, R., Vanhoudt, W., Winkel, T., Lanoix, J., and Barth, F. 2018. *Hydrogen from Renewable Power: Technology Outlook for the Energy Transition.* Abu Dhabi,

UAE: IRENA. Retrieved from https://www.irena.org/-/media/Files/IRENA/Agency/Publication/2018/Sep/IRENA_Hydrogen_from_renewable_power_2018.pdf, July 11, 2019.

Tanrioven, M., and Alam, M. 2005. Reliability modeling and assessment of grid-connected PEM fuel cell power plants. *Journal of Power Sources* 142: 264–278.

Tran, M., Scribano, G., Chong, C., Ho, T., and Huynh, T. 2018. Experimental and numerical investigation of explosive behavior syngas/air mixtures. *International Journal of Hydrogen Energy* 43(16): 8152—8160.

Tse, L. 2005. Molten Carbonate Fuel Cell [MCFC]. *Vision Engineer.Com*, http://www.visionengineer.com/env/mc.php, accessed August 15, 2005.

United Nations Environmental Programme. 2003. Indian Solar Loan Programme, http://www.uneptie.org/energy/act/fin/india/, accessed November 27, 2005.

U.S. Department of Energy. 2019. *Alternative Fuels Center*. Washington, DC: U.S. Department of Energy. Retrieved from https://afdc.energy.gov/fuels/laws/ETH?state=US, June 19, 2019.

U.S. Energy Information Administration. 2019b. Oil: Crude and Petroleum Products—Explained Use of Oil. Washington, DC: U.S. Energy Information Administration. Retrieved from https://www.eia.gov/energyexplained/index.php?page=oil_use, June 19, 2019.

U.S. Environmental Protection Agency. 2018. Electrified vehicles continue to see slow growth and less use than conventional vehicles. *Today in Energy*, May 22. Retrieved from https://www.eia.gov/todayinenergy/detail.php?id=36312, June 19, 2019.

———. 2019. Diesel Standards and Rulemaking. Washington, DC: U.S. Environmental Protection Agency. Retrieved from https://www.epa.gov/diesel-fuel-standards/diesel-fuel-standards-and-rulemakings#main-content, June 19, 2019.

U.S. Government Accountability Office. 2015. *Defense Energy: Observations on DODs Investments in Alternative Fuels*, GAO 15–674. Washington, DC: U.S. Government Accountability Office. Retrieved from https://www.gao.gov/assets/ 680/671667.pdf, June 19, 2019.

Vaitheeswaran, V. 2004. Unraveling the great hydrogen hoax. *Nieman Reports* 58(2): 14–17.

Van den Broek, H. 1993. Research, development, and demonstration of phosphoric acid fuel cell systems, in Blomen, L. and Mugerwa, M., eds. *Fuel Cell Systems*. New York: Plenum Press, 245–270.

Vandepaer, L., Amor, B., and Cloutier, J. 2017. Environmental impacts of lithium metal polymer and lithium-ion stationary batteries. *Renewable & Sustainable Energy Reviews* 78: 46–60.

Vignola, F., Hocken, J., and Grace, G. 2000. *PV in Schools*. Eugene, OR: Oregon Million Solar Roofs Coalition.

Wald, E. 2018. Trump's new ethanol rule explained (and what it means for gasoline). *Forbes*, October 9. Retrieved from https://www.forbes.com/sites/ellenrwald/ 2018/10/09/=trumps-new-ethanol-rule-wont-change-your-gasoline/ #503afb187d96, January 11, 2019.

Wald, M. 2004. Report questions Bush plan for hydrogen-fueled cars. *New York Times*, 6 February, A20.

White House, 2003. Fact sheet: Hydrogen fuel—a clean and secure energy future, http://www.whitehouse.gov/news/releases/2003/02/20030206-2.html, accessed November 27, 2005.

Wilson, R. 2013. The future of energy: Why power density matters. *Energy Central*, August 9. Retrieved from https://www.energycentral.com/c/ec/future-energy-why-power-density-matters, July 23, 2019.

Woodson, M., and Jablonowski, C. 2008. An economic assessment of traditional and cellulosic ethanol technologies. *Energy Sources Part B Economics Planning and Policy* 3(4): 372–383.

Wustenhagen, R. 2003. Sustainability and competitiveness in the renewable energy sector, *Green Management International* 44(Winter): 105–115.

Yilmaz, C. 2017. Thermoeconomic modeling and optimization of a hydrogen production system using geothermal energy. *Geothermics* 65: 32–43.

Zuttel, A. 2003. Materials for hydrogen storage. *Materials Today* 6(9): 24–33.

8

Historical Precedents: Alternative Energy/Fuels and Legitimacy Issues

★　★　★

A review of alternative energy would not be complete if due regard were not offered to historical precedents in the field of alternative energy. Considering the various forms of alternative energy discussed thus far, it is evident that each has experienced a period of intense development with relatively strong public and private policy and financial commitment. In the early stages of growth, many energy alternatives were viewed by skeptics as a bit far-fetched, only to be later recognized as highly valuable contributions to the overall energy paradigm.

Much the same could be said for reaction to other technological breakthroughs. Consider for a moment the possibility of a "horseless carriage" called the "Puffing Devil" (Trevithick, 1872) powered by steam (invented in 1801) or a corkscrew-shaped pumping system used for bringing groundwater to the surface called Archimedes' screw (Waters and Aggidis, 2015). Better still, how about a water-well camera that can take interpretable pictures inside a well borehole even though the water therein is murky (https://www.lavalunderground.com/, accessed July 15, 2019)? I had to add the last invention because, as a young man, I once met a man who invented a camera of that type—Claude Laval Jr. of Fresno, California, now deceased—and heard, directly from him, the source of his inspiration—namely, he was driving a car on a foggy day and noticed that he could always see clearly from the driver's seat to the front of the car hood if the headlights were switched on. At one time or another, each one of these innovations was likely viewed with some skepticism, but it is indeed the case that that which has yet to be experienced is often viewed with skepticism at best, and undue fear at worst.

Over time, that which was inconceivable may prove to be quite practical and useful; familiarity and utility lead to broader public acceptance, at times ignoring the real risks that innovative technologies may pose—taking the good with the bad, so to speak, even when a better alternative may be on the horizon or readily available. There may be practical reasons for those needs to be considered. Once a technology has been accepted and adopted, there are sunk costs that shape future choices and direction. It is not easy to simply discard an old technology if one has already invested heavily in it, in the process, building a life, a community, and societal economic sector around it as well. There are also behavioral considerations—the fact is, technology shapes our habits and our preferences, and may even shape our perception of personal status.

Using certain technologies—even if out-of-date and inefficient—may make us feel good about ourselves in honoring the past. Abandoning a technology may mean a loss of personal property, job loss, and social upheaval. On an individual level, abandoning technology might even cause us varying degrees of stress and anxiety. Change, therefore, may be incremental at times, but at other times a broader social, economic, or political shift must occur to move society toward new and more positive innovation and opportunities for a better future. Such shifts may occur as a result of crisis, leading to a punctuated equilibrium and rapid change in a new direction involving new technologies and novel ways of doing things.

In the case of each form of energy generation or fuel, the technical, economic, and political feasibility dimensions were discussed with the intent of informing a healthy dialogue about movement toward an alternative energy future. Much of the discussion resolves around what we can do (technical feasibility) and for what price (economic feasibility), but political and social values play a substantial role in the path we chose to take in the past and choose to take in the future. The birthright of many forms of alternative energy cannot be claimed by the private sector alone—sociopolitical forces can have much to do with either continued commitment or the fraying of commitments.

The swift transition from the environmentally friendly Obama presidency to a decidedly fossil energy friendly Trump presidency represents a salient example of the underlying concern about alternative energy—the need for consistent policy signals during a critical century, likely to witness the decline of fossil energy, the growing dangers from climate change and accelerated resource demands due to population growth, and growing affluence in some selected countries. What we value, how we define risk, our level of acceptance of change, and the quality of democratic dialogue may help us to understand better why we accept, fail to accept, or change our collective thoughts about energy sources, their use, and desirability. By understanding how two historically important forms of alternative energy fell out of favor, it helps us to understand that just because it is not carbon-based does not mean that alternative energy is politically and socially acceptable to significant portions of society.

RISK AND CULTURE: ALTERNATIVE ENERGY AND HIDDEN COSTS

In their now famous account *Risk and Culture: An Essay on the Selection of Technological and Environmental Dangers* (1983), authors Mary Douglas and Aaron Wildavsky come to terms with public policy direction through a study of risk assessment. Ultimately, they argue persuasively that our selection of public policy, particularly in areas such as the environment, crime control, and public health, are a function of what is feared most—judged to be a serious risk—by the public.

Many risks are judged, consciously or not, to be of little importance. Risks may be brushed aside, despite the fact that substantial evidence points to a high level of risk. Times change and perceived or real levels of risk are adjusted. For example, smoking cigarettes was once thought to be good for one's health. Since the 1960s, however, public policy efforts have focused great attention on informing smokers of the potential dangers to their health and those around them. In essence, as Douglas and Wildavsky (1983) would say, "Risk should be seen as a joint product of *knowledge* about the future and *consent* about the most desired prospects (p. 5)."

As Douglas and Wildavsky (1983) argue—and Deborah Stone (2011) echoes this point—knowledge can be contested, thus making it very difficult to establish agreed-upon facts shaping risk assessment in many situations. A great example of this dilemma arises in the contemporary global warming debate. Scientists, politicians, interest groups, and interested citizens all can have quite disparate views on whether global warming is occurring, and likewise whether the ubiquitous use of fossil fuels is negatively impacting the global environment. The basis of our knowledge is uncertain and relevant facts are frequently disputed by interested parties.

In other cases, information is fairly certain and is not contested in the risk assessment process. A good example comes from the economics of energy. Few would disagree that the basic economic principles of supply and demand will impact energy prices. While the amount of available fossil energy is contested, it is generally accepted that, ceteris paribus, as demand increases in relation to supply, fuel prices will increase and likely impact economic outcomes for individuals, nations, and the world as a whole.

The second dimension in the analysis of risk assessment is related to political *consent*. While likely to exist on a continuum, level of consent ranges from *complete* to *contested*. An example of complete consent might be found in the area of energy economics—specifically, in energy policies for the indigent. Very few individuals would openly deny access to energy for poor citizens, and most would accept the idea that the poor should either pay reduced rates or nothing at all for access to the electrical energy necessary to live in the contemporary world. Few, for example, would not favor the recreation of the power grid in Puerto Rico in the wake of the most recent devastating hurricane.

According to Douglas and Wildavsky (1983: 5), when information is certain and not contested, then problems associated with a risk are thought to be *technical* in nature (figure 8.1). The "solution," therefore, is viewed as a matter of "calculation." Risks associated by rising global demand for fossil fuel—particularly petroleum—and its cascading effects can be studied through economic modeling (e.g., Bernal et al., 2019). Similar studies can be conducted to study the economic "risk" associated with the integration of intermittent renewable energy sources as well as methods to overcome "risk" through energy storage (e.g., Connolly et al., 2012).

When knowledge is certain and consent is contested, frequently there exists significant disagreement in risk assessment. According to Douglas and Wildavsky, the definition of risk and policy solutions to limit defined risk becomes a function of political coercion or discussion. Thinking back to an earlier discussion of Lowi's policy typology, public policy of this type is often subject to the influence of interest group politics as consent to risk assessment develops. In Lowi's typology, policies most likely to be a function of interest group politics are either redistributive or regulatory. As will be discussed later

Figure 8.1   Risk and Policy Solutions

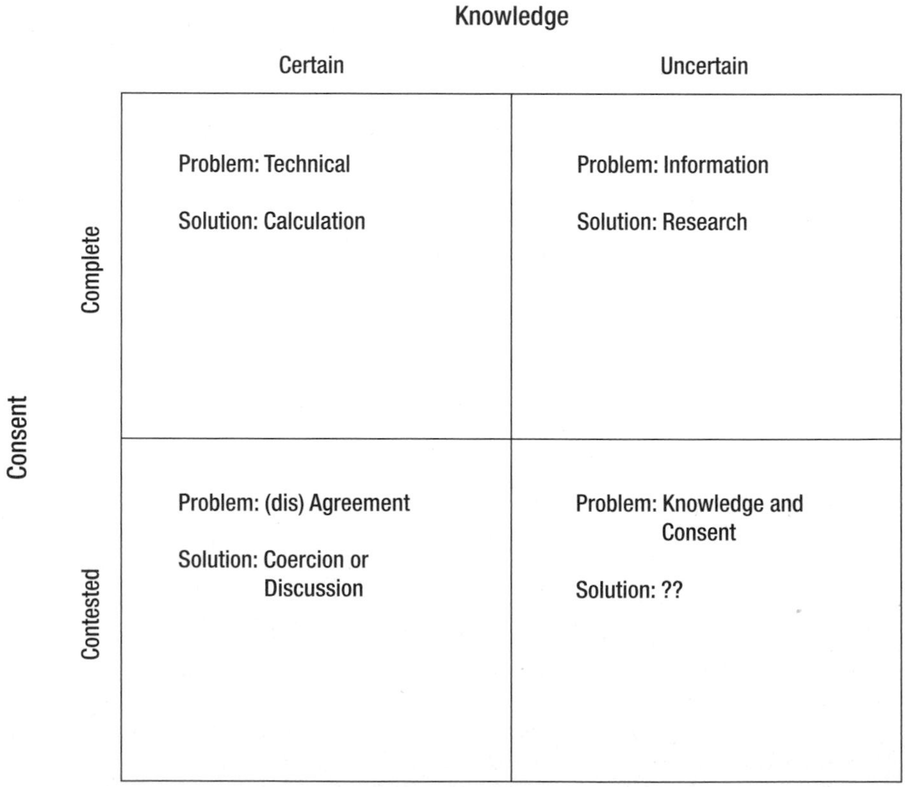

After Douglas and Wildavsky (1983: 5). Art reproduced by author.

in the chapter, proponents of nuclear energy would argue that the knowledge undergirding nuclear energy is certain, but that consent is highly contested; from the perspective of a nuclear energy proponent, the primary reason why nuclear energy has not been able to develop further in the United States is directly related to interest group politics.

When knowledge associated with risk assessment is uncertain and consent is complete, then the primary problem facing risk assessment is a lack of information to deal with limiting or ameliorating the impact of a risk that proves to be real. The solution, therefore, is to pursue or encourage research associated with a particular risk. In the case of energy policy, significant resources are being directly toward R & D of alternative energy solutions to a perceived risk of energy supplies not being capable of meeting demand, and the resulting risk (or certitude) of facing higher energy costs, lower economic growth, and greater dependence on energy imports from a world wherein political instability is rife.

Government research funds for energy development are by no means a recent development. Research funding for fossil fuel research has been going on for nearly a century, with the establishment of the Coal Research Center by the Bureau of Mines (BOM) in 1910 representing an early example. In 1918, the Bureau of Mines, a subunit within the U.S. Department of Interior, established the Petroleum Experiment Station in Bartlesville, Oklahoma (see http://www.netl.doe.gov/, accessed June 23, 2019). With increased emphasis on accessing petroleum and natural gas reserves in Alaska, the National Energy Technology Laboratory opened its Arctic Energy Office in 2001. In all instances, the focus has been on continued R & D of fossil fuel sources and production technologies, and beneficial home and industry applications, effectively reinforcing its role in the energy paradigm for some time to come.

According to the Douglas and Wildavsky (1983) model, when knowledge is uncertain and consent is contested, there is no easily predictable solution to the "problem" to be addressed. In fact, the problem is itself contested in definitional form. For some individuals and groups, it might not be a problem at all, while other individuals and groups find that the problem is paramount and must be addressed with dispatch. It is in this fourth quadrant of the model of risk assessment where Douglas and Wildavsky are most interested, and it is an area that becomes of critical importance to any individual studying or thinking about U.S. and global energy policy of the future. It is a decisional region, a quadrant in which nearly all energy policy first emerges, a region where science is viewed as unclear and the nature of consent or contestability has yet to be determined.

When it comes to risk assessment, the "center" (Douglas and Wildavsky, 1983) is complacent. For the most part, most individuals are not deeply interested in the scientific foundations of public policy, nor do they have deep-seated ideologically driven value structures that lead to the complete embrace or outright rejection of policy (or lack thereof) in relation to a level of risk.

While Douglas and Wildavsky (1983) do not directly emphasize this point, it is clear from the temper of their writings that the "center" is driven primarily by the maintenance of established political, social, and economic patterns of behavior. The individuals and groups along the fringes of society and politics, the "border" (Douglas and Wildavsky, 1983), tend to be more interested in defining risk either through the lens of new scientific theory or in relation to a set of core values divergent from the majority, or both. In any event, the "border" tends to be more risk adverse when it comes to departure from the status quo.

Douglas and Wildavsky (1983) conclude that the border is what tends to be more active in shaping the policy process, from initial agenda setting through formulation, implementation, and evaluation, while the "center" tends to be largely disinterested in risk assessment. The "border" seeks to gain the attention and interest of the "center" not through direct appeals to a deep-seated knowledge base or deeply held values; rather, the "border" attempts to influence the "center" by appeals to an interest in maintaining economic, social, and political *conditions and benefits*, which—it is advocated—can only be achieved through marginal (or possibly even radical) change in *methods* of existence.

At times, things are made easier for the "border" through societal (perhaps global) shifts in basic values (see Inglehart, 1990), changes that lead to shifts in consent and alter the nature of risk assessment and public policy. Increased levels of education may shape individuals' ability to comprehend risk assessment, to conceptually identify multiple perspectives of risk, and to proactively critique and accept/reject its validity and generalizability. In other instances, events occur that provide individuals and groups along the "border" opportunities to employ narrative as a basis of their claims to knowledge or a core set of political, social, or economic values. For example, a series of exceptionally warm summers in a particular semiarid region may provide an opportunity for certain actors along the "border" to promote green energy as solution to climate change, while identifying fossil energy firms as "devils" standing in the way of a better future for all and putting at risk the survival of the entire planet. Ultimately, the center remains complacent, concerned primarily with its political, social, and economic self-interest, the maintenance of and continued improvement of a particular lifestyle.

Contemporary policy models and frameworks owe a great deal to the theoretical developments of Douglas and Wildavsky (1983); to Herbert Simon (1957), who described human reason as limited or "bounded"; and to E. E. Schattschneider (1960), who described the interrelationship of political conflict, interest groups, and policy agenda setting. With limits on rational decision-making, Simon (1957) concludes that it is unlikely that human beings will be able to make optimal policy decisions in many situations where choice needs to be exercised. In other words, our efforts to create policy solutions are limited by our ability to fully understand problems and identify optimal solutions. Furthermore, Schattschneider (1960) concludes that the policy agenda and process are typically heavily influenced by a narrow group of interests. In theory, pluralism would produce a broad range of organized interest groups representative of the citizenry, but Schattschneider argues that the array of interests is often biased toward the articulate, well-educated and elite classes. Applying the conclusions of Simon (1957) and Schattschneider (1960) to the risk and culture model of Douglas and Wildavsky (1983), it becomes clear that the likelihood of policy problems—particularly in the case of alternative energy—to fit into the upper left quadrant (policy is politically uncontested and knowledge of policy is complete)—is extremely limited. Our collective knowledge of alternative energy is growing tremendously, without a doubt, but nonetheless remains far from complete. In fact, knowledge is often contested in the energy and environmental policy arena, particularly by powerful interest groups who, through lobbying efforts and campaign funding, may create opportunities for access to elected officials. Access to elected officials offers an opportunity to influence public policy direction. In the case of energy policy, energy interests seek to shape everything from climate change policy, air and water quality policy, land-use policy, transportation policy, science and technology R & D funding, energy market regulations, production tax credits, property tax codes, to environmental policy, to name but a few major policy areas of interest. With limited and contested knowledge, it is difficult to choose optimum solutions. Add to that, risk assessment varies tremendously with policy actors on one side advocating for fossil and nuclear energy, while other policy actors call for reductions in carbon emissions to prevent irreversible climate change through the timely adoption of renewable energy solutions.

Historically, energy policy has sought to fill unmet energy supply needs in a variety of ways. For President Franklin D. Roosevelt, hydropower was a feasible energy solution to fill the needs of a largely agrarian nation that was soon to witness tremendous economic prosperity, expanded industrialization, and urbanization. Two decades later, then-President Dwight D. Eisenhower was a strong proponent of nuclear energy as a sound method of producing large quantities of electrical energy in a post–Second World War United States. A half-century later, renewable energy policy advocates called for greater development of solar, wind, biomass, geothermal, and tidal energy to meet the energy needs of a planet seeking to stave off the worst effects projected for climate change. And only three short years ago, President Donald Trump reversed direction in favor of the greater development, extraction, and use of fossil energy.

Once touted as energy solutions, hydropower and nuclear energy remain prominent parts of the U.S. energy portfolio, but both sources of energy face somewhat uncertain futures. When it comes to the public acceptance of hydro- and nuclear power, or at least their social and economic utility, knowledge and consent have changed over time. Public support for energy policy tends to fluctuate due to both changing sociopolitical values and economic

A Tidal Energy Turbine (30–50 ft diameter)
E+ / shaunl

calculus-based considerations as marginal social and environmental costs become increasingly apparent, legitimized through public policy and often subject to regulation and associated costs.

HYDROELECTRIC DAMS

Hydropower, or water power, is one of the oldest sources of energy used in human civilizations. For millennia, water power was primarily used to operate mechanical equipment in the processing of grain. While electricity-related research had occurred for centuries, it was not until the application of scientific and technological breakthroughs of the 1870s that commercial electricity from impounded waters became practical.

The first hydroelectric dam in the United States began operations on September 30, 1882. The dam was built over the Fox River in Appleton, Wisconsin (http://www.eia.doe.gov, accessed March 22, 2006). Other dam projects quickly followed in the late nineteenth century, most of them either privately owned or controlled by nascent urban public utility boards. The images associated with hydropower during the late nineteenth and the early twentieth centuries were those of greater freedom and heightened prosperity. Electricity was synonymous with urban development and the replacement of much manual work with power-assisted tools and devices. Electric-powered urban mass transit systems appeared. Electric light meant that workers could operate machines during nighttime hours. Previously, homes were lit by expensive candles and oil, but electricity reduced the cost of illumination and made possible the development of many electricity-consuming domestic appliances in due course. While it is the case that electricity was not generated solely by hydropower, it became and has remained an important source of electrical energy supply (see Jonnes, 2004).

Electric energy generation was initially controlled by state and local utilities and private electric companies, which worked in conjunction with state and local utility boards and oversight commissions that typically both promoted and controlled utilities so that they promoted the public interest. The electrical energy market was seen as a combined local government and private corporate function in most of the country. The political feasibility of federal government involvement in energy generation expanded with the passage of the Tennessee Valley Authority Act of 1933 (16 U.S.C. 12; also see Abrams 1937) and the Bonneville Project Act of 1937 (16 U.S.C. 832) in the U.S. Pacific Northwest. Signed by President Franklin D. Roosevelt in 1935, Executive Order 7037 established the Rural Electrification Administration, providing for a strong federal role in the management of electric power generation and distribution (Campbell, 2000). Despite movement toward partial deregulation in the 1990s, the 1930s policy shift remains, with its impact most visible in the large hydropower projects throughout the U.S. West and in the Tennessee Valley in the South.

In 2005, hydropower accounted for approximately 45 percent of all forms of renewable energy used in the United States (Sale, 2005)—less than 3 percent of all energy consumed. By 2017, hydropower had declined to just 25 percent of all renewable energy in the United States. In 2005, solar, wind, and geothermal sources made up less than 1 percent of the total energy consumption in the United States (Sale, 2005). By 2017, solar, wind, and geothermal provided an estimated 29 percent of renewable energy in the United States (EIA, 2019a). The sharp decline in hydropower as a percentage of renewable energy is partially related to the meteoric rise of other renewable energy sources, as well precipitation shortfalls, particularly in the West. It is also a function of the contested nature of hydropower as an energy source in some regions of the country.

The economic, technical, and political feasibility of hydroelectric and flood control dam projects has been questioned for quite some time (Howarth, 1960; National Wildlife, 1984; Baker, 1988), and alternative plans for balancing human needs with ecological realities are most decidedly called for (see Marts and Sewell, 1960). The Sierra Club, the Nature Conservancy, the Environmental Defense Fund, and other environmental interest groups historically have been quite active in opposing the installation of new dams.

Early on, environmentalists and ecologists questioned the hidden costs of dam installation and subsequent operation in general, and hydroelectric dams in particular. All dams act as natural barriers to stream flow and the migration of both soil sediment and fish and wildlife in streams and along river and stream banks. Hydroelectric dams are particularly damaging to salmon seeking to move upstream to lay eggs in ancestral spawning grounds. While systems of fish ladders have been designed to encourage salmon migration upstream and bypass the dam, only limited success has been achieved in this regard in most dam locations. This is likewise the case with the use of fish hatcheries and selective netted catch-and-release upstream efforts. Dam breaching is another method of improving salmon movement through once unobstructed streams and rivers (Tatro, 1999).

State-level ecology movements in Oregon in 1980s and 1990s, for instance, effectively culminated in statewide migratory fish protection efforts in the 1990s to bring attention to the issue of technical feasibility as well as the dynamics of public consent to a standing policy favoring hydropower and impoundments (see Nicholas, 1997). The state policy offers clear evidence that grassroots policy efforts can have a significant role to play in offering legitimacy to scientific/technical feasibility as well as offering or withholding political/social consent. The technical feasibility and consent may not exist entirely on separate dimensions, as the Douglas and Wildavsky model would indicate—in essence, there is an interaction effect in ultimately assessing policy risk and benefit. Furthermore, state and local grassroots efforts in shaping the risk-and-benefit dialogue may be birthed out of provincial concern, but the dialogue can expand and grow. A bottom-up policy dimension emerged from Oregon's evolving consideration of its long association with the hydroelectric paradigm. Federal–state partnerships have emerged since the National Marine Fisheries Service (now NOAA Fisheries) listed Coho salmon as an endangered species (see American Forests, 1999). As Steel et al. (1999) found in their study of salmon recovery in relation to the hydroelectric policy paradigm, policy implementation surrounding the issue of policy balance is tied directly to knowledge and values, and energy policy is by no means exogenous to policy developments in related arenas.

In combination the Pacific Salmon Treaty Agreement, the Endangered Species listings of salmon and steelhead, and the Pacific Coast Salmon Recovery Fund (see 16 U.S.C 56A §3645 and P.L. 106–113) tested the political feasibility of hydropower and effectively exposed some of the heretofore less visible economic costs of hydropower electricity generation. By redefining the issue of technical feasibility to include the ability of hydropower to eschew large-scale damage to the environment, the act effectively sends hydropower experts back to the drawing board to meet new standards of technical feasibility—standards that will meet the political and social values of a new era seeking a reduced level of environmental risk. At the very least, the salmon issue and subsequent policy adjustments related to hydropower generation have "moved" hydropower from the upper left quadrant in Douglas and Wildavksy's model to the lower left quadrant.

The report *Hydropower Vision: A New Chapter in America's 1st Renewable Electricity Source* (2018) represents an attempt to recommence a new strong U.S. commitment to hydropower. The report calls for optimization of existing hydropower facilities to increase generator capacity and enhance efficiencies, as well as to take actions designed to reduce damage to the environment. The plan also calls for some "responsible growth" of hydropower (Zayas, 2018: 8). A large part of the report is dedicated to addressing the marginal social and environmental costs that have traditionally been associated with hydroelectricity generation. Recognizing that marginal costs are only one part of addressing a policy dilemma is also a major feature of the plan—the other part involves convincing policy actors that there is a technical solution to those problems once thought insurmountable. In effect, the advocates of hydropower are interested in moving back to the top left quadrant in the Douglas and Wildavsky (1983) model. The hydropower vision document does just that by addressing "transformative technical innovations" (Zayas, 2018: 7). One method of particular note is a more aggressive pursuit of pumped storage hydropower. In a green energy application, water is pumped into reservoirs using renewable energy. When the hydropower facility is called upon to generate electricity for the power grid, water is released from storage, spinning generator turbines.

The report also calls for a more broadly inclusive stakeholder collaboration than is normally witnessed in developing hydropower policies for the future, clear evidence of the need to effectively incorporate a broad range of concerns about the environmental risks of hydropower. Emphasis is placed on the potential for both sustainability as well as the anticipated economic growth emerging from the implementation of a next-generation hydropower paradigm. Again, there is clear evidence here of an ambitious attempt to broaden the stakeholder base to create successful and long-lasting hydropower policy in the United States after several decades of decline and of suffering the constricting effects of policy and legal constraints.

Hydropower is also witnessing the rebirth of an old idea. In *Environmental Impacts of Increased Hydroelectric Development at Existing Dams* (Railsback et al., 1991), the authors argue that retrofitting nonhydroelectric dams for electricity production could substantially increase power generation in many locations. The authors concluded that many environmental concerns regarding habitat impacts and fish depletion could be mitigated through commonly known, widely tested, and understood techniques. In 2017, the Office of Energy Efficiency and Renewable Energy published a richly researched report entitled *Five Promising Water Power Technologies*. Along with pumped storage and modular hydro (run-of-the-river micro hydropower), the dam retrofit innovation, a topic broached in the aforementioned 1991 report, resurfaced claiming a similar 12 GW increase in renewable electricity generation. Coincidentally, the

1991 report and the 2017 report both emerged during Republican presidential administrations—those of George H. W. Bush and Donald Trump.

Other areas of growth in water power are tidal and wave energy, and ocean thermal energy conversion (OTEC). Tidal power converts the kinetic energy of the falling and rising of tides into electrical energy. The U.S. state with the greatest tidal power capacity is Alaska, but all coastal states in the United States have some tidal power potential (Georgia Tech Research Corporation, 2011). Commercially available tidal generators are turbine systems typically built into existing piling structures for bridges or are stand-alone systems submerged beneath the water's surface. The first major tidal power system for the generation of grid-quality electricity was installed by Bangor Hydro Electric Company in Maine using TidGen tidal turbines. At peak power production, the system could provide electricity to meet the needs of twenty-five to thirty homes—roughly 180 kW. As with nearly all energy innovations, things start small to provide proof of concept and can be scaled up for commercialization (Levitan, 2012). Unlike wind and solar energy, tidal power is very highly predictable and could be used as a replacement for fossil energy power plants that provide back-up power plants (Conca, 2017).

In terms of U.S. public policy, OTEC was more broadly addressed in the *Ocean Thermal Energy Conversion, Research, Development, and Demonstration Act* (42 USC 9001, P.L. 96–310) passed and signed into law in 1980. While ocean thermal energy had been the subject of interest before 1980, the aforementioned law was a major step in OTEC policy development.

In OTEC systems, higher temperature ocean surface waters are used to heat secondary fluids that have a lower boiling point to create steam, and then power a turbine with that steam. At the end of the cycle, the secondary fluids are cooled with deeper ocean waters with lower average temperatures. The secondary fluids, which had become steam, condense to become liquid. The cycle begins anew with the now liquid-state secondary fluids again absorbing heat from higher temperature ocean surface waters, and once again become steam to be used to power a turbine. The greater the temperature difference between the higher temperature ocean surface waters and the secondary fluid—known as the heat gradient—the greater the energy available to power the turbines and create electricity.

With the aforementioned facts in mind, it is easy to guess where OTEC would be more feasible—anywhere where ocean surface temperatures are consistently high in temperature, and much warmer than deep water ocean temperatures. Temperature differences between surface waters and deeper waters make OTEC more feasible. Attaching geographic names to these locations: the Caribbean, the Indian Ocean, Hawaii, and the South China Sea represent optimal sites, to name a few. I suppose that as you read this section about OTEC, you are probably saying to yourself, "This is a form of solar energy since the sun often shines in these tropically located bodies of water." In a way, you would be absolutely correct! It is, at its origin, solar energy since the surface ocean waters absorbed heat from a higher-quality source, in this case the sun. Besides the potential to produce electric energy, commercially available OTEC systems can be used to desalinate ocean water for human use where water is scarce. The same basic principle used in OTEC can also be operated in reverse, where heat from air is absorbed by cooler ocean water, which could be used for cooling the interior climate of office buildings, factories, or residences. The system for doing this is known as Seawater Air Conditioning (SWAC).

NUCLEAR ENERGY

Nuclear energy is largely a twentieth-century phenomenon. The theoretical work of Albert Einstein, and critical demonstration projects of Enrico Fermi and Leo Szilard in 1940 showed that while very small in size, atoms contain a tremendous energy potential, particularly when broken apart in a process known as fission. Uranium-235 was particularly interesting to physicists studying nuclear energy because when the element encounters an additional neutron, it becomes unstable and breaks apart, or "decays," and in the process releases a great quantity of energy. In the process of decay, uranium releases large bursts of both thermal and radioactive energy. The decay process becomes a chain reaction, as neutrons released from one fission event impact other uranium atoms.

The thermal energy released from fission reactions is quite significant (approximately, 315°C), which can be used to turn liquid water into steam. Steam can be used to operate turbines for the generation of AC current. In most U.S. reactors, the water in piping that comes in contact with nuclear material is in a closed loop (frequently, these systems are pressured water reactors) and thus more likely to be contained in the event of a reactor failure. The heat from the steam produced in the closed loop is transferred via heat exchanger to another system, usually water-based, that creates the steam used to operate the electricity-generating turbine system (http://hyperphysics.phy-astr.gsu.edu/hbase/nucene/reactor.html#c3, accessed February 13, 2019).

Nuclear energy proponents argue that, based on a long track record in the United States and elsewhere around the world, nuclear energy is relatively safe. Nuclear energy plants cannot blow up like nuclear bombs, but they could conceivably produce small explosions and fires if the energy plant system overheated or in some other way malfunctioned in operation. If a reactor core became supercritical and there were no functional safety protocols in place, it is possible that the radioactive material would find its way into the subsurface below a reactor unit leading to environmental contamination. Of course, functional safety protocols exist in all such plants and are operational. Through peer-reviewed publications, demonstration projects, and everyday evidence from commercial plant operations, nuclear engineers and nuclear physicists lay claim to a well-grounded scientific knowledge base regarding the operations of nuclear power plants in commercial energy production settings.

Perhaps the strongest piece of evidence in the quivers of nuclear energy proponents relates to the empirical reality that nuclear safely provides approximately 20 percent of the base power needs in the United States currently and produces the vast majority of electrical energy needs in many European nations—for instance, 69.5 percent of the electrical energy needs in France are met by nuclear energy (EIA, 2019b).

There are, however, many aspects of nuclear technology that remain somewhat elusive. Perhaps the most commonly discussed issue is how to process and manage the radioactive waste products of nuclear energy plants (see Ojovan and Lee, 2005; Dolan and Scariano, 1993). In 2000, the U.S. government itself shipped approximately 2,467 metric tons (approximately 2,719 short tons) of spent nuclear fuel (SNF) (Department of Energy, 2001: 2) to nuclear waste repositories in the United States. The vast majority of this spent nuclear fuel (SNF) is stored at the U.S. Department of Energy site at Hanford, Washington. According to Ojovan and Lee (2005), the active nuclear power plants in the United States (producing approximately 1 GW_e annually) yield thirty tons of nuclear waste per nuclear facility per year.

Risk factors associated with nuclear waste management and disposal are of significant concern because dangerous levels of radioactivity are present in commercial nuclear energy waste products for, quite literally, tens of thousands of years. At one time, the Hanford Site in Washington State accepted the vast bulk of nuclear waste from government sources and some medical- and research laboratory-related radioactive wastes in the United States. The facility did this while simultaneously operating one of the nation's largest nuclear waste decontamination operations on the facility lands—a remnant of several decades of nuclear weapons facility operations for the production of plutonium during the Second World War and the subsequent Cold War.

In November 2004, the voters of Washington State passed a ballot initiative with a 69 percent majority in favor of banning nuclear waste imports into the Hanford Site. The U.S. Department of Justice challenged the ballot initiative in federal court (*U.S. v. Hoffman*), arguing that federal law governing nuclear waste shipments should prevail over state law, and asserted "sovereign immunity" over the waste generated by weapons production (Steele, 2004: B1). The federal court ordered a temporary injunction against the ballot initiative's implementation, requesting a decision from the State Supreme Court of Washington State with regard to the intent of the initiative in terms of challenging federal authority over Hanford Site management. In July 2005, the Washington State Supreme Court rejected the federal government's argument. The Washington Court concluded that the ballot initiative "'was drafted to prevent the addition of new radioactive and hazardous waste to the Hanford nuclear reservation until the cleanup of existing contamination is complete.'" (Cooper, 2005). In 2006, the U.S. District Court for Eastern Washington struck down the Washington State initiative, but the decision was moot because of an agreed settlement between the then U.S. Secretary of Energy Bodman and the state of Washington wherein Hanford (a U.S. Department of Energy–operated facility) would eliminate most of its waste imports (Triay and Manning, Settlement Agreement, 2006).

Beyond the issue of government-created nuclear waste is, of course, a much larger concern over the commercial spent nuclear fuel (SNF) that is produced by nuclear power stations across the nation. Since the Three Mile Island incident in 1979 in which a reactor core overheated, there has been a net loss in the number of commercial nuclear power plants in the United States. Critics of nuclear energy argue that these waste materials have the potential added cost of destroying the environment and harming animal and plant life well into the foreseeable future, quite possibly beyond the existence of human beings as a species. The Government Accounting Office estimates that as of 2019, there are approximately 90,000 tons of spent commercial nuclear fuel stored on-site at commercial nuclear power and Department of Energy facilities—at eighty sites in thirty-five states—spread across the whole nation (U.S. GAO, 2019).

U.S. government responsibility over the regulation and management of nuclear fissile materials can be traced back to the Atomic Energy Act of 1954. In 1982, Congress passed, and President Reagan signed into law, the Nuclear Waste Policy Act (NWPA). The NWPA directed the U.S. Department of Energy to conduct studies of appropriate locations for the storage of commercial and government-generated nuclear waste in a "permanent" repository. In 1987, Congress amended the NWPA and required the U.S. Department of Energy to consider only Yucca Mountain, Nevada, as a potential site for such a repository. "In 2002, the President recommended to the Congress and the Congress approved, Yucca Mountain as a suitable site for the development of a permanent high level waste repository" (U.S. GAO, 2003: 5).

In 1995, the U.S. Department of Energy, the U.S. Navy, and the state of Idaho entered into a precedent-setting agreement on the movement of nuclear waste material within the state. In essence, the DOE agreed to limit shipments into waste repositories within the state, and in return promised to remove nuclear waste from the state sites and to safely transport it from the Idaho National Engineering and Environmental Laboratory (INEL) to a permanent repository. The time line established in the document indicates that all nuclear waste will be removed from INEL by 2035. The agreement essentially established a time line for, and the removal and transportation of SNF to, the permanent waste repository. The agreement pushed forward the process of permanent nuclear waste disposal and reduced the likelihood that waste will continue to be transported and stored at temporary repositories.

Despite the growing sense that there needs to be a permanent repository established, there remains significant controversy over the use of Yucca Mountain as such a nuclear waste depository. Environmental interest groups have historically been opposed to nuclear energy because of the potential for harm to humans and to the environment in energy production and waste storage; such concerns are fueled by power plant incidents at Three Mile Island in 1979, at Chernobyl in the former Soviet Union in 1986, and at Fukushima in Japan in 2011.

Nuclear waste repositories exist at the aforementioned eighty storage sites in the United States. The Nuclear Regulatory Commission (NRC) has approved dry pellets stored in steel containers within cement structures or in shallow cooling pools constructed of several feet of steel and cement designed to prevent contamination. Concerns remain over the ability to manage nuclear waste spread over so many different sites, but there are equal concerns about the transportation to and safe storage of nuclear waste materials at a repository site such as Yucca Mountain, Nevada.

In 2003, the GAO conducted a study to determine the level of risk associated with the transportation of nuclear waste via truck or rail to Yucca Mountain. In the past, major concerns had focused on nuclear waste spills produced by the occurrence of transportation accidents. The GAO report recounted these analyses, finding that vehicle/rail accidents impacting the transportation of fissile waste materials would occur in the range of four to seven times per 100,000 rail or truck trips, which were considered minimal likelihood events. Another major concern that emerged in the report was related to a terrorist attack on the transportation of commercial nuclear waste to Yucca Mountain. The GAO study concluded that the cement and steel casks in which the nuclear materials were transported would most likely survive a terrorist or sabotage attack, and that only a series of highly improbable events would result in the release of any injurious radioactive contaminants. Citing DOE research evidence, the GAO found that many experts' confidence in the very high level of safety associated with the transportation of nuclear waste to Yucca Mountain has continued to grow due to increased amounts of data and growing sophistication of simulation programs employed to study potential weaknesses in both the transportation and disposal process models (U.S. GAO, 2003: 11–12).

Despite the evidence that a centralized waste depository at Yucca Mountain is both safe and feasible, one strategy for preventing the depository from ever receiving nuclear waste would involve appeals made to the Environmental Protection Agency. Appellants would ask EPA to develop secondary risk assessments to prevent the NRC, which is more closely tied to energy producers than to environmental interests, to regulate nuclear waste and plant decommissioning activities. At least for the moment, the policy "door" remains closed to interest groups pursuing the aforementioned strategy because of a 2002 Memorandum of Understanding in which the EPA expressly denies itself the ability to regulate the activities of the NRC in relation to nuclear material transportation and commercial nuclear energy plant-related environmental measures, most specifically those associated with plant decommissioning (Whitman and Meserve, 2002). If that policy door were to open, nuclear power and waste management would likely face a more hostile policy environment.

Risk assessment, however, remains the central focus of concern with regard to nuclear waste, as detailed in the National Research Council report *Risk and Decisions: About the Disposition of Transuranic and High-Level Radioactive Nuclear Waste* (2005). The NRC eschewed offering specific recommendations, focusing instead on the ways in which risk is defined in relation to nuclear waste. The NRC has reviewed a number of previous studies conducted by both government and nongovernmental organizations regarding the level of risk associated with the transportation and storage of nuclear waste. NRC paid particular attention to the politically charged atmosphere surrounding the definition of risk, identifying the level of angst, expressed through ballot initiatives and litigation, occurring in a multitude of state and local communities: bluntly stated, there is very little trust in the process of dealing with nuclear waste and NIMBY sentiments tend to prevail.

Perspectives on nuclear waste management vary significantly across policy stakeholder groups. Native American tribes, numerous so-called "downwinder" communities—communities that were adversely impacted by past nuclear radioactive contamination—and environmental groups demonstrate a high level of distrust of scientifically defined risk assessments produced by governmental agencies and by nuclear industry policy analysts. One thing that can be agreed upon is the need to remove nuclear contamination and waste from where it is currently being stored, but the big questions relate to the designation of a final repository location and modes of transportation thereto. The "not-in-my-backyard" effect as well as historically demonstrated and now legally recognized damaging impacts of nuclear energy development and waste storage appears to cast a long shadow over the U.S. nuclear industry and its advocates (Washington Department of Public Health, 2004).

With multiple stakeholders on both sides of the nuclear waste disposal issue, the prospect of a central nuclear waste facility were dimmed by President Obama, who cut funds to the Yucca Mountain program in 2011 (Northey, 2011). The politics surrounding Yucca Mountain are often closely associated with the policy priorities of then-Senate Majority Leader, Senator Harry Reid (D-Nevada) (Kormarow, 2015). Following Reid's retirement from the U.S. Senate and congressional election outcomes, a Republican Senate majority considered formulating a $120 million budget expenditure to restart construction of the Yucca Mountain facility. According to Ferguson (2017), the Republicans retreated and then eliminated the Yucca Mountain budget line in order to protect U.S. Senator Dean Heller (R-NV), saving him the politically charged decision to vote in favor of a nuclear waste depository that remains unpopular with a large majority of Nevada voters. The Republican reversal on Yucca Mountain, a facility that will likely never open and which has cost approximately $15 billion for preliminary exploration, may have dimmed the chances for safe, centralized storage for nuclear waste in the United States. In the absence of safe long-term SNF storage, it is unlikely that nuclear energy will expand significantly in the United States in the coming decades.

The economics of nuclear energy are quite revealing, and offer a different view of how risk is assessed in the case of this form of alternative energy. Nuclear energy as a source of electricity generation represents a significant portion of the net power generation portfolio in the United States despite the nuclear waste problem. Currently, there are ninety-eight commercial nuclear power plants in operation in the United States. The newest plant is Watts Bar 1, which began operations in 2016. There are two additional new plants expected to be completed and operational in a few years (Southern Company, 2018). In the past decade, five nuclear plants were retired due in large part to political pressure from opponents of nuclear energy. Nuclear power plants produce approximately 20 percent (as of 2017, 805 billion kWh) of grid-supplied electricity in the United States (U.S. Census, 2004–2005: 587), which makes nuclear energy the third-largest commercial electricity-producing sector behind those of natural gas and remaining coal-fired electricity plants (https://www.eia.gov/tools/faqs/faq.php?id=427&t=3, February 14, 2019).

The ratio of operating capacity to generation capacity has increased tremendously over recent years. In 1990, operating capacity was 99 percent, and it has remained above that threshold for the last twenty-nine years. But energy production comes at a price in terms of nuclear material used. The process of mining, enriching, and fabricating nuclear fuel is estimated at $1,491 (in 2019 dollars) per kilogram, which would yield 315,000 kWh. In terms of uranium concentrate purchases alone, current nuclear energy costs are around $0.0045 per kWh (in 2007 dollars) (World Nuclear Association, 2008).

Capital costs for the construction of nuclear power facilities are not presently being factored into the cost of nuclear-produced electricity in the United States because only a handful of new plants are coming online and older plants are largely bought and paid for at this point. Nevertheless, if new plants were to be built, overnight capital costs would largely be a function of the number of plants being built, the size of the plant, time to completion, and the expected life span of the facility. Plant costs for a next-generation gigawatt light water reactor are estimated to be as much as $ 4.2 billion (in 2011 dollars) (Rosner et al. 2011, 5). Capital costs per kWh for power generation would decline significantly if a commitment to large-scale plant construction was ever undertaken nationwide.

Technological developments, such as the pebble bed modular reactor (PBMR) design, may one day lead to lower plant costs. PBMR is an energy option that has been used globally. The system relies on nuclear fuel "pebbles" composed of uranium oxide and graphite, the latter intended to help manage the fission process and reduce the chance of overheating (although overheating associated with graphite and graphite fires was part of the problem in the Chernobyl nuclear plant accident in 1986). An encouraging PBMR analysis conducted at the University of Michigan claimed that the cost of these advanced reactor units is much smaller than a conventional nuclear plant, requiring less downtime for fuel replacement and considerably fewer operating personnel. These two cost factors alone, it is claimed, will significantly reduce operations and maintenance costs for electricity generation on a per kWh basis. The plant facilities are modular and require a smaller land "footprint," which will also reduce capital cost expenditures. Anti-PBMR studies, however, claim that the plant design is unsafe and could result in the release of radioactivity into the atmosphere. Critics find that the pebbles have been shown to have at least one defect per pebble, which could result in uncontrollable fission reactions and thus overheating. Due to heightened concerns about the safety of the technology, the major South African firm engaged in PBMR reactor development—Pebble Bed Modular Reactor Ltd.—has experienced significant decline in activity and disinvestment by the South African government (Nuclear Engineering International, 2017).

The United States has not commercialized PBMR domestically, but the technology is being adopted elsewhere—most notably in China. The Institute of Nuclear and New Energy Technology, Tsinghua University, has developed two PBMR reactors using a design originally developed in Germany. A German firm is currently supplying the "pebbles," which contain nuclear fuel encased in graphite spheres. Each of the reactors has a nameplate capacity of 105 MW. Tsinghua University has invested over a decade of research time leading up to the construction of their PMBR research-oriented reactors (Martin, 2016).

The debate over the quality of pebble materials, the relative safety of nuclear power generation, and the "true cost" per kWh of nuclear energy remains mired in politically charged analysis in the United States. The issue of managing nuclear waste, however, is an area where pronuclear forces have, in recent years, provided new analysis that might change the nature of debate for next-generation nuclear power.

In terms of nuclear waste issues, European innovations have resulted in significant reductions in spent nuclear fuel (SNF) through the reprocessing and reuse of radioactive material. Reprocessing recovers usable plutonium and uranium; these provide the basis of a product known as mixed oxide fuel (MOX). MOX does not require enrichment because it has already been processed as a fuel source, reducing production costs of fuel. Additionally, the resulting SNF, which cannot be used as a source of MOX, is estimated at only 35 percent of the "volume, mass, and cost of disposal" when compared to traditional SNF not subject to the MOX recovery process. In many European nations, nuclear reactors are designed to include MOX as part of the energy generation process, and it is claimed that the process substantially reduces the cost of energy generation (see U.S. Nuclear Regulatory Commission, 2017). In the United States, MOX is not used in commercial nuclear power plants, but there are plans for future use. In the United States, MOX will not be generated from reprocessed nuclear waste but rather from weapons grade plutonium either inventoried as surplus or from decommissioned nuclear weapons (U.S. Nuclear Regulatory Commission, 2019).

An MIT interdisciplinary study report, *The Future of Nuclear Power* (2003, updated 2009), rejected the use of reprocessed commercial fuel rods into MOX and calls for continued "once-through fuel cycle" (Ansolabehre et al., 2003, updated 2009: x). The authors' reasoning is that large-scale reprocessing of nuclear fuel would lead to large-scale material security problems for which the world is not adequately prepared. All the while, the report advocated for a threefold increase in nuclear power generation. The MIT report called for streamlining facility costs, NRC preapproval of modern power plant designs to streamline the development process, and inclusion of nuclear power in state renewable standards portfolio—even though nuclear is, strictly speaking, not a renewable energy source. The plan also recommended increased public education to sway public opinion toward nuclear energy as an option for the reduction of greenhouse gas emissions. Nevertheless, despite all of these well-based arguments, the MIT report concluded that nuclear power is on the decline.

The Economic Future of Nuclear Power (2004), a report produced by a team of economists and other public policy analysts at the Harris School of Public Policy, is a widely referenced analysis of nuclear energy at the dawn of the twenty-first century. The report was delivered to the U.S. House of Representatives and has been subjected to peer review as well as government administrator review. The University of Chicago study focused on the levelized cost of electricity for current and next-generation nuclear power plants when compared with projected costs for other major sources of electrical energy

Nuclear Power Plant
PHOTOS.com>> / Getty Images Plus / Jupiterimages

generation likely to be used in the twenty-first century. The study found that initial analysis of the levelized cost of electricity of nuclear energy is somewhat higher than electricity from "conventional" energy sources (i.e., coal, gas-fired, and oil-fired plants). At the time of the study, it was estimated that a 1,000 MW nuclear power plant would cost between approximately $550 million and $600 million in terms of overnight capital costs (for seven-year construction time), compared to coal and gas generation plants, which were, at the time of the study, estimated to have overnight capital costs of between $275 million and $375 million. On a per MWh basis, the range for nuclear is between $47 and $62, while the range for coal- and gas-fired plant capital construction costs is between $33 and $45. The University of Chicago report, however, demonstrated that capital costs are expected to decline significantly *if* there is a commitment to build multiple nuclear power plant units.

THE REBIRTH OF NUCLEAR ENERGY?

Over the past fifteen years, there has been a growing interest in the expansion of nuclear energy as part of the national energy portfolio. The Nuclear Energy Task Force (NETF) report *Moving Forward with Nuclear Energy: Issues and Key Factors* (2005) built on themes similar to those set forth in the University of Chicago study. The report sought to streamline the process of permitting for new nuclear power facilities. The study outlines methods of achieving this goal, calling on the U.S. Department of Energy to preapprove nuclear facility designs to reduce the time commitment necessary for each facility application and approval process. The process of design and site approval is costly, and the litigation that is likely to appear during the operations approval phase is an obstacle to firms interested in building and operating nuclear power facilities.

Reducing the uncertainty of plant design and operations through preapproval of plant designs and facility operations plans was found by NETF members to be a significant step forward in developing nuclear energy plants in the future. Critics would likely charge that the NETF recommendations are simply methods of reducing public response time to the development of nuclear power plant facilities. The report does spend minimal effort to promote the principles of sustainable communities with regard to public visions of acceptable energy development. In other words, the role of consent is firmly embraced in the study, rather than a narrow focus on technical feasibility.

The NETF study was a substantial step forward for the future development of nuclear energy as a macro top-down energy policy solution to meet short- and long-term needs. Political outcomes over the next decade will likely determine if a macro top-down solution, such as the further development of nuclear power, will or will not become a policy reality. Given the need to remain competitive in an international market-driven economy, the report's author anticipates that a resurgence of nuclear energy in some form will occur, but remain part of a larger mixed-source energy portfolio.

Nevertheless, according to the Secretary of Energy Advisory Board (SEAB), "there is no shortcut to reestablish a vigorous U.S. nuclear power initiative that could be a major source of carbon-free generation" (Deutch, 2016: cover letter). The SEAB report went on to state that power plant construction costs must be reduced by about half in order to make the levelized cost of nuclear energy more competitive. The report also recommended that nuclear energy should be recognized as a carbon-free form of energy. The combined effects of a well-structured carbon market (and a carbon pricing policy) and production tax credits would go a long way toward making nuclear energy more market competitive. Additionally, the report finds that dispatch rules are biased in favor of renewable energy, and that rate structures of nuclear energy are not sufficient to allow for investment recovery. The SEAB noted that the issue of nuclear waste management must be both secure and meet the prevailing standards of public acceptability. Finally, the SEAB recommended more aggressive government funding and policy to support the development of advanced nuclear power plants, noting that the United States lags far behind the rest of the world in developing next-generation nuclear energy—the development of a "significant nuclear power option" (Deutch, 2016: cover letter) in the United States would more likely occur by mid-century.

All other issues aside, the SEAB report's conclusions regarding nuclear waste management have proven to be a significant dilemma for the future development of nuclear energy. The development of a centralized nuclear waste storage facility at Yucca Mountain in Nevada was intended to address the exact issues regarding nuclear waste mentioned in the SEAB report in 2016. While the GAO has concluded that the facility does meet the standards of safety and security, public acceptability was not forthcoming and the issue became highly politicized. As previously noted, nuclear waste storage was effectively stopped before it ever got started by the combined efforts of the Obama administration and then-U.S. Senator Harry Reid (D-NV), but the Trump administration has indicated a desire to reopen the facility. It is likely that politics—namely, Republican concern about losing a U.S. Senate seat in Nevada—led to a policy retreat by President Trump. Regardless, the Senate seat was lost in the 2018 election cycle as Nevada continues to move toward becoming a Democrat-leaning state. That said, there remains no long-term politically viable solution to the disposal of nuclear waste in the United States. Restarting the licensing process for Yucca Mountain as a permanent nuclear waste repository will require restaffing the facility and reengaging key stakeholders in the process, requiring at minimum several years (U.S. GAO, 2017). Barring the adoption of such a policy, nuclear waste continues to remain on-site at over one hundred power plant and research sites throughout the nation.

Despite there being no major U.S. nuclear energy safety issues since Three Mile Island in 1979, international nuclear disasters continue to focus public attention on the perceived dangers of nuclear power. The Chernobyl disaster in 1986 and the Fukushima Daiichi disaster in 2011 are enduring images in the minds of policy makers and stakeholders. At least for the foreseeable future, nuclear energy in the United States is offered a zero-tolerance threshold for system operational failure. Only a large-scale policy shift will likely lead to a revival of nuclear energy policy in the United States. The event that might produce such an effect is a massive grid failure—given proenvironmental values and risk-adversity, even a major grid failure might prove insufficient in moving energy policy direction. Under such conditions, however, there would likely be insufficient time to construct and put into production large-scale nuclear power. Other parts of the world, however, do not face the same policy maker and stakeholder constraints as currently faced in the United States policy-making arena; nuclear power will likely proliferate in areas where barriers to disposal, reprocessing, and plant construction are so much lower. Commercial nuclear technology and industrial development will likely gravitate to nations welcoming of nuclear power, and wither away domestically, save for military applications and maintenance of existing commercial nuclear plant and waste storage infrastructure.

CHAPTER SUMMARY

Hydropower and nuclear energy are two excellent examples of the intersection of politics and science in the energy policy arena. In both cases, the energy sources were initially viewed as grounded in solid scientific knowledge and were largely uncontested, but are today viewed as highly risky endeavors that can endanger humans and the environment, or both. In the 1970s the energy policy paradigm was shaken significantly as science and political and social consent for these two energy sources began to unravel. The science of hydropower was questioned as ecological evidence increasingly documented the adverse impacts of hydropower dams on the natural environment. Political and social consent to the risks associated with hydropower was significantly eroded. Nuclear energy faced a similar set of changes in risk assessment, particularly following the aforementioned nuclear accidents. Hydropower has staged a limited comeback in the form of pumped hydro storage, micro hydro, and hydro-refitting plans. All three methods can overcome the major barrier to hydropower—the destruction of native fish populations (e.g., wild salmon) and the destruction of habitat through water level changes, erosion, and turbulence. Nuclear power, however, has yet to discover a long-term tenable policy solution to overcome the political and social barriers standing in the way of its future development.

REFERENCES

Abrams, E. 1937. Your stock in TVA. *Saturday Evening Post* 210(16): 27, 77–82.
American Forests. 1999. Salmon efforts jumping. *American Forests* 105(1): 11–12.
Ansolabehere, S., Deutch, J., Driscoll, M., Gray, P., Holdren, J., Joskow, P., Lester, R., Moniz, E., and Todreas, N. 2003 (updated 2009). *The Future of Nuclear Power: An*

Interdisciplinary MIT Study. Cambridge, MA: MIT. Retrieved from http://energy. mit.edu/wp-content/uploads/2003/07/MITEI-The-Future-of-Nuclear-Power.pdf, February 25, 2019.

Baker, J. 1988. Letting the rivers flow. *Sierra* 73(4): 21–24.

Bernal, B., Molero, J., and Perez De Gracia, F. 2019. Impact of fossil fuel prices on electricity prices in Mexico. *Journal of Economic Studies* 46(2): 356–371.

Campbell, D. 2000. When the lights came on. *Rural Cooperatives* 67(4): 6–9.

Conca, J. 2017. Tidal energy—all renewables are not created equal, *Forbes*, July 27. Retrieved from https://www.forbes.com/sites/jamesconca/2017/07/27/tidal-energy-all-renewables-are-not-created-equal/#53b32d7d4f4e, February 8, 2019.

Connolly, D., Lund, H., Mathiesen, B., Pican, E., and Leahy, M. 2012. The technical and economic implications of integrating fluctuating renewable energy using energy storage. *Renewable Energy: An International Journal* 43: 47–60.

Cooper, B. 2005. State supreme court upholds key provisions of Hanford cleanup initiative 297. http://www.hoanw.org/PDF/7_28_5.pdf, accessed August 29, 2005.

Deutch, J. 2016. *Secretary of Energy Advisory Board Report of the Task Force on the Future of Nuclear Power*. Washington, DC: U.S. Department of Energy. Retrieved from https://www.energy.gov/sites/prod/files/2016/10/f33/9-22-16_SEAB%20Nuclear%20 Power%20TF%20Report%20and%20transmittal.pdf, June 24, 2019.

Dolan, E., and M. Scariano 1993. *Nuclear waste: The 10,000-year challenge*. New York: Franklin Watts, Inc.

Douglas, M. and Wildavsky, A. 1983. *Risk and Culture: An Essay on the Selection of Technological and Environmental Dangers*. Berkeley, CA: University of California Press.

Energy Information Administration. 2019a. U.S. Energy Consumption by Source, 2017. Retrieved from https://www.eia.gov/energyexplained/?page=us_energy_home, July 23, 2019.

———. 2019b. Country Analysis Briefs: France. Retrieved from https://www.eia.gov/ beta/international/data/, June 23, 2019.

EPA. 2000. *Federal and California Exhaust and Evaporative Emissions Standards for Light Duty Vehicles and Light Duty Trucks*, EPA420-B-00-001. Washington, DC: U.S. Environmental Protection Agency.

Ferguson, R. 2017. Republicans play politics on Yucca Mountain. *Wall Street Journal*, August 16, A15.

Georgia Tech Research Corporation. 2011. *Assessment of Energy Production Potential from Tidal Streams in the United States*, Award DE-FG36-08GO18174. Savannah, GA: Georgia Tech Research Corporation.

Howarth, D. 1960. Giant in the jungle. *Saturday Evening Post* 232(40): 26, 97–100.

Inglehart, Ronald. 1990. *Culture Shift in Advanced Industrial Democracies*. Princeton, NJ: Princeton University Press.

Jonnes, J. 2004. New York unplugged, 1889. *New York Times*, August 13, A21.

Kormarow, S. 2015. The king of Yucca Mountain. *CQ Weekly*, March 30, p. 6.

Levitan, D. 2012. First tidal power in U.S. starts flowing to the grid. *IEEE Spectrum*, September 18. Retrieved from https://spectrum.ieee.org/energywise/green-tech/ge-othermal-and-tidal/first-tidal-power-starts-flowing-to-the-grid, February 8, 2019.

Martin, R. 2016. China could have a meltdown-proof nuclear reactor next year. *MIT Technology Review*, February 11. Retrieved from https://www.technologyreview. com/s/600757/china-could-have-a-meltdown-proof-nuclear-reactor-next-year/, February 14, 2019.

Marts, M., and Sewell, W. 1960. The conflict between fish and power resources in the Pacific Northwest. *Annals of the Association of American Geographers* 50(1): 42–50.

National Energy Technology Laboratory. 2005. History. Washington, DC: U.S. Department of Energy, http://www.netl.doe.gov/, accessed August 19, 2005.

National Wildlife. 1984. Power vs. wildlife. *National Wildlife* 22(3): 35.

Nicholas, J. 1997. *The Oregon Plan: Coastal Salmon Restoration Initiative*. Salem, OR: State of Oregon.

Northey, H. 2011. GAO: Death of Yucca Mountain caused by political maneuvering. *New York Times*, May 10. Retrieved from https://archive.nytimes.com/www.nytimes.com/gwire/2011/05/10/10greenwire-gao-death-of-yucca-mountain-caused-by-politica-36298.html?pagewanted=2, February 13, 2019.

Nuclear Energy Task Force. 2005. *Moving Ahead with Nuclear Energy: Issues and Key Factors*. Washington, DC: Secretary of Energy Advisory Board, U.S. Department of Energy.

Nuclear Engineering International. 2017. Second thoughts on South Africa's pebble-bed reactor. *Nuclear Engineering International*, April 2. Retrieved from https://www.neimagazine.com/news/newssecond-thoughts-on-south-africas-pebble-bed-reactor-5776340, February 25, 2019.

Ojovan, M., and Lee, W. 2005. *An Introduction to Nuclear Waste Mobilization*, 2nd edition. Oxford, UK: Elsevier.

Railsback, S., Cada, G., Petrich, C., Sale, M., Shaakir-Ali, J., Watts, J., and Webb, J. 1991. *Environmental Impacts of Increased Hydroelectric Development at Existing Dams*, Environmental Sciences Division Publication No. 3585. Oakridge, TN: Oakridge National Laboratory/Washington, DC: Department of Commerce, National Technical Information Service.

Rosner, R., Goldberg, S., Hezir, J., and Davis, E. 2011. *Analysis of GW-Scale Overnight Capital Costs*. Chicago, IL: Energy Policy Institute, University of Chicago. Retrieved from https://epic.uchicago.edu/sites/default/files/EPICOvernightCostReportDec14 2011copy.pdf, February 14, 2019.

Sale, Michael J. 2005. *An Overview of Hydropower Resources in the U.S.* Oak Ridge National Laboratory. Renewable Energy Modeling Project, May 10.

Schattschneider, E. 1960. *The Semisovereign People: A Realist's View of Democracy in America*. Chicago, IL: Holt, Reinhart, and Winston.

Simon, H. 1957. *Models of Man*. New York: Wiley.

Southern Company. 2018. All four Vogtle 3 & 4 project co-owners have voted to continue construction of the two new nuclear units. *Southern Company News Center Stories*, September 26. Retrieved from https://www.southerncompany.com/ newsroom/2018/sept-2018/all-vogtle-owners-vote-to-move-forward.html, February 14, 2019.

Steel, B., Lovrich, N., and O'Toole, E. 1999. Public perceptions and preferences concerning pacific salmon recovery: An Oregon "voluntary grassroots" perspective. *Social Science Journal* 36(3): 497–513.

Steele, K. 2004. Nuclear waste initiative targeted. Challenge contends federal laws prevail over state rules. *Spokesman Review* (Spokane, WA). December 2, B1.

Stone, D. 2011. *Policy Paradox: The Art of Political Decision Making*. New York: Norton.

Tatro, S. 1999. Dam breaching. *Civil Engineering* 69(4): 50–55.

Tolley, G., and Jones, D. 2004. *The Economic Future of Nuclear Power*. Chicago, IL: Harris School of Public Policy, University of Chicago.

Trevithick, F. 1872. *Life of Richard Trevithick with an Account of His Inventions*. London: E. & F. N. Spon Publishers.

Triay, I., and Manning, J. 2006. Settlement agreement re: *Washington v. Bodman*, civil no. 2:03-cv-05018-AAM. Washington, DC: U.S. Department of Energy. Retrieved from https://www.energy.gov/sites/prod/files/em/144113SettlementAgreement-FINAL-01-06-061.pdf, February 13, 2019.

U.S. Census Bureau. 2004–2005. *Statistical Abstract of the United States 2004–2005*. Washington, DC: U.S. Census Bureau.

U.S. Department of Energy. 2001. *DOE Current Year Waste/Contaminated Media and SNF Inventories by Site (Sum-3)*. Washington, DC: U.S. Department of Energy, Office of Environmental Management, Central Internet Database.

U.S. Government Accountability Office. 2003. *Spent Nuclear Fuel: Options Exist to Further Enhance Security*. Washington, DC: U.S. Governmental Accountability Office.

———. 2017. *Commercial Nuclear Waste: Resuming Licensing of the Yucca Mountain Repository Would Require Rebuilding Capacity at DOE and NRC, among Other Key Steps*, GAO-17-340. https://www.gao.gov/assets/690/684327.pdf, June 24, 2019.

———. 2019. *Disposal of High-Level Nuclear Waste*. Washington, DC: U.S. GAO. Retrieved from https://www.gao.gov/key_issues/disposal_of_highlevel_nuclear_waste/issue_summary, February 13, 2019.

U.S. Nuclear Regulatory Commission. 2017. *Backgrounder on Mixed Oxide Fuel*. Washington, DC: U.S. Nuclear Regulatory Commission. Retrieved from https://www.nrc.gov/reading-rm/doc-collections/fact-sheets/mox-bg.html, February 14, 2019.

———. 2019. Frequently Asked Questions about Mixed Oxide Fuel. *Nuclear Regulatory Commission*. Retrieved from https://www.nrc.gov/materials/fuel-cycle-fac/mox/faq.html#2, February 25, 2019.

Washington Department of Public Health. 2004. An Overview of Hanford and Radiation Health Effects, http://www.doh.wa.gov/hanford/publications/overview/overview.html, accessed November 27, 2005.

Waters, S., and Aggidis, G. 2015. Over 2,000 years in review: Revival of the Archimedes' screw from pump to turbine. *Renewable and Sustainable Energy Reviews* 51: 497–505.

Whitman, C., and Meserve, R. 2002. *Memorandum of Understanding between the Environmental Protection Agency and the Nuclear Regulatory Commission: Consultation and Finality on Decomissioning and Decontamination of Contaminated Sites*. Washington, DC: EPA & NRC.

World Nuclear Association 2008. *The Economics of Nuclear Power*. London, UK: World Nuclear Association. Retrieved from http://www.world-nuclear.org/uploadedfiles/org/info/pdf/economicsnp.pdf, February 14, 2019.

WTRG Economics. 2005. *Oil Price History and Analysis*. London, AR. WTRG Economics, http://www.wtrg.com/prices.htm, accessed August 20, 2005.

Zayas, J. 2018. *Hydropower Vision: A New Chapter in America's 1st Renewable Electricity Source*. Oak Ridge, TN: U.S. Department of Energy, Office of Scientific and Technical Information.

9

Conceptualizing Alternative Energy Policy and Future Directions

★ ★ ★

We have in the United States an abundance of fossil energy in the forms of coal, crude oil, shale oil, and natural gas to last through the current century, and possibly into the twenty-second century. The business-as-usual model is one approach the United States could take, but global climate change and the eventual depletion of carbon-based energy sources make the business-as-usual model unrealistic. The evidence is clear that carbon emissions caused by human activity are related to significant rises in global temperatures. The Intergovernmental Panel on Climate Change (IPCC) recommends energy and policy changes seeking to rein in rising temperatures to 1.5°C above preindustrial levels so as to minimize the growing likelihood of some irreversible adverse global climate impacts. A panel comprised of 195 member nations, created in 1988 by the World Meteorological Organization and the United Nations Environment Program, the IPCC represents a very broad international scientific and political consensus on climate change, its causes, its effects, and the policy solutions available to policy makers in the United States and around the world.

Beyond issues of fossil energy use, there is the issue of fresh water availability. Over two billion gallons of water are used every day in the United States just for the refinement of petroleum products such as gasoline. Over 40 percent of all water supply withdrawals in the United States—approximately 133 billion gallons of water per day—are used in the generation of electricity (Water Calculator, 2019). Billions of gallons more water are used to grow agricultural crops, the major one of which is corn. Corn is used as the principal feedstock for ethanol production. The reduction of water use—a renewable resource in extremely high demand—would reduce pressure on water systems to meet the needs of multiple sources, including species of threatened and endangered fish that require minimum instream flow levels for habitation and reproduction. In short, there is a pressing need to balance the needs of our natural environment with human needs.

FUTURE DIRECTIONS

The future of alternative energy and climate change policies is deeply mired in international and national politics. By definition, politics involves the articulation of values and the distribution of benefits and costs through governmental decision-making processes. Two critical lines of reasoning encapsulate separate but related sets of values. One value set and related line of reasoning is grounded in issues of present and future scarcity and distributional equity. Those ascribing to these values gravitate to postmaterialist values and a concern for aesthetic qualities of life as well as a concern for equality, broadly defined, emphasizing social and environmental justice. For simplicity's sake, I will refer to these individuals as Greens, although a range of viewpoints exists within this category.

For Greens, climate change, the limits of growth, global climate migration, peak oil (and natural resource depletion, in general), and the anticipated Holocene extinction weigh heavily in their thoughts and shape policy preferences. For Greens who operate on the "border" rather than in the political "center" (Douglas and Wildavsky, 1983), the energy future relies heavily on a sense of collective action brought about through public policy. The energy future would be built on a green energy paradigm of net-zero carbon emissions attained through the exclusive use of renewable alternative energy sources. Through regulation, the provision of incentives, and direct investment, fossil and two alternative energy sources, namely nuclear power and certain forms of hydroelectricity, would be largely supplanted by solar, wind, geothermal, and tidal renewable energy systems. Hydrocarbon fuels would be replaced entirely by renewable biofuels.

As noted earlier, Greens focus significant attention on environmental and social justice. Greens tend to emphasize the point that the business-as-usual approach to international industrial capitalism has contributed mightily to environmental degradation, water and air pollution, and the destruction or endangerment of species. Beyond the broader issue of environmental concern, Greens often point to the human effects of the business-as-usual model claiming that industrial capitalism has destroyed traditional societies throughout the developing world. Furthermore they often argue that climate change and resource depletion too often leads to climate migration as individuals seek better lives for themselves and their families elsewhere. Climate migration is, according to many among the Greens, a form of displacement producing forms of social injustice as individuals lose contact with their traditional communities, their language, culture, and value-structure, finding themselves frequently transplanted in developed nations where they are valued solely for their labor.

In some despicable cases, they are victimized by human traffickers, often face discrimination and bigotry, and often are threatened with and experience deportation by powerful privileged classes.

In February 2019, Democratic congresswoman Alexandria Ocasio-Cortez—a millennial generation representative from Brooklyn—took the lead in proposing H.R. 109 "Recognizing the duty of the Federal Government to create a Green New Deal." It was considered by proponents and opponents alike to be a bold legislative step, and it engendered much public debate. In fact, the plan was not a completely new idea, but rather represented a response to growing knowledge and understanding about climate change and its anticipated impacts on human populations within the United States and across the globe. In 1990, Congress passed the Global Change Research Act, a statute that tasked the U.S. Global Change Research Program, with the participation of a number of federal agencies, with producing a National Climate Assessment every four years to provide evidence on environmental and public health impacts that should be documented for Congress as it considers new legislation.

Initially, the assessment was the collaborative effort of a sixty-member panel; by the third national assessment the collaboration involved approximately 300 researchers. The assessment draft reports were subject to public comment and peer-organization review, and were redrafted in response to these comments and critical reviews. In other words, a great deal of effort was made to increase transparency and create a foundation of shared assumptions about "facts on the ground" in the United States. The four highly vetted national assessments that have been published are clear in their call for a response to growing evidence of climate change and the need for ameliorating its impact on human society and the environment.

In response to these assessments, Representative Ted Deutsch (D-FL) and Senator Dianne Feinstein (D-CA) have, independently, sought to advance legislation in both the U.S. House of Representatives and the U.S. Senate that would lead to the systematic reduction of carbon emissions, the promotion of clean energy, the enhancement of energy efficiency, and the implementation of a carbon market wherein emissions are limited by federal statute—also known as "cap and trade" (see *Congressional Digest*, 2019). The Green New Deal, therefore, builds on an existing climate change policy agenda as well as acknowledges the recommendations of decades' worth of climate change studies and policy initiatives.

The Ocasio-Cortez plan called for increased investment in renewable energy and for dramatically more rapid progress toward a 100 percent renewable energy paradigm. The premise of the plan is that the social and environmental costs of carbon-based energy must be recouped through government policy. The ambitious plan calls for the protection of the individual, particularly working and middle classes that are most vulnerable to the costs imposed by climate change, over the needs of the wealthy, big business, and transnational corporations.

Workers' rights and the right to organize and collectively bargain for better working conditions and salaries is a critical part of the Green New Deal. The HR 109 demands that the federal government ensure a family wage and related benefits such as quality health care, education, and housing; clean water and air; and access to healthy food for every American. The legislative resolution also called for the protection of domestic industry in the United States.

While much of the Green New Deal goes beyond the scope of this book, which is alternative energy and its feasibility, the plan does highlight the fact that the future of energy is closely related to a broad range of social, political, and economic changes as well. Some of these changes will be, as the Green New Deal indicated, a result of climate change, while others will be the effect of value shifts, the relationships between and among nations, evolving public policies, economic cycles, technological breakthroughs, and demographic change. All of this raises the core question: What will the future look like, and how will we, a nation built on the primacy of the individual and his or her civil and private property rights, decide to live in the future?

U.S. Senator Edward Markey (D-MA), a strong advocate for environmentalism, a member of the U.S. Congress Freshman Class of 1973, a baby boomer, and a living symbol of the culture shift of the late 1960s, was an ardent supporter of the Green New Deal. In a Pro & Con editorial in the *Congressional Digest*, Senator Markey summarized his support in a manner that echoes a good many of the foundational principles undergirding the value shift and resulting social and political movements discussed earlier in this book:

> Our Green New Deal resolution outlines an historic 10-year mobilization that will mitigate climate emissions and build climate resiliency. We can create high-quality jobs and enforce labor standards, guarantee rights to retirement security and health care, and conduct inclusive decision-making in this Green New Deal. I thank Representative Ocasio-Cortez [NY-D] for her partnership and leadership on this resolution, and I look forward to elevating the issue of climate change as the highest of congressional priorities. The Green New Deal has struck a powerful chord in this country, and it is igniting the movement of young people who are ready to make this the organizing issue for their generation. And with a mission to save all of creation by investing in massive job creation, the Green New Deal is the kind of generational commitment we need to transform our economy and our democracy. (Markey, 2019: 14)

Senator Markey's words are profound indeed, and serve as a reflection of the values of many millennial and Generation Z voters. These voters tend to be intensely aware of climate change, and are very supportive of public policy designed to counter climate change and to promote social and economic justice (Woodward, 2019; Simon, 2017).

In a CNN editorial, Jeffrey Sachs, director of Columbia University's Center for Sustainable Development, argued that the Green New Deal was an affordable and realistic plan. Sachs argued that a sustainable future required that the Green New Deal be implemented (Sachs, 2019). Writing in *New Labor Forum*, Sean Sweeney (2019: 74) argued that the Green New Deal represents a direct challenge to mainstream Democratic politics by "open[ly] socialist" Alexandria Ocasio-Cortez, Ed Markey, and Bernie Sanders. Essentially, the Green New Deal relies less on markets and more on direct government policy and investment. The Green New Deal would lead the United States to become a zero-emission, clean energy economy within two decades. The massive change required has labor unions concerned about the economic pain that would likely emerge short term (Sweeney, 2019: 75). As Sweeney (2019) points out, the rejection of carbon-based energy sources opens the door to renewable and nuclear (alternative) energy sources.

Short of the moratorium on fossil energy development, as proposed in the "100 by '50" Act (S. 987, 115th Congress), introduced by Senator Jeff Merkley, it is unlikely that fossil energy development in the United States will abate any time soon. The other option, as noted by Sweeney (2019), would be cap and trade, but there are at least two challenges facing the establishment of a well-functioning and effective carbon market. First, establishing an internationally agreed-upon price on carbon emissions is no simple matter. As noted by Sweeney (2019), the price of carbon emissions would have to increase significantly to have any significant effect on the use of fossil energy. Second, international agreement on carbon emission targets must be more than voluntary, as was established in the Paris Agreement. Also, please recall that the United States is no longer bound by the Paris Agreement due to President Trump's decision to pull out of the agreement. Regardless, progress toward meeting voluntary emission targets has slowed rather than accelerated international efforts to limit carbon emissions.

Some scholars have argued that not only is the Green New Deal affordable, but it can also can be implemented in a way that prevents an economic crisis as the United States and global economies implement one of the single largest changes in human society in millennia. Sweeney (2019) argues that the federal government could simply create the money needed to finance the Green New Deal through deficit spending, in very much the same way that Franklin Delano Roosevelt responded to the Great Depression and in ways similar to how the U.S. government responded to the Great Recession through stimulus policies, bailouts, and the use of sustained low interest rates (see Blinder and Zandi, 2015; Grusky et al., 2011). Proponents of the Green New Deal view climate change as a crisis; and a crisis, as you learned in studying punctuated equilibrium theory earlier in this volume, is typically characterized by a significant change from the status quo, eventually establishing a new equilibrium, a "new normal" in the future.

Beyond the issue of crisis, however, are the issues of social justice and moral imperative (see Roewe, 2019). For advocates of the Green New Deal, issues of social justice for migrants, minorities, and the working class, for example, are issues that may transcend the long-term impacts of climate change. The disadvantages faced by the aforementioned often marginalized groups are, according to advocates of the Green New Deal, issues of the here and now, and circumstances and conditions of deprivation are likely to worsen in the years and decades ahead absent forceful government action (see Faist, 2018).

According to Pollin (2019), annual government investments of about 2 percent of GDP in clean energy over a three- or four-decade time frame would produce a seamless transition to a clean alternative energy economy that continues to grow and meet individual and collective needs and goals. World GDP in 2019 was approximately $20.4 trillion. Therefore, a 2 percent annual expenditure in clean energy would have an annual cost approximately of $408 billion, or $16.32 trillion (2019 USD) over forty years—a far lower estimate than the $93 trillion (over ten years) that critics claim the Green New Deal would cost (Neuhauser, 2019). In terms of U.S. Federal government spending, the increased expenditure would equate to a roughly 5 percent increase over current total government spending in the United States—up from roughly 37.8 percent of GDP to nearly 40 percent of GDP (see Heritage Foundation, 2019), assuming constant spending levels for all other government programs.

But, is this the right time for the Green New Deal? There are two different responses to this question. The more moderate response comes from mainstream Democrats such as the Speaker of the House, Nancy Pelosi (D-CA) (see Friedman and Gabriel, 2019). Pelosi formed a study group to explore climate change and has not been supportive of the Green New Deal. First, the Green New Deal lacks specifics on how its ambitious progressive policy goals will be realized. For a seasoned policy maker such as Pelosi, the lack of detail might have posed one of the biggest hurdles. Second, the Green New Deal came with an unspecified but arguably hefty price tag and requires a significant change in how the economy and society functions. Undoubtedly, Pelosi, who steered through Congress the $787 billion American Recovery and Rehabilitation Act in the wake of the Great Recession, is aware that agenda setting—as discussed in the multiple streams model—requires the merging of the problem stream, the politics stream, and the policy stream, and the opening of a policy "window" due to a focusing event.

And, in a much more sophisticated treatment of policy making, the ACF model helps us understand that coalition building is an important part of gaining traction in the process of successfully advancing public policy goals. In the current political climate, Republicans hold the Senate and the presidency, while the Democrats hold the House of Representatives. Additionally, Republican presidents have appointed a majority of the U.S. Supreme Court justices and have appointed several other federal judges in the U.S. Courts of Appeals and the U.S. District Courts. While party control of Congress and the presidency will change over time, impacting the short-term constraints on and resources available to subsystem actors, the longer-term constraints are impacted by the lifetime appointment of federal judges. To date, President Trump has appointed two Supreme Court justices, over forty appellate court judges, and over eighty district court judges. While judges are apolitical, they do hold judicial philosophies impacting their judicial opinions. Additionally, a strong economy with low unemployment and relatively stable energy prices may also limit the success of a coalition advocating for policy change.

As Douglas and Wildavsky (1983) would likely note, the political "center" is complacent and tends to support a status quo or possibly incremental movement along an existing or evolving policy path. Rapid change in policy direction tends to be supported to a greater extent by those on the "border." The Green New Deal represents a massive investment in a broad range of policy goals. On the coalitional periphery of the Green New Deal, some individuals advocate for economic degrowth (see Pollin, 2018), in other words, the shrinking of the economy through reduced production of goods, such as fossil energy. Some critics refer to this as "keep it in the ground." Yet, some groups within the degrowth movement tend also to see a much broader rollback on societal demands on natural resources and an intentional policy for the slowing of economic growth so that natural resources will be protected for all species, in general, and for future human populations, more specifically. Critics, even those who are vocally proenvironment, argue that degrowth is "unrealistic" and not a viable option (see Pollin, 2018: 25).

Policy theories and frameworks would tend to lead us to the conclusion that the "border" and its view of risk and the acceptability of policy solutions is a function of the policy agenda; the nature of the times (i.e., crisis, social movements); the capacity to organize into an effective coalition of interests in both the short and the long term; and the capacity of coalitions to win when conflict arises and shifts to different venues, as conflict inevitably does. Finally, it is imperative to understand the disposition and values of policy decision makers and the organizational rules, incentives, and constraints that shape their choices in both agenda prioritization and decision outcomes. Ideology, elections, and institution role and power all contribute to the behavior of policy decision makers. While not elected to their positions, bureaucrats also encounter the impact of elections on their capacity to implement and to garner funding for policies, and to draft and successfully enforce administrative rules that govern policy in practice.

Senate Majority Leader Mitch McConnell (R-KY), was undoubtedly as aware of the aforementioned issues as was Speaker Pelosi and Senate Minority Leader Chuck Schumer (D-NY), who was also hesitant to support the Green New Deal. McConnell saw an opportunity to show the cleavages (again, think back to the ACF) that exist between Ocasio-Cortez/Merkley Democrats and more mainstream Democrats through a formal vote in the U.S. Senate. The Green New Deal went down to defeat in the U.S. Senate with a vote tally of 57–0. Forty-three Democratic Senators voted "present" on the resolution, perhaps the least damaging way to demonstrate a cleavage within the Democratic caucus, while still maintaining status as a mainstream Democrat (Grandoni and Sonmez, 2019).

The outcome is, perhaps, not a surprise. Federal energy law of recent decades has generally arrived on the heels of key agenda-setting events—such as the Rio Conference in the 1990s and post–September 11 concerns about energy supply and security. At the current time, there is no specific agenda-setting event. When that event will occur is anyone's guess. Clearly, the world is an unsafe place with numerous threats to energy supply. Conflict in the Middle East, for instance, brings with it the potential for price spikes and supply concerns. Massive climate events may also raise awareness and concerns, winning over those who are skeptical about climate change and its impacts. The growing distance between the United States and China could complicate international cooperation at a time when such cooperation is sorely needed.

THE MOVEMENT OF PUBLIC OPINION

But perhaps even more influential will be any future social and political movement in support of climate change and social justice policies in legislation such as the Green New Deal. There is some evidence to show that the public is already highly supportive of clean energy, and holds negative views of fossil energy. A March 2019 Gallup poll found that 60 percent of Americans surveyed supported policy proposals to reduce the use of fossil energy. There was a sharp ideological divide in the opinion responses, with only 37 percent of self-identified Republicans supporting the reduced use of fossil energy and 80 percent of Democrats supporting the reduced use of fossil energy. Approximately 60 percent of Independents were supportive of policies to reduce fossil energy. While 60 percent of survey respondents thought that the United States would dramatically reduce fossil energy use within the next decade, slightly less than 40 percent felt that the reduction in fossil energy use within a decade was unlikely. The vast majority of Americans polled are supportive of increased emphasis on renewable energy, with 80 percent and 70 percent of Americans, respectively, supporting increased emphasis on solar and wind energy. Nuclear energy has mixed levels of support, with 32 percent indicating that greater emphasis should be placed on nuclear energy, while 35 percent of survey respondents indicated that less emphasis should be placed on nuclear energy. In all forms of fossil energy mentioned in the survey (natural gas, coal, and oil), a minority of respondents say that more emphasis should be placed on fossil energy. According to the Gallup poll, support for fossil energy has been trending downward for more than a half-decade (McCarthy, 2019).

In terms of government policy to reduce global warming and reduce the effects of climate change, the plurality of Americans polled felt that the policies "definitely" or "probably hurt" the economy (see McCarthy, 2019). The finding is particularly interesting because political science literature indicates that vote choice is usually impacted by economic conditions, although to what degree remains up for debate (see Downs, 1957; Lewis-Beck, 1988; Wlezein et al., 1997). Candidates who are able to convince voters that their policy preferences promote economic growth normally gain political supporters. Framing green policy and economic growth as opposing forces may be the position of actors on the "border," whereas those seeking to win the "center" often seek to convince voters that clean energy and economic growth are complementary and achievable. It is a point, I maintain, to which Pollin (2018) was alluding in his article, albeit not in these exact terms. One of the great successes of the Obama energy policy was the ability to take advantage of a policy window provided by an economic crisis to demonstrate that large-scale investment in clean energy and an economic policy guided by the goal of steady growth was achievable in much the way that Pollin (2019) foresees in his future-oriented essay.

A second line of reasoning is governed by a different set of values. I shall refer to this line of reasoning as *democratic liberalism*. Liberal democrats identify many of the same concerns that prompt Greens to action. Liberal democrats accept the ideas of resource scarcity and the need for wise use and just distribution to meet the needs of multiple stakeholders. Climate change and its impacts are viewed as a Tragedy of the Commons requiring increased efficiency and reasonable distribution and use of limited, possibly nonrenewable, resources. Concerns for environmental and social justice writ large are not the exclusive central focus in the value structure or policy priorities of the democratic liberal, and assume different forms. From the perspective of a democratic liberal, environmental and social justice could be advanced through the wise structuring of rules and processes shaping the use of resources, with due consideration given to the marginal social and environmental costs associated with resource management and use. Historically, liberal democrats conceptualize social and environmental justice through the metaphors of conservation and balanced or wise use of resources rather than metaphors emphasizing near-apocalyptic human-caused climate disaster, imperial Western capitalist extraction and consumption of developing nations' natural resources, and victimization of workers. Liberal democrats view the issues of energy, water, and climate as requiring collective action to the degree that individual abeyance to rules and processes governing resource use and allocation occurs in a regular and orderly fashion. Ultimately, however, individual commitment to agreed-upon rules and processes, rather than elevating the scope of conflict to more powerful venues operating at a distance from the local or regional level, will produce the most useful and lasting outcomes.

Liberal democrats tend to accept the idea that individuals will pursue their self-interest through the marketplace. In short, costs matter, and individuals and corporations will seek low-cost, high-benefit options and will factor in marginal social and environmental costs when they see it as beneficial to do so. Liberal democrats tend to look to methods that rely less heavily on penalty and punishment, preferring approaches that are built around collaboration and discovery of mutual benefit.

Liberal democrats are found on both the left and right center of the political spectrum; they are strongly committed to investing in alternative energy sources of various types. President Franklin Delano Roosevelt advanced hydroelectric power through the construction of a series of dams in the Pacific Northwest (BPA) and the Tennessee Valley (TVA). In 1946, Congress passed and President Truman signed the Atomic Energy Act of 1946, which led to the creation of the Atomic Energy Commission and opened the possibility of a nuclear power industry. Nuclear power was advanced further when Congress passed and President Eisenhower signed the Atomic Energy Act of 1954. In similar fashion, Congress passed and President George W. Bush signed the Energy Policy Act of 2005 and the Energy Independence and Security Act of 2007, laws intended to increase the supply of renewable energy as well as seek further advancement in accessing shale oil and tapping gas reserves. Hydroelectricity and nuclear energy are essentially carbon-neutral forms of energy, and newer design versions reduce the possibility of environmental degradation and water consumption.

From an energy, water, and environment policy perspective, the democratic liberal narrative has been fairly clear over a long period of time—a potential Tragedy of the Commons can and should be avoided. This can be accomplished through institutional rules and processes established through good faith negotiations and legislative deliberation, with agreements reached being administered by an effective and empowered bureaucracy, and disputes that arise being settled in federal courts of known commitment to the rule of law and a fair hearing of disputed claims. The democratic liberal narrative further holds that we should pursue policy processes that reduce rather than raise the specter of an enlarged scope of conflict, emphasizing the capacity for individuals to act reasonably and socially responsively if the marginal social and environmental costs of preferences is illuminated, and pursue and possibly collectively invest in more desirable energy alternatives while keeping in mind that no private or public policy choice is without risk of some type.

In many ways, the Environmental Protection Agency can be seen as an attempt to check markets and individual and private business choices so as to reduce the prospect of a Tragedy of the Commons. The EPA is a federal regulatory body at the national level, and as such is a centerpiece institution for democratic liberals whose faith in science and the federal courts provides confidence that laws governing environmental and public health protection will be well administered and upheld in court if challenged. That said, for liberal democrats there are other important institutional rules and processes in place at state and local levels that may achieve similar regulatory goals, but with the potential for lower levels of conflict and with due consideration for differences in access to knowledge and diversity of values, and conducted in possibly a more collaborative manner.

For liberal democrats, there are many state and local level governments that continue to advance the goals of a green energy future with effectiveness.

Renewable energy portfolio standards, for instance, began in the early 1980s when Iowa passed the first state law of its kind—currently, twenty-nine U.S. states, the District of Columbia, and Puerto Rico have RPS standards. Five of these states have met their RPS standards, with Texas meeting and exceeding its goal of 10,000 MW of electricity generated by renewable energy fifteen years ahead of its 2025 time frame. Nearly 21 percent of electricity generated in Texas uses nonhydroelectric renewable energy sources. Texas is the "leading producer of crude oil and natural gas . . . and produces more electricity than any other state . . . [Texas] produced one-fourth of all the U.S. wind powered electricity in 2017" (EIA, 2019).

State- and local-level collaborative governance involving public, private, and nonprofit partnerships engaged in meaningful policy dialogue has proven to be an effective way of advancing a clean energy and sustainable community paradigm. State offices for economic development, county and city planners focusing on both development and transportation infrastructure, state demographers, social and workforce services, and education all play key roles in helping markets evolve to meet changing demand and to shape consumer choice and values. An office often overlooked, the role of state and local auditors, is central to effective policy implementation and outcome monitoring. Auditors help government to implement policy and evaluate program performance in meeting the goals of effectiveness, efficiency, and equity. The great advancements made in cost/benefit analysis have revolutionized a good deal of the work of state auditors and their colleagues working in U.S. counties throughout the country (see Sunstein, 2018).

Policy innovation in states and local governments, as addressed earlier in relation to the policy diffusion model, invite policy adoption in other states along the lines of the laboratories of democracy conception of federalism. In other words, if it works in State A, maybe it will also work in States B, C, and so on. Unlike top-down, one-size-fits-all policy approaches, the diffusion model allows states to consider how the implementation of innovative policy will work given the unique values, needs, and circumstances of their state. Nicholson-Crotty and Carley (2016: 93) found that when considering the adoption of innovative policy modeled after that implemented in other locales, states take into consideration the "conditions under which those policies were implemented." A state is more likely to adopt and implement a policy if the policy innovation is occurring in a state that has a similar regulatory structure.

State ideology plays a significant role in the likelihood of state adoption of climate change and energy policy innovations, and impacts the relative strength of those policies (Nicholson-Crotty and Carley, 2016; Bromley-Trujillo et al., 2016; Vasseur, 2014; Carley and Miller, 2012). In a pooled event history analysis of state adoptions of climate change mitigation and energy policy innovations in the United States, Bromley-Trujillo et al. (2016) found that policy diffusion in the states can be largely explained by state ideology and membership levels in environmental interest groups. States with similar ideological stances and environmental group membership rates are more likely to adopt climate change and energy policies of a similarly situated neighboring state. The level of Democratic power in state government helps explain the likelihood of renewable portfolio standards in the states (Vasseur, 2014). Republican support for renewable portfolio standards tends to be "reactive," with less support in highly progressive states with significant environmental coalition strength, and greater support for renewable portfolio standards in states with lower median incomes and weaker environmental coalition strength (Coley and Hess, 2012; see also Hess et al., 2016).

Taking it to the next level, how do state ideology and interest group strength impact climate change and energy policy at the state level? Believing in something does not, by itself, lead to change. Rather, it is the actions taken by those who believe in something that leads to desired and positive change. Reflecting back to the *Federalist Papers*, American politics is built on the idea that individuals with similar beliefs and values have a tendency to coalesce into groups (Hamilton et al., 2019). Those groups might be political parties or interest groups. Through interaction in groups, individuals establish policy networks. Networks allow for the efficient exchange of ideas and the possibility of collaborating with individuals and groups that represent related interests in the world of technology, finance, law, politics, and even community-based stakeholders (Iskandarova, 2017). Networks make it more feasible for technology experts and related business interests to educate citizen stakeholders and policy makers about the technical, economic, and political feasibility of emerging and established energy technologies (see Gjefsen, 2017), and such networks cross not only state lines but also often transcend international boundaries (Schmidt and Dabur, 2014). Taxes, incentives, regulatory environment, market structure, and demand levels all contribute to the feasibility of renewable energy options. Networks often serve as the basis of coalitions that pressure government to adopt policy (see Mander, 2007).

Successful adoption is often a function of effective participation in the planning process, the building of compromise, and policy timing (Rowlands, 2007). With some urgency due to the anticipated effects of climate change, there is a need to balance the needs of democratic deliberation and participation with the need to accelerate the implementation of green energy and sustainability policies and technologies (see Lammers and Arentsen, 2017). Political compromise is particularly critical in order for large-scale institutional changes to occur in a timely and effective manner. The substantial deregulation of state electricity markets, for example, was facilitated by negotiated policy compromises that led to market-friendly renewable energy policies such as renewable portfolio standards, tax credits, and incentives (see Kim et al., 2016). Furthermore, policy environments shape decisions to invest in renewable energy (Polzin et al., 2015); thus, innovative policy acts to stimulate the development and adoption of new technologies and the shuttering of older technologies (Negro et al., 2008) have taken place on a number of occasions. This is particularly the case in states and communities that possess a strong sense of collective action around community dilemmas. The promise of shared positive policy impacts and innovation testing under conditions of close monitoring by an inclusive set of stakeholders offers at least the reasonable possibility of reversing environmental, social, and economic inequities in a community (see Fowler and Breen, 2013).

Collective action at the community level is a recognition that in the modern world energy is, in many cases, a marketable public good. While we, as consumers, make choices to purchase energy products in many forms, and then use those products for private personal benefit, the supply of energy goods societally considered is limited. In some cases, such as fossil energy, the supply of the good is ultimately limited because fossil energy is a nonrenewable resource. Yet, in other cases, such as electrical energy, the supply of energy is limited by transmission line congestion regardless of energy source or intermittency. In either case, energy consumption patterns in the modern, increasingly urbanized world are such that our individual energy consumption patterns have a direct impact on the availability of energy for all. Affordable and readily available energy is a central facet of our very existence in modern society. The ability to overcome this dilemma rests largely with our ability to conceptualize energy as a marketable public good, as well as our political and social values, and capacity to cooperate and to work toward mutually beneficial outcomes.

In the case of electricity and intermittency, community characteristics play a significant role in the ability of policy makers and markets to respond to the introduction of renewable energy onto power grids while simultaneously seeking to reshape load patterns. Until solutions to the energy storage dilemma have been adequately implemented and adequate clean energy baseloads have been established, intermittency issues will impact the power grid.

In their meta-analytic study of demand response (DR) programs that rely on the above-referenced methods of reducing demand, Srivastava et al. (2018) found DR programs witness their greatest success in economically successful, rapidly growing urban areas that were supportive of renewable energy policy innovations. As is known from public opinion studies conducted in the United States, urban areas tend to have higher rates of progressively minded voters and are generally somewhat more likely to view problems within their communities as collective action problems.

As the discussion of innovation moves toward the promise of economic development, the role of ideology may become less relevant as economic development and its benefits may have a transcendent effect (see Wiener and Koontz, 2010). That said, it is critical that policy dialogue between competing coalitions remain focused on a desired outcome rather than differences in normative policy beliefs. Evidence gathered in the environmental conflict resolution literature has shown that when normative differences are elevated over shared interests, then conflict often arises between environmental coalitions and economic development coalitions (see Rietig, 2018). As alluded to earlier in this volume, industrial powers often have a vested interest in "business as usual," and are resistant to change for economic reasons—a focus on economic development has been shown to tip the balance toward environment clean energy coalitions when the "technology and financial sector" sees a benefit in financing a new clean energy path (see Hess, 2014: 278). Furthermore, the reins of government change hands overtime. Shifts in party control and changing policy priorities may weaken government support for renewable energy and for related budget expenditures. Continued innovation and development of renewable energy technology require consistent and credible commitment from federal, state, and local government—industry will be hesitant to invest in renewable energy if short- and long-term government commitment is not in sufficient evidence (Liang and Fiorino, 2013).

The historical evidence at our disposal indicates that the liberal democratic clean energy agenda has been largely successful in its innovative efforts at the state and local levels, and at a lower cost in terms of conflict. In Western democracies, lowering levels of conflict in policy making and implementation has been shown to be a critical method of increasing public acceptance of green technology, thus facilitating more rapid ultimate widespread utilization (Parag and Butbul, 2018). According to the National Conference on State Legislatures, "roughly half the growth in U.S. renewable energy generation since 2000 can be attributed to state renewable energy requirements." The RPS requirements have contributed mightily to the $64 billion market for renewable energy (NCSL, 2019).

The NCSL study is further supported, yet qualified, in the peer-reviewed energy policy literature. Shrimali and Kniefel (2011) conducted a panel study of the fifty U.S. states from 1991 to 2007 to determine if state energy policies had a positive effect on the market penetration of renewable energy sources. Their study found that the effect of RPS standards on required state capacity and required sales of energy generated using renewable energy was dependent on renewable energy source. Voluntary RPS standards had no significant impact on renewable energy market penetration, nor did either socioeconomic conditions in a state or the price of competing energy sources, such as natural gas. In general, however, RPS standards are best viewed as effective state-level policy to advance the clean energy agenda (contra Carley, 2009), taking into account the level of political support in a state for environmental policy generally (see Delmas and Montes-Sancho, 2010). A caveat to this conclusion is in order, however, relating to the market trading of renewable energy credits (RECs).

RECs, or green tags, are a way of accounting for the generation of 1 MWh of electricity using a renewable energy source. A REC is very much like currency, and it can be traded on open markets. RECs are traceable, and have serial numbers. When a REC is purchased, it cannot be resold for the obvious reason that once electricity is used, it cannot be reused. In a practical sense, if a utility operates under a requirement that it must generate a certain percentage of renewable energy and it fails to do, it can purchase RECs to make up the difference. When states allow utilities to purchase RECs to make up for renewable energy generation shortfalls, state renewable generation tends to lag in renewable energy generation, whereas states that do not allow interstate REC purchases tend to witness in-state renewable energy electricity generation grow faster than RPS standards require (Yin and Powers, 2010: 1147).

Energy policy innovation at the state level, particularly in relation to RPS standards, has proven to be a highly effective way of implementing a clean energy agenda. Despite years of energy policy enactments that have helped renewables make tremendous strides in R & D, national policy makers have yet to enact a federal-level RPS. In many respects, it might prove unwise to do so, as a national RPS might disrupt ongoing state-level policy implementation. Approximately 40 percent of greenhouse gas emissions result from electricity generation, and state-level progress toward meeting RPS standards is having a positive effect on the environment. The substantial growth in the renewable energy power sector is largely attributable to state-level public policy. The proliferation of RPS standards is, to a great extent, a function of policy diffusion and effective advocacy efforts by green energy coalitions comprised of citizen stakeholders, renewable energy industry leaders, environmental groups, scientists, and academicians. Undergirding policy advocacy, and the safe energy policy choices made by elected/appointed government institutional actors, there exists a set of shared social proenvironmental concerns and values that unites the center-left and center-right elements of American political life.

Furthermore, social proenvironmental values shape individual-level support for the adoption of renewable energy and related systems in the United States (Home and Huddart, 2019) and internationally (Bashiri and Alizadeh, 2018; Dato, 2018). A study of renewable energy system installation decisions by California farmers found that personal values are a key factor in shaping decisions on both the initial adoption of renewable energy and likewise the size of renewable energy systems installed. California farmers and ranchers who displayed interest in protecting the environment through conservation were more likely to have renewable energy systems on their property (Beckman and Xiarchos, 2013). The price of energy was not a statistically significant factor shaping renewable adoption; proenvironmental values were the critical elements of decision-making on system installation.

Not all paths to a renewable energy future need rely directly on public policy. At the local level, there are opportunities for individuals accessing common pool resources to build their own solutions to resource allocation. The energy–water nexus is a particularly critical juncture that offers opportunities to build resource governance bodies to govern resource user behavior and choices. The IAD framework discussed in some detail in chapter 2 allows resource stakeholders to access common pool resources for personal gain, but in a way that does not deplete the resource or make it inaccessible to other users. Run-of-the-river hydropower generation, for example, requires sufficient water flow to operate micro-hydropower turbines. A water user upstream with prior appropriation water rights could, in accessing his or her water right, significantly reduce stream flow, particularly in times of drought. Stakeholder engagement under the IAD framework allows stakeholders to acknowledge and better understand the multiple uses of a resource and its potential for depletion through overuse. Through responsible resource governance and negotiated agreements facilitated by interest-based dispute resolution experts, the IAD framework offers natural resource users an opportunity to manage shared resources effectively and equitably.

CONCLUDING REMARKS

The transition to large-scale use of alternative energy in the United States will not be easy, nor will it constitute a quick fix to our energy problems. A state- and local-based approach bridging federal, state, and local government working in partnership with key stakeholders from industry, nonprofit (to include regional transmission operators), interest groups, and university scholars is the most likely path to be taken in the decade ahead. This is the approach advocated by liberal democrats (politically, those in the center-left and center-right; in Douglas and Wildavsky's "center"), and it may prove to be an effective method of moving to a clean energy future. Whether driven by a desire to promote economic development or to serve the goal of combating climate change, the American political system necessitates open dialogue and collective decisions built on constructive compromise. Compromise means producing outcomes where all parties realize some benefit. If energy is a marketable public good, then we must understand our rate of use in relation to rate of production, and given these two rates, we can develop a better understanding of optimal consumption patterns in the short and long term with the ultimate goal of sustainability.

The liberal democratic approach may, in fact, prove to be more effective for yet another reason: we simply do not have the resources needed to quickly implement a large-scale shift to renewable energy. As Moriarty and Honnery (2009) discussed in their article "What Energy Levels Can the Earth Sustain?," a rapid move—that is, a ten-year time frame—to renewable energy would result in a spike in the demand for fossil energy needed to fabricate renewable energy systems. Reliance on renewable energy to construct renewable energy systems would take a significantly longer period of time and would not be feasible. Effectively, we would deplete fossil energy supplies and produce more climate harming emissions.

Furthermore, Moriarty and Honnery (2009) point out that the large-scale use of renewable energy systems—systems designed to meet rapidly increasing energy demands—would cause environmental damage and reduce natural habitats. Massive solar and wind farms could cause environmental damage to native flora and fauna. The use of hydropower and biomass would damage habitat and, in the case of biomass, emit impurities into the air and water. Furthermore, the cost of energy produced would be much higher than consumers pay for energy today, leading to predictable social and economic hardship. It might be the case that rapid deployment of a clean energy agenda would seek to reduce some hardships, but would simultaneously produce new hardships.

In the case of nuclear power, Moriarty and Honnery (2009) conclude that nuclear power will be unable to meet projected energy needs thirty years hence. The authors also discuss the potential for fission nuclear energy, but argue that it is not commercially feasible at this time, and that even if it were, the cost of electricity produced would be much higher than current energy prices.

The bottom line to all of this, however, relates to the central issue of feasibility. Is alternative energy politically, socially, and economically feasible? Without focusing on any specific energy source, the three-part answer is that many energy alternatives are indeed feasible, and are becoming more so every day. The decades-long road to the development of new renewable energy sources has, thus far, been made possible by the strong and effective intergovernmental relationships that emerge from federalism, and which allows for careful deliberation, well-considered decision-making, the building of knowledge, market adjustments, and the evolution of social values necessary for a long-term commitment to clean energy and sustainability.

Politically, the states and local governments have demonstrated that it is possible to establish a long-term energy goal (RPS standards) and to make steady progress toward the renewable energy goals set forth. Progressive states, such as California, have made bold moves to advance renewable energy, but the same could be said for the traditionally "red state" of Texas with its large wind energy infrastructure. Many states and localities have established their own unique renewable energy narrative through policy dialogue. Some are driven by a desire to reduce emissions due to the visibly polluting effects of fossil energy used in their communities, while others focus greater attention on the effects of climate change on a global level. State and local policy dialogue and solution-building allow for diversity of narrative and the creation or adoption of unique solutions that will likely change as new knowledge and values are incorporated into our public policy debates over time.

The federal government plays a slightly different role in renewable energy development. International climate change agreements as a policy driver have been attempted, but the U.S. public and leadership have alternately embraced and rejected this approach. The Reagan administration was not supportive of renewable energy development, but in the decades since, Republican and Democratic elected officials at the federal level have increasingly identified ways in which to invest in renewable energy. Renewable energy production tax credits help level the playing field between renewable energy and fossil energy sources. Federal rule changes governing electricity markets have enlarged market access for renewable energy, facilitated by FERC regulations regarding access to the grid by third-party providers. Additionally, public land and mining policies that historically served the interests of fossil energy development have evolved to increasingly provide opportunity for renewable energy development. In 1974, the federal government established a renewable energy R & D infrastructure through the creation of the National Renewable Energy Laboratory.

The federal government has played a significant role in establishing the market rules that allow renewable energy to gain market access to finance R & D, to establish environmental regulations that realize the true costs of fossil energy, and to recoup the social and environmental costs of its continued use. The Trump administration's rollback of key environmental regulations impacting fossil energy use throws out of whack that long-established delicate intergovernmental balance in renewable energy and environmental policy. Furthermore, U.S. withdrawal from the Paris Agreement—a voluntary emissions agreement—may reduce the opportunity for international dialogue and persuasion of other countries to reduce their carbon emissions. For those most knowledgeable and concerned about global climate change, the Trump policy shifts come at the worst possible time.

The Trump policy shift may, however, turn out to be a brief blip as there is clear evidence that the social movements of the 1960s and 1970s that drove the environmental and renewable energy policy shifts have not disappeared, and live on in a new generation of American youth. State and local policies, and many federal-level policies, are at a fairly mature state with strong scientific support and are not easily disrupted by a single presidency. The technical and economic feasibility of alternative energy continues to advance, both domestically and internationally. Much has already been done in terms of foundational work, and many pieces of the alternative energy future are moving into place—a sizable event (social unrest, political uprising, economic shift, international conflict, etc.) could very easily lead to a massive shift in the energy policy equilibrium. Regardless of current political conditions, a half-century of developments around alternative energy may indicate that the pressure for change remains present and is building.

One of the largest challenges we face, long term, is how we view risk and how we either come to terms with risk or reduce perceived risk. At times, this book refers to alternative energy, while at other times it refers to renewable energy. As a point of reminder, one of the proverbial elephants in the room is nuclear energy—a form of alternative energy. The fact is that the nuclear fission process has an extremely high energy density, multiple times higher than the renewable energy sources currently being pursued. Should public policy and technological advancements address public concerns with nuclear energy, and should it become a more accepted source of "clean" energy, particularly through the effective processing, reprocessing, and storage of nuclear waste, then the politics of energy will look substantially different. That day, however, is not on the horizon, at least in the contemporary U.S. policy context.

Political and social feasibility issues have played and will continue to play a very prominent role in the U.S. energy future. Public commitment to renewable energy has been critical to the rise of renewable energy. As figure 9.1 shows, however, such commitment must continue if renewable energy should surpass the electrical energy output of fossil- and nuclear-powered generation. Technological breakthroughs in storage that overcome intermittency issues may very well be one of the keys to making the clean electric energy dream a reality. Liquid fuels, however, are another matter. Great strides have been made in the area of biofuels, but it is likely that electric-powered vehicles with next-generation storage capacity (batteries, hydrogen fuel cells) are more realistic, along with revolutionary rethinking of transportation systems.

Figure 9.1   Electricity Generation by Source (2009–2019)

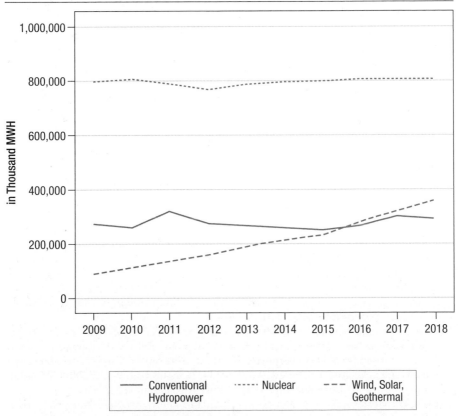

Data Source: Energy Information Administration

REFERENCES

Bashiri, A., and Alizadeh, S. 2018. Knowledge factors affecting prospective residential PV system adoption. *Renewable & Sustainable Energy Reviews* 81(2): 3131–3139.

Beckman, J., and Xiarchos, I. 2013. Why are California farmers adopting more (and larger) renewable energy operations? *Renewable Energy* 55: 322–330.

Binder, A., and Zandi, Mark. 2015. The financial crisis: Lessons for the next one. *Policy Futures—Center on Budget and Policy Priorities*, October 15. Retrieved from https://www.cbpp.org/sites/default/files/atoms/files/10-15-15pf.pdf, June 27, 2019.

Bromley-Trujillo, R., Butler, J., Poe, J., and Davis, W. 2016. The spreading of innovation: State adoptions of energy and climate change policy. *Review of Policy Research* 33(5): 544–565.

Carley, S. 2009. State renewable energy electricity policies: An empirical evaluation of effectiveness. *Energy Policy* 37: 3071–3081.

Carley, S., and Miller, C. 2012. Regulatory stringency and policy drivers: A reassessment of Renewable Portfolio Standards. *Policy Studies Journal* 40(4): 730–756.

Coley, J., and Hess, D. 2012. Green energy laws and Republican legislators in the United States. *Energy Policy* 48: 576–583.

Congressional Digest. 2019. Legislative background on the Green New Deal: Recent action by Congress on climate change proposals. *Congressional Digest*, April 1. 98(4): 12–13.

Dato, P. 2018. Investment in energy efficiency, adoption of renewable energy and household behavior: Evidence from OECD countries. *Energy Journal* 39(3): 213–244.

Delmas, M., and Montes-Sancho, M. 2010. U.S. state policies for renewable energy: Context and effectiveness. *Energy Policy* 39: 2273–2288.

Douglas, M., and Wildavsky, A. 1983. *Risk and Culture: An Essay on the Selection of Technological and Environmental Dangers*. Berkeley, CA: University of California Press.

Downs, A. 1957. *An Economic Theory of Democracy*. New York: Harper.

Energy Information Administration. 2019. Texas Net Electricity Generation by Source, March 2019. Washington, DC: Energy Information Administration. Retrieved from https://www.eia.gov/state/?sid=TX#tabs-4, June 28, 2019.

Faist, T. 2018. The socio-natural question: How climate change adds to social inequalities. *Journal of Intercultural Studies* 39(2): 195–206.

Fowler, L., and Breen, J. 2013. The impact of political factors on State's adoption of Renewable Portfolio Standards. *Electricity Journal* 26(2): 79–94.

Friedman, L., and Gabriel, T. 2019. A new deal at once possible and problematic. *New York Times*, February 22, A1-A17.

Gjefsen, M. 2017. Crafting the expert-advocate: training and recruitment efforts in the carbon dioxide capture and storage community. *Innovation: The European Journal of Social Science Research* 30(3): 259–282.

Grandoni, D., and Sonmez, F. 2019. Senate defeats Green New Deal, as Democrats call vote a "sham." *Washington Post*, March 26. Retrieved from https://www.washingtonpost.com/powerpost/green-new-deal-on-track-to-senate-defeat-as-democrats-call-vote-a-sham/2019/03/26/834f3e5e-4fdd-11e9-a3f7-78b7525a8d5f_story.html?noredirect=on&utm_term=.570f250baac4, June 25, 2019.

Grusky, D., Western, B., and Wimer, C. eds. 2011. *The Great Recession*. New York: Russell Sage Foundation.

Hamilton, A., Madison, J., and Jay, J. 2019. *Federalist Papers*. CreateSpace Independent Publishing Platform.

Heritage Foundation. 2019. *2019 Index of Economic Freedom*. Retrieved from https://www.heritage.org/index/explore?view=by-variables, June 25, 2019.

Hess, D. 2014. Sustainability transitions: A political coalition perspective. *Research Policy* 43: 278–283.

Hess, D., Mai, Q., and Brown, K. 2016. Red states, green laws: Ideology and renewable energy legislation in the United States. *Energy Research & Social Science* 11: 19–28.

Home, C., and Huddart-Kennedy, E. 2019. Explaining support for renewable energy: Commitments to self-sufficiency and communion. *Environmental Politics* 28(5): 929–949.

Iskandarova, M. 2017. From the idea of scale to the idea of agency: An actor-network theory perspective on policy development for renewable energy. *Science and Public Policy* 44(4): 476–485.

Kim, S., Yang, J., and Urpelainen, J. 2016. Does power sector deregulation promote or discourage renewable energy policy? Evidence from the States, 1991–2012. *Review of Policy Research* 33(1): 22–50.

Lammers, I., and Arentsen, M. 2017. Rethinking participation in Smart Energy system planning. *Energies* 10: 1–16.

Lewis-Beck, M. 1988. *Economics and Elections*. Ann Arbor, MI: University of Michigan Press.

Liang, J., and Fiorino, D. 2013. The implications of policy stability for renewable energy innovation in the United States, 1974–2009. *Policy Studies Journal* 41(1): 97–118.

Mander, S. 2007. Regional renewable energy policy: A process of coalition building. *Global Environmental Politics* 7(2): 45–63.

Markey, E. 2019. The pros of the proposed: Should Congress pass a resolution recognizing the duty of the Federal government to create a Green New Deal? *Congressional Digest* 98(4): 14–26.

McCarthy, J. 2019. Most Americans support reducing fossil fuels. *Gallup*, March 22. Retrieved from https://news.gallup.com/poll/248006/americans-support-reducing-fossil-fuel.aspx, June 27, 2019.

Moriarty, P., and Honnery, D. 2009. What energy levels can the Earth sustain? *Energy Policy* 37: 2469–2474.

National Conference on State Legislatures. 2019. State renewable portfolio standards and goals. *National Conference on State Legislatures*, February 1. Retrieved from http://www.ncsl.org/research/energy/renewable-portfolio-standards.aspx, June 28, 2019.

Negro, S., Hekkert, M., and Smits, R. 2008. Stimulating renewable energy technologies by innovation policy. *Science and Public Policy* 35(6): 403–416.

Neuhauser, A. 2019. The Green New Deal and the strength of ambiguity. *U.S. News—Civic Report*, March 1, C1–C4.

Nicholson-Crotty, S., and Carley, S. 2016. Effectiveness, implementation, and policy diffusion: Or "Can we make that work for us?" *State Politics & Policy Quarterly* 16(1): 78–97.

Parag, Y., and Butbul, G. 2018. Flexiwatts and seamless technology: Public perceptions of demand flexibility through smart home technology. *Energy Research & Social Science* 39: 177–191.

Pollin, R. 2018. De-growth vs a green new deal. *New Left Review* 112: 5–25.

Pollin, R. 2019. Advancing a viable Global Climate Stabilization Project: Degrowth versus the Green New Deal. *Review of Radical Economics* 51(2): 311–319.

Polzin, F., Migendt, M., Täube, F., and von Flotow, P. 2015. Public policy influence on renewable energy investments—a panel data study across OECD countries. *Energy Policy* 80: 98–111.

Rietig, K. 2018. The links among contested knowledge, beliefs and learning in European climate governance: From consensus to conflict in reforming biofuels policy. *Policy Studies Journal* 46(1): 137–159.

Roewe, B. 2019. Catholics see hope in Green New Deal goals: Faith-based environmentalists examine ambitious climate agenda. *National Catholic Reporter*, June 14, 11.

Rowlands, I. 2007. The development of renewable electricity policy in the province of Ontario: The influence of ideas and timing. *Review of Policy Research* 24(3): 185–207.

Sachs, J. 2019. Green New Deal is feasible and affordable. *CNN Opinion*, February 26. Retrieved from https://www.cnn.com/2019/02/22/opinions/green-new-deal-sachs/index.html, June 25, 2019.

Schmidt, T., and Dabur, S. 2014. Explaining the diffusion of biogas in India: A new functional approach considering national borders and technology transfer. *Environmental Economic Policy Studies* 16: 171–199.

Schrimali, G., and Kniefel, J. 2011. Are government policies effective in promoting deployment of renewable electricity resources? *Energy Policy* 39: 4726–4741.

Simon, C. 2017. *Public Policy: Preferences and Outcomes*, 3rd Edition. New York: Routledge.

Srivastava, A., Van Passel, S., and Laes, E. 2018. Assessing the success of electricity demand response programs: A meta-analysis. *Energy Research & Social Science* 40: 110–117.

Sunstein, C. 2018. *The Cost-Benefit Revolution*. Cambridge, MA: MIT Press.

Sweeney, S. 2019. The Green New Deal's magical realism. *New Labor Forum* 28(2): 74–78.

Vasseur, M. 2014. Convergence and divergence in renewable energy policy among the U.S. states from 1998 to 2011. *Social Forces* 92(4): 1637–1657.

Water Calculator, 2019. Water Footprint of Energy. Retrieved from https://www.water-calculator.org/water-use/the-water-footprint-of-energy/, March 3, 2019.

Wiener, J., and Koontz, T. 2010. Shifting winds: Explaining variation in state policies to promote small-scale wind energy. *Policy Studies Journal* 38(4): 629–651.

Wlezen, C., Franklin, M., and Twiggs, D. 1997. Economic perceptions and vote choice: Disentangling the endogeneity. *Political Behavior* 19(1): 7–17.

Woodward, A. 2019. Millennials and Gen Z are finally gaining ground in the climate battle—here are the signs they're winning. *Business Insider*, April 27. Retrieved from https://www.businessinsider.com/signs-millennials-gen-z-turning-tide-climate-change-2019-4, June 25, 2019.

Yin, H., and Powers, N. 2010. Do state renewable portfolio standards promote in-state renewable generation? *Energy Policy* 38: 1140–1149.

Index

★ ★ ★

Note: Page references for figures are italicized.

Adams, William, 102
advocacy coalition framework (ACF) model, 57
agenda setting, 41–42
agriculture, use of geothermal energy in, 164–66
Agriculture Department, 11
Ahlstrom, A., 140
Alagappan, L., 51
Alam, M., 197
Alaska:
    energy law in, 67
    Permanent Fund, 67
    tidal energy in, 228
alkaline fuel cells (AFCs), 201
alternative fuels:
    alkaline fuel cells (AFCs), 201
    alternative-fuel motor vehicles (AFVs), 188
    biodiesel, 191–92, 192
    clean diesel, 191
    defined, 68
    direct methanol fuel cells (DMFCs), 201–2
    ethanol, 192–94, 193, 195
    hydroelectric energy, 224–29
    hydrogen fuel cells, 196–201
    Hydrogen Initiative and, 194–96
    innovation in, 81–82
    methyl tertiary-butyl ether (MTBE), 194
    molten carbonate fuel cells (MCFCs), 202–3
    natural gas as, 189–90
    nuclear energy, 229–37
    ocean thermal energy conversion
        (OTEC), 228–29
    phosphoric acid fuel cells (PAFCs), 203
    solid oxide fuel cells (SOFCs), 204
    tidal energy, 228
    wave energy, 228
    See also specific fuel
American Recovery and Reinvestment Act of
    2009 (ARRA):

alternative fuels and, 188
Green New Deal and, 248
historical background, 21, 24
innovation and, 69, 92–93
public policy and, 35, 45
punctuated equilibrium (PE) model and, 58
wind energy and, 151
American Wind Energy Association (AWEA),
    132, 150–51
Arctic Energy Office, 221
Arctic National Wildlife Refuge (ANWR),
    23–24, 87, 90
Argonne National Laboratory, 25, 194
Arizona:
    concentrated solar power in, 115
    geothermal energy in, 177
Atomic Energy Act of 1946, 252
Atomic Energy Act of 1954, 83, 231, 252
Atomic Energy Commission (AEC), 117, 252

"baby boomers," 16–17
Bacon, Francis, 196
Bangor Hydro Electric Company, 228
Barhelmie, R., 6
Batchman, Ted, xi
Becquerel, Alexandre, 103
binary geothermal systems, 168–72
biodiesel, 191–92, 192
Bipartisan Budget Act of 2018, 123, 175
Bobrow, D., 75
Bodman, Samuel, 230
Bonneville Power Administration (BPA), 38, 252
Bonneville Project Act of 1937, 225
bottom-up policy making, 48–49
BP Deepwater Horizon oil spill, xii
British Petroleum, 15
Broers, G. H. J., 202
Bromley-Trujillo, R., 253

265

Brown, D., 2
budgetary commitment to alternative energy, 52
Bureau of Mines (BOM), 221
Bush, George H. W., 23, 69, 80–84, 228
Bush, George W., 23–24, 69, 80, 87–92, 96,
    194–95, 252

California:
    California Innovation Group (CIG), 73
    concentrated solar power in, 115
    Energy Commission (CES), 124
    energy law in, 72–74
    geothermal energy in, 160–61, 164,
        167, 177–78
    Miller-Warren Energy Lifeline Act of
        1972, 72, 96
    MTBE in, 194
    Public Utilities Commission (PUC), 72, 125
    renewable energy in, 259
    Revenue and Taxation Code, 124
    solar energy in, 124–25
    Solar Rights Act (SRA) of 1978, 124
    State Assembly Bill 1905, 177
    Warren-Alquist State Energy Resources
        Conservation and Development Act of
        1974, 72
Canada, Kyoto Protocol and, 5
carbon emissions, 4–7, 247
Carley, S., 253
Carter, Jimmy, 22, 47, 56, 68, 75–76, 78
Chen, J., 145
Chernobyl nuclear disaster, 232, 234, 238
China:
    energy demand in, 26, 188
    fuel cells in, 206
    GDP in, 1, 42
    geothermal energy in, 164
    nuclear energy in, 235
    photovoltaic manufacturing in, 113
    renewable energy in, 1
    wind energy in, 132
Clean Air Act of 1970, 22, 24–25, 188
Clean Air Act of 1990, 194
Clean Cities Program, 23, 81, 85
clean diesel, 191
Clean Power Plan, 45–46, 93–95
Clean Water Act of 1972, 11
Clean Water Act of 1977, 22, 24
climate change:
    innovation and, 84
    National Climate Assessments, 245
    public opinion and, 250–51
    public policy and, 243
    as rationale for alternative energy, 4–7
    risk assessment and, 219
    Trump on, 188
Clinton, Hillary, 41
Clinton, William J., 23, 25, 48, 69, 80,
    84–87, 96
club goods, 36

coal:
    Clean Power Plan, 93–95
    disposal of coal combustion residuals from
        electric utilities, 93
    innovation in, 83
    mercury and air toxics standards (MATS), 93–95
    Obama era coal rules, 93–94
    resurgence of, 94–96
    US, consumption in, 12, 14
Coal Research Center, 221
collaborative policy making, 49–51
Colorado, concentrated solar power in, 115
commercial applications for alternative fuels, 206
Conant, T. T., 167
concentrated solar power (CSP), 110–11, 115
concentrated solar PV (CPV), 107–8
Connecticut, renewable portfolio standards
    (RPS) in, 79
constituent policy, 46–47
Conti-Ramsden, John, 140
Conway, Michael, 73
corporate production tax credit (PTC), 122–23
cultural shifts, 16–17

Daniilidis, A., 173
Defense Department, 206–7
Defense Procurement Act of 1950, 207
definition of alternative energy, 65–68
Deloitte Consulting LLC, 200
democratic liberalism, 251–53
Democratic Party, 20–21
deregulation, 77–80
Deutsch, Ted, 245
direct methanol fuel cells (DMFCs), 201–2
distributive policy, 47–48
District of Columbia, renewable portfolio
    standards (RPS) in, 253
DOE. See Energy Department (DOE)
Douglas, Mary, 219–22, 226–27, 249
Drake, Edwin, 189
Dyer, Kirsten, 140
dye-sensitized solar cells (DSCs), 106

economics:
    alternative energy and, 35–39
    of geothermal energy, 172–75
    of hydrogen fuel cells, 199–201
    innovation, economic growth and, 84
    of nuclear energy, 234–37
    of solar power, 111–15
    of solar thermal, 115
    of wind energy, 144–49
Edison, Thomas, 189
EERE. See Office of Energy Efficiency and
    Renewable Energy (EERE)
Einstein, Albert, 103, 229
Eisenhower, Dwight D., 223, 252
electricity:
    innovation in, 83

production figures, *261*
solar energy, levelized cost of electricity
    and, 112–15
electric motor vehicles, innovation in, 82
Emmanuel, Rahm, 35
Endangered Species Act of 1973 (ESA), 22
Energy and Conservation Standards for New
    Buildings Act of 1976, 81
energy density, *186,* 186–88
Energy Department (DOE):
    advocacy coalition framework (ACF) model
        and, 57
    biodiesel and, 191
    budgeting commitment to alternative energy, 51
    geothermal energy and, 161, 166,
        173–74, 176–77
    Geothermal Technologies Office (GTO), 176
    historical background, 21–22, 25–26
    innovation and, 75, 81–82, 89–90
    molten carbonate fuel cells (MCFCs) and, 202
    nuclear energy and, 230–32, 237
    Office of Fossil Energy, 202–3
    Office of Indian Energy Policy and
        Programs, 61
    phosphoric acid fuel cells (PAFCs) and, 203
    public policy and, 47–49
    research and development (R & D) and, 185
    solar energy and, 101, 112, 116–17
    wind energy and, 149
energy efficiency, 81
Energy Independence and Security Act
    of 2007, 24, 252
Energy Information Administration:
    geothermal energy and, 176
    overview, xii, 2–3
    on petroleum, 204–5
    solar energy and, 101, 112
    on US energy supply and use, 13–15
Energy Policy Act of 1992:
    alternative fuels and, 188
    ethanol and, 192
    historical background, 21, 23–24
    innovation and, 69, 80–84, 96
    solar energy and, 122
    wind energy and, 132
Energy Policy Act of 2005:
    alternative fuels and, 188
    democratic liberalism and, 252
    historical background, 24
    innovation and, 69, 80, 88–90, 96
    Office of Indian Energy Policy and
        Programs, 61
    public policy and, 45
Energy Policy and Conservation Act of 1975,
    74–75, 80, 188
Energy Research and Development
    Administration (ERDA), 73
Energy Security and Independence Act of 2007
    (ESIA), 69, 80, 90–91, 93
Energy Star, 67

Environmental Defense Fund, 225
Environmental Protection Agency (EPA):
    clean diesel and, 191, 204
    coal rules, 93
    democratic liberalism and, 252
    EnergyStar, 67
    ethanol and, 194
    historical background, 24–25
    nuclear energy and, 232
    public policy and, 45, 48–49
    water resources and, 11
environmental public interest groups, 17–19
Ericsson, John, 102
ethanol, 192–94, *193, 195*
evaluation of policy, 44–45
excludable goods, 35
Executive Order 7037, 225
Executive Order 13149, 85
Executive Order 13693, 65
Executive Order 13783, 95

Federal Energy Regulatory Commission (FERC):
    innovation and, 69, 83, 85–87, 89–92
    natural gas and, 189
    public policy and, 49
    solar energy and, 121
    wind energy and, 141
federalism:
    alternative energy and, 51
    intergovernmentalism and, 60–61
Feinstein, Dianne, 245
Ferguson, R., 233
Fermi, Enrico, 229
Fingersh, L., 139
flash steam power, *160,* 166–67
Florida, concentrated solar power in, 115
Ford, Gerald, 74–75
Ford, Henry, 95
formation of policy, 42–43
fossil energy:
    availability as rationale for alternative
        energy, 11–12
    US supply and use as rationale for alternative
        energy, 12–15
Foundational Program to Advance Cell Efficiency
    (F-PACE), 121
Framework Convention on Climate Change
    (UNFCCC), 94
fuel cells:
    alkaline fuel cells (AFCs), 201
    direct methanol fuel cells (DMFCs), 201–2
    hydrogen fuel cells, 196–201
    molten carbonate fuel cells (MCFCs), 202–3
    phosphoric acid fuel cells (PAFCs), 203
    solid oxide fuel cells (SOFCs), 204
Fukushima Daiichi nuclear disaster, xii, 232, 238
future directions of public policy:
    demand response (DR) programs, 255
    democratic liberalism and, 251–53
    Green New Deal and, 245–50

"Greens" and, 244–45
ideology and, 255–56
institutional analysis and development (IAD)
    model and, 257–58
moral justice considerations, 247–48
overview, 243–44, 258–61
political considerations, 244–50
public opinion, importance of, 250–58
renewable energy credits (RECs), 256–57
social justice considerations, 247–48
state and local efforts, 252–56

Gallup, 250
Geological Survey, 3, 9
geothermal energy, 159–79;
    agriculture, use in, 164–66
    binary systems, 168–72
    case study, 160–61
    costs of, 172–75
    defined, 159–60
    economics of, 172–75
    emission-related issues, 161–63
    environmental issues, 161–63
    federal programs, 175–77
    flash steam power, 160, 166–67
    FORGE program, 148
    greenhouses, use in, 164–66
    heat pumps, 163–64, 169
    mechanics of, 159–60
    overview, 159, 178–79
    production figures, 159
    renewable portfolio standards (RPS) and, 160–61
    research and development (R & D) in,
        171, 175–77
    safety issues, 161–63
    state and local efforts, 177–78
    tax credits, 174–75
    technical feasibility of, 163–72
    turbines, 169–70, 172, 175
    use in US, 165
    US geothermal provinces, 162
    wells, 170
Geothermal Energy Association, 161
Geothermal Resources Council, 161
Geothermal Technologies Office (GTO), 176
Germany:
    nuclear energy in, 235
    renewable energy in, 1, 42
Global Change Research Act, 245
Global Change Research Program, 245
global demands and conflicts, 26–27
Goldberg, R., 174
Gore, Albert, Jr., 84–85
Gorsuch, Ann, 96
Gorsuch, Neil, 94, 96
Government Accounting Office (GAO),
    231–32, 238
Goyal, K. P., 167
Green, Henry L., 9
greenhouses, use of geothermal energy in, 164–66

Green New Deal, 18, 245–50
Green Party, 5, 17–18
green politics, 16–17
Griffin, Dayton A., 139, 144–45
Grove, William, 196

Hanford nuclear waste storage site, 230–31
Hansen, A., 139
Harder, A., 151
Harris School of Public Policy, 236
Hasager, C., 142–43
Hawai'i:
    concentrated solar power in, 115
    geothermal energy in, 177
Hawai'i Electric Light Company, 125, 177
heat pumps, 163–64, 169
Heller, Dean, 233
Hoen, B., 152
Holttinen, Hannele, 141
Honnery, D., 258–59
Honolulu, Hawai'i, solar energy in, 124–25
Housing and Urban Development Department, 81
Hurricane Katrina, 190
hydraulic fracturing, 3, 190
hydroelectric energy, 224–29;
    feasibility of, 225–28
    historical background, 224–25
    innovation in, 89
    overview, 239
    risk assessment and, 223–24
hydrogen fuel cells, 196–201;
    costs of, 199–201, 200
    diagram, 196
    economics of, 199–201, 200
    "green" power model, 198–99
    proton exchange membrane fuel cell (PERFC)
        power plants, 197
    pyrolysis, 199
    storage issues, 199–201
    technical feasibility of, 196–99
Hydrogen Initiative, 23–24, 87–88, 88,
    96, 194–96

Idaho National Engineering and Environmental
    Laboratory (INEL), 89, 231
implementation of policy, 43–44
independent system operators (ISOs), 85–87, 86
India:
    energy demand in, 26, 188
    GDP in, 1, 42
    geothermal energy in, 168
    photovoltaic manufacturing in, 113
Indian Mineral Development Act of 1982, 61
inelasticity of demand, 38
Inglehart, Ronald, 16–17, 19
innovation, 65–97;
    alternative energy and, 68–70
    in alternative fuels, 81–82
    ARRA and, 92–93
    Bush I era, 80–84

Bush II era, 87–92
cheaper petroleum, resurgence of, 77–80
Clean Power Plan and, 93–95
climate change and, 84
Clinton era, 84–87
in coal, 83, 94–96
coal rules, 93–94
deregulation and, 77–80
disposal of coal combustion residuals from electric utilities, 93
economic growth and, 84
in electricity, 83
electricity markets and, 91–92
in electric motor vehicles, 82
energy efficiency and, 81
environmental factors, 70
EPAct reauthorization (1992) and, 80–84
EPAct reauthorization (2005) and, 88–90
ESIA and, 90–91
FERC orders and, 85–87, 91–92
first oil shock period, 71–75
historical background, 68–70
in hydroelectric energy, 89
ideology and, 70
mercury and air toxics standards (MATS), 93–95
in natural gas, 81
Obama era, 92–94
oil vulnerability, reduction of, 84
overview, 65, 96–97
Paris Climate Agreement and, 94
post-EPAct reauthorization, 84–87
pre-PURPA, 71–75
promoting equity through energy, 95–96
public utilities commissions and, 71, 79
PURPA and, 76–79
in radioactive waste, 83
in renewable energy, 83
research and development (R & D) and, 69, 75, 83, 87, 92
reversal of climate policy and, 94–96
RTO/ISOs and, 85–87
secondary oil shock period, 75–77
Trump era, 94–96
in uranium, 83
values and, 70
waves of, 70–96
institutional analysis and development (IAD) model, 53–55, 257–58
institutional change and influence, 19–26
intergovernmentalism, 60–61
Intergovernmental Panel on Climate Change (IPCC), 4, 243
Interior Department, 11, 49, 151, 221
Internal Revenue Service (IRS), 123
Iowa:
renewable portfolio standards (RPS) in, 79
wind energy in, 132
Iranian Revolution, 27
Ivanpah Solar Electric Generating System, 115

Jackson, K. J., 138–39
Japan:
fuel cells in, 206
Kyoto Protocol and, 5
Johns, S., 24
Jones, Charles O., 40
Justice Department, 230

Kansas, wind energy in, 132
Ketelaar, J. A. A., 202
Keystone Pipeline, 70
Kingdon, John, 43, 55–56
Kniefel, J., 256
Koch Industries, 150–51
Kudrle, R., 75
Kyoto Protocol, 4–5, 43, 51, 204

Laval, Claude, Jr., 217
Lazard (firm), 173–74
LeBlanc, Steve, 151
liquefied natural gas (LNG), 187, 189–90
Louisiana, liquefied natural gas (LNG) in, 190
low-emission vehicles, 205
Lowi, Theodore, 46, 220
Lukawski, M., 174
Lund, J., 164, 167
Lund, Peter, 142

Macknick, J., 10
Maine:
geothermal energy in, 177
renewable portfolio standards (RPS) in, 79
Maine Maritime Academy, 177
Malaysia, photovoltaic manufacturing in, 113
Malcolm, D., 139
marketable private goods, 36
Markey, Edward, 246–47
Marshall, Christine, 152
Marxism, 17–18
Massachusetts, renewable portfolio standards (RPS) in, 79
Massachusetts Institute of Technology (MIT), 235–36
McConnell, Mitch, 249
mercury and air toxics standards (MATS), 93–95
Merkley, Jeff, 247, 249
methyl tertiary-butyl ether (MTBE), 194
military applications for alternative fuels, 206–7
Mitsubishi Hitachi Power Systems, 88
mixed oxide fuel (MOX), 235–36
molten carbonate fuel cells (MCFCs), 202–3
Morbarak, A., 2
Moriarty, P., 258–59
Morocco, concentrated solar power in, 115
motor vehicles:
alternative-fuel motor vehicles (AFVs), 188
electric motor vehicles, innovation in, 82
low-emission vehicles, 205
zero-emission vehicles (ZEVs), 205

Mouchout, Auguste, 102
multiple streams (MS) model, 55–57

narrative policy framework (NPF), 59–60
National Academy of Sciences, 84
National Aeronautics and Space Administration (NASA), xii 205
National Ambient Air Quality Standards (NAAQS), 25
National Climate Assessments, 245
National Conference on State Legislatures, 256
National Energy Technology Laboratory, 221
National Environmental Policy Act of 1969 (NEPA), 22, 24, 61
National Housing Act, 81
National Marine Fisheries Service, 226
National Petroleum Council, xi
National Renewable Energy Laboratory (NREL):
    Batteries and Electrification R&D Program, 185
    historical background, 20, 25, 260
    solar energy and, 115, 118
    Vehicle Technologies Office, 185
    wind energy and, 146
National Research Council (NRC), 87, 233
National Science Foundation (NSF), 73
National Wind Watch, 136
Native Americans:
    alternative energy and, 61
    nuclear energy and, 233
natural gas:
    as alternative fuel, 189–90
    consumption of, 189
    innovation in, 81
    liquefied natural gas (LNG), 187, 189–90
    US, consumption in, 12–14, 15
Natural Gas Act of 1938, 189
Natural Gas Act of 1978, 81
Nature Conservancy, 225
Navy, 231
NEG Micon, 154
Nevada:
    concentrated solar power in, 115
    geothermal energy in, 177–78
    renewable portfolio standards (RPS) in, 79
New Deal, 38
New Environmental Paradigm (NEP), 19, 19, 23
New Jersey, renewable portfolio standards (RPS) in, 79
NextEra, 151
next-generation alternative fuels, 185–208;
    alkaline fuel cells (AFCs), 201
    biodiesel, 191–92, 192
    clean diesel, 191
    commercial applications, 207
    direct methanol fuel cells (DMFCs), 201–2
    ethanol, 192–94, 193, 195
    fuel as concept, 186–88
    hydrogen fuel cells, 196–201
    Hydrogen Initiative and, 194–96
    liquefied natural gas (LNG), 189–90

methyl tertiary-butyl ether (MTBE), 194
    military applications, 206–7
    molten carbonate fuel cells (MCFCs), 202–3
    natural gas as, 189–90
    overview, 185–86, 207–8
    phosphoric acid fuel cells (PAFCs), 203
    residential applications, 207
    solid oxide fuel cells (SOFCs), 204
    transportation applications, 204–6
Nicholson-Crotty, S., 253
NIMBY effect, 50, 152, 233
9/11 attacks, 87
Nixon, Richard, 22, 68, 74–75, 78
Noor Complex Solar Plant, 115
North American Electric Reliability Corporation (NERC), 86–87
North Dakota, natural gas in, 190
NREL. See National Renewable Energy Laboratory (NREL)
nuclear energy, 229–37;
    alternatives to, 73
    economics of, 234–37
    historical background, 229–30
    mechanics of, 229
    mixed oxide fuel (MOX), 235–36
    overview, 239
    pebble bed modular reactors (PBMRs), 234–35
    rebirth of, 237–39
    risk assessment and, 223–24, 233
    spent nuclear fuel (SNF), 231, 235
    waste storage, 230–32, 238
Nuclear Energy Task Force (NETF), 237
Nuclear Regulatory Commission (NRC), 232
Nuclear Waste Policy Act (NWPA), 231

Oakland Project, 43
Obama, Barack, 5, 21, 24, 35, 42, 45–46, 65, 69–70, 92–94, 96–97, 163, 190, 218, 238
Ocasio-Cortez, Alexandria, 18, 245, 247, 249
Occupational Safety and Health Act of 1970 (OSHA), 22
ocean thermal energy conversion (OTEC), 228–29
Office of Energy Efficiency and Renewable Energy (EERE), 25, 116, 121–22, 166, 227
Office of Fossil Energy, 202–3
Office of Indian Energy Policy and Programs, 61
oil. See petroleum
Oklahoma, wind energy in, 132
Oregon, geothermal energy in, 177
organic and polymer solar cells (OPSCs), 106
Organization of Petroleum Exporting Countries (OPEC), 22, 26, 41
Ostrom, Elinor, 53–54

Paatero, Jukka, 142
Pacific Coast Salmon Recovery Fund, 226
Pacific Salmon Treaty Agreement, 226
Paris Climate Agreement:
    carbon emissions and, 247

US position on, 24, 41, 51, 92, 94–95, 260
"peak oil," 2–3
Pebble Bed Modular Reactor Ltd., 235
pebble bed modular reactors (PBMRs), 234–35
Pelosi, Nancy, 21, 248–49
Pennsylvania, natural gas in, 190
Perovskite solar cells (PSCs), 106–7
personal tax credit, 123
petroleum:
    cheaper petroleum, resurgence of, 77–80
    first oil shock period, 71–75
    "peak oil," 2–3
    secondary oil shock period, 75–77
    US, extraction in, 13, 13–15
    vulnerability, reduction of, 84
Petroleum Experiment Station, 221
Pew Research Center, 149
phosphoric acid fuel cells (PAFCs), 203
photovoltaics:
    concentrated solar PV (CPV), 107–8
    dye-sensitized solar cells (DSCs), 106
    infrastructure of, 112–15
    levelized cost of electricity and, 112–15
    manufacturing of, 114
    organic and polymer solar cells (OPSCs), 106
    Perovskite solar cells (PSCs), 106–7
    price of, 114
    production figures, 102, 113–15
    silicon-based photovoltaic cells, 103–5, 104
    tax incentives for, 123
    technical feasibility of, 105–8
    thin film technology, 106–7
Poet LLC, 150
Poland, geothermal energy in, 168–69
policy diffusion model, 58–59
Pollin, R., 248, 251
postmaterialism, 18–19
power, energy distinguished, 66
Pressman, Jeffrey, 43
price controls, 74, 78, 78
process of policy, 39–46
Pruitt, Scott, 46
Pryfogle, P. A., 167
Pryor, S., 6
public policy, 35–62;
    advocacy coalition framework (ACF) model, 57
    agenda setting, 41–42
    bottom-up policy making, 48–49
    climate change and, 243
    coercion and, 47
    collaborative policy making, 49–51
    constituent policy, 46–47
    distributive policy, 47–48
    economics and, 35–39
    evaluation of, 44–45
    federalism and, 51
    formation of, 42–43
    future directions (See future directions of public policy)
    implementation of, 43–44

institutional analysis and development (IAD) model, 53–55
intergovernmentalism and, 60–61
multiple streams (MS) model, 55–57
narrative policy framework (NPF), 59–60
Native Americans and, 61
overview, 35, 61–62
policy diffusion model, 58–59
policy frameworks and models, 52–61
process of, 39–46
punctuated equilibrium (PE) model, 58
redistributive policy, 47
regulatory policy, 48
research and development (R & D), 45
risk assessment and, 220, 222–23
roles for, 35–39
termination or change of, 45–46
top-down policy making, 48–49
types of policy, 46–48
water resources and, 243–244
public utilities commissions, 71, 79
Public Utilities Holding Company Act of 1935 (PUHCA), 83, 89, 96
Public Utility Regulatory Policies Act of 1978 (PURPA), 76–81, 83, 89, 96
Puerto Rico, renewable portfolio standards (RPS) in, 253
punctuated equilibrium (PE) model, 58

R & D. See research and development (R & D)
Rabe, B., 51
radioactive waste, innovation in, 83
Rand, J., 152
rationales for alternative energy, 1–28;
    availability of fossil fuels, 11–12
    carbon emissions, 4–7
    climate change, 4–7
    cultural shifts, 16–17
    environmental public interest groups, 17–19
    global demands and conflicts, 26–27
    green politics, 16–17
    institutional change and influence, 19–26
    New Environmental Paradigm, 19, 19
    overview, 1–4, 27–28
    US supply and use of fossil energy, 12–15
    water resources, 7–11
Reagan, Ronald W., 12, 17, 19, 22–23, 44, 57, 68–69, 72, 77–79, 84, 231, 259
redistributive policy, 47
regional transmission operators (RTOs), 85–87, 86
regulatory policy, 48
Reid, Harry, 21, 233, 238
renewable energy credits (RECs), 256–57
renewable portfolio standards (RPS):
    geothermal energy and, 160–61
    public policy and, 59
    solar energy and, 123–24
    state and local efforts, 51, 67, 79, 89, 253, 256, 259

Republican Party, 20
research and development (R & D):
  DOE and, 185
  federal government, role of, 260
  in geothermal energy, 171, 175–77
  historical background, 21, 23
  innovation and, 69, 75, 83, 87, 92
  public policy and, 45
  risk assessment and, 221
  in solar energy, 106, 108, 119, 121
  in wind energy, 132, 140
residential applications for alternative fuels, 206
Rifkin, Jeremy, 195
Rifle, Colorado, solar energy case study, 117–18
Rio Earth Summit, 4, 21, 250
risk assessment, 219–24;
  "center" versus "border," 221–22
  climate change and, 219
  consent and, 219–21
  hydroelectric energy and, 223–24
  nuclear energy and, 223–24, 233
  policy solutions and, 220, 222–23
  research and development (R & D) and, 221
rivalrous goods, 35, 36
Roberge, P. R., 203
Roosevelt, Franklin D., 48, 76, 95, 223, 225,
  247, 252
Roosevelt, Theodore, 21
RPS. See renewable portfolio standards (RPS)
Rural Electrification Act of 1936, 95, 133
Rural Electrification Administration, 225
Russia, Kyoto Protocol and, 5
Rystad Energy AS, 15

Sachs, Jeffrey, 246–47
Saint Olaf Wind Turbine, 152–54
Sandberg, Pete, 152, 154
Sanders, Bernie, 247
San Diego, California, solar energy in, 125
Santa Rosa, California, geothermal energy in, 167
Saudi Arabia, petroleum reserves in, 3
Scalia, Antonin, 94
Schattschneider, E. E., 222–23
Schrimali, G., 256
Schumer, Chuck, 249
Secretary of Energy Advisory Board (SEAB), 238
Shaheen, Jeanne, 9
Shevenell, M., 174
Sierra Club, 225
silicon-based photovoltaic cells, 103–5, 104
Simay, Gregory, 73
Simmons, Matthew, xi, 2–3
Simon, Herbert, 222–23
solar energy, 101–26;
  case study, 117–18
  commercial incentives, 121, 122–23
  concentrated solar power (CSP), 110–11, 115
  concentrated solar PV (CPV), 107–8
  dye-sensitized solar cells (DSCs), 106
  economic development impacts, 116

economics of, 111–15
federal incentives, 122–23
infrastructure of photovoltaics, 112–15
levelized cost of electricity and, 112–15
manufacturing of photovoltaics, 114
mechanics of, 101–3
organic and polymer solar cells (OPSCs), 106
overview, 101, 125–26
parabolic dishes, 110–11, 111
Perovskite solar cells (PSCs), 106–7
power towers, 110
price of photovoltaics, 114
production figures, 101, 102, 113–15
renewable portfolio standards (RPS)
  and, 123–24
research and development (R & D) and, 106,
  108, 119, 121
silicon-based photovoltaic cells, 103–5, 104
Solar Energy Technology Program
  (SETO), 118–22
state and local efforts, 123–25
Stirling engines, 109–11
tax incentives, 122, 123
technical feasibility of photovoltaics, 105–8
technical feasibility of solar thermal, 108–11
thin film technology, 106–7
Solar Energy Industries Association, 113
Solar Energy Technology Program
  (SETO), 118–22
solar investment tax credit (ITC), 122–23
solar thermal:
  concentrated solar power (CSP), 110–11, 115
  economics of, 115
  parabolic dishes, 110–11
  production figures, 102
  Stirling engines, 109–11
  tax incentives for, 123
  technical feasibility of, 108–11
solid oxide fuel cells (SOFCs), 204
South Africa, nuclear energy in, 235
South Dakota, wind energy in, 132
Southeast Geysers Effluent Recycling Project
  (SEGEP), 167
South Korea, photovoltaic manufacturing in, 113
spent nuclear fuel (SNF), 231, 235
Srivastava, A., 255
Stanford Research Institute, 4
Stirling engines, 109–11
Stone, Deborah, 43, 219
SunEdison, LLC, 117–18
SunShot Initiative, 121
Supremacy Clause, 60–61
Swan, J., 151
Sweeney, Sean, 247
Szilar, Leo, 229

Tanrioven, D., 197
Tennessee Valley Authority Act of 1933, 225
Tennessee Valley Authority (TVA), 38, 252
termination or change of policy, 45–46

Texas:
  energy law in, 67
  Land Commission, 67
  liquefied natural gas (LNG) in, 190
  Railroad Commission, 67
  renewable energy in, 259
  renewable portfolio standards (RPS)
    in, 79, 253
Texas Instruments, 202
Thailand, photovoltaic manufacturing in, 113
Thomas, Clarence, 41
Three Mile Island nuclear disaster, 20, 22, 77,
    231–32, 238
Thunberg, Greta, 18
tidal energy, 224, 228
top-down policy making, 48–49
Toyota Motor Corporation, 196
"Tragedy of the Commons," 251–52
transportation applications for alternative
    fuels, 204–6
Transportation Department (DOT), 82
Tribal Energy Projects Database, 61
Truman, Harry, 252
Trump, Donald, xiii, 6, 12, 24, 41, 45–46, 56, 69–
    70, 94–96, 114, 121, 151, 188, 194, 218, 223,
    228, 238, 247–49, 260
Tsinghua University, 235
Turkey, geothermal energy in, 164–65

Union Carbide Corporation (UCC), 117
United Arab Emirates, concentrated solar power
    in, 115
United Nations:
  CEO Water mandate, 11
  Environmental Programme, 4, 243
  Framework Convention on Climate Change
    (UNFCCC), 94
United States. See specific entity or topic
United States Enrichment Corporation, 83
University of Chicago, 236–37
University of Maine, 177
University of Michigan, 234
uranium, innovation in, 83
Uranium Mill Tailings Radiation Control
    Act, 117
Utah:
  Advanced Clean Energy Storage project, 88
  concentrated solar power in, 115
  geothermal energy in, 177–78

Vestas, 154
Vietnam, photovoltaic manufacturing in, 113

Washington, geothermal energy in, 177
water resources:
  energy, nexus with, 7–11
  public policy and, 243–244
  as rationale for alternative energy, 7–11
  in US, 8–10
Water Resources Group 2030, 11
Watts Bar 1 nuclear power plant, 234
wave energy, 228
Wildavsky, Aaron, 43, 219–22, 226–27, 249
wind energy, 132–55;
  case study, 152–54
  costs of, 144–49, 145, 147–48
  defined, 132–36
  economics of, 144–49
  imaging SAR in, 142–43
  land-based systems, 147
  Lidar in, 144
  mechanics of, 132–36, 133–34
  nacelles, 135, 135
  offshore systems, 142, 143, 146, 148, 148–
    49, 150
  overview, 132, 155
  political feasibility of, 149–52
  production figures, 133
  propeller blades, 134, 134–35, 137, 137–39
  research and development (R & D) and,
    132, 140
  rotors, 135, 139
  siting of, 141–43
  social feasibility of, 149–52
  technical feasibility of, 136–44
  towers, 135–36
  turbines, 147–48, 150
Windlogics, 153
Wisconsin, renewable portfolio standards
    (RPS) in, 79
Wiser, R., 140–41
World Bank, 11
World Economic Forum, 196
World Health Organization, 9
World Meteorological Organization, 243
Wyoming, energy law in, 67

Xcel Energy, 152–54

Yucca Mountain nuclear waste storage site,
    231–33, 238

zero-emission vehicles (ZEVs), 205
Zhou, H., 106
Zinke, Ryan, 151